Sociocultural Studies in Education

Sociocultural Studies in Education

Critical Thinking for Democracy

RICHARD A. QUANTZ

Paradigm Publishers

Boulder | London

Copyright © 2015 by Paradigm Publishers

Published in the United States by Paradigm Publishers, 5589 Arapahoe Avenue, Boulder, CO 80303 USA.

Paradigm Publishers is the trade name of Birkenkamp & Company, LLC, Dean Birkenkamp, President and Publisher.

Library of Congress Cataloging-in-Publication Data

Quantz, Richard A., 1947–
    Sociocultural studies in education : critical thinking for democracy / Richard A. Quantz.
        pages cm
    Includes bibliographical references and index.
    ISBN 978-1-61205-693-7 (hardcover : alk. paper)
    ISBN 978-1-61205-694-4 (pbk. : alk. paper)
    ISBN 978-1-61205-695-1 (e-book)
    1. Educational sociology—United States.   2. Democracy and education—United States.
3. Education—United States—Philosophy.   4. Education and state—United States.
5. Education—Social aspects—United States.   6. Education—Economic aspects—United States.
I. Title.
    LC191.4.Q83 2014
    306.43'2—dc23

                                                                                        2013049604

Printed and bound in the United States of America on acid-free paper that meets the standards of the American National Standard for Permanence of Paper for Printed Library Materials.

Designed and Typeset by Straight Creek Bookmakers.

19 18 17 16 15   1 2 3 4 5

This book is dedicated to all the students and instructors of
EDL 204: Sociocultural Studies in Education,
whose struggle to learn and teach about education in a democracy
has helped to sharpen and strengthen these essays;
and
to Kathleen and Kate,
colleagues who have contributed heavily to the evolution of EDL 204 and
to many of the essays that constitute this book.

Contents

Introduction

PORTLAND—Joining the growing ranks of students and teachers protesting standardized testing, over 60 Grover Cleveland High School students walked out of their classes on Thursday April 18. The students, who are members of the Portland Student Union (PSU) see the tests as an unreliable way to evaluate their actual knowledge, as well a useless stick for measuring students, teachers, and schools. They urged their classmates both in Cleveland High School and the rest of Portland's high schools to "opt-out" of taking the Oregon Assessment of Knowledge and Skills (OAKS).

Flanked by banners reading "Education Is Not a Commodity," "Think Outside the Bubble!" and "I Am A Student, Not A Test Score," Cleveland junior Ian Jackson said, "We will not stand by as the arbitrary, biased, and bigoted tests assess our knowledge, evaluate our teachers, and determine our education."[1]

PROVIDENCE—Spattered with blood, their eyes blackened, their T-shirts torn, a line of teenaged zombies zigzagged through downtown during the afternoon rush. Chanting, "No education, no life," more than 50 Providence teenagers marched on the state Department of Education to protest its decision to link test scores to high school graduation.

"To take away the diploma is to take away our life, to make us undead," said Cauldierre McKay, a Classical High School student. "That's why we're here today ... dressed as the zombies that this policy will turn so many of us into."[2]

TUCSON—A Tucson school board meeting was shut down after a rowdy mob of student protesters took over the school board meeting room, running out the school board, chanting, yelling, screaming, and banging desks for two hours. Some even

---

1. Pete Shaw, "Local High School Students Stand against Standardized Testing," *Portland Occupier,* April 30, 2013, www.portlandoccupier.org/2013/04/30/local-high-school-students-stand-against-standardized-testing/.

2. Linda Borg, "Student 'Zombies' March on R.I. Department of Education in Protest," *Providence Journal,* February 13, 2013, http://news.providencejournal.com/breaking-news/2013/02/student-zombies-march-on-ri-department-of-education-in-protest.html.

chained themselves to desks—all because they [the student protesters] are demanding a history course that teaches history from a Mexican-American perspective.[3]

WOODLAWN [CHICAGO]—Witnesses to a Wednesday afternoon protest over city efforts to close schools said at least five students were taken into custody by police.

The protest was designed to highlight a situation the protestors say is being created by the proposed closings—that students moved to new schools will be forced to cross dangerous gang lines....

Matt Ginsberg-Jaeckle, an organizer with Southside Together Organizing for Power, and others called the event—in which students blocked traffic in the intersection of 61st Street and Cottage Grove Avenue—a "die-in."

Students wore mock-bloody clothes in an effort to show the effect they believe school closings will have: more violence and death for the young students forced to cross new gang territories.

"The message is that school closings are killing people," Ginsberg-Jaeckle said. "Everyone knows what will happen when these kids start crossing these gang lines."[4]

CHICAGO—Hundreds of Lane Tech College Prep students staged a sit-in this morning inside the school in response to Chicago Public Schools' controversial announcement last week that it would remove the graphic novel "Persepolis" from its seventh grade curriculum.... Today's sit-in comes on the heels of a Friday afternoon demonstration outside the school, where about 100 Lane Tech students and teachers gathered to protest CPS' decision, which they say is censorship.

One participant held a sign during Friday's protest reading "Banning books ... Closing schools. What's next?"[5]

Portland; Providence; Tucson; Chicago; Detroit; San Anselmo and San Rafael, California; Danvers, Massachusetts; and many more communities have experienced students' taking to the streets to protest standardized tests, school closings, teacher firings, banned books, and banned courses and more. And they are not alone; teachers, parents, and community members have joined with them to protest some of the most controversial issues of our day. What is going on here? Are we no longer willing to work within our democratic process to resolve conflicts? Or perhaps we have abandoned democratic process so significantly that citizens must take to the streets to be heard? Are these protests signs that democracy is not working or that it is?

And why now? What is going on that has led this particular moment in history to call forth such strong emotions about education? For more than thirty years the United States has been implementing an unprecedented educational experiment backed by huge amounts of money and near universal support from legislatures, yet what have these reforms accomplished? What

3. Joe Newby, "La Raza Student Mob Storms Tucson School Board, Shuts Down Meeting," *Examiner.com*, April 11, 2011, www.examiner.com/article/la-raza-student-mob-storms-tucson-school-board-shuts-down-meeting.

4. Darryl Holliday, "Students Stage 'Die in' at School-Closing Protest," *DNAinfo Chicago*, May 15, 2013, www.dnainfo.com/chicago/20130515/woodlawn/students-stage-die-at-school-closing-protest.

5. Ellen Fortino, "Lane Tech Students Hold Morning Sit-in to Protest *Persepolis* Book Ban," *Progress Illinois*, March 18, 2013, www.progressillinois.com/quick-hits/content/2013/03/18/lane-tech-students-hold-morning-sit-protest-persepolis-book-ban.

are they intended to accomplish? In this age of marketing and mass media, which often cloud meaning as often as they clarify it, can anyone really know what is going on? Should students, teachers, parents, and community members be supporting these reforms or opposing them? Surely, there is one thing we can claim to know: today, education is a controversial field.

But we would make an important mistake if we were to think that education is a stranger to controversy. From the founding of the nation, education has been the center of differing opinions and the site of strong political efforts. Thomas Jefferson's "Bill for the More General Diffusion of Knowledge," presented to the Virginia Assembly in 1779, was defeated, perhaps for including such controversial ideas as providing some education (three years' worth) for poor free children, including girls; because his bill created a process by which even poor boys could find a way to advance through secondary education and even college; or because his bill explicitly required the education provided by the public to be secular and even excluded the teaching of the Bible. In the early part of the 1800s, southern states forbade the teaching of reading and writing to people held in slavery (although they were certainly permitted job training in work such as carpentry, blacksmithing, and cooking so their labor could be exploited).

In the middle of the nineteenth century, Horace Mann became the first secretary of education of any state in the union (Massachusetts). After building a strong state system, Mann crisscrossed the United States meeting with business leaders, labor leaders, religious leaders, political leaders, women's groups, and any community group whom he could gather to convince a reluctant public to develop and fund a full public school system in every state. By obscuring the different interests among these groups, Mann covered up, rather than solved, their conflicts. Then as now, people see the public schools as a solution to very different, often opposing, problems. In fact, in every historical moment, education has been a lightning rod for controversy.

This should hardly be surprising. Education is one process that forms adults from children and in doing so helps determine what kind of adult a society promotes as well as the kind of society these adults create. In a democracy, it seems, almost any issue can create disagreement, but what is so controversial about education? We could start with what we mean by education itself, what we think makes a strong democracy, and how the two are connected. Differing opinions of one or the other will inevitably lead to conflict. We might not be surprised to find out that in every age people have had different philosophical understandings that lead to different beliefs about how schools should operate. Nor should we be surprised that in every period different political parties have developed contrasting senses of how public schools should be run. And certainly we know that the cleavages of our society at large are bound to create division within our schools as well. Issues around social class, race and ethnicity, gender, and sexuality are just some of the issues that have led to struggle in the field of education.

These divisions and public struggles are important because they affect the lives of students and their teachers in very significant ways. We can see some of the effects of today's conflicts in education in the decision of so many groups of students, teachers, parents, and community members to take to the streets to protest what they understand to be intolerable conditions. Unfortunately, too few people have taken the time to actually study the issues and understand what the fundamental disagreements are. And even many who have tried to come to grips with the issues have a hard time separating out the real arguments from the fog created by marketing firms to sell one position or another.

This book is designed to fill a void in the education of both educators and citizens who have an interest in education. It explores some of the fundamentals around which disagreements in education arise. It presents a process with which those new to these debates (or perhaps not yet well versed in the subtleties of the debates) can pull apart an otherwise confusing and entwined set of facts. This book leads the reader through some general concepts and intellectual skills that provide the basis for making sense out of the debates about public education in a democracy such as the United States.

In many ways, this book can be seen as a primer on how to read educational texts. It may be the first book written for undergraduate courses in sociocultural studies in education—such as social foundations of education, educational studies, and cultural studies in education—located in general education rather than professional education. It takes a humanities approach to the study of education by addressing how education is represented in the texts of our society, including books, newspapers, movies, the Internet, and any other place where people represent a vision of public education. This book does not present a scientific view of the world of education (though it does certainly take those research findings into consideration), but rather presents the various themes and currents found within the arguments and narratives that people use to represent public education. It assumes that the more those interested in education know about how to see through the rhetoric and recognize the basic philosophical and ideological positions embedded in the texts, the better they will be at discerning whose interests are served by which texts. It should be of interest to future teachers not as a toolbox of teaching techniques but, as Paulo Freire and Donaldo Macedo might say, as a way to read the world in order to read the word.[6] It ought to be of interest to citizens of a democracy because the future of that democracy inherently depends on the quality of the education of its youth. It should be of interest to any college student because they are in a unique moment in their own lives where they have some control over what their own time in college will accomplish.

The book is divided into four parts. Part I lays out a few basic concepts and skills upon which the rest of the book draws. The four chapters of this section provide the elements needed as a foundation to read the rest of the book. Parts II and III develop in more depth ideas of philosophy and of ideology that permit an astute reader to better interpret educational texts. Finally, Part IV zeroes in on some of the most controversial issues of our day, including social class, race, gender, and sexuality. I strongly recommend that the reader read this book in the order that the chapters are laid out because each builds on those that go before.

My hope is that when the reader finishes the text, he or she will have a better idea what is happening to education that has led so many students in Portland, Tucson, Detroit, Chicago, and so many other cities and towns to gather in protest. I hope that the reader will be in a better position to decide whether to support these movements or not based on a clear understanding of the issues and interests at hand.

DETROIT—Students suspended for walking out of class at Detroit's Western International High School earlier this week to protest school closures and demand

---

6. Paulo Freire and Donaldo P. Macedo, *Literacy: Reading the Word and the World*, Critical Studies in Education Series (South Hadley, MA: Bergin & Garvey Publishers, 1987).

a better education, are holding a "freedom school" Friday in Clark Park, across the street from their official school building.

Students left class Wednesday morning to protest the closing of Southwestern High School, which many fear would lead to overcrowding at Western, and to demand more resources and greater teacher engagement for the district's schools....

[Suspended student, 17-year-old Raychel] Gafford said students are organizing the freedom school for the same reasons they walked out. "We're sticking together and we're not backing down from this," she said. "We were thrown out of school for fighting for an equal education and we're doing this to show we're still going to be learning even if we got kicked out of school."

Classes at the freedom school will be held with help from community volunteers for the duration of the students' suspensions, including over the weekend.

A Facebook page promoting the freedom school puts the number of participating students at more than 150:

> We do not understand why we are being punished with a loss of educational opportunity when that is exactly what we were fighting for. To further demonstrate our commitment to education, we will be attending our own school taught by ourselves and community educators for the duration of our suspension.[7]

Acknowledgments

All books require the collaboration of many people, but this book was created by an unusually large number of people. Even though I am the author whose name appears on the cover, I owe much to many, many others, starting with the thousands of students enrolled in EDL 204: Sociocultural Studies in Education at Miami University who, over the past several years, read the many drafts of the essays that form the foundation of this book. Through their questioning, confusions, misunderstandings, frustrations, and willingness to share their thoughts, I have been able to hone, refine, and completely rewrite each essay into a form that has shown to be successful with undergraduate students. Thanks to the many of you for your openness and your spirit in the struggle to gain an honest education.

I also owe much to the dozens of instructors of that same course who have taught the many versions of these essays that resulted in this book. Through their real-world trials that helped reveal their strengths and weaknesses, those essays have been much strengthened as they were converted to chapters for a book. I also owe much to colleagues Kathleen Knight Abowitz and Kate Rousmaniere, who have shared the duty of coordinating the course and who authored and coauthored many of the original essays from which this book was built. One of the true joys of my work is the opportunity to work with such intelligent, engaging, and supportive colleagues as Drs. Kathleen and Kate. I owe a particular thanks to Kevin Talbert, whose good thinking and easy manner led to our coauthoring what became Chapter 4 in this book. I also owe much to Josh Fletcher, who worked with me to develop the concepts and the content of

---

7. David Sands, "Detroit Walkout: High School Students Suspended for Leaving School Start Freedom School," *HuffPost Detroit,* April 27, 2012, www.huffingtonpost.com/2012/04/27/detroit-walkout-high -school_n_1459253.html.

Chapter 17. Kathleen, Kate, Kevin, and Josh surely should be credited with much that is strong in these chapters, but I alone should be assigned responsibility for when these chapters misstep.

Thanks to Don Felty, whose dissertation, "The Bully Pulpit: Presidential Rhetoric and National Education Agenda in the Reagan Administration, 1981–1984," helped me see a different approach to teaching undergraduates about sociocultural studies of education. Also many, many thanks to João Paraskeva, friend and former colleague here at Miami University, who after using many of the essays to teach undergraduates was the first to encourage me to publish the collection as a book and continued his gentle encouragement through the years that followed. I owe a deep appreciation to my good friends and colleagues, Dennis Carlson, Thomas Dutton, Henry Giroux, and Peter McLaren, whose own work and insights have maintained my hope for a renewed revival of education in this country and who helped me forge a unique critical lens with which to make sense out of education in our world today.

I have a particular gratitude and unique appreciation for my daughter Elizabeth, who served as a guinea pig by reading through the first drafts of several of the original essays and by helping me understand how they might be read and misread by college students. I also owe much to Betty, whose daily conversations about her high school English classes have helped me winnow out what is and is not important in the everyday life of our elementary and secondary schools and to daily renew my appreciation for the very difficult job of teaching in today's public schools. And, finally, I have so much appreciation for Rick and Allison, who, though distant in geography, are close in spirit and continue to provide the encouragement needed to attack and complete a project such as this. Without any one of the individuals named above, this would be a very different book.

Part I

Basic Concepts

CHAPTER ONE

On Education and Democracy

Everyone seems to have an opinion about education: whether it is worth having; whether it is necessary; whether they've had enough of it, not enough of it, or too much of it; how bad it is; how to make it better or less expensive; or how to make a profit from it. But even though everyone seems to have an opinion about it, few stop to reflect about what education might actually be.

Is education a privilege or a right? If it is a privilege, how do we decide who is to have it and who is not? If it is a right, why is it that some people have so much more access to it than others? When does education begin? At birth, or at age five or six when a child starts school? When does it end? At age sixteen; eighteen; twenty-two, when a young adult leaves school; or when a person simply decides to stop pursuing it regardless of age? Perhaps it never ends until we die? Is education something to "have" (that is, a thing) or is it something that is "done" (that is, a process)? What does it mean to be educated? Does it mean a person now has the skills necessary to get a good job? Does it mean that a person knows how to learn through reading and reasoning? Does it mean that a person knows the primary knowledge that it takes to be a well-functioning, adult member of a particular community? How do we know when a person is making progress toward being educated? How do we know when a person has made sufficient progress that she or he can stop?

The Latin root, *ēducātiō*, refers merely to the process of bringing up children. And, of course, the upbringing of children begins when they are born and ends when they are recognized as adults. This idea that education is the process of raising children into adulthood remains one of the major uses of the term in English today, but it is hardly the only way the term *education* is used in contemporary English. At least since the sixteenth century, English speakers have used the term to refer to the cultural development of knowledge, understanding, and character.[1]

John Dewey began his 1887 educational manifesto, "My Pedagogic Creed," by stating,

> I believe that all education proceeds by the participation of the individual in the social consciousness of the [human] race. This process begins unconsciously almost at birth, and is continually shaping the individual's powers, saturating his consciousness, forming his habits, training his ideas, and arousing his feelings and emotions. Through this unconscious education the individual gradually comes to share in the

---

1. *Oxford English Dictionary* (online), s.v. "education," March 5, 2013, www.oed.com.proxy.lib.muohio.edu/view/Entry/59584?redirectedFrom=education.

intellectual and moral resources which humanity has succeeded in getting together. He becomes an inheritor of the funded capital of civilization.[2]

Dewey's understanding of education adds some specificity and clarity to the traditional understandings mentioned above. He understands education to be something that begins at birth and does not require schools. He also understands education as a process by which individuals become members of a larger community. Typically, of course, this refers to children who wish to become members of good standing in the adult community within which they are raised, but a careful reading of the above quotation suggests that Dewey's community includes all humanity, which, it would seem, requires all of us to pursue education throughout our lives as our circle of humanity widens as we grow, age, and learn. To "share in the intellectual and moral resources which humanity has succeeded in getting together" is surely a lifelong project.

Dewey's conception of education also clearly refers to the process through which individuals become integrated into human society. It is a process that seeks the development of the whole person in a multitude of knowledge, skills, habits, and attitudes. It is primarily, though not exclusively, intellectual and moral. It is the preparation of the individual to accept their responsibility and perform their part in continuing the ever-evolving improvement and growth of our communities. It is the process by which human civilization itself grows and progresses.

Education versus Training

In today's world, many people equate education with training, but education is much more. We can train a dog, but we cannot educate a dog. We can train a person, but we can also educate a person. Mere training may be sufficient for dogs, but people deserve more: they deserve education. *Training* is the process through which we learn a technique or a skill or a job. It is the process of learning to reason technically—to solve given problems by applying set rules. It comprises specialized knowledge and technical learning. In training, we typically learn how to do very specific things, such as operate a computer or balance a budget. Learning about computers becomes *educational* when it moves beyond the mere techniques of using the computer to a broader understanding through a critical inquiry into computers; their uses; their problems and possibilities; and their multiple social, ethical, and other meanings. In a similar way, although balancing a budget may be important training, it only becomes educational when budgeting comes to be understood as a way of thinking and approaching the world.

Certainly, teachers need some training, but they need much more than training if they are to be successful teachers—they need education. Teacher training only becomes teacher education when the techniques taught in methods courses are understood within broader philosophical, ethical, political, historical, and sociocultural contexts. Part of the purpose of this book is to help students gain a better understanding of the broader contexts of education. Its purpose, then, includes helping students, whether in a teaching major or not, move beyond mere training to gain part of what is necessary to become educated about education.

---

2. John Dewey, "My Pedagogic Creed," *School Journal* 54 (1897): 77–80, http://dewey.pragmatism.org/creed.htm.

Education versus Schooling

All societies educate their young even if they don't have schools. They teach their young the customs, language, traditions, myths, and knowledge that their society upholds as true, good, or normal. Similarly, these societies teach their young what they believe to be false, bad, or abnormal. Traditional societies use educational practices that are mostly integrated into everyday life, controlled closely by the members of the local community, and only sometimes situated outside of daily life. An example of this would be coming-of-age rituals when an age group of boys or girls is often removed from the community for a period of time where, under the tutelage of an adult, they are introduced to the special knowledge of the community.

On the other hand, even though modern societies certainly have many educational practices in the everyday family and community life of the child (such as dietary and moral education), modern societies rely heavily on institutions that are removed from the practices of family and community life, such as schools and the media. In traditional societies, the customs, language, traditions, and knowledge considered true or false, good or bad, and normal or abnormal arise in the daily practices of interacting with one's parents and other adults integrated into a common culture. In these societies, education is assumed to be an integral part of daily life. But in modern societies, much of what is learned takes place outside of the family in a public space controlled by public institutions, such as schools and the media, leading many people to equate education with formal institutions, as something separate from ordinary daily living. Equating education with schooling, however, is inappropriate; traditional societies may not have schools, but they have education. Also, much of the education in the contemporary, modern world still occurs in the ordinary daily life of families and communities.

If we follow Dewey's reasoning as explained above, to be educated involves a lifelong process of learning and growth; to be schooled is a formal process of instruction organized by a particular institution (typically the state, but sometimes religious or other private organizations) and usually lasting for a limited time in a person's life span. In the contemporary world, schooling is typically compulsory, sequential, and ends in young adulthood. To become an educated person, however, requires learning after schooling ends. It is a long-term, lifelong goal. If a person has received good schooling, he or she will have developed the knowledge, skills, reasoning, creativity, and dispositions necessary to continue the process throughout life. If all a person received through schooling is a set of acquired knowledge and skills, that schooling will not have prepared her or him well for a life in pursuit of education.

Even though many people in today's modern societies equate education and schooling, education is a larger concept. Education encompasses both informal and formal learning. It involves our everyday lived experiences as well as what we learn in such formalized institutions as schools. *Schooling* is an institutionalized system that we hope leads to education. Unfortunately, too often schools focus on training, on mere knowledge and skill acquisition, and not on a full education.

Even worse, much schooling is *mis*educative. That is to say, rather than coming "to share in the intellectual and moral resources which humanity has succeeded in getting together" (to use Dewey's phrase above), too often schooling leads students to confuse their training with education, to embrace their ignorance and reject the intellectual qualities that are inherent in education, or to denigrate themselves as someone unable to become educated. In other words, schools have the potential to educate, but education does not always occur in schools.

Colleges and universities are schools. Whether or not students gain mere training while being schooled in college, or whether they gain some education, depends partly on their instructors, but largely it depends on them. Do they want an education, or do they just want to be trained for a job? Do they even know what one needs to do to gain an education?

Many educational scholars, myself included, believe that most American students have spent at least twelve years in schools dedicated to training them to be good technical readers, technical writers, and technical thinkers, but not interpretive readers, analytical writers, and critical thinkers. Having spent twelve years gaining "knowledge and skills," most American students are well prepared for continuing their training. But having had little in the way of education beyond training, many American college students may be at a loss as to how to move beyond the technical requirements of knowledge and skill acquisition to the intellectual and moral prerequisites required to gain an education. Too often these well-trained students treat education as if it were a consumer product—something to pay for, ingest, and master. They wait eagerly, perhaps, but futilely, for their instructors to train them to be educated. Unfortunately for them, education is not a consumer good, and it is not something that one can gain through training. It is something that students have to do for themselves.

Nonetheless, that doesn't mean they have to do it alone. In fact, there is good reason to think that trying to gain an education alone is futile. Students must have the help of other students and their instructors; otherwise, how can they possibly become integrated into the larger community? Part of being a member of a community is the ability and inclination to engage others in the pursuit of education. To gain an education in college requires that students move beyond mastery of knowledge and skills and learn to read the world, to reason critically, and to engage others in a joint pursuit of wisdom. These are the purposes of this book: to help students learn to read the world in order to read the word,[3] to learn to reason critically in order to critique the world of education, and to stimulate engagement with others in the sociocultural process that leads to wisdom.

Liberal Education

Many colleges and universities in the United States require that students not only engage in a specialized course of study (i.e., a major) but take courses in liberal education as well. When asked why they are required to do this, most college students respond that a liberal education broadens students' knowledge so that they know about more than just their own major area of study. But when asked why this is desirable, few can give a good reason. And why a broad education is considered "liberal" is equally unclear.

One of the primary reasons for this confusion is that in ordinary usage, the term *liberal* tends to describe a particular political orientation that is primarily understood as the opposite of conservative. Later in this book, that usage will be explored and complicated, but here I wish to explore an earlier, more fundamental, and original meaning for the term *liberal*. If

---

3. See Paulo Freire and Donaldo P. Macedo, *Literacy: Reading the Word and the World*, Critical Studies in Education Series (South Hadley, MA: Bergin & Garvey Publishers, 1987).

we think about it for a moment, we should notice that the word "liberal" appears to have the same root as some other English words such as *liberty, liberalize,* and *liberate,* all words that in one way or another have something to do with freedom. We shouldn't be surprised at this because the root for all of these words is the Latin word *liber,* which means "free."

We should suspect from this that a liberal education has something to do with freedom. But what is that connection? To understand it, we need to know that the idea that we refer to as liberal education is inspired by the education provided to free citizens of ancient Athens. Whether true or not, in American mythology,[4] the American democracy was inspired by the democracy of ancient Athens, where all free, adult males were members of the governing Athenian senate. From this sense, a "liberal" education should be understood as the education needed by a free citizen who must accept and carry out his or her responsibilities in the governing of the city-state.

Mortimer Adler, one of America's best known classical philosophers, argues that a liberal education, in the classic sense, is the education one needs to pursue a fully human life in one's leisure time, that is, outside of one's vocation. According to Adler, education for work is the kind of education one provides slaves who have no right or responsibility to the governing of public space. In contemporary America, where slavery is no longer legal, nearly all of us must have some sort of occupation, so, Adler concedes, we all need some sort of vocational training. However, he also vigorously argues, we are all also citizens and share both the right and the responsibility to actively participate in the governance of public life. This is the purpose of liberal education—to provide the kind of education needed by everyone in a democratic society in order to provide the knowledge, skills, values, and dispositions necessary to fulfill their roles as citizens in a democratic society.[5]

Education and Democracy

Earlier in this chapter, I pointed out that Dewey understands education to be a lifelong pursuit "to share in the intellectual and moral resources which humanity has succeeded in getting together." But Dewey's emphasis on "humanity" should not be taken to mean that he was unaware of social and cultural differences among different communities and nations. Clearly, a child needs to be integrated into a successive series of different communities, starting with the family, then the local community and the nation. For Dewey, one of the key differences among nations is their different political systems, and of all political systems, according to Dewey, democracies are the most dependent on education. In fact, for Dewey,

---

4. Many scholars point out that the Hau de no sau nee (also known as the Six Nations or the Iroquois Confederacy) may actually be the oldest democracy. Certainly the founding fathers of the American experiment drew inspiration from ancient Athens, but they also drew inspiration from the Hau de no sau nee nations who occupied the New England territory when the Europeans arrived. The reality of an actual democracy among a confederacy of nations on the North American continent was influential in their own commitment to develop a democratic confederacy from the thirteen English colonies. For a good and accessible discussion of the Hau de no sau nee democracy and its contribution to the American conception of democracy, see David T. Ratcliffe, *The Six Nations: Oldest Living Participatory Democracy on Earth* (Roslindale, MA: Rat Hous Reality Press, 1995–2013), www.ratical.org/many_worlds/6Nations/.

5. Mortimer Adler, "Labor, Leisure, and Liberal Education," *Journal of General Education* 6 (1951): 35–45.

democracies not only require education, true education requires democracy—not just at the national level, but also at the school and classroom levels.

To understand why democracy and education are so intertwined, we must gain a better understanding of what Dewey meant by "democracy." Put simply, "A democracy is more than a form of government; it is primarily a mode of associated living, of conjoint communicated experience."[6] Dewey argued that there were two aspects of democracy that people often confused. One aspect he referred to as "the idea of democracy," or the wide commitment to a way of living together as expressed in the definition above. One might think of the democratic idea as a commitment to a process where everyone is respected and included as we all figure out ways for all of us to live and work together.

The idea of democracy should not be confused with the political mechanisms of democracy found in such institutions as government, secret ballots, majority rules, constitutions, courts, and any mechanism used to try to institutionalize democracy. These mechanisms are just tools that we agree upon in the hopes of achieving democracy. When these mechanisms fall short and fail to help us achieve a form of association marked by "conjoint communicative experience," they must be rejected, and the democratic community must continue its search for ways to move forward democratically.[7]

For Dewey, democracy is a way in which people come together to deliberate in order to adjust to the ever-changing world that we inhabit. It should be clear that a community that depends on conjoint deliberation needs to ensure that its citizens are competent and capable in this process. A society that wishes to be democratic but fails to ensure its children are brought into adulthood with the necessary intellectual, moral, and dispositional elements of democratic engagement will soon lose any chance of true democracy. In other words, for democracy to succeed, its citizens must be educated to democracy.

But, also consider that for people to come together to deliberate about adjusting to an ever-changing world requires that those people and that society must commit to their own continuous education. After all, what is the end result of honest deliberation if not the shared learning of all involved? When public discussion is merely my side beating down your side and pushing our thinking onto you, we do not have democracy. For that matter, when all we do is let everyone "do their own thing" and each "go our own way" and in doing so fail to learn or teach each other, we also do not have democracy. For a society to survive, it must learn. And for it to learn, it requires that as many of its citizens as possible be willing to learn, to teach, to reason, and to commit. Democracy is not easy. It is not sitting around a campfire and holding hands. It is often quite combative. But, ultimately, at least according to Dewey, democracy is a commitment to the idea that by working, thinking, speaking, and learning together, we can continually grow as a society and meet whatever challenges the future might bring.

The Public and the Private

Dewey also makes a distinction between public events and private events. Private events refer to all of those interactions among people in which the effects of their actions affect no one

---

6. John Dewey, chapter 7 in *Democracy and Education* (New York: Teachers College, Columbia University, 1994).

7. John Dewey, *The Public and Its Problems: An Essay in Political Inquiry* (Chicago: Gateway Books, 1946).

beyond themselves. When a committee of people makes a decision and acts on it, if only the members of that committee are affected, it is, according to Dewey, a private act. Public events refer to all of those interactions among people in which their action affects people beyond those participating in the decisions and actions. When a committee of people makes a decision and acts on it, and people who are not a part of that committee are affected, we have a public event. In a democratic society, public events must be held in the spirit of democracy.[8]

Private events, because they are private, can be democratic or not. If a nuclear family wishes to organize its family democratically, it may. If, however, the family chooses to be an oligarchy of adults, that is permitted as well. In a society such as the United States, certain institutions are generally understood to be private, including families and churches. Some churches organize themselves in a manner committed to democratic association, whereas others are quite hierarchical. In the same way, private schools, because they are private, may or may not organize themselves in a manner congruent with democracy.

Public schools, however, because they are public, must always operate with the idea of democracy at their center. Here is a good example to clarify the distinction between the idea of democracy and the mechanisms of democracy. Public schools are a mechanism that hopefully fulfills the need of democratic societies to educate their citizens into democratic public life. That is their purpose; they are not public schools just because the government runs them. They are not public schools because they are tuition free. They are public because they serve the interests of the public to have an educated populace in order for a democratic society to continue to grow and develop democratically. Their purpose is to serve as a mechanism for a democratic society to create and maintain its democracy.

Conclusion

The national debate about education in the United States seems to address a very narrow set of questions. First of all, it equates "education" with "schooling." Second, it equates "public schools" with "free schools paid out of taxes." Third, it focuses on job training. Fourth, it zeroes in on schools' effectiveness at promoting student knowledge acquisition. In other words, despite the wide variety of questions and answers about what education should be in a democracy, the debate around education in this country acts as if these are all settled questions and no longer up for debate. But such an assumption is premature, at best, and downright wrong, at worst. This book opens up these questions so that anyone interested in public education (including teachers, parents, and citizens) or their own education (i.e., students) might gain a better understanding of what the fundamental debates are actually about, in the hope that by learning to recognize the fundamental issues and a variety of positions possible around these issues, we can begin to have an honest and vigorous debate about the purposes and practices of public education in a democratic society.

---

8. Ibid.

CHAPTER TWO

Understanding Culture as Text

Because education includes learning how to participate in our community, education must reflect the culture of the community. But even though education may *reflect* the community's culture, it also helps *construct* the community's culture. So, education is both formed by its society and at the same time helps to form that society.

Human life has some basic shared characteristics around the world—human beings speak, eat, grow, work, dance, fight, get sick, love, hate, and die, among other things. But the way in which these activities are performed within a group and the meanings that any one society ascribes to these activities is a reflection of their culture. For example, whereas nearly all groups ritualize birth and death, the ways in which they are ritualized differs from group to group.

And just as with death and birth, education shows the influence of the culture within which it occurs. Different cultures present diverse understandings of intelligence, curriculum, discipline, teacher, and student. For example, in most of the industrialized nations, higher education is seen as a public good and so college students' education is highly subsidized by the government. In many of these nations, a university education is free for all who desire or so heavily subsidized that anyone can attend who gains admittance without having to take out a loan, something once done in some states such as California, but which no US states do today. Today, American culture seems to suggest higher education is more a private good accruing to individuals than a public good accruing to the community. Recent decades have seen a steady reduction of government support of higher education and an increasing inequality by social class in American universities as well as a higher level of indebtedness of today's young Americans.[1] The difference between, for example, Finland's complete support of students' expense for higher education and America's requirement that the cost of higher education be borne primarily by the students and their families is at least partly a reflection of some important differences between the two nations' cultures.

But it would be a mistake to assume that the belief that higher education is a private rather than a public good, resulting in the responsibility of the student to bear the primary cost of her or his education, merely reflects a long-standing American cultural trait. In fact, this is a very recent change in American culture. In the middle of the twentieth century, Americans largely shared the Finnish cultural belief that higher education was a public good. As a result, state universities were affordable for nearly all students who could obtain admission. For example,

---

1. John Bound, Michael F. Lovenheim, and Sarah Turner, "Increasing Time to Baccalaureate Degree in the United States," in *Education Finance and Policy*, NBER Working Paper Series (Cambridge, MA: National Bureau of Economic Research, MIT Press, 2012), 375–424, www.nber.org/papers/w15892.

in the 1965–1966 school year, California's university system cost $245 per year ($1,903 in constant 2005 dollars, the year the study was conducted). In 2005, the cost had increased to $6,312.[2] Several states have committed to moving toward "charter universities," which reduces state support for state universities in exchange for releasing those universities from certain state regulations. The idea of charter universities indicates that higher education is a private, not a public, good.[3] Many believe the continued privatization of public education will inevitably lead to a greater and greater burden being placed on students because of the newly constructed American cultural assumption that education is something for the individual rather than the community.

Although the change from considering education as a public good to considering it a private good has happened recently, it did not happen spontaneously. In other words, American culture has not just happened to change over the past forty years on its own. The change in culture resulted from a concerted effort by certain political interests to change the way Americans understand the purpose of education.[4] One of the mechanisms these interests used to change American culture is education through the media. By organizing the media to speak repeatedly about schools as if their only benefits accrue to individuals through obtaining good jobs, the other purposes of education that had traditionally been part of American culture, such as making a strong democracy through having an educated populace, began to wan in the public's mind. In other words, that so many in the United States today place primary responsibility on students to pay for their own university education resulted, at least partly, from education itself: education taught by the media. In this way, education both reflects culture and participates in its construction.

But we should not consider any nation to be made up of a single culture. All nations include multiple subcultures. The United States, for example, includes subcultures associated with ethnicity, race, language, sexuality, gender, social class, geographic region, religion, and many others. These American subgroups share many cultural practices and understandings that mark them as Americans, but they also differ in some ways. These differences often lead to dissimilar understandings of the purpose of education, the appropriate content of curriculum, and the most suitable classroom pedagogy (*pedagogy* refers to the art and practice of teaching).

Because schooling usually takes place outside of the family, the culture that is taught in the school may or may not differ in some important ways from that which the students bring with them into the classroom. In other words, schooling tends to treat the culture of some subgroups as legitimate and good while treating the culture of other subgroups as not legitimate and deficient, if it acknowledges their existence at all. What counts as "correct" English in American schools? The English spoken by the upper middle classes or that spoken by the working classes? As British sociologist Basil Bernstein and American anthropologist Shirley Brice Heath have shown, schools clearly favor and reward students who come to school speaking middle-class

2. California Postsecondary Education Commission, "Changes in Student Fee Levels in California's Public Postsecondary Education Systems," *Commission Fact Sheet 04-02*, 2004, www.cpec.ca.gov/FactSheets /FactSheet2004/fs04-02.pdf.

3. David Harrison, "Are 'Charter Universities' the Future of State-Funded Higher Ed?" *Stateline* (Washington, DC: Pew Charitable Trusts, 2011), www.pewstates.org/projects/stateline/headlines /are-charter-universities-the-future-of-state-funded-higher-ed-85899376842.

4. Richard A. Quantz, *Rituals and Student Identity in Education: Ritual Critique for a New Pedagogy*, Education, Politics, and Public Life series (New York: Palgrave Macmillan, 2011).

English.[5] For this reason, some scholars understand schooling to be an institutionalized process that legitimizes certain cultures and delegitimizes others. This process of favoring certain cultures helps explain why some students do well in school while others do poorly. It also helps explain why some students seem to think schools are fair, while others don't, and why some students are eager to do well in school, while others resist what the school teaches.

On Culture

In ordinary language, we often use the term "social" to refer to transitory or frivolous aspects of life, as when we talk about students' "social life" as opposed to their "academic life." In this ordinary way of speaking, "social" refers to our downtime. In contrast, we often think of the term "culture" as referring to the heavy weight of those generations that came before us and who seem to direct our lives from their graves. In this way of speaking, "culture" means the same thing as "heritage." But sociologists and other social scientists use these terms very differently from this ordinary usage; in fact, in some ways these terms may be not just different but also contradictory to how we use these terms in everyday language.

Many scholars use the term *culture* differently from other scholars as well. Sociologists, anthropologists, artists, writers, and literary critics often differ in their meaning of the term. This book situates culture in the humanities and so will emphasize a humanities usage of the term. But it is also situated in a field called Cultural Studies, a field that is both the humanities and the social sciences. Even though the book uses a humanities conception of culture, it will temper that usage with many insights from Cultural Studies normally found in the social sciences.

Having emerged in the United Kingdom in the 1960s, Cultural Studies is multidisciplinary and has as its focus issues of power, knowledge, and culture. Although many different fields may study culture, that does not mean all fields engage in Cultural Studies. For example, anthropologists study culture, but most anthropologists do not engage in Cultural Studies. For an anthropologist to work in the field of Cultural Studies, he or she must bring a particular set of understandings to the study of culture. To help signal when I am referring to the scholarly field of Cultural Studies, this book will capitalize the words and, hopefully, that will help the reader recognize that we are talking about a specific approach to the study of culture.

Culture as Text

Historically, two broadly different ideas of culture have predominated. The older concept of culture derives from the same root as the word "cultivate" and implies the improvement of a person through the careful "planting" of ideas, dispositions, and skills. To be cultured has

---

5.   Basil Bernstein, *Class, Codes and Control*, 2nd ed., Vol. 3: *Towards a Theory of Educational Transmissions*, Primary Socialization, Language and Education series (London: Routledge & Kegan Paul, 1977); Shirley Brice Heath, *Ways with Words: Language, Life, and Work in Communities and Classrooms* (New York: Cambridge University Press, 1996).

traditionally meant to be educated in the finer things of life, such as art, literature, philosophy, and etiquette. In the past, there had always been a bias in this understanding of culture toward that of upper-class Europeans, so for something to be considered "art," it required that thing to be favorably appreciated by the European upper classes. Traditionally, art from "the colonies" (i.e., the Americas, Africa, and Asia) and from the middle and working classes of Europe were seen as interesting, perhaps, but as "primitive" and not worthy of the designation "art." Similar opinions were held of texts and social norms valued by the less elite and foreign cultures.

One of the important influences of the twentieth century was the gradual recognition that such an understanding of culture is ethnocentric and classist because it devalues others' cultures as deficient rather than respecting other cultures as different but not less valuable. One of the central goals of Cultural Studies, as it developed during the latter part of the twentieth century, was to change the biased understanding of culture as being equivalent to the high culture of Europeans and to begin to bring the same methods of scholarship to the culture produced by nonelites and non-Europeans as traditionally used to study high culture. Cultural Studies, as a field, helped promote the idea that the study of television, Hollywood, Bollywood, rock and roll, blues, salsa, romance novels, magazines, and all the other formerly denigrated forms of cultural production are worthy of serious scholarly study.

Besides shifting attention from the culture of society's elites to that of ordinary people, Cultural Studies also changed the way that we understand the products of culture by focusing upon reading and interpreting these *products* as *texts*. This textual meaning of culture is associated primarily with the arts and humanities; courses in English, French, or German literature; courses in literary, music, or art criticism; or courses in philosophy often adopt some version of this textual meaning of culture. In the arts and humanities, "culture" is typically used to refer to material texts created by artists and scholars. The focus of art criticism, art history, or the humanities, in general, is on how we ought to "read" these material products, whether they are word, image, or social texts. Much of the scholarship in the humanities is a dialogue about the value or lack of value of a particular text. Often referred to as "criticism," this dialogue is performed by a critic of music, film, art, or some other kind of culture. (See the left-hand column of Table 2.1.)

Table 2.1 Two Concepts of Culture

Humanities	Social Sciences
texts	everyday life
(e.g., essays, books, paintings, movies, architecture, musical recordings)	(e.g., life on a particular street corner, in a specific bar, in a specific school)
products	shared values, dispositions, patterns of action
criticism	ethnography and scientific study

Culture as Everyday Life

Even though the humanities have traditionally used a text-based understanding of culture and engaged in criticism of text, the social sciences have developed an understanding of culture as the way in which people make sense out of the patterns of their daily lives and have traditionally attempted to study people and their lived culture "scientifically" by conducting ethnographies or conducting surveys. (See the right-hand column of Table 2.1.)

The social sciences developed their understanding of culture as a result of the rise of the social sciences near the end of the nineteenth century and during the first part of the twentieth century. These social sciences attempt to develop theories to explain what their ethnographies and surveys have found. One thing that any social theorist immediately realizes when she or he tries to develop a comprehensive theory to explain findings is that some parts of sociocultural life are clearly apparent and can change relatively easily across time or distance. On the other hand, other parts of sociocultural life are often obscure and seem relatively impervious to change even across great lengths of history or across great geographic distances. For example, Larry Cuban suggested that the basic way in which classroom teachers taught in the United States at the beginning of the twentieth century was pretty much the same as the way teachers taught at the end of the twentieth century.[6] And, in a photo-essay, Kate Rousmaniere showed how schools are visually similar throughout the world and across time.[7] There is something about a school that makes it immediately recognizable, whether it is in the United States or in Denmark, in the nineteenth or in the twenty-first century. While there is a tendency for some things to change very slowly, there is also a tendency for different things to change relatively quickly. If we look at the photos in Rousmaniere's photo-essay, we see many similarities from place to place and time period to time period, but we also see some things that are strikingly different. For example, schools in Brazil may have similarities to schools in Norway, but they also have many differences (see pages 10–11 of the photo-essay). Any complete social theory needs to explain those things that change relatively quickly, while simultaneously explaining those things that change relatively slowly. The linguistic tradition in the social sciences has been to label those things that change very slowly the "social" and those that change relatively quickly as the "cultural" part of the *sociocultural*.

But nonetheless, we must always keep in mind that we mean *relatively* slow and *relatively* fast. That is to say, even though the social may be slow to change, it does change; the cultural may be quick to change, but it also has some long-lived legacies that seem to hold on and on to mark a group. When Cuban argued that teachers teach the "same" at the end of the twentieth century as they did at the beginning, he didn't mean identically, but rather that the art of teaching was largely and noticeably the same. And while culture changes quickly, there are some who would argue, for example, that the American suspicion of intellectuals is something that has persisted nearly throughout its history.[8] So, while culture typically changes relatively quickly, sometimes it does persist across great spans of time.

The social (i.e., more static) part of the sociocultural is often understood as being located in deep structures that are underneath the notice of ordinary people. These structures influence our societies whether we realize it or not. *Structure* refers to the persistence of certain role relations (such as mother/daughter, teacher/student, principal/teacher, or broader relations such as social class) or to different forms of economic or social formations, such as capitalism or socialism. These social factors are understood to influence the form of our society in ways that are not always recognized by the very people who live in it. For example,

---

6. Larry Cuban, *How Teachers Taught: Constancy and Change in American Classrooms, 1890–1990*, 2nd ed., Research on Teaching series (New York: Teachers College Press, 1993).

7. Kate Rousmaniere, "Questioning the Visual in the History of Education: Or, How to Think about Old Pictures of Schools," 1998, www.units.muohio.edu/eduleadership/kate/kate1.html.

8. Richard Hofstadter, *Anti-Intellectualism in American Life* (New York: Knopf, 1964).

the change in American culture that redefined higher education as a private good is said by some scholars to result from the increased power of corporations and the very wealthy in our capitalist society. Or, in a different example, social factors such as racism, sexism, and heteronormativity[9] have become institutionalized in the practices of our media. Sometimes these social influences are obvious and noticed, but at other times they are subtle and obscure so that people do not even recognize their effects.

Here is one way to imagine how social structure works. Picture a modern city with all of its skyscrapers stripped of their facades, so we can see them as nothing but girders and beams. These girders and beams provide the structure upon which the different buildings attach their facades. Normally, of course, we don't see these internal structures, but these girders and beams form the skeleton around which the building is built. Buildings can look very different from each other, but they cannot violate certain necessities laid out by their internal structures. Social structures can be thought of as the girders and beams of societies around which societies must construct everyday life. Everyday life in a particular society may look different from one decade to the next, but each society's everyday life cannot violate its underlying structures.

On the other hand, whereas the skyscrapers of a modern city may share certain structural necessities, even a quick look at the city will show us that not all buildings look the same. In fact, they can look amazingly different from each other. The facades of the buildings might be made of brick, stone, or steel. They might have a lot of or a little glass. They might suggest massiveness or lightness. They might be colorful or dull. Like the facades of buildings, the surface life of societies can change more easily than the deep structures; a society might maintain the same structures but look different from decade to decade or from region to region.

This surface and dynamic part of the sociocultural may not be able to violate the underlying structures, but it might change if people begin to alter how they make sense out of their world. A society may maintain the same class structure from one generation to the next, but what meanings are given to those class divisions can change as people begin to interpret things differently in the different periods of history. In the 1950s and even into the 1960s, students in the United States were often forbidden from wearing jeans and T-shirts to school because such dress indicated working-class status, but as rock and roll and the youth culture developed during these decades, middle-class youth rebellion borrowed working-class dress, so that today, few schools would even think about banning such clothes. On the other hand, we find many schools today forbid hip-hop dress from school, even as we find middle-class, white, suburban kids adopting the dress of the poor and working-class, black, urban youth who spawned hip-hop culture. In other words, even though the cultural form of class and race might have changed from the 1950s to today, the social formation of class and race has remained much the same. Classism and racism as *social structures* may persist through the decades, but class culture and racial culture may change significantly during the same time period. So in the social sciences, the term "culture" has traditionally referred to this more surface, dynamic, interpretive set of meanings, whereas the term "social" has traditionally referred to the deeper, more static, more fixed set of relations.

---

9. "Heteronormativity" refers to the practices that treat heterosexuality as normal and all other sexual orientations as not normal.

Given these two aspects of society (i.e., the social and the cultural), if we wish to describe a society, we should describe both. And, if we were to try to describe the cultural aspects of a nation, we would certainly need to describe the culture against the background of the social. In other words, we must always understand that the cultural and the social go together. In this way, we come to realize that culture may make people quite different from each other in some ways, but we can understand those differences as distinctive ways to respond to their own structural constraints. Culture is something that can allow people to ignore social differences and embrace each other as alike, as when Americans come together despite their different class positions or identified racial categories and embrace each other as American. But it also can make people who are very much alike in their need to navigate through the same social structure understand each other as so different from each other. Despite the fact that African Americans, Asian Americans, European Americans, Hispanic Americans, and Native Americans may share more than they differ culturally, we often look at them as fundamentally different from each other. And yet Asians in Asia and Africans in Africa sometimes use the same racial term to describe Americans, regardless of our American racial categorization, because we appear more alike than different to the Asians and Africans. Culture is what makes one suburban high school appear to be so different from another; students in one school may actually believe that their archrivals really are cheaters and unsportsmanlike even while the two student bodies look identical to students from the inner city or the rural communities.

This social science approach to culture differs from the arts and humanities approach in that the social sciences are focused on how people make meaning of their lives, or how they actually live their lives, rather than being focused on the products that they produce. The approach associated with the social sciences focuses on everyday lived culture and the meanings that people make of their lives, whereas the approach associated with the humanities focuses on the texts that societies produce.

Culture in Cultural Studies

Which of these two approaches does Cultural Studies embrace? Both of them. Perhaps the most important contribution Cultural Studies makes to the study of culture is its recognition that these apparently different approaches to culture are really just two sides of the same coin. Cultural Studies suggests to those in the social sciences that one cannot really understand everyday lived culture outside of the texts that people in those cultures produce. If we want to try to understand a traditional society, we cannot merely study their values and norms; we also have to critique their cultural products, such as utensils, tools, weapons, art, and myths. Furthermore, if we want to understand the culture of the contemporary United States, we cannot just study our values and norms but must also critique our cultural products, such as our popular music, movies, television, and magazines.

Furthermore, Cultural Studies suggests to those in the humanities that one cannot really read, analyze, and critique the texts of culture without also understanding the lived culture within which those texts are produced. To try and make sense out of a tribe's pots or clothes without understanding how people make sense out of and live their ordinary lives is likely to lead to much misreading of those texts. In the same way, to try to comment upon *Modern*

Family, Abercrombie & Fitch ads, or the Kindle without understanding the everyday lives of ordinary Americans today is likely to lead to much misunderstanding.

But Cultural Studies goes one step further. It suggests that when we study culture we not only must study both the lived and textual culture, but we must also place culture (both the lived and the textual) in the larger social context. Cultural Studies works to not only understand cultural texts and everyday life but also to understand both senses of culture given the structural constraints that organize the social world. In other words, Cultural Studies develops a very complex, multifaceted understanding of culture.

The Circuit of Culture

Several models of a complex, multifaceted culture exist. Richard Johnson, a former director of the Centre for Contemporary Cultural Studies at Birmingham University in Birmingham, England, created one of the first (and still quite useful) models.[10] Johnson's model presents culture as repeated processes of production and reading. Figure 2.1 shows a modified version of how the circuit flows.

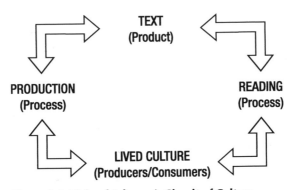

Figure 2.1 Richard Johnson's Circuit of Culture

One can begin an analysis of culture at any spot on the circuit and can move in any direction. The important factor is that each spot on the circuit should be addressed in any cultural critique. In Johnson's circuit of culture, the "text" phase of the circuit corresponds to the produced culture as used in the arts and humanities, whereas the "lived culture" phase corresponds to the way culture is used in the social sciences. The phase in the circuit called "production" addresses the "social" or "structural" part of society that the social sciences also address. Johnson's model suggests that individuals must "read" cultural objects in order to give them meaning. This implies that certain forces of production might create a text, but what that text comes to mean depends as much on how it is made sense of by the individuals who "read" it as it does on those who produce it. So the cultural meaning

---

10. Richard Johnson, "What Is Cultural Studies Anyway?" *Social Text* 16 (1986/87): 38–80. Another slightly more recent, but also even more complex, model was developed by another former director of the Centre for Contemporary Cultural Studies, Stuart Hall. Hall is now a professor at the Open University in England and probably the foremost scholar in the field of Cultural Studies. See Paul Du Gay, *Doing Cultural Studies: The Story of the Sony Walkman,* Culture, Media and Identities series (Thousand Oaks, CA, and London: Sage, in association with the Open University, 1997).

of *Girls* (the television series created by and starring Lena Dunham) is not just what the writers and actors put into the series, but what the TV viewers put into their reading of the series. To the extent that Johnson's circuit captures the concept of culture as used in the field of Cultural Studies, culture becomes a never-ending process that both produces and reads cultural texts as they come out of and help form everyday life.

Conclusion

As the above discussion should make clear, a humanities approach to the study of the sociocultural world of education will center on texts. It will examine the forces related to the production of texts as well as the consumption or use of texts. It will closely examine the texts themselves using techniques of analysis, interpretation, and critique that permit us a deeper appreciation of the meaning and implications of various texts about education in today's world.

CHAPTER THREE

Text Critique

This book addresses sociocultural studies in education as a study in the humanities both in the content knowledge it addresses and in the process skills it uses. The *content knowledge* of this book includes the textual representation of education in a democracy. The *process skills* address how to critique such texts. Throughout this book, readers need to keep in mind this two-pronged thrust and pay attention to the process skills of text critique as well as the content knowledge found in texts themselves. Reading (and creating) texts is the heart of the humanities, and education texts are no different from texts found in the fields of philosophy, literary studies, and Western civilization. The content of humanities texts makes few empirical claims about the way the world actually is (as a social or behavioral science course does, e.g., educational psychology). Instead, the humanities make claims about the way in which people represent their worlds in texts. In other words, its focus is people's meaning, their words, images, and texts.

In this book a *text* is any representation produced and engaged by people in which the interactive process between people and the text creates meaning. There are at least three different kinds of texts: word, image, and social, each of those representing through its specific medium. *Word texts* are what most people understand texts to be—books, newspapers, poems—anything where words are doing the representation. *Image texts* refer to anything that represents through images—drawings, paintings, sculptures, photographs, architecture. *Social texts* refer to representations found in the live engagement of humans in social interaction with each other—ordinary daily life, special ceremonies, extraordinary events. Of course, many texts are a mixture of the three basic types bringing together words, images, and social action in all possible combinations, such as movies, plays, and songs.

All three kinds of texts have been used for centuries to produce and represent education. Education has been a topic of debate at least since the ancient Greeks and Chinese. For 4,000 years, scholars, parents, ordinary citizens, and students have been struggling with what education is, how it should proceed, and why we have it. And their debates have been represented in texts. Today we find many of the same arguments that existed in the distant past. Of course, we might ask why we should bother thinking about these things if people can't ever agree. If the experts haven't figured it out in 4,000 years, how can one person do so simply by reading one book? Obviously, they can't. But such a question misses the point because understanding how education has been and is represented in texts is not about finding the one "correct" text; it is about clarifying for ourselves and for others what basic issues are at stake in the enactment of education in our society.

If people do not have a clear understanding of what they think education is and is not, how can teachers know what or how to teach, unless they are little more than robots following what they are told? How can parents know what to ask of their children and what to ask of their children's schools? How can citizens know how to demand school reform from their politicians? How can undergraduates know what to ask of their professors and of themselves? This book is about the meaning of education in a democracy as read in texts, and it is about the meaning of our own education as each of us constructs it through engaging educational texts.

How to Read Texts

To "read" any type of text means to *create meaning(s)* out of the representations in the text. Whereas representations are found in a text, "meanings" are not. Instead, meaning is located in the reading of the text—the act in which a reader engages the text. For this reason, we can never claim to have found the "true" meaning of a text, for there is no one true meaning. The best that can be hoped for is to construct a strong or good meaning for a text. Claims must, therefore, always be qualified—such as "This is what I believe the author intended"; "this is what I read in this text"; or "if we juxtapose this text with this other text, we can gain a new understanding of this passage." Gaining both knowledge and skills to help readers construct strong readings is one of the main objectives of this book.

In order to accomplish the construction of one's own meaning of education, the skills and knowledge are necessary to engage the texts to help one figure it out. So, besides presenting a variety of educational texts to provide a content to engage, this book also develops those skills necessary to critique those texts as generally accepted by scholars in the field of educational studies. To accomplish this task, this book will examine how to critique texts through reading analytically and interpretively with a particular emphasis on the normative aspects of reading educational texts. Stated very simply, *analytic reading* identifies the elements of a text, while *interpretive reading* places a text into a larger context. Paying attention to the normative elements requires bringing ethical or political values to the analysis and interpretation of the text. Part of *normative reading* asks the reader to reflect on how their own ethical or political values influence how they read the text.[1] The next section of this chapter will address text analysis, and the final section will address text interpretation.

Text Analysis

To analyze a text is to break it down into its important elements. This book will focus on two different ways to analyze a text: argument analysis and rhetorical analysis. This book makes a distinction between argument and rhetoric, but not every discipline treats the two things differently. For example, most first-year English composition courses treat argument

---

1. "Standards for Academic and Professional Instruction in Foundations of Education, Educational Studies, and Educational Policy Studies," Council of Learned Societies in Education, 1996, www.unm.edu/~jka/csfe/standards96.pdf.

as just one kind of rhetoric. But on this particular issue, this book is more influenced by the discipline of philosophy, which tends to treat the two differently. Here I wish to make a distinction between the two for particularly heuristic reasons. I have found that it is generally easier for someone to learn distinctions first and then to begin to muddy the boundaries than to start off with unmarked distinctions, which too often just leads to confusion.

Argument Analysis

In this book, *argument* refers to the use of reason or logic to make a claim. It might be called a "chain of reasoning."[2] Its purpose is to get at "truth," "right," the "good," or simply the "best answer" using reason. There are always, at least, two aspects to an argument: the claim (or conclusion) and the premises (also called *grounds, evidence,* or *support*). A claim without premises is not an argument; rather, it is an assertion. Many philosophers of informal logic also identify two other elements of arguments: warrants and backing. Warrants will be further discussed below. Backing will not be addressed in this book. The purpose of argument analysis is to identify the claim, the premises, and when helpful, the warrant used or assumed in a text and to judge the strength of the argument or the degree to which the premises and logic support the claim.

Claims. A *claim* is what the author attempts to convince us to accept. In ordinary conversation, people often mistake a claim for the whole argument. When asked to find an argument in an article, people often point to what the author is attempting to convince us to accept but fail to point out the evidence for the claim. But, as mentioned above, a claim without evidence is an assertion, not an argument. Being able to distinguish between assertions and arguments is an important tool in deciding whether or not to accept a text's claim.

Although most texts present claims, not all do. Even when there is a claim, it is not always obvious. Sometimes the claim may be implicit rather than explicit; in fact, occasionally the authors may even deny they are making a claim, even when the reader may believe that they are clearly doing so. Some texts, especially image texts, may not be putting forward a claim at all. So, when reading a text, one first must decide whether or not the text actually puts forth a claim. If the text does make a claim, then the reader should identify the premises presented to support the claim in order to identify the argument. If a claim is present but its premises are not, then there is no argument.

Premises. There are several different types of premises in an argument. *Empirical premises* appeal to facts about the world obtained through observing or measuring the world. Arguments that make an empirical claim rely on empirical premises and are called *empirical arguments*. The quintessential empirical arguments are found in science where the scientific claim depends on observations or measurements of the world for their evidence. For example, we could ask a question such as, "Which method for teaching reading works better: 'phonics' (i.e., part-to-whole methods) or 'whole language' (i.e., whole-to-part methods)?" Because such a question makes a claim about how the world actually works, it is an empirical claim

---

2. Steven Toulmin, Richard D. Rieke, and Allan Janik, *An Introduction to Reasoning*, 2nd ed. (New York: Macmillan, 1984).

and requires some kind of empirical evidence gathered by observing or measuring the learning of students who have been taught one or the other reading method.

But while science provides the prototypical empirical argument, not all empirical arguments are scientific. For example, if someone were to tell me that his daughter's teacher is really good because his daughter loves to go to school for the first time in her life, he would be making an empirical argument. His claim: his daughter's teacher is really good. His premise: his daughter loves to go to school for the first time in her life. We might raise objections to this argument. It could be something else that attracts her to school (perhaps the chance to play field hockey at recess), but that is our judgment of the argument's strength (that is, we judge the argument to be weak). Weak or strong, it is still an empirical argument because it makes a claim about the way the world is and provides empirical evidence to support that claim. Or, in a different example, if a student told her teacher that she knew Jimmy cheated on the test because she saw Jimmy looking at Albert's paper, then the student would be making an empirical argument. Her claim is that Jimmy cheated, and her empirical evidence gathered through observation was that she saw him look at Albert's paper. In both the "good teacher" argument and the "cheating student" argument, an empirical argument has been made, but neither is scientific.

Conceptual premises use evidence based on concepts and definitions and are not dependent on facts about the world but are dependent on the meaning we give to aspects of the world and life. For example, when Chapter 1 explores what we should mean when we talk about "education" and how education differs from training and from schooling, it is making a conceptual argument because it is trying to clarify the meaning of something that exists in our ideas, our concepts, our definitions. Conceptual arguments often reveal the different ways words or concepts can be understood and then attempt to use one of those ways to support some particular statement.

If, for example, we were to return to the empirical question asked above, "Which method for teaching reading works better: 'phonics' (i.e., part-to-whole methods) or 'whole language' (i.e., whole-to-part methods)?" we would have to answer some conceptual questions *before* we could answer the empirical question. For one thing, we would have to make an argument as to what "works better" means. Can a score on a comprehensive reading test be sufficient for deciding which "works better"? This is certainly the evidence that policy-makers seem to be using to determine everything from a school's report card to teacher retention. However, some might raise objections to such an indicator as being sufficient for determining what works better. They might prefer to know which method leads to further love of reading and which leads to a dislike of reading. What if, for example, part-to-whole approaches such as so-called phonics approaches (or what Constance Weaver calls "phonics first and in isolation") lead to slightly higher test scores for early readers but turn students off to reading, while whole-to-part approaches such as whole language (or what Weaver calls "teaching phonics and other cue systems and strategies in context")[3] lead to slightly lower test scores but turn students on to reading? Which would "work better"? No amount of empirical evidence can answer that question because it depends on what counts as "better"—higher test scores or love of reading. Does this mean that our answer is merely a matter of opinion? Should we just walk away and say, "Oh, you believe what you want to believe and I'll believe what I want to believe!" I would argue no, that it requires a well-reasoned conceptual

---

3. Constance Weaver, *Reconsidering a Balanced Approach to Reading* (Urbana, IL: National Council of Teachers of English, 1998), 8.

argument using conceptual premises to make claims about the most defensible meaning of "work better" before we can choose phonics or whole language to teach reading.[4]

Because understanding conceptual evidence and conceptual arguments is difficult for many people, let me give you one more example. Most of us would agree that education can occur without teaching. Most of us have had an experience in our lives when we gleaned an important lesson out of it even though no one was there attempting to teach that lesson to us. But while education can occur without teaching, can teaching occur without learning? This is a conceptual question and requires us to think carefully about what the necessary conditions might be for something to be called teaching. To accomplish this, we might want to start with a model case. Consider the following:

> Mr. Sommers, a sixth-grade language arts teacher, presents a lesson to his mixed-ability sixth-grade class on the difference between "there," "their," and "they're" by writing the three words on the board and asking students to find examples of each spelling in a short story that they have previously read together. After they find examples, he asks for volunteers to come to the board and write one of the sentences they found under the appropriate word. When at least one example of each spelling has been written on the board, he invites a discussion from the students about what the differences among the three spellings might be. Finally, he asks the students to write their own short story using each of the three words and, after collecting their individual essays, he returns them to the students letting them know which spellings they have used correctly and which they have not.

We could consider this a model case because most people would agree that this is an example of teaching. They might say, "If this is not teaching, than nothing is." What do we learn from this? P. H. Hirst and R. S. Peters might say that this model exhibits three necessary characteristics of activities that they describe as teaching:

> (i) they must be conducted with the intention of bringing about learning, (ii) they must indicate or exhibit what is to be learnt, (iii) they must do this in a way which is intelligible to, and within the capacities of, the learners.[5]

If you reread the above case, you will find that all three of these necessary conditions can be found.

We could then examine the question, "If no student learns after a teacher's lesson, is it still teaching?" by providing an example that might represent this question. Consider the following example:

---

4. Many research studies have found that whole-to-part reading methods, often referred to in the media as "whole language approaches," are better at leading students to like reading than part-to-whole approaches, (i.e., phonics) without diminishing reading test scores. If part-to-whole approaches do outperform whole-to-part approaches on tests, that superiority is lost by second grade. For a good summary of research that supports these statements, see Margaret Moustafa, "Foundations of Universal Literacy," in *Reading Process and Practice*, ed. Constance Weaver (Portsmouth, NH: Heinemann, 2002), 365–377.

5. Paul Heywood Hirst and R. S. Peters, *The Logic of Education*, The Students Library of Education (New York: Humanities Press, 1970), 81.

Dr. K. Pavlichenko, a professor of Russian literature at the local university, reads a 19th century Russian poem in Russian to Mr. Sommers's sixth-grade class of English-speaking students with the intention of developing in them an interest in Russian poetry. When she finishes reading it, she explains to them its meaning while continuing to speak in her fluent Russian.

Given the three necessary conditions identified by Hirst and Peters, this example appears to meet the first two criteria, but certainly fails to meet the third. Her presentation seems not to have been performed in a manner that was likely to have been intelligible to or within the capacities of the sixth-graders. It would, therefore, be reasonable to claim that whatever Dr. Pavlichenko was doing, she was not teaching—at least if we agree with Hirst's and Peters's three necessary conditions.

American culture is highly biased toward empirical arguments and is skeptical of conceptual arguments. This cultural bias is not universally shared. For example, the ancient Greek philosopher Plato was quite skeptical of empirical arguments, and German culture is known for its bias toward conceptual argument. In truth, however, Americans use conceptual evidence just as frequently as Germans; we just tend not to pay much attention to such evidence, assuming instead that everyone shares our understanding. For example, Americans will frequently say things such as "that is not democratic," or "he is a conservative." And certainly every student has exclaimed, "That is not fair." These are examples of concepts that require conceptual argument to clarify what we mean by "democratic" or "conservative" or "fair" before we can accept the claim; however, we rarely find someone following up their claim that something is undemocratic or conservative or fair with an explanation as to what those terms mean.

Warrants and Normative Arguments.   Generally, normative arguments use a normative warrant and make a normative claim. Warrants (along with claims and premises) are one of the three basic elements of an argument that this book addresses. A *warrant* is a rule or principle that connects the rest of the premises to the claim. A warrant authorizes us to move from the evidence provided in the premises to the conclusion found in the claim.[6] *Normative* arguments typically use an ethical or political principle or rule as a warrant. For example, return to the problem raised above when the hypothetical empirical study of teaching methods led us to the following finding: phonics helped students score higher on the tests but led many students to dislike school, while whole language resulted in lower test scores but led to students being happier in school. One might want to make the following argument:

P_1:   Part-to-whole language approaches ("phonics") help students score high on tests in first grade, but lead them to dislike reading and school.

P_2:   Whole-to-part language approaches ("whole language") help students to like reading and school, but may result in lower test scores in first grade.

therefore,

C_1:   We should use whole-to-part language approaches in teaching reading so students are not led to stop reading or to dislike school.

---

6. Toulmin, Rieke, and Janik, *Introduction to Reasoning.*

But why should we accept such an argument? Why should we choose based on whether or not children are happy in school? There has to be a normative *warrant* in the argument that authorizes the claim by connecting the empirical evidence "that students are happier in school" with the claim "we should use whole language." In other words, what warrant do we use to authorize the "therefore"? In order to justify the whole language approach over the phonics approach in this example, we would have to come up with an ethical or political principle to justify such a choice. For a warrant, perhaps we could adopt the principle of nonmaleficence taught in medical ethics: "First, do no harm." If we were to insert the principle, "first, do no harm," into our argument as a warrant, we might be able to justify our claim.

P_1: Part-to-whole language approaches ("phonics") help students score high on tests in first grade, but lead them to dislike reading and school.

P_2: Whole-to-part language approaches ("whole language") help students to like reading and school, but may result in lower test scores in first grade.

W_1: We accept the principle of nonmaleficence (first, do no harm).

therefore,

C_1: We should use whole-to-part language approaches in teaching reading so students are not led to stop reading or to dislike school.

Before leaving this discussion of warrants and normative arguments, I must address the terms *moral, ethical,* and *political.* Each of these terms will be more fully developed later in the book, but for now a brief clarification might be helpful. While many people make a distinction between the moral and the ethical, most philosophers (though not all) make no distinction whatsoever—after all, the root of the word *ethical* is just the Greek for the Latin root of the word *moral.* This book will mostly use the terms *moral* and *ethical* as synonyms. One exception to this will be when later in the book I discuss the ethic of care as developed by the philosopher Nel Noddings. But other than this one exception, I will treat the terms *ethics* and *morals* as having the same meaning.

The term *political* refers to the struggle for power. *Cultural politics* will refer to the struggle for power through seeking recognition and legitimacy for one's culture or refusing to recognize as legitimate other cultures. This certainly includes the struggle over elective state office and the struggle over legislation or the struggle over the enforcement of laws by the state executive, but it also includes the struggle over which curriculum will be seen as legitimate or which version of English will be accepted in schools or whether males and females should expect equal experiences in schools or not.

Politics is typically organized around principles and interests. Political principles are used as warrants in the same way the moral principles are. In fact, many political principles are also moral principles. For example, a commitment to the principle of democracy could be used as either a moral or a political warrant. But other political principles might not be about morality at all, such as a commitment to the American principle of majority rule, which is just a mechanism used to attempt to achieve democracy.

Identifying the moral or the political warrants in a normative argument is an important tool for analysis. My experience after nearly thirty-five years of college teaching is that for most students, the requirement that they become self-reflective about the relationship between their own ethical and political values and the ethical and political values of public spaces is new for them and that they often enter this process without a strong background in ethics or politics. Though I will present much of the content needed to identify normative warrants, readers of this book may find that they need to do work beyond that which is presented in these materials in order to develop more fully their understanding of the ethical and political principles used as warrants in American educational texts.

Premises and Subarguments. An argument typically has several premises supporting its claim, and each premise may itself be the claim of its own argument. When a premise of the overall argument is the claim of its own argument, I refer to it as a subargument.

In 2006, former Supreme Court Associate Justice Sandra Day O'Connor, a Republican, and the then-superintendent of the Los Angeles City Schools and former Democratic governor of Colorado, Roy Romer, coauthored a commentary in the *Washington Post* titled "Not by Math Alone."[7] Before reading the rest of this chapter, you might want to read the commentary, which can be found on the *Washington Post* website (noted in the endnote).

One way to state the argument of "Not by Math Alone" follows (all quotations are directly from the commentary):

P_1: Preserving democracy requires we promote civic learning. (argued)

P_2: "Understanding society and how we relate to each other fosters the attitudes essential for success in college, work and communities; it enhances student learning in other subjects." (asserted)

P_3: "America's economy and technology have flourished because of the rule of law and the 'assets' of a free and open society." (asserted)

therefore,

C_1: "We must restore education for democracy to its central place in school."

This argument has three premises in support of its final claim; however, if you actually read the commentary, you will find that only P_1 is itself argued; P_2 and P_3 are both assertions (claims with no supporting evidence). The authors provide neither empirical nor conceptual reasoning for P_2 and P_3; they merely assert them and expect their readers to accept them. On the other hand, P_1 is given much support by a subargument. If we were to summarize the subargument for P_1, it might look like this:

P_{S1}: There is evidence of the neglect of democracy in the United States.

P_{S2}: A healthy democracy requires an educated population.

P_{S3}: The effect of reduced civic learning on civic life is not theoretical but is having real effects.

P_{S4}: Education is more than taking classes: much effective civic learning takes place beyond the classroom in extracurricular and other experiences.

P_{S5}: A nation that invests in advancing democracy elsewhere must not neglect it at home. (warrant)

therefore,

C_1: Preserving democracy requires we promote civic learning.

7. Sandra Day O'Connor and Roy Romer, "Not by Math Alone," *Washington Post*, March 25, 2006, www.washingtonpost.com/wp-dyn/content/article/2006/03/24/AR2006032401621.html.

Here we see a set of conceptual and empirical premises in a subargument advancing the claim that "preserving democracy requires we promote civic learning," which is then, in turn, used as the first premise in the overall argument of the commentary. And, if we wanted to, we could develop another sub-subargument for some of the premises in this subargument. For example, the authors provide evidence that American education is neglecting the teaching of democracy. In this example, we can see that an argument is a set of premises in support of a claim and that any premise can itself be a claim of a subargument presented to ultimately convince the reader to accept the overall claim.

By breaking a text into the elements of its argument, an astute reader is able to make a judgment about the strength or weakness of the argument. Do the premises support the claim? Are the premises consistent with each other or might some contradict one or two of the others? Is the argument coherent (that is, do all the parts fit together as a whole)? Does the argument present sufficient evidence (either empirical or conceptual) to convince us that the reasoning is strong?

If we look at the O'Connor/Romer argument stated above, we find quite a clear set of premises for P_1, but little evidence to support P_2 and P_3. How should we regard the strength of this argument? First, recognize that any short commentary is too short to provide all of the evidence we might desire, so perhaps we should take the space limitation into consideration. Doing so, one might say that given the space limitations, the subargument for P_1 is pretty strong, but that the lack of support for P_2 and P_3 makes the overall argument less strong. Having analyzed the argument, we are in a position to decide whether reason should lead us toward supporting O'Connor and Romer's claim or not.

Rhetorical Analysis

Most first-year composition courses subsume argument under rhetoric, whereas this book treats argument as different from rhetoric. English composition courses are influenced by the field of literary studies, which typically recognizes argument as just another technique for persuading readers of the worth of the author's text. This book separates argument out from rhetoric because the field of educational studies is more heavily influenced by philosophy than literary studies, and philosophy has a tradition of treating argument as an aspect of reasoning, not persuasion. In philosophy, an argument is judged on its strength of reasoning—its logic—not by whether or not people are persuaded by it. Too often people are persuaded through rhetorical tricks to accept a bad argument and just as often people are not persuaded by a good argument simply because they find the language boring or complicated. But while the field of educational studies differs from that of literary studies on the issue of argument, the two agree about the rest of the elements of rhetoric.

While argument analysis identifies the elements of an argument that make it strong or weak, rhetorical analysis breaks down the elements found in a text that make it more or less persuasive. A text may have a strong argument but be unpersuasive, or it may have a weak argument and still be very persuasive. Even though most scholars would agree that the strength of an argument is the crucial element in reading another's work, they frequently find that rhetoric often trumps argument. In other words, many readers make their judgments of texts based more on the rhetoric than the argument. Advertisements would be ineffective if it were the other way around.

Rhetorical Appeals to Reason. To clarify the distinction between the approach to rhetoric found in literary studies and that found in educational studies, let us return to the question of argument for just one moment. In literary studies argument is just another element of rhetoric sometimes identified as "rhetorical appeals to reason." In this book, any real use of reason will be considered part of a text's argument and not part of its rhetoric, but there are times in which the appeals to reason are more apparent than real. For example, consider those advertisements for medicines in which an actor dressed in a white lab coat and wearing glasses speaks in a scientific sounding language about the worthiness of the product being sold. Often graphs will be projected with numbers and shapes and colors suggesting that studies have shown this product to be superior to other similar products. This is not a real use of reason but rather an *apparent use of reason.* The apparent use of reason is what this book will call a "rhetorical appeal to reason" and might make for a very persuasive advertisement, even though its argument (i.e., the real use of reason) is weak. In this example, it should be clear that there is a distinction between the rhetorical appeal to reason and the actual use of reason in an argument, because one is clearly present and the other clearly absent. But in other texts, it might be less clear whether the argument is actually using reason or merely appearing to do so.

Traditional academic writing has valued the presentation of strong arguments, but it has also privileged rhetorical appeals to reason by insisting on certain rhetorical forms and devices in published academic journals. In other words, in traditional academic writing, we find not only real arguments being presented, but these arguments being presented with a rhetoric whose form shows that it values rhetorical appeals to reason. This is especially true in any of the scientific literature but can also be found in the humanities as well. Although scholars are trained to see through the rhetoric to get at the argument, sometimes academic texts are accepted more on their rhetoric than their argument.[8] A strong reader will be able to recognize the distinction between a text that puts forth a strong argument and one that puts forth only a persuasive "rhetorical appeal to reason."

Rhetorical Elements of Style. While rhetorical appeals to reason are important to note, this book focuses more often on rhetorical elements of style. And while there are many different kinds of style elements that readers should pay attention to, this book will emphasize only three of them: cultural narratives, tropes, and ideographs. What follows is a summary describing each.

Cultural Narratives. Whether or not a text makes an argument, it likely uses a cultural (also called a *root* or *stock*) narrative. A narrative is simply a story. Some texts place the narrative at the center of the text, focusing on making the story interesting, exciting, and intriguing. This focus on narrative sometimes causes authors not to care about developing a strong argument but to rely on the narrative to persuade the reader. However, just because an author has emphasized the narrative at the expense of the argument does not mean that

---

8. It must be pointed out, however, that in today's world of academia, including educational studies, many scholars reject the notion that there is anything called a "real argument." Instead, they agree with those in literary studies that all arguments are little more than rhetorical appeals to reason. This book continues to maintain the distinction between real argument and rhetorical appeals to reason for heuristic reasons—by maintaining the distinction, those new to text analysis are more readily able to see some of the important illusion-creating effects of rhetoric found in texts on education.

there is no argument. A persuasive narrative may still have an argument, even if it is a weak one. In the same way, just because an author de-emphasizes narrative and works to develop a clear and strong argument does not mean that there is not a story being presented or, at least, a cultural narrative assumed. This is the heart of the analysis techniques in this book. This book argues that identifying cultural narratives is the single most important reading skill required in analyzing educational texts. Chapter 4 will focus exclusively on cultural narratives, clarifying and developing this technique for text analysis, but a beginning exploration of cultural narrative is presented here.

As stated above, narratives are just stories, accounts, reports, chronicles, or records. There are at least two different levels of narratives: surface narrative and cultural narrative. The *surface narrative* of a short story or a movie is easy to recognize. If asked to tell the narrative of *The Breakfast Club*, a reader would have little trouble laying out the basic plot where a group of high school kids from different social groups serving Saturday detention forges an uneasy camaraderie resulting from their common experience. But this surface story is only a particular version of a very common underlying *cultural narrative* that director John Hughes returned to again and again (for examples, see *Sixteen Candles*, *Pretty in Pink*, and *Ferris Bueller's Day Off*). We might call the underlying narrative in all of these movies the Teenage Angst cultural narrative. This cultural narrative presents a story in which the teenagers find themselves in opposition to adult authority while undergoing the trials and tribulations of teen social life, all the while struggling for an identity they can be comfortable with. The surface narrative is just the plotline, but in rhetorical analysis we are interested in the deeper foundational, deep-seated, or underlying storyline, a cultural narrative that organizes the surface narrative. We can think of *Sixteen Candles*, *Pretty in Pink*, and *Ferris Bueller's Day Off* as each presenting a different surface narrative while sharing an underlying cultural narrative. We are searching for the underlying narrative that *The Breakfast Club* used to tell its story. Perhaps we could call it a formula. What is the cultural narrative (or storyline or formula) that John Hughes used in making these movies?

Or, to take a different example, whenever we watch a romantic comedy, we know basically what is going to happen before we sit down to watch because we know the cultural narrative that romantic comedies use. Within five minutes we know which actor has been assigned which role in the story because we already know the basic elements of a romantic comedy, including the major roles as well as the basic plot development that builds to the ending. We already know the cultural narrative; we don't watch romantic comedies to find out what happens but because we enjoy watching the execution of this familiar underlying storyline and the particular details of the narrative that change from text to text and that we may have learned to appreciate. Most texts have familiar cultural narratives supporting them, though sometimes the cultural narratives used are not familiar or, at least, conscious in our minds as we read them. However, a good reader will know the basic cultural narrative supporting the surface narrative of a mystery compared to a police procedural or a romance versus a coming-of-age story. A good reader will be able to recognize, for example, that the recent vampire genre is really only a variation of the traditional romance narrative. A good rhetorical analysis will be able to penetrate the surface and identify the underlying narrative.

In fact, most arguments gain some of their rhetorical persuasiveness because they are couched within a commonly accepted story. Ronald Reagan often located his arguments within a cultural narrative called a *jeremiad*. Reagan's arguments can be understood better when you are aware that underlying them is a storyline stating that the United States was built into a great country because it followed true and moral actions; however, lately America has gotten off track and, as a result, we have started downhill. But, like Jeremiah in the Bible, we can get ourselves back on track, if we return to the tried and true virtues of the American past.[9] This jeremiad narrative helped make Reagan's speeches more persuasive to those people who already believed the basic story regardless of the particular facts that Reagan was advancing. Take a close look at the rhetoric of today's social conservatives such as Sarah Palin, Mike Huckabee, and Michele Bachmann, and you'll find Reagan's jeremiad. All three of these politicians often use the same cultural narrative to support many of their own surface narratives. In other words, because people are familiar with the storyline of the jeremiad narrative, they accepted Reagan's claims and are also attracted to the arguments of contemporary social conservatives such as Palin, Huckabee, and Bachmann whether or not their arguments are strong or weak. The cultural narrative of these politicians persuades many people more than their arguments convince them.

Some would argue that the McCain-Obama presidential campaign was largely contested around cultural narratives rather than policies. John McCain was presented *as a narrative*: a tough soldier who sacrificed for his country as a prisoner of war and who as a senator acted as a "maverick." Sarah Palin was also presented *as a narrative*: a tough hockey mom from Alaska who stood for old-fashioned family values. Palin's narrative was brilliantly captured in her quip that, in Alaska, a hockey mom was a pitbull with lipstick. Candidate Barack Obama was presented as the American dream come true—the proof that America's dream is still alive—that the son of a black African immigrant and a white mother from Kansas can grow up to be president of the United States. If Obama can do it, anyone can grow up to be president if they have the drive and talent. All three of these candidates attempted to persuade Americans to support them through these three narratives. And, in fact, many people voted for one or the other because they liked the narrative that the candidate represented. Naturally, opponents attempt to replace these positive narratives with negative counternarratives. Obama was presented as a secret Muslim working in the interest of al Qaeda who would take our guns away and leave America unsafe. McCain was presented as an old man whose time has passed (check out *The Daily Show*'s clip of McCain at the debate wandering around the stage like a doddering old fool talking to himself[10]). Politicians know that people are more likely to be persuaded by a good cultural narrative than by reasoned argument.

In the Obama-Romney election, President Obama's campaign re-narrated him as the president who saved Detroit and the American economy, while Governor Romney's campaign tried to re-narrate Obama as someone who doesn't understand business and has failed as president. In the meantime, Romney's campaign presented him as the businessman who saved the Olympics and, therefore, would be able to save America using the same business sense. In turn, the Obama campaign worked to re-narrate Romney as a cold businessman whose fortune was founded by shipping American jobs overseas, not paying his fair share of taxes, and hiding money offshore; who was born wealthy and was only interested in helping

---

9. Don Felty, "The Bully Pulpit: Presidential Rhetoric and National Education Agenda in the Reagan Administration, 1981–1984" (PhD diss., Miami University, 1992).

10. See minute 07:50 of this clip: www.thedailyshow.com/watch/wed-october-8-2008/word-war-ii.

the wealthy. "He is not one of us," they might have said. Of course, many Romney support-ers continued the McCain narrative that tells us that President Obama is a secret Muslim working in the interest of al Qaeda who would take our guns away and leave America unsafe. Or, in other words, "he is not one of us." Because presidential campaigns have primarily focused on telling stories, many people are turned off to elections. They long for candidates to actually use argument and not mere rhetoric. They want candidates to tell them what they would do and why and mean it. But, the politicians have come to believe that argument does not work particularly well, whereas rhetoric does and so, for now, elections are primar-ily about telling stories that appeal to cultural narratives that members of the electorate are already inclined to accept.

The important debates around education in the United States are not much different from those of the politicians. Policy-makers and politicians seem more interested in persuad-ing people through narrative than in convincing them through well-reasoned arguments supported by evidence. True, part of their stories include the "rhetorical appeal to reason" mentioned above, but keep in mind, just because their story tells us that they are interested in research-based decision-making does not mean that they actually pay attention to the research. If they did, most of the elements of the reform movement for the past forty years would have been dropped decades ago since nearly all of them have little to no empirical evidence to support their effectiveness.

So, many arguments in education use a cultural narrative instead of argument to persuade people to support their solutions to the problems of schools. Some use a cultural narrative that its supporters might call the "Great School Equalizer" and its opponents might call the "Great School Legend."[11] The Great School Legend cultural narrative suggests that our wise forebears, desiring a true and equitable democracy, built a system of schooling designed to give a common education to all Americans, rich or poor, in order to give every child an equal chance for success in life. This cultural narrative suggests that while schools may have some faults, they have largely been successful in creating the most equitable nation on earth. This narrative, whichever name we give it, has created a cultural narrative, an underlying story, that many Americans believe: America's democracy is strong and society is equitable due to its historically strong public school system. Of course, the Great School Legend has been vigorously opposed by alternative narratives that suggest alternative stories such as the public schools are broken or schools are about the economy, not democracy. Chapter 4 will explore these and several other cultural narratives that influence education today.

We can better understand educational arguments when we can find the cultural narratives that make the argument more persuasive. We can also better understand why some argu-ments, though logically compelling, do not seem to be effective when they present a cultural narrative that is not already familiar to the reading audience. In fact, as most politicians understand and as our elections continue to show us, the narrative may be more important in the persuasiveness of an argument than the argument itself.

Tropes. *Tropes* are rhetorical devices such as metaphors, similes, irony, satire, paralipses, puns, aphorisms, hyperbole, and dozens of other words and phrases that change the basic meaning of a word. That is, tropes (or figures of speech) alter a word from its common

---

11. Colin Greer, *The Great School Legend: A Revisionist Interpretation of American Public Education* (New York: Basic Books, 1972).

meaning to some other meaning. Most tropes are used merely to make the writing more interesting to prevent the reader from becoming bored, but some tropes are used to persuade the reader to accept a particular claim that is not well supported by argument. Most cultural narratives use specific tropes so that when the trope is used, the cultural narrative is evoked in the mind of the reader.

In contemporary academic writing, much attention has been placed on the metaphors people use to give meaning to their world. In education, you will often find writers using metaphors from the military (e.g., war on drugs), sports (e.g., pep rallies before proficiency tests), factory (e.g., students are the "raw material" to be turned into "products"), marketplace (e.g., students are consumers), or gardening (e.g., kindergarten is German meaning "garden of children") realms. Using health metaphors has become particularly popular when referring to educational problems, such as "at-risk" or "learning disabled" students. Plato likened teachers to midwives assisting in the birthing of knowledge that comes out of the student rather than something that is put into the student. By locating the tropes used by an author, we can often gain insights into the controlling logic or emotional appeal of a text. This book is less interested in those tropes used to merely make a text interesting, but is very interested in those tropes, especially metaphors, used to make the claim more persuasive. Perhaps today the most popular tropes used by politicians evoke the marketplace, and lead readers to think of students or their parents as consumers, and education as a consumer good, and that schools have to market themselves and brand themselves and sell themselves. These tropes are so common that it may be hard for some people to realize that the cultural narrative they evoke (that government is the first step to tyranny and that all problems can be solved through the market) is a relative newcomer to the narratives of schooling—one that barely was told a mere fifty years ago. Many people have a hard time even imagining a different cultural narrative and part of that reason derives from the ubiquitous use of marketplace tropes when talking about education.

Ideographs. An *ideograph* is an idea that evokes strong emotion in a large number of people and that writers and speakers use to bolster their position. In educational policy, Ronald Reagan appealed to the ideographs "choice" and "excellence." Bill Clinton accepted the ideograph of "choice" but tied it to an ideograph of "fairness" by requiring that government-supported school choice be limited to the public schools. George W. Bush used "no child left behind" and "research-based instruction" as ideographs. President Obama's Department of Education speaks of a "race to the top" as an ideograph. In all of these cases, these presidents attempted to sell their education program by attaching an ideograph to it.

The trick of ideographs lies in the fact that readers must disassociate themselves from the ideograph before they can reject the argument. For example, when the Reagan administration argued that their education plan provided choice and excellence, it placed the opponent to their plan in the position of appearing to be against choice and excellence. When George W. Bush advanced his plan as designed to leave no child behind and to favor pedagogy that is research-based, it placed the opponent in the position of appearing to favor leaving some students behind and being against the rational basis of research. And today, anyone who wishes to argue against President Obama's race to the top, must be willing to settle for being at the bottom. Of course, opponents of Reagan's plan might also be in favor of choice and excellence and still be against his plan and the opponents of Bush's education policy might be very much in favor of leaving no children behind and in favor of research, but still be against the Bush policy. And naturally, one doesn't have to be willing to settle for the bottom to object to Obama's educational policy.

This rhetorical device is very powerful. You will find that authors in the field of education frequently use the ideographs "democracy," "diversity," and "the child." By appealing to choice, excellence, fairness, democracy, diversity, or the child, an author hopes to convince the reader that the author and reader are interested in the same common goals. Watch for those who argue that they are only interested in helping the kids while the other guys are in it for themselves. Many different groups use this ideograph, but it is a particularly effective rhetorical device to use against teachers. Claiming their own position is "for the kids" while that of the teachers or their unions is only "for themselves" is a very effective technique even if the teachers and their unions are also arguing for the interest of the kids. People are just more likely to believe that teachers or their unions don't have their students' best interests at heart. Perhaps this comes about from people's experience in schools in which they felt that too many of their teachers did not really care about their students. In fact, the recent well-publicized (and well-financed by conservative moguls) movie, *Waiting for Superman*, depends heavily on the negative ideograph "teacher union" and the positive ideograph "choice," which help to persuade viewers to support the idea that the problem with schools is bad teachers and the unions that support them. Of course, that the wealthy financiers might be less interested in helping the kids and more interested in weakening the power of unions and, therefore, having nothing to do with education, let alone the effectiveness of schools, is likely to be unseen by the unreflective viewer. If an author can appeal to an ideograph that the reader subscribes to, the reader will often overlook a poor argument, since s/he is already emotionally committed to the ideograph.

Text Interpretation

Analytic readings examine texts and identify the arguments and rhetoric found in the text and make judgments about the strength of the argument and the persuasiveness of the rhetoric. Its purpose is to focus on the text itself and not to bring our own arguments and rhetorical strategies to replace those of the text. In a way, when we conduct an *analytic reading*, we are trying to understand the text as a thing by itself, not connected to other texts or to the world itself. Of course, no one is ever able to actually understand a text isolated from the rest of the world. At the very least, the very process of analyzing a text in terms of its argument and its rhetoric brings a dichotomy and set of methods from the outside of the text. But, in analysis we are really focusing on the text in front of us. We are breaking it down into its elements. We are talking about what we see on the page or on the screen or on the canvas or in the event right in front of our eyes.

Perhaps too many students in our secondary schools are not ever taught how to analyze texts; instead, they are asked to do little more than read for information. Certainly the requirements of standardized tests require little more than this. But when students are asked to go beyond remembering the information presented in a text, few are asked to go beyond a simple analysis that requires them to identify a plot and theme. Very few are taught that a complete reading requires that they go beyond the text in front of them. Few learn that in order to be a good reader, they have to bring material outside of the text to it. In fact, I believe most high school students would believe that a teacher who required that they know something not actually stated in the text would be unfair. Unfortunately, American students are no longer taught that the reader has a responsibility to bring all of their knowledge about the world to the text if they are actually going to be a good reader. But to read the word, as Paulo Freire and Donaldo Macedo tell us, requires that we also read the world.[12] The necessity of reading the world to read the word is rarely taught in secondary schools and, perhaps, even in higher education. This aspect of good reading is what we mean by interpretation.

Text interpretation is the specific and conscious act of bringing outside contexts to the text in order to deepen and broaden our understanding of it. It means to place a text into different contexts to see how these new contexts influence our understanding of the text. The "con-" in "context" simply means "together" and so "context" refers to the act of bringing a text together with other texts or knowledge or understandings. Text critique requires that we analyze texts within themselves and that we interpret texts by connecting them to other contexts.

But which other contexts should we connect the texts to? There could be hundreds of different contexts, from science and economics to sports or television or even our own personal experiences. The best context to use in interpreting a text is the one that provides the reader with the most important or interesting reading. The best readings draw on contexts that help reveal meanings that would otherwise go unnoticed. There is no right context to use to interpret a particular text, but some contexts provide much more insight into the text than others, and so some contexts are better to use in an interpretation than others. Some contexts help provide us a depth of understanding that we just could not have without it or open up our understanding to make connections that go far beyond our initial understanding of the text. Perhaps we see so little interpretive reading required in high schools because it requires both the student and the teacher to search for nuance and to accept complexity. Interpretation certainly does not lend itself to multiple-choice tests, and it requires teachers to use judgment in determining the quality of one student's interpretation. It is so much easier, for both the teacher and the student, to ask questions about things that can claim to be right or wrong. But requiring students to only read for information or to analyze texts is settling for a schooling that produces poor readers. Good reading requires interpretation.

So, one cannot answer which context is the best context to use for interpreting texts until we know the text, the readers, the situation, and the purposes involved in reading the text. Selecting the best context is always contingent. However, I recognize there is a heuristic benefit for limiting the range of contexts for those beginning to learn how to read the world as context for reading educational texts. For that reason, this book will focus primarily on four contexts: historical, philosophical (especially in the realm of education), economic-political ideological, and sociocultural contexts. After an in-depth discussion of cultural narratives in the next chapter, the rest of this book elaborates each of these four contexts as possibly useful for interpreting educational texts.

---

12. Paulo Freire and Donaldo P. Macedo, *Literacy: Reading the Word and the World,* Critical Studies in Education Series (South Hadley, MA: Bergin & Garvey Publishers, 1987).

CHAPTER FOUR

Cultural Narratives

Richard A. Quantz, with Kevin M. Talbert

Chapter 3 introduced narrative as an element of rhetoric. This chapter will extend the discussion of narrative through a more complete and focused elaboration of cultural narratives. The last chapter presented narrative as a rhetorical technique used to persuade readers rather than to reason with them. As such, what makes a narrative persuasive is not whether it is true or not, but whether it rings true to the reader. Rather than using a line of reasoning based on premises, warrant, and claim, narratives bring the reader into the order and organization and setting of a storyline. Of course, we might want to argue (using claims, premises, and warrant) that one narrative is true and that another is false, but narratives persuade through the nonrational effects of rhetoric rather than through the rational logic of argument. *Nonrationality* refers to all of those factors that push, pull, or sway people to believe or act without the use of rationality. Nonrational factors include emotional ties, prejudices, ritual expectations, and rhetorical devices. Nonrationality is *not* irrationality. Irrationality goes against reason, whereas nonrationality just doesn't use reason. Rhetoric works for reasons other than its rationality. This chapter will explore cultural narratives frequently found in educational texts that serve to persuade people nonrationally and, therefore, it is less interested in the truth or untruth of a cultural narrative and more interested in its meaning and power. The first part of the chapter will explain further the important aspects that make a cultural narrative and present a useful way to analyze the structure of a narrative. The second half will present some examples of cultural narratives that are influential in educational texts.

The Structure of Cultural Narratives

A narrative is just a story. As a story, it has particular structure, most notably plot, characters, and theme. One can understand the power of a narrative to persuade people by recognizing the patterns found in its structure. Different narratives favor certain plots, characters, and themes and use them to influence people nonrationally.

There are at least two different kinds of narratives. The *surface narrative*, as discussed in Chapter 3, refers to the individual and unique qualities of a specific story. The *cultural narrative* refers to a generic story from which surface narratives build their unique story. Sometimes the cultural narrative is explicit in the surface narrative as *Ever After: A Cinderella Story,* the 1998 movie starring Drew Barrymore, is built from a Cinderella cultural narrative and as *Clueless,* the 1995 movie starring Alicia Silverstone, consciously creates a new version of Jane Austen's book, *Emma.* But more frequently the relevant cultural narratives are implicit in the surface narrative and may be missed by the reader. For example, the surface narrative of the 2012 musical comedy *Pitch Perfect* presents a story in which a girls' a cappella group at fictional Barden College known for their star-quality good looks and tired covers of pop songs brings in newcomers who don't appear to fit into the traditional Barden Bellas mold. The oddball newcomers create disruption, discord, and drama that must be overcome before successfully competing for a national championship. Most obviously, *Pitch Perfect* exemplifies the musical comedy in which songs sung by the characters connect a lighthearted story often focused around romance. In particular, *Pitch Perfect* presents that subgenre of musical comedy built around a cast of young people who put on a show. Think of the sixteen Andy Hardy movies starring Mickey Rooney that began in the Depression years of the 1930s and continued for almost thirty years, or the recent television version, *Glee.*

The *Pitch Perfect* surface narrative draws on many underlying cultural narratives in order to stitch together the story. Is anybody surprised at the end when we find out that Anna Kendrick's character, Beca, ends up with the male lead, Skylar Astin's character, Jesse? We see other common plot devices such as the stressed relationship between Beca and her father; the beautiful and bossy Chloe, played by Anna Camp, who eventually gets her comeuppance; or the narrative of college life as being about everything except book learning. We also see stock characters in *Pitch Perfect* including the nerd; the oversexed and underbrained Stacie, played by Alexis Knap; and the butch lesbian played by Ester Dean. Even when the surface character plays against type, the stock character we know from the cultural narrative provides us with the humor, such as Rebel Wilson's Fat Amy who apparently has a ton of boyfriends. Surface narratives draw on underlying cultural narratives to hold the story together. Sometimes the surface narrative does it quite well; *Pitch Perfect* received an 81 percent from critics on RottenTomatoes.com, perhaps the largest aggregator of movie criticism. Contrast that with a movie that draws from the same basic cultural narrative, *Glee: The 3D Concert Movie,* which scored only 60 percent. The master creator of texts understands and uses the cultural narratives that circulate in society as a foundation for the creation of his or her surface narrative.

Plots and Arcs

One of the three structural elements of cultural narratives used in this book, *plot,* refers to the pattern, or trace, of events found in a story. A plot follows a trajectory and often implies a cause-effect sequence—event A happens, and then event B happens, which causes event C to happen. Plots typically introduce a problem or conflict that the characters must solve or resolve. So we might think of plots as events that proceed along a path where various new events disrupt or create imbalances that demand attention from the characters. Plots employ arcs to organize the movement through the story. A *plot arc* is a pattern of stages through which a reader is lead. (Plot arcs can also be called narrative arcs, story arcs, or just plain arcs—without any adjective.) The most common plot arc is a three-part pattern that begins with a setup that develops through some kind of escalating action and climaxes in some sort of resolution or solution. Of course, not all arcs follow this typical pattern, but, especially in popular culture, this is overwhelmingly the most common. Being able to recognize particular plot arcs can help clarify which cultural narratives a surface narrative is drawing upon in its construction.

Cultural narratives typically employ a cause-effect plot arc, which suggests certain events are linked to other events. These plots suggest that we can understand certain aspects of the world by understanding their connection to other aspects of our world. A cultural narrative will have a basic plot, which provides a structure to the specific surface stories told. In other words, a particular text will have its own unique variation of the plot, but if you are familiar with the cultural narrative, you will recognize that underlying the individuality of the plot in the text you are reading is a plot from a cultural narrative. For example, we all know the adage "crime does not pay." But this is more than an adage; it is also a cultural narrative. We know that there are plenty of criminals walking around who never get caught and who actually do benefit from their crimes. But in Hollywood, the Crime Does Not Pay narrative is king. When have you seen a movie where someone commits a crime and does not pay for it in the end? Except for heist movies (e.g., *Ocean's 11*) and sting movies (e.g., *The Sting*), most frequently criminals end up getting their just desserts in the end. And most heist and sting movies go to great lengths to let us know that the victims of the crime deserve it, the victims are themselves criminals, and the perpetrators of the crime are really more vigilantes than criminals. Consider Showtime's series *Dexter,* in which a serial killer kills other serial killers. Could we really have a television series in which the lead character is a serial killer who kills innocent people and gets away with it? Well, we could, but for some reason, makers of commercial movies do not want to stray too far from the Crime Does Not Pay narrative and knowing that, the astute moviegoer can recognize that movies with surface narratives as different as *High Noon* and *Avatar* still share the same cultural narrative.

While every cultural narrative has a plot arc, often the cultural narrative is so well understood by its readers that it is represented through other rhetorical devices such as tropes and ideographs (see Chapter 3). In other words, the plot often gets shorthanded and is only indicated by certain elements that everyone realizes. For example, I do not have to outline the whole plot of the movie *The Matrix* if I wish to appeal to its narrative, all I have to do is to mention "the matrix" and people will know what I mean. The same is true with the plots of cultural narratives. I do not always have to outline the whole plot every time I wish to evoke it, I only have to use some clear indicators of the narrative and the reader will fill in the plot. All one has to do, for example, is state, "Bush is a fascist," or "Obama is a socialist," and the listener can fill in the whole plot found in the cultural narratives associated with fascism or socialism that exist deep in the American culture.

Stock Characters

Besides a plot, cultural narratives have stock characters. *Stock characters* consist of a set of qualities, habits, mannerisms, traits, and so forth typically associated with certain positions or identities. The idea of stock characters is similar to the idea of characterization as used in theatre. Stock characters may be little more than stereotypes or can be more complex and nuanced and sophisticated representations of recognizable characters. The individual and specific characters found in a surface narrative are typically drawn from an underlying stock character found in a cultural narrative. For example, consider how the Johnny Galecki and Jim Parsons characters in *The Big Bang Theory* draw on the stock character of "the nerd." While their two characters are unique in themselves, they each are built upon a common stock character.

Stock characters can typically be identified as good guys or bad guys. Cultural narratives often present characters as heroes or villains. One way to better understand a surface narrative is to recognize the cultural narrative that it draws upon and therefore to recognize who is the hero and who the villain. This becomes particularly effective in persuading people to like or dislike a person based on the role they are assigned in the cultural narrative. President Bush and President Obama can each be a hero or a villain depending on which stock character they are assigned in the cultural narrative used in the construction of the surface narrative being told.

Theme

Whereas arguments have claims, narratives have themes. Theme is one of the most useful elements of cultural narratives for the astute reader. Most cultural narratives imply some sort of moral, some sort of lesson to be learned from the characters' experiences throughout the plot arc. In this sense, cultural narratives are allegorical. Consequently, many cultural narratives have a normative orientation to them. That is, through a moral they communicate how someone (or all of us) is supposed to behave or, perhaps, should not behave. The theme or moral of a cultural narrative is largely why narrative is so persuasive.

One aspect of the plot arc of the Crime Does Not Pay cultural narrative is that due punishment results when we commit a crime or, more generally, when we commit an immoral act. People get their just desserts. The crime or immoral act *causes* the retributive punishment; therefore, the story links the crime to the punishment. The villain deserves punishment; the hero brings about the punishment, reinforcing the theme that we should not sin against the community. In the 2001 version of *Ocean's 11,* the "ruthless" casino owner, Terry Benedict, not only takes the easy money that comes to casinos (casinos simply take money from easy prey—legal perhaps, but hardly moral), but he has the audacity to try and steal Danny Ocean's wife while Danny is in jail. Could there be a more dastardly deed! Could there be anything more Benedict Arnold than watching Terry Benedict stealing a man's wife while he is in prison? What deserves more punishment than that? So we see that in *Ocean's 11,* we have the plot line that connects the consequences to its causes (trying to steal a man's wife while he is in prison), the characterization of the villain who deserves the punishment that is coming (Benedict a ruthless and immoral man, even given the name of America's most notorious traitor), and the theme (live honorably or pay).

But *Ocean's 11* is Hollywood, and casinos are not schools—or, at least not the kind of schools we normally mean when we use that term. So, let's look at how cultural narratives might work in educational texts. While I think that the Crime Does Not Pay narrative is sometimes appealed to in educational texts (for example, there have been plenty of news reports about teachers and administrators getting caught doctoring tests), it is probably not the most frequently appealed to. There are other, equally powerful cultural narratives that those writing about education are more likely to use to persuade their readers to accept their view. For example, consider the cultural narrative we call American Exceptionalism. Here we will lay out, in accordance to the structure identified above, the plot, stock characters, and theme of this narrative. Keep in mind that the truthfulness or falsity of the narrative is not the point here. Some Americans accept this as true and others reject it as false, but when it is persuasive, its effectiveness is not based on its truth, but on its ability to capture readers' belief. The American Exceptionalism narrative tells us the following (this narrative will be elaborated more fully later in this chapter):

Plot. The United States was founded as a model to other nations. We have always been, and continue to be, envied for our freedoms, for our political system, and for our economic prosperity. Our best days are always ahead. When we do fall behind, we always have the potential to win again because of our greatness; therefore, we must do whatever it takes to ensure our success. America is always the exception due to its exceptional goodness and destiny.

Stock Characters. Americans are the smartest, strongest, bravest, best educated, most inventive, most morally upright and freedom-loving/patriotic people in the world. Americans are down-to-earth, without aristocratic airs, and have innate sense. In a world of tyranny and brutality, freedom-loving Americans are here to show the rest of the world how to do it.

Theme. America is the major exception in the history of the world. It is unique in history. America must win, must be first among nations of the world. It is its destiny.

Do you recognize this narrative? It is frequently invoked in American culture. The cultural narrative of American Exceptionalism underlies a great deal of American political rhetoric. For example, here is former Republican presidential nominee Mitt Romney appealing to this narrative by claiming that President Obama does not believe in American Exceptionalism:

> "Our president doesn't have the same feelings about American exceptionalism that we do," Romney said. "And I think over the last three or four years, some people around the world have begun to question that. On this Tuesday, we have an opportunity—you have an opportunity—to vote, and take the next step in bringing back that special nature of being American."[1]

For Romney, being American is special. To be American is to be unique in the world. He seems to be asking how a president can work in America's interests if he does not believe that America and Americans are unique and special in the world? Obviously, Romney had hopes that by attaching the narrative of American Exceptionalism to himself and detaching it from Obama, he would be able to persuade some people to vote for him. Evidence is not what is important here. He need not provide real evidence. He need only to provide an appeal to a narrative that some people will find persuasive.

---

1. Philip Rucker, "Romney Questions Obama Commitment to 'American Exceptionalism,'" *Washington Post*, March 31, 2012, www.washingtonpost.com/blogs/election-2012/post/romney-questions-obama-commitment-to-american-exceptionalism/2012/03/31/gIQA7xKUnS_blog.html.

Also remember that many tropes, ideographs, and other rhetorical devices are closely identified with particular cultural narratives so that a speaker need not tell the whole plot to evoke the narrative; all that is needed is to mention one or two tropes or ideographs and the reader will fill in the rest of the plot themselves. Here, Romney need not actually tell the story of American Exceptionalism, he merely needs to name it for the whole narrative to be invoked in the mind of the audience.

If a speaker wished to evoke American Exceptionalism without naming it, how might he or she do it? What tropes and/or ideographs could she or he use that will suggest this cultural narrative to the listener? One common phrase in American political discourse is the "[shining] city upon a hill." This phrase is a trope originally written in 1630 by a Puritan leader named John Winthrop, but in recent history Ronald Reagan frequently used this trope. Here is how President Reagan used it in his farewell speech to the nation on January 11, 1989:

> I've spoken of the shining city all my political life, but I don't know if I ever quite communicated what I saw when I said it. But in my mind it was a tall proud city built on rocks stronger than oceans, wind-swept, God-blessed, and teeming with people of all kinds living in harmony and peace, a city with free ports that hummed with commerce and creativity, and if there had to be city walls, the walls had doors and the doors were open to anyone with the will and the heart to get here. That's how I saw it, and see it still.[2]

As a cultural narrative, American Exceptionalism can often be found framing and supporting (though hidden underneath) a specific text. President Reagan is not the only American president to appeal to American Exceptionalism. Despite Romney's claim to the contrary, Obama has also evoked American Exceptionalism. Consider Obama's major education policy proposal, "Race to the Top." Who is racing whom, and to what top are they racing? "Race to the top" is an ideograph that softly evokes American Exceptionalism. Why is it so important for the United States to be on the top, to be number one? Notice how even though the ideograph "race to the top" does not explicitly detail every element of American Exceptionalism in such an obvious way as Reagan did in the above quotation, it does not need to. The ideograph "race to the top" shortcuts our understanding. Obama does not need to lay out why the United States must be on the top, the phrase itself appeals to the American Exceptionalism narrative that so many Americans seem to accept. Even if Americans cannot call to mind the name of this narrative, even if they do not realize there is a cultural narrative at all, this cultural narrative works to persuade many Americans.

In fact, specifically *because* people do not recognize it as a narrative with a history, this cultural narrative is persuasive. One of the powers of nonrational persuasion is that it works best when people do not realize it is working at all. When people begin to see that a text is attempting to persuade them through nonrational mechanisms, the power to persuade is reduced. The narrative becomes less persuasive. People don't like to be manipulated.

The appeal to American Exceptionalism is so pervasive in American cultural discourse today that most Americans only take it as a matter of course—of course, America was

---

2. Ronald Reagan, "Farewell Address to the Nation," *The American Presidency Project,* January 11, 1989, www.presidency.ucsb.edu/ws/?pid=29650.

number one once and should be number one again and must be number one in the future! There is no need for the Obama administration to explicitly recount the entire plot; we are already so familiar with the larger cultural narrative, the administration only needs some well-placed tropes or ideographs and many Americans respond. So, we see that both Romney and Obama can call on this narrative to attempt to persuade voters to support them.

In sociocultural studies of education, we want to understand and critically analyze cultural narratives. In particular, we want to understand how they pose as evidence (notice I said "pose"). These narratives are not real evidence for an argument, but only pseudo-evidence. Rather than serve as premises in an argument, they are but rhetorical mechanisms used to persuade through emotion and commonsense.[3] By learning common cultural narratives, we can begin to understand how they come to be used to promote particular interests.

Some Common American Cultural Narratives

There are hundreds of cultural narratives that serve as resources for the surface narratives found in educational texts. Below, some of the more popular or influential cultural narratives will be analyzed using the three structural elements discussed above: plot, stock characters, and theme. Many of the analyses will also include some common tropes and ideographs that evoke the cultural narrative. The following analyses will not argue for the truth or falseness of any of them, but will only attempt to show what these narratives assume to be true and false, important and not, or moral and immoral. The analyses will attempt to merely outline some of the important elements that make them persuasive for some people. It will begin with a repeat of American Exceptionalism with some added elements, followed by outlines of other cultural narratives.

American Exceptionalism

Plot. America was founded as a model to other nations. We have always been, and continue to be, envied for our freedoms, for our political system, for our economic prosperity. Our best days are always ahead. When we do fall behind, we always have the potential to win again because of our greatness; therefore, we must do whatever it takes to ensure our success. America is always the exception due to its exceptional goodness and destiny. (Other narrative variations: Manifest Destiny, City on a Hill, the American jeremiad.)

Stock Characters. In this narrative the hero is the "true American" because Americans are the smartest, strongest, bravest, best educated, most inventive, most morally upright and freedom-loving/patriotic people in the world. Americans are down-to-earth, without aristocratic airs, and have innate sense. In a world of tyranny and brutality, freedom-loving Americans are here to show the rest of the world how to do it (e.g., Captain America, "Greatest Generation,"

---

3. When *common sense* is written as two words, it refers to sense held in common by all sensible people. When *commonsense* is written as one word, it refers to beliefs manufactured by some and claimed to be held in common by all sensible people, but, in fact, not all sensible people agree with the belief. This book is not interested in *common sense* but is very interested in *commonsense*.

the American soldier, the American Olympians). The villain is anyone who doubts America's moral, economic, and political superiority (e.g., American apologists, "Frenchified" American intellectuals, Harvard professors, antiwar peace-niks).

Theme. America is the major exception and unique in the history of the world. America must win, be first among nations of the world. It is its destiny. "Winning isn't the most important thing, it's the only thing." America is uniquely good, moral, and strong. God blesses America.

American Jeremiad

Plot. Perhaps a variation of the American Exceptionalism narrative, the American jeremiad is a lament that expresses the deep dissatisfaction of an America that is not living up to the promise expressed in the American Exceptionalism narrative. Its name derives from the Christian, Islamic, and Judaic prophet Jeremiah. Its plot is of a once-great nation with strong moral values that has lost its way by abandoning the virtues that made it great, but its lost greatness can be reclaimed by a return to the traditional values that made it great in the past. The 1998 movie *Saving Private Ryan* showed America the road back after the decades of lament following the national shame of the Vietnam War by appealing to a war that the United States not only helped win, but that nearly everyone agrees was fought for good reasons. In Christianity, a jeremiad is told when a sinner has been said to have been reborn by a return to the true Christian faith.

Stock Characters. The hero is the prophet who leads us out of our wrongful ways and especially the former sinner who becomes saint-like (e.g., Phil, Bill Murray's character in *Groundhog Day*; Rocky, the title character from the movie of that name; Vivian Ward, Julia Roberts's character in *Pretty Woman*; Ronald Reagan, an American president who success-fully led a revolution to re-vision America and return it closer to the vision of its founding fathers). The villain is the liberal who celebrates and languishes in immoral pleasures such as drugs and sex and those who protect them (e.g., Hollywood, a trope for the entertain-ment industry; Bill Clinton; Barack Obama; Nancy Pelosi; San Francisco, a trope for an openly gay community; limousine liberals, a trope for multimillionaires who supposedly drive around in their limousines representing themselves as caring about the poor when, this trope implies, their own lives and actions work against the interests of the poor—supposedly like the Kennedy family, the Clintons, and Al Gore).

Theme. The persecutions we are experiencing at present result from our wandering off the righteous path. We must return to our traditional values before it is too late.

Conspicuous Consumption

Plot. You may have problems such as bad relationships, unsuccessful marriages, meaning-less jobs, but you can find happiness through consumption. Almost all advertisements push this narrative.

Characterization. The heroes may or may not work hard, but they definitely play hard by living "The Good Life" through their expensive clothes, jewelry, cars, homes, brand of liquor and beer, and luxurious vacations (e.g., Carrie Bradshaw, Sarah Jessica Parker's character in *Sex and the City*; Danny Ocean, the lead character in the *Ocean's 11* series). The villain is anyone who is poor (especially if they complain about being poor) or anyone who attempts to moderate good living through imposing their narrow and uptight or politically correct personal moral code on those having a good time.

Theme. It's okay to be rich. Happiness is found in spending money and displaying wealth, bling.

Rags to Riches

Plot. Horatio Alger is born poor, but through working hard in school, minding his lessons, and cultivating his character through hard work, he attains financial security. The Rags to Riches narrative differs from the Conspicuous Consumption narrative due to the insistence in the Rags to Riches narrative that wealth results from good values, especially hard work, and that there is a kind of modesty in their well-deserved wealth. There is not much modesty in the Conspicuous Consumption narrative.

Stock Characters. The hero is obedient, hardworking, righteous, perseverant, and ingenious but not devious (e.g., Horatio Alger; Willy Wonka; Chris Gardner, Will Smith's character in the movie *The Pursuit of Happyness*). The villain is anyone who makes excuses for failures, anyone who does not believe that everyone can make it in America if they work hard and have talent and good values.

Theme. With hard work, perseverance, and ingenuity, anyone can rise from poverty to the middle class. (*Subtheme*: poverty is the result of laziness/moral failures.)

Individualism (Stand on Your Own Two Feet)

Plot. The main character (usually a masculine man) is in a situation where he is alone, left to his own devices, detached, able to roam free, surviving on his wits and his fists. It is often a gendered narrative having to do with being a "real man."

Stock Characters. The hero is rugged, terse, scrappy, inventive, detached, a doer, not a thinker (e.g., gunslinger, gangster, Marlboro Man, John Wayne, Clint Eastwood as "the Man with No Name" in the so-called Spaghetti Westerns and as Dirty Harry, and any "real man"). The villain is anyone who promotes the idea that people need relationships and community, anyone who might quote, "It takes a village to raise a child" (e.g., psychologists, women who emasculate their men such as in classic Westerns, men who hide behind their women). There is also frequently a clown or fool in these narratives, a weak and ineffectual man whom we laugh at such as the tenderfoot on the "dude ranch," the male schoolteacher in Westerns, metrosexuals, men who cry, or men who eat quiche.

Theme. Moral individuals stand on their own two feet and depend on no one else.

The Good, Wholesome, Middle-Class American Life

Plot. This is a counternarrative to the Conspicuous Consumption narrative. It typically follows a person as he or she builds a good, wholesome life. There are trials and tribulations along the way, but by building a family, working well in an ordinary job, and remaining committed to friends, everything works out in the end. Often these stories pit the big city as Gomorrah and the small town as wholesome. This narrative is found in all those feel-good movies, such as *Father of the Bride, The Family Man,* and *It's a Wonderful Life.*

Stock Characters. The hero does okay in school (not an intellectual, but a person with good character); gets an honest job or goes to a respectable college; graduates and then secures a stable job; marries a hometown sweetheart; starts a family; and repeat. Or they do not do all of that and are unhappy until they realize their mistake. The measure of an individual's success is their ability to sustain a stable, middle-class lifestyle, exemplified by home owner-ship, a respectable (upwardly mobile) job, a nice car, and a close, stalwart family (e.g., the Huxtables from *The Cosby Show,* the Bradys from *The Brady Bunch,* the varied but ultimately loving *Modern Family*). The villains are all those heroes from the Conspicuous Consumption narrative who confuse success and bling with happiness.

Theme. Humble, middle-class stability and modesty get one through life's travails and bring happiness.

Culture of Poverty

Plot. While the Good, Wholesome, Middle-Class American narrative gives us a narrative of stability and happiness, we often find it side-by-side with a Culture of Poverty narrative that tells us that people who live in poverty may not be genetically preconditioned to failure (as suggested in the Stand on Your Own Two Feet narrative), but they live in a culture that teaches them the wrong values for success. This plot lays the cause of poor people's poverty in their culture, which may help them survive poverty, but dooms them never to get out of poverty either. Whereas, according to this narrative, middle-class culture teaches hard work, good morals, family commitment, the value of school, and individual responsibility, poverty teaches how to game the system by taking advantage of government handouts, improper behavior (especially when dealing with alcohol, drugs, and sex), the refusal to take respon-sibility for one's children, the irrelevance of school, and individual irresponsibility. What the poor need is to learn middle-class values, and they too will be able to get themselves out of poverty. Providing economic support in the form of welfare, health care, and food stamps only provides incentive for the poor to remain poor. Government benefits are a trap.

Stock Characters. We know these characters well. They inhabit most movies and television shows that deal with the inner city because this narrative seems to represent poverty as an inner-city problem. Poverty in the suburbs, small towns, and rural areas must be different. Here we find the welfare queens who keep having children in order to get more money from Aid to Families with Dependent Children (AFDC), the pimps, the drug lords, the drunks and druggies, the homeless, and the petty thieves. We find unruly students and uncaring parents. The heroes are those who don't fall for the sad stories of the poor but demand that they pick themselves up and start living with proper middle-class morals and good habits. The heroes practice "tough love." This narrative is one of the principle producers of that well-known pop culture figure, the teacher as savior. The savior teacher is a stock character in books, movies, and television at least from the 1950s, with *Blackboard Jungle,* and is regularly recreated through the decades, such as *To Sir with Love* (1967), *Stand and Deliver* (1988), *Dangerous Minds* (1995), and *Freedom Writers* (2007). The villains include all of the do-gooders and well-intentioned but misled liberals who don't realize that as long as the poor don't have to work for anything, they won't. The heroes and villains are the same as found in the Minority as Problem narrative discussed below. In fact, there is a lot of overlap between these two narratives, which vary primarily by whether the "problem" is defined as "poverty" or "race."

Theme. The problem of poverty does not result from an economic system that depends on having poor people, but results from the culture of poverty itself. The only solution to poverty is to educate poor people in such a way as to teach them the proper values of the middle class.

Minority as Problem

Plot. At one time, America was a diverse people who found a common cause and created a common language, common history, and common culture and as a result became a great nation. Any group of people who put their group identity first will not learn to appreciate our values, our ways, and will ultimately become problems. They will demand that we do something for them rather than realizing that all they have to do is do it for themselves. The Minority as Problem narrative differs from the Balkanization narrative because it does not fear the division of the nation into "tribes" as much as it calls attention to what it sees as the undeserved demands and the unfair advantages that accrue to members of minority groups who appear to them to refuse to assimilate to the dominant culture.

Stock Characters. This narrative focuses on villains who are those members of minority groups who are a drain on the rest of us. They play the "race card" or the "woman card" or the "gay card." Other villains include anyone who advocates for affirmative action and "political correctness." The heroes would be those members of minority groups who assimilate into the mainstream. Heroes would also include those who demand that a person be judged as an individual rather than as a member of a group. As in the Culture of Poverty narrative, one of the common heroes is the teacher who comes into the school and saves the children by showing them tough love. Examples of heroes would be Principal Joe Clark, a real person portrayed by Morgan Freeman in *Lean on Me*; Jaime Escalante, a real person portrayed by Edward James Olmos in *Stand and Deliver*; Michelle Rhee, the chancellor of Washington, DC, public schools from 2007 to 2010 and one of the heroes in *Waiting for Superman*; and

Tom Horn, the former superintendent of Public Instruction for the state of Arizona who was largely responsible for the Arizona law banning ethnic studies courses that promote racial identity over individual identity and used it to close down the Mexican-American Studies program in Tucson High School. As Horn stated,

> They [the teachers in the Mexican-American Studies program] are people to whom race is very important in self-identity and they want to instill that in the kids. My view of what America is all about is the opposite. I think that what is important about us is that we're individuals, that what matters is what we know, what we can do, and what is our character, and not what race we happened to be born into.[4]

Theme. Members of minority groups—including the poor, immigrants, people of color, and youth—are intransigent problems that must be managed by tough love or "conservatism with a conscience," or they will explode into bigger problems. Minority groups create a strain on society until they become assimilated into the mainstream American culture.

Balkanization

Plot. A unified and successful nation becomes divided against itself because of cultural differences and collapses into civil war. Civil war can only be avoided through the construction of a common culture. Its name comes from the historical warring found among people living in the Balkans, of which the wars in Bosnia (1992–1995) and Kosovo (1998–1999) following the collapse of Yugoslavia are typical examples.

Stock Characters. The hero of this narrative is the one who focuses on what people have in common or the one who works to erase cultural differences and create a common people (e.g., the color-blind teacher). The villain is the one who focuses on what makes people different from each other and demands the right to maintain minority identities (i.e., multicultural-ists, angry feminists/blacks/Latinos/gays/lesbians, the teachers in Tucson High School's Mexican-American Studies program, etc.).

Theme. Diversity is a problem. Commonality is the solution.

Minority as Victim

Plot. An alternative to the Minority as Problem and Balkanization narratives, the Minority as Victim narrative portrays members of minority groups as not being at fault for the problems accompanying cultural diversity. Instead, in this narrative, members of minority groups are victims. This is especially true for the children, who cannot be held responsible for their situation. Perhaps they have a poor home life growing up or are forced to attend a low-functioning school or live in a crime-infested neighborhood. The best way to help people,

---

4. "Banned in Arizona," *Need to Know,* PBS, 2013, http://video.pbs.org/video/2335625906.

especially children, to escape the unfair situation they have been put in is to provide them with love and care and charity. This narrative is a kind of "salvation" narrative: the powerful, through their benevolence, help those in need (rather than those in need taking control of their own affairs to help themselves). We see this narrative frequently in some advocates of service learning. Most, though not all, urban education movies use this narrative (e.g., *Blackboard Jungle, To Sir with Love, Dangerous Minds, Freedom Writers*).

Stock Characters. The heroes are the innocent victims, especially youth, who struggle against a system that is stacked against them. We see this particularly with disabilities and, lately, with gay teens. We strip them of agency and make them childlike innocents and, therefore, victims of bullies who need us to protect them (e.g., Mother Teresa; Patch Adams, Robin Williams's character in the movie *Patch Adams*; social workers/community organizers; inner-city teachers). The villains are those who oppose public health care, welfare, housing, and good public schools for the poor.

Theme. Minorities and the poor are victims who need us to help them out of their situation.

Minority as Exotic Other (Orientalism)

Plot. The Minority as Exotic Other narrative might be called a travelogue narrative in that it tells the story of those who leave the safety and protection of their privileged environment to visit and live (temporarily) in the communities of the poor and the Other. As a result of this trip the person is fundamentally changed and returns home newly enlightened and ready to continue the struggle for their newfound friends. We often see this narrative in advocates of service learning and semester abroad. It is sometimes called *orientalism* because of the way in which Westerners created an exotic, exciting, sensual, dangerous image of Asia that does not have much in common with the reality. Read Tracy Kidder's book about Paul Farmer's experiences in Haiti called *Mountains beyond Mountains* and Greg Mortenson's *Three Cups of Tea*, the story of Mortenson's travel to Afghanistan that led to his return to build schools. The Teach for America program draws on this narrative as a way to recruit college students receiving degrees from elite universities to spend a few years teaching in inner cities.

Stock Characters. The heroes are those who are different from us because they are interesting, mysterious, glamorous, and we learn more about ourselves by visiting them as well as the privileged individual who leaves the safety and comfort of their privileged communities to live and work among the poor. In many ways the hero is constructed as (white) student-as-tourist. Like a tourist, a student travels to another community for short and exciting visits filled with adventure and then returns a better, wiser person (e.g., Indiana Jones, Marco Polo, the authors of the *Lonely Planet* and *Rough Guide* books, Paul Farmer in *Mountains beyond Mountains*). The villains are those homebodies who never want to travel, or those who tell Minority as Problem, Balkinization, American Exceptionalism, or Nativist narratives.

Theme. Travel to other countries or poor communities is good, the more different than one's own community, the better. Minorities are interesting for their "difference," and so we should honor their culture by honoring their difference (by consuming it—food, dress, festivals, etc.). It is their very difference that we find interesting, entertaining, and self-improving.

Nativist (Xenophobia)

Plot. Americans built a nation with a common language and common culture (see Minority as Problem narrative above) that values such virtues as honesty, industry, religious commitment, and cultural tolerance. Americans are the most culturally diverse and culturally tolerant people on Earth, but they must be constantly on guard against the soiling influence of immigrants whose inherent immorality, backwardness, and un-American beliefs have resulted in corruptness all around us. These immigrants take our jobs, corrupt our politicians, rape our women, import drugs and potential terrorist bombs, and kill us while car-jacking us on the interstate highways. See the following political ads from fall 2010 for examples: John McCain's "Complete the Danged Fence" ad,[5] Dan Fanelli's "This Is a Terrorist" ad,[6] and Tim James's "English-Only Driver's Exams" ad.[7]

Stock Characters. The heroes are people such as John McCain, Dan Fanelli, Tim James (as seen in the videos above), and other politicians and media personalities who work to keep America safe from undesirable illegal immigrants. The villains are those foreigners, whether here or in their home country, who are slothful, greedy, sinister, sneaky, non-English speaking, and non-Christian. Also all those advocates of bilingual education, "amnesty" for "illegals," and those who resist the Patriot Act and the measures taken by our security forces to protect us from foreign terrorists.

Theme. In general, people who are like us are superior to those not like us; we should be suspicious of those different from us. While not all foreigners are trouble, we must protect our borders from those who are and so must work to restrict the corrupt influence of those immigrants who hold on to their national or ethnic identity and refuse to assimilate to American language and culture.

Melting Pot/*E Pluribus Unum*

Plot. The melting pot is a trope taken from the name of an early twentieth-century play by Israel Zangwill and promotes that play's primary storyline which tells us that America has always been a place that welcomes immigrants and eventually assimilates their best parts. Immigrants have always come to America seeking moral and economic freedom and opportunity. They have been welcomed. They have worked hard, assimilated, and become American. Like those who tell the Balkanization stories, tellers of the Melting Pot narrative are suspicious of groups who refuse to assimilate to the dominant common culture. The

---

5. www.youtube.com/watch?v=r0lwusMxiHc.

6. www.youtube.com/watch?v=umTITWQuXwY.

7. www.youtube.com/watch?v=S9hZO-dQYww.

Melting Pot narrative and the Balkanization narrative are often told by the same people. However, the Melting Pot narrative is distinct from the xenophobic Nativist narrative in that the former welcomes immigrants into our society to "melt" into becoming one of us, whereas the latter is less welcoming to immigrants who do not look and act "like us."

Stock Characters. The heroes are the ethnic "everyman"; persons who themselves or whose ancestors are of varied national origins, but who think of themselves primarily as American. They have affection for their or their ancestor's land of origin, but have unquestioned loyalty to America (e.g., John F. Kennedy, Senator Marco Rubio). The villains are those who refuse to accept the assimilation of others into the American family (e.g., white supremacists, "birthers") and the cultural pluralists who insist that immigrants do not have to assimilate (see the Cultural Pluralism narrative).

Theme. *E Pluribus Unum* ("from many, one"), celebrate diversity as long as it doesn't cleave the fundamental American culture.

The Radical Promise of Democracy

Plot. The United States was created on the promise of democracy, a radical plan to let public decisions be made by the public. But from the very beginning this promise has been thwarted by the privileged to turn the system to their personal advantage. Our nation's short history has been a series of struggles to expand who counts as a citizen as well as struggles to counter the coalescence of power into the hands of the few. While much progress has been made, today we must continue to struggle because the wealthy and the corporations continue to use the mechanisms of democracy for their own personal ends instead of for the good of all. Public schools are one of the primary sites of struggle over democracy. For too long, the public schools have been used to *reproduce* the class, race, and gender inequalities and it is time for the public schools to be harnessed to *transform* the class, race, and gender systems.

Stock Characters. The heroes are those who work tirelessly without the promise of personal gain and often with personal risk to advance the idea of democracy (e.g., Founding Fathers, suffragettes, Rosa Parks, freedom riders, Bob Woodward and Carl Bernstein in *All the President's Men*). The villains are the super wealthy, corporate executives, and the politicians who work in their interests.

Theme. Democracy requires vigilance and continued struggle against the privileged in order to realize its possibilities.

Cultural Pluralism

Plot. America is stronger because it not only welcomes immigrants but it encourages them to maintain their heritage, their ways, their culture. By having a nation in which people are free to dress, worship, and work within their own groups, we have forged a nation of many voices, which strengthens our public sphere and allows us to adjust to new situations better than other countries trapped in their traditional ways. This is a counternarrative to the Melting Pot narrative discussed above. The Melting Pot narrative tells a story of how immigrants assimilate and lose their ethnic identities melting into a common American culture. The Cultural Pluralist narrative tells the story of a people who hold on to their cultures while joining hands engaging others in public space in order to make America stronger and better for everyone regardless of their group identities. Some refer to this narrative with a "mosaic" or "salad bowl" metaphor rather than the "melting pot."

Stock Characters. The heroes are those who celebrate their group memberships through honoring their rituals and symbols of identity (e.g., the students and teachers of the Mexican-American studies program in Tucson High School, the Harlem Renaissance, Malcolm X, Tupac Shakur, the Amish, Hasidic Jews, Little Haiti, Chinatown). The villains are those who define America as a white and Christian nation, segregationists, opponents of multicultural education and bilingual education, advocates of a "common curriculum," and of English-Only (see Tim James in the Nativist narrative above).

Theme. Maintaining one's ethnic/national heritage is a good thing. Cultural plurality enriches a democratic nation. Difference is a positive, not a negative. Diversity is not the problem, the forced assimilation and erasure of diversity is.

Man as Predator/Woman as Victim

Plot. This narrative presents the idea that males are by their nature defined by their sexual appetites that must be sated. Females by their nature are "innocents" and regularly subject to (unwelcomed) male advances. This narrative is often used as a way to excuse improper male behavior as in "boys will be boys" or in the Glen Ridge Rape case in which school authorities initially refused to sanction the high school football players responsible for the gang rape of a low-IQ girl. Think *American Pie, Animal House, Not Another Teen Movie.* But it is also used as a warning to teen girls that boys are by nature dangerous and girls should not allow themselves to get into situations in which they might be victimized such as all of those stories of date-rape drugs.[8]

Stock Characters. Guys are the villains. They are all the same. They are out for only one thing.

Theme. "Boys Will Be Boys" or "Girls Watch Out!"

Woman as Virgin, Mother, or Whore

Plot. The unmarried woman who fails to hold out for marriage before having sex becomes a social pariah. Married women have sex, but are identified by the offspring of such behavior

---

8. For an example, see "Date Rape PSA," YouTube video, www.youtube.com/watch?v=2zMAm_eHnhk.

and never the behavior itself. Today, a variation of this narrative is that girls need not wait for marriage but do need to be in a steady relationship before having sex. Having sex with guys while not in a steady relationship makes her a "whore" or a "slut."

Stock Characters. Good girls wait until marriage. Those who can't wait are bad girls. Mothers may have sex (obviously), but they are sexless.

Theme. Girls, be in a steady heterosexual relationship, or be a saint!

Market Fundamentalism

Plot. Since America's founding, economic competition in free markets has laid the foundation for unprecedented prosperity. Moments of government intervention have invariably destroyed prosperity, including the government protection of unions, environmental regulations, taxes, etc. When government has stayed out of things, the United States has expanded its wealth and power. When government has intervened, it has screwed things up. The solution to any economic challenge is low taxes and low regulation. In fact, the solution to any public problem can be found in a minimally regulated marketplace. This narrative plays a central role in the conservative economic-political ideology "classical liberalism/neoliberalism." This ideology will be extensively discussed in a later chapter.

Stock Characters. The heroes are our business leaders because they know how to get things done and keep government out of our business and off our backs ("captain/titan of industry," Andrew Carnegie, Bill Gates, Donald Trump). The villains are all those who want "big government," taxes, and regulations (e.g., union leaders, liberals, "Harvard professors"). Governor Romney used this narrative as one of his central advertising narratives when he ran for president.

Theme. Market competition is a universal good; government is undesirable.

Small-Town America (America's Hinterland)

Plot. In this very common narrative, the hero moves away from the town where she grew up and finds economic success in the big city, but does not find happiness. In fact, the story's hero may have lost her/his soul in gaining success. The hero has certainly lost her/his way. When the hero moves home back to the small-town community where her/his family and childhood friends and neighbors live, s/he rekindles his/her inner goodness and finds true fulfillment (and often a romantic partner).

Stock Characters. The hero of this narrative is a good person at heart, raised in a small town or on a farm with middle-class, middle-America, Christian family values (e.g., Dolly Parton, Garth Brooks, Sarah Palin). The villains are "fast-talking city types," "Washington politicians," "limousine liberals," atheists, Eastern college professors.

Theme. America's greatness is a result of inherent goodness/uprightness of ordinary people in "small-town America." It is important to always remain "of the people," representing "average people" and their values and interests. Be authentic!

Yeoman/Small-Business Owners

Plot. The narrative of the wisdom of the yeoman farmer was central to the thinking of Thomas Jefferson. This narrative relates that small, independent farmers and artisans have built America's moral, economic, and political structures and formed its character. Farmers are, because of their connection to the earth and because their decisions must be focused on performance and not ideology, inherently virtuous. Today, small business owners have replaced the yeoman farmer in this narrative, which then tells us that they, the small business owners, form the backbone of America's character and economy.

Stock Characters. The heroes are those whose economic livelihood depends on hard work and smart decisions in the real world (e.g., the independent, yeoman farmer; the Mom and Pop storekeepers; the Main Street business owners). The villains are those people who get something for nothing, such as corporate executives, Wall Street traders, union workers, liberal college professors and other intellectuals, any government bureaucrat, welfare queens.

Theme. The innate wisdom of people who produce for themselves, make for themselves, work for a living rather than talk or get others to do the work for them.

The Conservative

Plot. Traditions develop over long periods of time because they help people survive and to thrive. Abandoning these traditions for the promise that things will get better is foolish, at best, and more likely disastrous. When people abandon the traditional ways, they lose their way; they get off-track. A return to tradition is necessary to move into the future on a good moral footing. (See related narratives above: jeremiad, Small Town). Some common ideographs found in this narrative include "family values" and "God-fearing."

Stock Characters. The heroes are the traditional heterosexual, religious, hardworking, virtuous, humble American man and woman and their family (e.g., Ronald Reagan, John Wayne). The villains include anyone who thinks that they can envision a better future that requires that we give up our traditions and those who tell us that the way we have always done things is backward or racist or sexist or some other "-ist" (e.g., Bill Clinton; Barack Obama; Hollywood producers, directors, and actors; "Progressives/Liberals").

Theme. Traditional, conservative values are good; progressivism may be well intended but leads to unintended disasters.

The Progressive

Plot. Progressivism became a strong and powerful narrative at the end of the nineteenth century and into the twentieth. It tells the tale of the rise of humankind from an animal at the mercy of the natural world to the present-day, modern humans who have learned to master their environment. While the history of humankind up to this point has been a story of success, we must continue to use science and reason to address the problems of life if we hope to continue into the future. Those people who have stood still and refused to move on, to advance, find themselves at the mercy of others. The only choice we have is to grow, learn, invent, and plan our future.

Stock Characters. The heroes are the men and women of reason—scientists, philosophers, artists, intelligent politicians, and other cultural leaders (e.g., Albert Einstein, John Dewey, Pablo Picasso, Franklin Delano Roosevelt). The villains are those who resist the application of reason to address contemporary problems: the "country bumpkin," the global warming deniers, the advocates of intelligent design being taught as if it were a science, and any other who advocates keeping things as they are or as they were in the (mythical) past (e.g., James Dobson, founder of Focus on the Family; Mel Gibson; Sarah Palin; Mike Huckabee; almost every on-camera personality on FOX News).

Theme. We either plan and conquer our future, or our past conquers us.

Wanderlust

Plot. One or two people travel as rootless drifters without a home but are searching for something—to escape the rat race, to find themselves, or just looking for adventure. A subgenre of this narrative places the travel in idyllic natural settings away from civilization. Another subgenre places the travel in a car that represents the freedom to travel the highways and byways (*Endless Summer*; *The Motorcycle Diaries*; *Easy Rider*; *O Brother, Where Art Thou?*; *Lord of the Rings Trilogy*). In education, this narrative is occasionally used to attract students to travel abroad programs or specialized nonformal educational experiences, such as Semester at Sea and Outward Bound.

Stock Characters. The adventurer, rugged hiker, biker, backpacker, road movie pals (e.g., frontiersmen such as Daniel Boone and Davy Crockett, cowboys such as Butch Cassidy and The Sundance Kid, drifting artists such as Woody Guthrie and Jack Kerouac). The villains are those who are afraid to leave the comfort of home, afraid of adventure, afraid to take a chance (e.g., the couch potato, the company man, the traditionalist).

Theme. Putting down roots, being tied down or encumbered is not good for the soul. Freedom is to be found in adventure.

Conclusion

Above are only a very few of the many cultural narratives that are used in the public rhetoric that addresses educational discussions as found in newspaper commentaries and politicians' statements and ads. Not every use of every narrative will include all its parts. As mentioned earlier in this chapter, some of these narratives will be appealed to indirectly through carefully selected tropes or ideographs. Please keep in mind that what makes the narrative persuasive or not is its emotional appeal and not whether it is "true." Critical readers will recognize these and other recurring narratives, which will enable them to read texts about schooling and education with much more depth of understanding and reveal more clearly what the politicians and the policy-makers and the commentators are doing when they create texts designed to persuade people to support their position.

Part II
Philosophy of Education

CHAPTER FIVE

Introduction to Philosophy for Educators

"The unexamined life is not worth living."
—Socrates (as reported by Plato, *Apology*, 38A)[1]

Whereas most of Chapter 3 addressed text analysis, the last several pages stated that a good critique had to not only analyze a text, it had to interpret it as well. As a reminder, *text interpretation* is the specific and conscious act of bringing outside contexts to the text in order to deepen and broaden our understanding of it. One of the most useful outside contexts to use to interpret many educational texts is that of philosophy, especially the philosophy of education. The next four chapters help clarify and develop philosophy and educational philosophy as interpretive contexts for texts in education. This chapter introduces general philosophy to those interested in education.

Which is more valuable for a person to have: knowledge or wisdom? If we look at the way in which students, teachers, and schools are being assessed these days, we might come to the conclusion that knowledge is valued more than wisdom. After all, we have yet to develop a standardized test that measures wisdom. In fact, wisdom is not really measurable in any standard way. However, I believe that even in this "information age," the truly educated person is the wise, rather than merely knowledgeable, person. So an important question for those who wish to educate and be educated is how does a person gain wisdom?

Many people recognize that a certain amount of wisdom is gained through living one's life. The school of hard knocks, if survived, can lead to the older and wiser person. On the other hand, there sure seem to be a lot of people who are merely older and not one bit wiser than when they were young. What leads to wisdom is not surviving and succeeding in the world but rather reflecting on one's experiences in the world. As one experiences more and reflects carefully on those experiences, wisdom can be produced. Schooling can contribute to this production, but only if its focus is to help people learn how, and to develop the dispositions to, reflect on experience. While all subject areas can help teach us how to reflect on experiences, perhaps more than any other academic discipline, philosophy has claimed living reflectively as its central purpose.

The ancient Greek and Latin languages contained words that acknowledged several different kinds of knowing. *Sophia* is a Greek word that refers to the kind of knowledge that we associate with wisdom; hence the word "philosophy" (*philo* + *sophia*) means "the love of

---

1. Plato, *Apology*, trans. Benjamin Jowett (Auckland: The Floating Press, 2011).

wisdom." While there is much information to be gained in the disciplinary study of philosophy, such as who Socrates was and what Plato's Allegory of the Cave refers to, the real purpose of the study of philosophy is to learn the skills and dispositions to live reflectively.

The discipline that we now call *philosophy* is built upon the reasoned exploration of concepts and meanings. Its tools include logic, analysis, and critique. As a discourse, philosophy has existed for more than 2,500 years. As you might suspect, any conversation that has gone on for that long has developed a large set of terms, ideas, problems, answers, canonical texts, heroes, and villains. We could mistake the knowing of these things as "knowing philosophy," but if one is to gain the love of wisdom, it is more important to develop the tools of "reasoned argument" and the dispositions to use reason than to merely "know" the names and most common beliefs of the most popular philosophers.

In this book, *reason* refers to the practice of supporting claims with justifiable premises, and *disposition to use reason* refers to the inclination to actually use reason. When one uses reason, one is being rational. To be rational requires that we be coherent and consistent in our questions and answers. *Consistency* refers to the agreement of each of the parts with each of the other parts. *Coherency* refers to the parts' fitting seamlessly into a unity or a whole. Because of the privileging of coherency and consistency, the kinds of questions philosophers ask and the order in which those questions are asked become quite important because after one asks and answers a question, all other questions and their answers should be coherent and consistent with the first. Sometimes, of course, we find out that our earlier questions or their answers were misplaced or weak, which requires that we go back and ask a different question or develop a new answer in order to remain coherent and consistent with later questions and their answers. Through the process of using reason to develop consistency and coherency, we become more confident in our arguments.

The history of asking and answering philosophical questions is so old that the field has been organized by the types of questions asked. Traditionally there have been four basic philosophical questions: ontology (or, before the modern age, metaphysics), epistemology, ethics, and aesthetics (also sometimes spelled "esthetics" and referring to the questions of art such as what we should consider to be art). This book will address ontology, epistemology, and ethics. I personally have a strong commitment to the importance of aesthetics, but I have had to make many choices of what to include and what to exclude in this book. Unfortunately, from my point of view, aesthetics is too frequently ignored in educational philosophy. The result is a field heavily dominated by ontology, epistemology, and ethics and that is where the next four chapters will focus. If you have an interest in aesthetics and education, an excellent place to begin a study of it is the website of The Maxine Greene Center for Aesthetic Education and Imagination at www.maxinegreene.org/.

Ontology

Ontology is that part of philosophy that addresses the question of what it means "to be." One way we can ask the ontological question is to ask what it means to be fully human (or, perhaps, what the essence of being a human being might be). Below are just a few of the many ways in which philosophers have attempted to address this question. In the spirit of the last section, these ontologies are not presented as a set of answers to be mastered but merely as examples of the kinds of answers to the ontological question that philosophers have considered. By studying a list such as this, the reader may gain a better understanding of the kinds of consideration needed to reflect upon their own developing ontological reasoning. Read through the list in the following section and identify which you think might make for a reasoned starting place for your philosophy.

Homo aestheticus

Some philosophers argue that humans are the only animal that constructs a world marked by value, sentiment, or taste; therefore, to be fully human requires that we become fully "civilized" in the arts of living so as to fully appreciate these aesthetic values. To be fully human requires us to use completely our creative abilities to participate aesthetically in life. Consider the following quotation from Beau Smith, an artist and blogger:

> I have a philosophy. I call it the Science of Originality. A fundamental truth in this philosophy is that art is life. I would go further to equate life with consciousness, perception, and creativity. All that is one for me: consciousness, perception, creativity, art, and life.
>
> What a figurative smack on my head I gave myself when I figured out that my chief goal as an artist was to participate in life! I kind of already knew that. But some things you don't really know until you think about them and give yourself that figurative smack on the forehead.[2]

Smith may not be a professional philosopher, but here we see some of the markings of philosophical thinking that this chapter has already mentioned. Smith not only is experiencing life, but he is reflecting on his experiences and eventually coming to the conclusion that to be fully human, at least for Smith, means to be an artist and to be an artist means to "participate in life." This is a good example of *Homo aestheticus*.

Homo bellus

The human is a martial animal. Although we might not wish this, we must acknowledge that committing war on others of our species is central to who we are and to the advancement of civilization. While recent animal studies have found that other species appear to engage in something that resembles war,[3] we cannot escape the centrality of war in human societies throughout history and must understand this characteristic as that which is central to our being and, therefore, the development of the arts of war is central to our becoming fully human. Though the ancient Spartans are best known for developing a public education system

---

2. For an example, see Beau Smith, "Art Is Life," *Ezine @rticles*, February 28, 2008, http://ezinearticles.com/?Art-Is-Life&id=1013832.

3. Nicholas Wade, "Chimps, Too, Wage War and Annex Rival Territory," *New York Times*, June 21, 2010, www.nytimes.com/2010/06/22/science/22chimp.html?_r=0.

for males designed to develop warriors (the *agoge*), the centrality of training in the arts and skills of war has hardly been limited to Sparta. In present-day United States, we find many military academies whose reason for being can only be to develop the warrior skills in their students, even if not every graduate is assumed to become a soldier. Furthermore, consider the role of sports in American society both in and outside of schools. In many ways, sport is ritual war and the characteristics that make for outstanding athletes are often considered equivalent to those that make outstanding soldiers.

Homo economicus

Humans are rational and self-interested animals who engage in social exchanges in a manner that works in their own self-interest. Because of the popularity of *Atlas Shrugged* on Advanced Placement reading lists, Ayn Rand may be the person most students know who advances this ontology, but it is also a central assumption of classical liberalism, an economic-political ideology that will be addressed in a later chapter, as well as libertarianism. Consider these two quotations from Ayn Rand:

> America's abundance was not created by public sacrifices to "the common good," but by the productive genius of free men who pursued their own personal interests and the making of their own private fortunes.

and

> To the glory of mankind, there was, for the first and only time in history, a country of money—and I have no higher, more reverent tribute to pay to America, for this means: a country of reason, justice, freedom, production, achievement. For the first time, man's mind and money were set free, and there were no fortunes-by-conquest, but only fortunes-by-work, and instead of swordsmen and slaves, there appeared the real maker of wealth, the greatest worker, the highest type of human being—the self-made man—the American industrialist.
>
> If you ask me to name the proudest distinction of Americans, I would choose—because it contains all the others—the fact that they were the people who created the phrase "to make money." No other language or nation had ever used these words before; men had always thought of wealth as a static quantity—to be seized, begged, inherited, shared, looted or obtained as a favor. Americans were the first to understand that wealth has to be created.[4]

Many students I have taught are surprised to discover that among the many self-identified conservative politicians, *Homo economicus* may be the most frequently asserted ontology of all.

---

4. Ayn Rand, "What Is Capitalism?" in *Capitalism: The Unknown Ideal*, ed. Nathaniel Branden, Alan Greenspan, and Robert Hessen (New York: Signet, 1967), 29; Ayn Rand, "The Meaning of Money," in *For the New Intellectual: The Philosophy of Ayn Rand* (New York: Signet, 1963), 93.

Homo ethicus

Humans are moral beings. To be fully human requires us to act in a manner that is ethically justified. While there may be many different understandings of what it means to engage in proper conduct, the goal of all persons must be to live a "good life" or to become a "virtuous person" or to "act rightly." Listen to former US secretary of education William J. Bennett speak about the centrality of virtue education for schools:

> It's about the virtues, it's about self-discipline and courage, compassion, faith, friendship, the other virtues. It's about the hard realities that constitute the virtues. We used to teach the virtues in the schools. They are very important things for young people to learn.[5]

Homo faber

Often *Homo faber* refers to humans as tool-users and has been attributed to many people, including Benjamin Franklin and Thomas Carlyle, who wrote "Man is a tool-using animal.... Without tools he is nothing, with tools he is all."[6] But neither Franklin nor Carlyle actually used the term *Homo faber*. And neither did Karl Marx, yet Marx is probably the best known advocate of *Homo faber* as the essential nature of being human. Marx argued that humans realize their full selves when they conceptualize things in their minds and then produce them in the world.[7] Hannah Arendt uses the term explicitly and does so in a manner similar to Marx. Arendt distinguishes between *Homo faber* and what she calls *Animal laborans*. *Homo faber* refers to the creation of humans through their freely conceived work in the world. *Animal laborans* refers to the dehumanization of people as mere labor—used for their body to execute the orders of others. In the following passage Arendt stated that "labor" (as opposed to "work," which is creative and spirit building) leaves people isolated and lonely and is worthy only of totalitarian regimes:

> Isolated man who lost his place in the political realm of action is deserted by the world of things as well, if he is no longer recognized as *homo faber* but treated as *animal laborans* whose necessary "metabolism with nature" is of concern to no one. Isolation then becomes loneliness. Tyranny based on isolation generally leaves the productive capacities of man intact; a tyranny over "laborers," however, as for instance the rule over slaves in antiquity, would automatically be a rule over lonely, not only isolated, men and tend to be totalitarian.[8]

Do not confuse *Homo faber* with a simple "vocational man." Though human vocations certainly require the use of tools, in today's world they tend more to "labor" than to "work."

5. William J. Bennett, "The Book of Virtues," *Booknotes*, C-SPAN, 1994, video interview.

6. Thomas Carlyle, *Sartor Resartus: The Life and Opinions of Herr Teufelsdrockh* (Project Gutenberg, 1890), paragraph 9, chapter 5, book 1, www.gutenberg.org/files/1051/1051-h/1051-h.htm.

7. Karl Marx and Friedrich Engels, *The German Ideology* (New York: International Publishers, 1970).

8. Hannah Arendt, *The Origins of Totalitarianism* (New York: Harcourt, 1966), 612.

In other words, vocational training would be consistent with *Animal laborans*, whereas *Homo faber* requires a more critical and political education than vocational training typically provides.

Homo sapiens

In Aristotle's biological classifications, humans were named the animal that reasons. This ontology emphasizes that the human ability to reason is its most central quality. Given Aristotle's influence during the eighteenth century as the modern biological classification was constructed, the human species was given the Latin name *Homo sapiens* by Aristotelian-influenced scientists.

Homo societus

Humans are social animals. Humans are certainly not the only social animals, but we develop a complicated social and cultural world within which all adult members of our species must participate or find themselves isolated in the world. To be fully human requires individuals to become integrated into the larger community and many educational philosophers, including John Dewey, had at least some allegiance to this conception of human ontology. In Chapter 1, I quoted Dewey as having stated, "I believe that all education proceeds by the participation of the individual in the social consciousness of the [human] race."[9]

Homo spiritus

Humans are spiritual beings. To be fully human requires that we connect to our spiritual self. For many, the spiritual self refers to a religious self and, in the United States, that religious spirit is generally associated with an Abrahamic God, but, of course, there are many highly spiritual Americans who define that spiritual self in a manner different than Christianity, Islam, or Judaism such as Buddhists, Hindi, Wiccas, New Agers, and the traditional religions of the indigenous people of America. Spirituality connects us with our self and with others and with the universe. Surely this is one of the primary reasons for the private religious schools in the United States, but one does not have to attend a religious school to locate the spirit at the center of human life.

It would be a grave mistake to assume that education for spirituality required a commitment to religion at all. Michael Dantley argued,

> A person's spirituality is that ethereal part that establishes meaning in one's life. It dares to ask the hard ontological and teleological inquiries that help people to determine who they are and what their contributions to life will be. Spirituality is the

---

9. John Dewey, "My Pedagogic Creed," *School Journal* 54 (1897): 77–80, http://dewey.pragmatism.org/creed.htm.

instrument in our lives through which we build connectivity and community with others. Spirituality differs from religion in that religion is an institutionalized space where spirituality may be nurtured and celebrated. Religion is often used to codify moral behavior that works in collaboration with civil authorities to domesticate a society's citizenry. Religion is the formally recognized space where spirituality is legitimately to reside. However, spirituality far transcends the boundaries of institutional religion. Spirituality may certainly be nurtured through the auspices of the religious experience and may be articulated by some through the use of religious language but the ethereal nature of our lives may also be fostered through life's experiences, a relationship with nature, an appreciation for music and the arts, or even the dynamics of family and friendships. It is from one's spirituality that compassion, a sense of equity, understanding and passion toward others as well as the life's work to which one has been "called" emanate.[10]

Spirituality, according to Dantley, is also a necessary aspect of all education, but most particularly to those, such as African Americans, who often express a spirituality that juxtaposes "the truth of social, cultural, and political realities with a hope of dismantling and constructing a different reality grounded in equity and social justice."[11]

Pragmatism

Above I point out how John Dewey seems to have some allegiance to the *Homo societus* ontology, but much more central to Dewey's conception of human existence was his understanding of humans as problem-solvers who must continue to grow and adjust to new situations if the species is to survive. Failure to learn leads to failure to adjust, and ultimately leads to extinction. Furthermore, because humans cannot be conceived of as essentially isolated individuals (as in *Homo economicus*), Dewey understood humans as always one with the society, so that it is not only individuals who must solve problems and grow and adjust, but societies that must as well. Integrating these ideas, we might suggest that pragmatism's ontology suggests that to live fully as a human, one must not only learn how to learn and solve problems but how to contribute to a democratic society that is geared to solving problems and growing and adjusting to new conditions. Of all the ontologies described here, Dewey's pragmatism requires democracy at its center for humans to realize their full human selves.

Existentialism

Existentialism rejects the idea that there is any essential characteristic of human beings but argues, instead, that humans are *radically free*. The idea of being radically free does not refer to political freedom (we know only too well that many people have little political freedom

---

10. Michael E. Dantley, "Successful Leadership in Urban Schools: Principals and Critical Spirituality, a New Approach to Reform," *Journal of Negro Education* 79 (2010): 214–215.

11. Ibid., 216.

at all), but that we are free from some predetermined essence prescribed by God or Nature or anything else other than what we are free to determine for ourselves both as individuals and as societies. We create what it means to be human as we move through our lives and make choices. Our choices and actions create not only our own individual selves, but contribute to the creation of what it means to be human for all humanity. In other words, when I choose to lie to gain advantage, I not only show through my actions that I am a liar, but that human beings are animals that lie to gain advantage. On the other hand, when I choose to tell the truth, even when it is not to my own advantage, I show through my actions that not only am I an honorable person, but that humans are animals that can maintain honor even when not to their advantage. For this reason, we live in both "possibility" and "dread"—possibility because in any situation, we can always do otherwise—we do not have to conform to that which our society and culture expect of us and dread because in our choices we carry the burden of acting not only for ourselves but for all humanity. Once we realize that "we can do otherwise" (i.e., that we are radically free), we must live in "good faith" by stopping the practice of "lying to ourselves" (i.e., living in "bad faith") and instead choose to "live in truth." When we live as unreflective members of our culture, we live in bad faith. For example, when we become blindly patriotic or complacently accepting of the status quo, we live in bad faith. We must either accept responsibility for the immorality of our society or act against such immorality as war, poverty, child hunger, ignorance, and lack of humane health care.[12]

Postmodernism

To be human means to find that you exist in a symbolically constructed world (i.e., a world of language and media) embedded in power relations that we turn to in order to "name" or "identify" our Self. There is no essence nor is there any existential freedom and we are, therefore, decentered and multivoiced. Of all of the ontological ideas discussed in this chapter, the postmodernists would object the most to the suggestion that they even have an ontology. Because postmodernists point out that all theorizing is trapped in language the suggestion that we can ever claim to get at the essence of what it means to be human ignores the reality that whatever we claim, we do so through language and are, therefore, ultimately trapped by it and in it.

How Ontology Relates to Educational Philosophy

The eleven answers to this ontological question are only some of the possible answers that philosophers and other theorists have advanced as the best and most reasoned claim to the fullness of human existence. Which is correct? That is the wrong question. Trying to decide which of the eleven answers is the correct one suggests that the answer is singular and exists outside of us waiting for us to discover it. Some people are discouraged by questions that

---

12. For a good discussion of Sartre's work on bad faith/good faith, see Ronald E. Santoni, *Bad Faith, Good Faith, and Authenticity in Sartre's Early Philosophy* (Philadelphia: Temple University Press, 1995).

have no single correct answer. Many wonder why we are bothering to ask a question that has no correct answer. Many suggest that it is just a waste of time.

But, to fail to explore this question and commit to one or some combination of answers is to live unreflectively. One way or another, we each commit to an ontology. Our only question is whether or not we are going to do so reflectively or unreflectively. Are we going to reason our way to the best answer we can or are we just going to commit based on nonreason? And make no mistake about it, which answer you pick or that we as a society pick makes profound differences in people's lives. This is particularly true for those who are invested in formal education because some of these ontologies are congruent with the reality of our present schools while others are not. To achieve most of these ontological goals will require a radical change in the nature of schools, because most schools are congruent with only a few of those mentioned in this chapter.

A democratic society requires that its citizens make decisions about the nature of its public education, but when its citizens have not reflected on the very purpose of living a life, how can it possibly decide what its schools should look like? Keep in mind that philosophy commits to a reasoned exploration of problems and that it values consistency and coherency, so, if we start with one or another or some combination of these ontologies or argue for a twelfth or thirteenth, our educational philosophy must be consistent and coherent with our ontology. When we accept one ontology and then work in a school system set up to realize a contradictory ontology, we must either work to change our schools, give in and accept a different ontology, or live in the soul-sucking condition that Jean-Paul Sartre called "bad faith."

For this reason, how you answer the question of what it means to be fully human should help guide your own pursuit of becoming educated and should also guide how we develop our public schools. If you commit to *Homo economicus*, for example, as being the essence of living a fully human life (as so many of our present policy-makers do), then you will pursue one type of education: one that teaches you how to succeed as an economic being. If you commit to pragmatism as the basis of living a fully human life (as many college professors do), you will pursue a different type of education: one that teaches you the skills and dispositions necessary to solve problems through continuous growth as part of a community. The commitment to a particular ontology or the failure to commit to any has real and profound impact on the everyday lives of our public school students even though few Americans, even few teachers, seem to realize it.

Epistemology

Given the importance of coherency and consistency, which philosophical question one asks and answers first becomes quite pivotal in all that follows. While many people will be comfortable asking and answering the ontological question first, others prefer to ask and answer the epistemological question first. *Epistemology* asks what counts as knowledge or, perhaps, how we justify what we claim as knowledge. It also asks how we obtain knowledge. Many people argue that we cannot answer the ontological question until we have developed a justifiable epistemology, because we cannot justify our claim to know what a fully human life is until we have decided what it means "to know." But whether one starts by asking what it means to be fully human or starts with what it means to know, the answer to both questions must be consistent with each other and coherent with the overall philosophy developed.

Below are a few of the ways in which philosophers have attempted to address the question of epistemology. The different epistemologies presented below were selected based on their popularity in educational texts but also to help clarify through comparison one to the others.

Correspondence (Classical)

One of the oldest approaches to epistemology is referred to as "classical" or "correspondence" and is most closely associated with the classical philosophies of the ancient Greeks and Romans. However, it is still found prominently today in a wide range of philosophies and, perhaps more importantly, in the commonsense of ordinary people. There are at least three different versions of classical epistemologies depending on what kind of classical philosophy is utilized: empiricist, idealist, realist. These classical epistemologies differ in some very important ways, but they also share some common conclusions about knowledge.

What is knowledge?

All three classical epistemologies share the claim that *knowledge* is that which we hold in our minds that corresponds to the world as it is. This is why it is called *correspondence epistemology*. The claim here is that there is a world that exists out there that humans can know as it is, and we can claim to know it when our ideas match that world as it actually is.

How do we obtain knowledge?

The three classical epistemologies differ on their understanding of how we obtain knowledge-in-mind that corresponds to the world.

Empiricists. The world is fundamentally material (i.e., the world exists in matter) and so we obtain real knowledge through empirical methods that guide and structure our observations of the material world so that our ideas correspond to the facts of the material world. Empiricists typically privilege science as the best way of knowing.

Idealists. Because the material world is always changing (living things age, nonliving things break down), the eternal world of ideas and concepts (e.g., theoretical knowledge or the world as God knows it) is the most fundamental world, and so we obtain real knowledge through conceptual methods, which guide and structure our reason so that our ideas correspond to the postulates and logic of the conceptual world. Idealists tend to favor philosophy or religion or art as a way of knowing.

Realists. Realism is a form of idealism that agrees that true knowledge is found in the world of ideas but argues that humans can discover those eternal concepts through observation of the empirical world. In other words, realists believe that the ideal world is revealed in the material world. Aristotle is the iconic example of a realist. While we tend to think of him as a philosopher, his work in the physical sciences was a central influence to the birth of modern science starting in the fifteenth century. Realists tend to favor theoretical science.

Pragmatic (Transactional or Interactional)

Pragmatism developed near the end of the nineteenth century and grew out of the American experience. It has been very influential in educational discourses and is often associated with the philosopher John Dewey.

What is knowledge?

Knowledge is constructed as we transact with our world. We act upon our world, and our world acts upon us (transaction). Knowledge helps us negotiate our lives in the world (i.e., solve the problems we identify as we engage our world). We gain knowledge through our reflective experiences with the world. Knowledge only counts when others, who have studied the questions and problems seriously, agree to accept it as knowledge until another idea or data gained from experience requires that we revise our knowledge. In this way, in pragmatism, truth is always tentative, never absolute. Humans can never really know the world as God knows it. It certainly would be arrogant for people to liken ourselves to God; we must settle for the very human, very useful, and very worthy goal of tentative, human, and pragmatic truths.

How do we obtain knowledge?

Because pragmatism claims that knowledge is the result of our transactions with the world, to gain knowledge we must engage our world (transact with it—both the material and the symbolic worlds) in an active and systematic manner. We must act on our world and observe the way the world acts back on us. We must, therefore, be comfortable and confident in the processes of knowledge production. The processes of science can be helpful in organizing this process, but so can the processes of the humanities and the fine arts. What distinguishes the expert from the novice is not that one gains knowledge through transactions with the world and the other does not, but that the expert transacts with the world through a studied and reflective method, whereas the novice does so through less reflective processes.

Phenomenological

Both pragmatism and phenomenology maintain a skepticism toward claims of absolute knowledge, and both understand that knowledge is located in a process of construction. Where they differ is in their understanding of what this constructive process is and how it works. If pragmatism is rooted in the American experience, phenomenology is rooted in the European experience.

What is knowledge?

Knowledge is that which is left after we strip away all our interpretations and get to the basic experience of something in particular. We can never know the world as it is, but only as we experience it. Knowledge is how we experience the world before our language and our culture enter into our interpretations of that experience, but we often fail to recognize the ways in which our culture colors or distorts what we are experiencing directly. The moment we name what is happening or interpret it, we insert culture into it and we distance ourselves from knowledge.

How do we obtain knowledge?

We must put our Self in an experience of something in particular and attempt through reflection or through intuition to "get back to the thing itself" as it presented itself to us before we started to make meaning out of it. We must search for that which the kernel of this experience has in common with the kernel of other experiences. Phenomenology requires much self-reflection of our experiences and the ability to step outside our cultural recipes for making meaning. For example, freedom is known through our experience of freedom. As we experience freedom, we must learn to strip away all of our cultural biases to get to the fundamental experience of freedom itself before we recognize it and called it "freedom."

Hermeneutical

Hermeneutics is a method developed by biblical scholars in the Middle Ages to cull out what were to be considered true books of the Bible from imposters. During the Renaissance, the techniques of hermeneutics began to be applied to all texts, not just the Bible.

What is knowledge?

Knowledge is that which is built up as we experience things in their context and return to them again and again each time with a new set of experiences within which to reconsider those things. Knowledge is a back and forth, circular process of comparing part to whole and whole to part.

How do we obtain knowledge?

We have an experience with "A," which gives us some sense of "A." We then have an experience with "B," which combined with our sense of "A" gives us some sense of "B." But now our knowledge of "B" requires that we reconsider our experience with "A," therefore changing our understanding of "A." We then have an experience with "C," which combined with our sense of both "A" and "B" influences how we understand "C." But now our new experience with "C" requires that we reconsider our understandings of both "A" and "B," resulting in a new understanding of those phenomena. This process is never-ending. All parts must be understood in light of all other parts or of the whole. It is sometimes referred to as the "hermeneutic circle."

Critical Theory

Critical theory is a social philosophy that developed following World War I and centered in Frankfurt, Germany. During World War II, many of the original critical theorists fled Nazi Germany and migrated to England and the United States. It has had much influence in educational philosophy since the 1980s.

What is knowledge?

Knowledge always represents interests and, therefore, is always integral with morality and politics. No knowledge is morally or politically neutral and objective. Much knowledge, especially that knowledge that passes as neutral and objective, actually serves the interests of the powerful to help them maintain the status quo. Critical knowledge results from the demystification of our myths about the world and works to transform our world. Only "critical knowledge" serves the general interest of emancipation and democracy.

How do we obtain knowledge?

Critical knowledge results from the elimination of the way societies make meaning of the world that distorts the way the world actually works. For example, Americans tend to accept an American narrative that the United States is the most socially mobile country in the world, that Americans, regardless of social class, have a better chance to succeed than citizens of any other nation. The facts suggest otherwise.[13] According to critical theory, as long as Americans accept this distortion of the facts, such knowledge will serve only to maintain the nation that has more inequality than any other major industrialized nation. Only when Americans demystify such myths and tell stories that match the actual material facts, will we have critical knowledge that will make it possible to create the democratic nation that we claim to want.

Postmodernism

According to postmodernism, all the epistemologies discussed above are "modern" except the classical epistemologies of correspondence, which are "ancient." Today's world requires a postmodern philosophy. According to postmodern philosophers, so-called modern epistemologies are locked into a mistaken belief that people can actually "know" a world outside of our language. Postmodernism argues that knowledge outside of language is not possible.

What is knowledge?

Knowledge is only that which we are able to convince others to accept as knowledge. There is no "real" knowledge but only that which the powerful have been able to assert as true and get others to accept.

How do we obtain knowledge?

This is the wrong question. What we really need to ask is, how is it that some knowledge has become accepted as true? The answer to this revised question is that some people are

---

13.   Jason DeParle, "Harder for Americans to Rise from Lower Rungs, *New York Times*, January 4, 2012, www .nytimes.com/2012/01/05/us/harder-for-americans-to-rise-from-lower-rungs.html?_r=2&pagewanted=1&hp.

able to convince others to accept knowledge claims because they have the power to do so either through control of the institutions that legitimize knowledge or because they have the ability to manipulate the language well enough to "win the game." That which counts as "knowledge" in school, according to some postmodern epistemologies, is that which those scholars, policy-makers, and teachers have determined counts as "knowledge" regardless of whether it is true or not. Whoever writes the textbooks and tests determines what is true. Or, as it is sometimes said, history is written by the victors. Postmodernists might be seen as having ambitions to foster the lions' version of the hunt.

Constructivism

In the field of education, many speak of "constructivist epistemology." Philosophically, *constructivism* is an imprecise term that might include pragmatic, phenomenological, and/or hermeneutic epistemologies. It implies that knowledge must be constructed by the knower or the community of knowers in some way. For this reason, constructivism in educational texts is consistent with pragmatism, phenomenology, hermeneutics, and several others as well.

Summary

The epistemologies discussed above are just some of the possible answers to the questions of what knowledge is and how we obtain it. There are many others, but whichever episte-mologies philosophically minded educators might accept, their epistemological reasoning must be consistent with their ontological reasoning and coherent with their philosophy as a whole. One would think that teachers, whose job it is to help students gain knowledge and understanding, would have thought deeply about what knowledge is and how it is pro-duced and learned. Unfortunately, too many teachers simply take a naïve, unphilosophical approach to knowledge. Essentially they accept that knowledge is whatever is tested. But to approach teaching without having reflected upon one's epistemology is, to use Sartre's concept explained above, to live in bad faith. Teachers must think carefully about epistemology and accept their own complicity in the construction of the nation's commonsense understanding as to what counts as knowledge and what does not.

Ethics

Ethics is that area of philosophy that asks about proper human conduct. Most philosophers use the terms *ethics* and *morality* interchangeably as synonyms (though there are some important exceptions among philosophers to this common usage). In contrast, some other fields, such as educational psychology, make clear distinctions between these two terms. This book will typically use these two terms interchangeably. The only exception is when discussing Nel Noddings's ethic of care because Noddings is one of the few who makes a careful distinction between ethics and morality in order to clarify what she believes are important conceptual distinctions.

Ethics versus Efficacy

American professional cultures tend to value efficacy over ethics. When trying to decide what to do, professionals typically ask about what works rather than what is moral. *Efficacy* simply means effectiveness or the power to get something done. In education, for example, many people ask how we can get test scores up. They ask, "What works?" That is a question of efficacy. Much less frequently do they ask an ethical question such as, "Is focusing on test scores good for students?"

To answer a question of efficacy, we make an empirical argument. In other words, if I wanted to argue that to get test scores up, we should have an exercise program in schools, I would be required to provide empirical evidence that showed that exercise programs raise test scores.[14] On the other hand, if I wanted to argue that focusing on test scores was unethical, I would need a normative argument. There is evidence that suggests that the focus on test scores results in a curriculum that emphasizes basic information rather than higher order thinking, and that leads some educators to argue that the focus on test scores is unethical because it diminishes the education of students' higher order thinking.[15]

Public Ethics

Many Americans assume that ethics (or morality) belong in the private sphere: that morality is not a subject for public engagement. Perhaps this excluding of ethics from public discussion follows from confusion over the place of religion in ethics.

If we assume that the only basis for ethical decision-making lies in religion, then we might think that, since religion is supposed to remain in the private sphere, we must also relegate ethics to the private sphere. Certainly there are some ethical problems that lie specifically in religion. For example, whether a man should cover his head or shave his face or a woman should cover her head or face or dress modestly might all indicate adherence to or rejection of specific religious understandings of morality. But one does not have to appeal to a specific religious belief to argue for the moral need to dress modestly in public or to refrain from stealing or murder or to educate our society's children. Contemporary Americans seem to have lost the language necessary for public discussions of ethics.

This book develops a couple of ways in which we can begin to recover such a public language of ethics: one that neither requires a person to bring religion to the conversation nor forbids someone to bring their religion to the debate. While we agree there are some primary questions that apply only to the private sphere and are not issues for public discussion, there are ethical issues in the public sphere that can be addressed from whatever an individual's private religious or personal moral system might be. Chapters 7 and 8 explore two ways to approach ethics that could be used to build a conversation on ethics in public spaces. These ethics neither require nor forbid individuals to bring their own personal religious or

---

14. For evidence that exercise does raise test scores, see "Active Living Research: Using Evidence to Prevent Childhood Obesity and Create Active Communities," www.activelivingresearch.org/files/Active_Ed.pdf.

15. Angela Engel, "Exposing the Myths of High Stakes Testing," *FairTest: The National Center for Fair and Open Testing*, 2007, www.fairtest.org/exposing-myths-high-stakes-testing.

nonreligious moral foundation to the discussion, yet provide a basis for an honest debate on the ethics of different schooling practices.

Conclusion

Philosophy is a discipline aimed at developing the skills and dispositions necessary to lead a reflective life. It is the process of asking and seeking answers to age-old questions, such as what does it mean to be fully human? (an ontological question), how can we justify the knowledge we claim? (an epistemological question), and what is proper conduct? (an ethical question). Philosophy privileges reason and demands consistency and coherency. Educators and others interested in education should be interested in basic philosophical questions because philosophy's requirement of being reasoned requires that any philosophical questions we might ask and answer related to education must be consistent and coherent with the questions we ask and answer in general philosophy. In fact, philosophers have been interested specifically in questions of education at least since Plato, whose *Meno*, written in the fourth century BCE, is one of the first and one of the most important explorations of educational philosophy.[16] Frequently, people confuse the end result of such philosophic reflection for philosophy itself. As Chapters 9–11 will clarify more fully, answers that are separated from the actual process of philosophic reasoning are better labeled "ideology" than "philosophy."

As people seeking education, students have generally not been asked to reflect on what they think they need to become "fully human." Instead, students are typically asked to just go along with the teachers and the rules and the bureaucracy and hope that at the end they will have gotten an education. I am skeptical that such unreflective processes lead to a person's becoming educated. My own educational philosophy requires students to think about where they would like to be *as a human being* when they complete their schooling. Surely they will not yet be fully educated when they graduate from college, but hopefully they will be on their way and, if they have actually reflected on where that path should lead (and *only* if they have reflected on where that path should lead), when their formal schooling is completed, their education will not end but rather continue through a lifetime of reflective living.

---

16. Plato, *Plato's Meno*, trans. Benjamin Jowett (Rockville, MD: Serenity, 2009), http://books.google .com/books?id=5VZYxRiErO0C&printsec=frontcover&dq=meno&hl=en&sa=X&ei=CJs_UdwKgdjSAby QgcgE&ved=0CDMQuwUwAA.

CHAPTER SIX

Philosophical Reasoning about Education

Three Common Approaches

Text critique requires readers to both analyze and interpret texts. To interpret educational texts requires a broad understanding of many different contexts. Certainly one of the most important contexts used in critiquing educational texts is the philosophy of education. Having knowledge of how different educators have theorized education philosophically provides an excellent context for opening up insights that might otherwise go unnoticed. The next three chapters will explore philosophy of education to provide some needed background to make such interpretation possible. But, philosophy is not just a backdrop for the interpretation of educational texts, it is also a window into how one reasons about education.

Philosophic reasoning is a process of building a consistent and coherent argument. The educator explores a philosophic question, and when satisfied with reasoning, moves to a second question and then a third until all of the most important philosophical questions have been examined, resulting in a strong conceptual argument. The next three chapters present five different reasonings commonly found in the educational literature: perennialism, essentialism, progressivism, caring/relational pedagogy, and social reconstructionism/critical pedagogy. Four of the five have decades of development behind them. The fourth, relational pedagogy, is relatively new, but is rapidly growing in influence.

This chapter will present one way to reason through each of the first three on the above list. Each of the three will be explored first by addressing their approaches to general philosophical questions as developed in Chapter 5 and then by considering some of the important questions that philosophy asks specifically about education including, What is the primary aim of education? What should be taught and how should it be taught? How do we know when something is learned?

Perennialism

While perennialism was not given its name until the twentieth century, its reasoning is as old as formal philosophy itself. As its name suggests, this educational philosophy comes back age after age after age in the same way that a perennial plant, such as a daylily or a black-eyed susan, returns season after season. Robert Hutchins and Mortimer Adler developed the basic argument for perennialism while Hutchins was president (1929–1945) and chancellor (1945–1951) of the University of Chicago, where Adler (1930–1952) was one of its most prominent and controversial philosophers. Both men identified with classical philosophy as the best and most reasoned approach to any question of philosophy and when they turned their classical reasoning to education, they found the public schools of this country lacking.

Perennialism and Ontology

As classical philosophers, perennialists tend to begin with an ontological question such as, What does it mean to be fully human? Although they might not agree on the classical response to that question, they generally agree that God or Nature has given humans an essential being. Among the essential descriptions presented in Chapter 5, a perennialist is most likely to commit to one of the following: *Homo aestheticus*; *Homo ethicus*; *Homo spiritus*; and, because most contemporary classical philosophers are strongly influenced by Aristotle, *Homo sapiens*. Certainly the Aristotelians Hutchins and Adler would be comfortable with placing *Homo sapiens* as the primary conceptualization of what it means to be fully human. In his 1953 essay "The Basis of Education," Hutchins wrote (in the male-centric language of the day), "Men are rational animals. They achieve their terrestrial felicity by the use of reason."[1]

Perennialism and Epistemology

Because perennialists accept that humans have a God-given or Nature-given essence, their epistemology must acknowledge at least two things: first, that there is a God-given or Natural world that owes its existence and meaning to something outside of human action; and, second, that humans are able to know that world as it really is. These two assumptions are quite consistent with the classical "correspondence" epistemologies explored in the last chapter. While perennialists might disagree among themselves as to which of the correspondence epistemologies has the strongest argument (empiricist, idealist, or realist), they would all reject any of the constructivist epistemologies as well as critical theory. Again, being Aristotelians, Hutchins and Adler advance a realist epistemology that argues that essences of the world exist in pure forms or in correct theories, and that these correct theories can be grasped through good empirical study combined with strong conceptual reasoning. In other words, we can know that the essence of being human is *Homo sapiens* because we are able to study the concrete human experience and correctly reason our way to revealing our essence. That is, through our observations of human beings, we are able to rationally conclude that, unique among all living things, the human being is the animal that thinks.

---

1. Robert M. Hutchins, *The Conflict in Education in a Democratic Society* (New York: Harper & Row, 1953), 67–76.

Perennialism and the Aims of Education

As classical Aristotelians, Hutchins and Adler argue for accepting *Homo sapiens* as the strongest ontological claim and realist correspondence as the strongest epistemological claim. These two commitments suggest that education should help people develop their observation and reasoning faculties so that they are able to develop into their full essence as reasoning beings; however, this process is not something to be mastered quickly. In fact, it takes a lifetime. As Hutchins wrote in his 1953 essay, "The Basis of Education,"

> The object of liberal education in youth is not to teach the young all they will ever need to know. It is to give them the habits, ideas, and techniques that they need to continue to educate themselves. Thus the object of formal institutional liberal education in youth is to prepare the young to educate themselves throughout their lives.[2]

And what youth need to educate themselves throughout their lives does not change from student to student, but remains the same whoever he or she might be. In a 1951 essay, Adler explained,

> The primary aim of education [is] the betterment of men [i.e., humans] not with respect for their differences but with respect to the *similarities* that all men [i.e., humans] have. According to this theory, if there are certain things that all men [i.e., humans] *can* do, or certain things that all men [i.e., humans] *must* do, it is with these that education is chiefly concerned.[3]

And what do all humans, men and women, share? The desire to live a good life. In fact, when Thomas Jefferson borrowed John Locke's triumvirate of rights (the right to life, liberty, and property), he substituted "happiness" for "property," based on the Aristotelian claim that happiness is the ultimate purpose of life. Unfortunately, few Americans are exposed to Aristotle today and so they do not realize that the term "happiness" is an imperfect translation of the Greek term *eudaimonia*. *Eudaimonia* is better translated as "well-being" because its roots (*eu* and *daimon*) refer to "good" and "spirit." In other words, when Jefferson writes for the right to pursue happiness, he means the right to pursue well-being, something that is much broader than the pursuit of pleasure and laughter—though surely both pleasure and laughter are part of creating well-being. Instead, Jefferson is arguing that all citizens have the right not only to life and liberty, but also to the lifelong process of creating and completing a well-lived life.

The purpose of education then, according to the classical Aristotelians Hutchins and Adler, must be to help individuals develop the intellectual capacities and disposition necessary for building a life of well-being. This requires an education that focuses on humans as human or, as Hutchins stated (again in the male-centered language of his day), "The aim of an educational system is the same in every age and in every society where such a system can exist: it is to improve man as man."[4] Or as Adler stated in his 1951 essay on liberal education,

---

2. Ibid., 151.

3. Mortimer Adler, "Labor, Leisure, and Liberal Education," *Journal of General Education* 6 (1951): 35–36 (emphasis in the original).

4. Hutchins, *Conflict in Education*, 149.

vocational training is "the education of slaves or workers, liberal education is the education of free men [i.e., free people]."[5]

Perennialism, What Should Be Taught, and How

So what are the capacities and dispositions necessary for building a life of well-being and how do people develop them? Remember that Hutchins and Adler argued that to be fully human requires us to develop our full ability to reason, both empirically and conceptually, and, given that commitment, the only answer possible to this question is that students should be taught how to reason as well as to develop the habits of mind to actually use reason in their pursuit of well-being. Furthermore, keep in mind that in perennialism, the aim of education is to prepare all young people for the same purpose: a lifelong pursuit of *eudaimonia*. Does this mean that each of us has to learn all that is important on our own? If so, this would be a daunting task.

Luckily, we have books and some of those books contain true wisdom. Given that truth is God-given or Nature-given, real truth, truly true ideas, are true for all time and all places. We might say that truth, if it is really true, is Truth and it makes no difference when, where, or by whom Truth is found; if that Truth is put into texts, others can have access to it. One of the central elements of a perennialist education, then, is a focus on reading, analyzing, critiquing, and discussing texts—though not just any books, the "Great Books," the texts that have stood the test of time and shown to still contain the wisdom we all desire in our pursuit of happiness.

All people—regardless of identity, background, or intelligence—must experience the same curriculum with the same educational goals because all people have the capacity to become fully human. Although different individuals may have to pursue these same goals at different rates or in different ways, if they have the capacity to become fully human, regardless of their abilities, their purpose must be the same. While perennialists may have problems with many aspects of the new Common Core curriculum being adopted across the country as a result of "Race to the Top," they would be pleased at the Common Core's insistence that higher order educational goals should be adopted for all students.

Contrary to most schools today, perennialists argue that we should not have subject specialization until after students have gained the basic abilities and dispositions for reasoning. They might argue as to whether that can be accomplished by age sixteen or twenty or twenty-two, but there is no argument among perennialists that until basic education has been accomplished, everyone should be getting the same education regardless of natural intellectual abilities, social class, or gender. Schools should not be tracked into honors, college prep, and general education nor should schools put all of one type of student in one track and all of another type in a different track. Instead, all students should be grouped heterogeneously and study the same curriculum. More than thirty years ago, Marva Collins started a school in inner-city Chicago designed for impoverished children based on the principle that all students can learn the classics. One of her best known statements spoke to this point: "I have discovered few learning disabled students in my three decades of teaching. I have, however, discovered many, many victims of teaching inabilities."[6]

---

5. Adler, "Labor, Leisure, and Liberal Education," 36.
6. Marva Collins, "Marva Collins Seminars, Inc.," www.marvacollins.com/comments.html.

The content of the perennialist curriculum had been the center of perennialist writing for a couple of decades before Mortimer Adler presented a clear statement of the perennialist approach to pedagogy. In his 1982 manifesto, *The Paideia Proposal*, Adler laid out a plan for perennialist education in the elementary and secondary schools that includes a clear statement about appropriate pedagogy. Adler argued that there were three kinds of learning goals, each of which required a different pedagogy. The first is the standard acquisition of knowledge, which requires didactic instruction supported with textbooks. The second goal was the development of intellectual skills, which requires coaching and supervised practice. And the third was an "enlarged understanding of idea and values," which requires the Socratic method of asking questions and active student participation. While today's schools exhibit plenty of didactic instruction, they are mostly absent of coaching and Socratic questioning.[7]

Perennialism and How to Know if Something Is Learned

Because perennialists such as Hutchins and Adler understand the aim of education to be to develop the qualities necessary for a lifelong pursuit of well-being, they clearly reject knowledge acquisition as little more than the very rudimentary beginnings of such an education. Much more important than "knowing-that" is "knowing-how," and equal to knowing-how is developing the habits of mind necessary to continue their education after schooling ends. Given this aim, tests of knowledge acquisition may be a necessary step in the very early years of schooling with the youngest of children and for the most basic aspects of knowledge and skills, but such tests should never be confused with measuring actual learning. Students must be required to practice and show through their actions their ability to reason empirically and conceptually and to show the inclination to actually do so. At St. John's College, one of the best known colleges consciously implementing perennialism today, students are expected to read original sources, engage in reasoned discussions in seminars, and produce well-researched and well-reasoned treatises as the measures of their learning starting in their first semester. You will not find multiple choice or short answer tests at St. John's. Students must demonstrate their learning, not prove their mastery of knowledge.[8]

Essentialism

Whereas many of today's educational theorists are influenced by classical philosophy, many more approach education by using a modern philosophy. Like classical philosophies, modern philosophies are quite interested in questions of ontology, but most of them privilege epistemology over ontology. Of the modern philosophies, perhaps only existentialism is strongly committed to questions of ontology. For this reason, educators who base their reasoning on one of the modern philosophies typically start with the questions of epistemology, such as, what counts as knowledge, and how do we claim to know? Against the classical philosophers who start with ontology, many modern philosophers argue that to know what the essence of

---

7. Mortimer J. Adler, *The Paideia Proposal: An Educational Manifesto* (New York: Macmillan, 1982).
8. For St. John's webpage, see www.stjohnscollege.edu/admissions/learnmore/admission/index.html.

being human might be requires one first decide what it means "to know." Without having developed a reasoned understanding of knowing, one cannot claim "to know" anything, let alone what it means to be fully human. One of the educational philosophies that begins with epistemology is essentialism.

If the mastery of knowledge and skills plays only an elementary role in a perennialist education, it is the heart of essentialist education. For essentialists, education is nothing if not the accumulation of knowledge and skills that are useful for both the individual's economic success and the nation's economic and military success in an increasingly competitive global world.

Essentialism and Epistemology

Essentialists are more likely to be found among educators influenced by psychology than by philosophy. In fact, William Bagley, the man most credited with naming and advancing the essentialist argument for education, was not a philosopher at all but an educational psychologist. Being a psychologist, Bagley begins his reasoning with a commitment to empirical ways of knowing, such as found in the social and behavioral sciences. Psychology has a long and continuing commitment to the scientific study of human behavior and the heart of science is empirical study. Bagley, like most essentialists, was skeptical of the kinds of conceptual reasoning found in philosophy and advocated by perennialists, and his development of an essentialist philosophy for education shows his empiricist logic.

For essentialists, knowledge must be able to be measured through observation or some instrument of observation, such as an experiment or test, or it does not count as knowledge. It has to be shown to be true in its results. Knowledge must be shown to work, to be useful in getting things done. The proof is in the pudding, we might say. In many ways, more than any of the other philosophical approaches to education, essentialism is the most anti-philosophical and relies heavily upon claims of efficacy built upon empirical study and supported by a good dose of what essentialism understands to be commonsense.

Essentialism and Ontology

Because most essentialists start with accepting that knowledge arises from empirical study and commonsense, we shouldn't be surprised to find Bagley arguing strongly for a commonsense understanding of what it means to be fully human—one that stresses success in the world. The best-educated people are the ones who achieve success in the world regardless of whether that education was gained in a school or not. There are, of course, many ways to achieve success, but surely one of them is through our vocations and that, more than anything, is where essentialism focuses. In many ways, essentialists might say, "We are what we do." In this way, essentialism is the direct opposite of perennialism, which argues that only slaves are defined solely through their work.

But it would be unfair to think that the only thing that essentialists are interested in is training good workers and professionals because they also find it important that students gain some of that commonsense that is so important to realizing which knowledge is worth knowing and which is not. Perhaps it goes without saying, but we should probably keep in mind that commonsense, at least in this usage, is "that sense held in common." For that reason, a full human being is not just successful at his/her work, but is also well integrated into the mainstream of his/her society—a society that must always be vigilant to maintain its competitive strength and protect itself in the global struggle for success. Essentialists appreciate winners because, they argue, winners make all of us better as we work to improve our own competitive abilities. Of all of the ontologies discussed in the last chapter, *Homo economicus* best represents the center of essentialist ontology, but other ontologies such as *Homo bellus* and *Homo societus* are at least partially consistent with essentialism as well.

Essentialism and the Aims of Education

Given that we live in a competitive world where the strong survive and the weak do not, and given that what counts as knowledge can primarily be found through empirical means tempered with commonsense, for essentialists, the aims of education must primarily build around creating graduates prepared to take their place in the competitive world and succeed. Unlike perennialists, who desire to educate everyone to think about the big ideas of life and to participate in civic life, essentialists are likely to argue that if we don't build a society that is able to meet the competition, there will be no need for big ideas or participation in civic life. It is much better, they typically argue, to create a schooling system designed to push everyone to gain as much knowledge and skill as possible and to complement that useful knowledge with the basic knowledge of our culture. By creating schools that teach a common culture, we create a population that can understand each other and work together for success. As Bagley stated in his 1938 "An Essentialist's Platform for the Advancement of American Education": "An effective democracy demands a community of culture. Educationally this means that each generation be placed in possession of a common core of ideas, meanings, understandings, and ideals representing the most precious elements of the human heritage."[9] A house divided is a house that falls; a society that speaks the same language, holds the same values, and knows the same knowledge is a society that can stand together as one and compete with any other in the world.

Bagley opened his 1938 platform by claiming that the learning of American elementary school students is inferior to that of their counterparts in other nations. In the third sentence of the platform, Bagley wrote, "Age for age, the average pupil of our elementary schools does not meet the standards of achievement in the fundamentals of education that are attained in the elementary schools in many other countries."[10] This claim that American schools fail to compete at the world level was also famously taken up and reflected in the title of the 1983 education report from the Reagan administration called *A Nation at Risk*.[11] This same claim

---

9. William C. Bagley, "An Essentialist's Platform for the Advancement of American Education," *Educational Administration and Supervision* 24 (1938): 247–248.

10. Ibid., 241.

11. *A Nation at Risk: The Imperative for Educational Reform: A Report to the Nation and the Secretary of Education, United States Department of Education* (Washington, DC: National Commission on Excellence in Education, 1983).

was presented as justification for the Bush administration's educational reform movement "No Child Left Behind" and as justification for the Obama administration's own reform plan, "Race to the Top."

According to Bagley and most essentialists, then, our fundamental aim must be to educate our young to develop their unique and individual abilities as they enter the competition of life found primarily in the workplace, but also to ensure that they share a common culture upon which to build a united nation in its competition with the rest of the world. Fail to do so, and risk failure.

Essentialism, What Should Be Taught, and How

According to essentialists, what is needed to compete in the world and what everyone must know to be members of a common society constitutes the foundations of learning. Yes, advanced learning is important for the society as a whole, but not for every individual. It is far more important to teach every child the basics. Make sure they can read, write, do arithmetic, and know the basic things that make our society what it is. When an educational text calls for "back to basics," it almost certainly builds its argument with essentialist reasoning. Essentialists focus like a laser beam on knowledge and skills. Ensuring all students have mastered the basic knowledge and skills is the hallmark of basic education and the fundamental elements of schooling for the essentialists.

One advantage of focusing on basic knowledge and skills is that they lend themselves to precise standards with which teachers can organize their curriculum and against which students can be held accountable. Knowledge and skills can also easily be broken down into their constituent parts and used as building blocks for teaching. Determine what the end knowledge or skill is to be; break it down into its building blocks; teach the most basic elements of those blocks and as those fundamentals are learned, add on more blocks until the student has climbed all of the blocks to the top and met the standard. It is planned, organized, and mapped. Students move to the next level when, and only when, they have mastered the lower-level blocks. Keeping students to those standards becomes essential to their success. In his 1938 essentialist platform, Bagley spoke clearly and emphatically that one of the major problems of schools was "The complete abandonment in many school systems of rigorous standards of scholastic achievement as a condition of promotion from grade to grade, and the passing of all pupils 'on schedule.'" Bagley claimed that this lowering of standards had had dramatic effects on schools: "Instead of having 'overage' pupils piling up in the intermediate grades, we now have 'overgraded' pupils handicapped in the work of the junior and senior high schools by their lack of thorough training in the fundamentals already referred to (i.e., the educational basics)."[12] Bagley's statements clearly show the essentialist reasoning at work: failure to maintain standards and require students to learn the primary building blocks before moving to the next set of building blocks is a formula for disaster.

---

12. Bagley, "An Essentialist's Platform," 243.

Essentialism and How to Know if Something Is Learned

Unlike the qualities needed for a lifetime pursuit of well-being, knowledge and skills are easily measured. Remember that essentialist epistemology privileges knowledge that can be measured. That which cannot be measured or shown to be true in its application does not count as knowledge. Such a claim lends itself to the idea that we can know if a student has learned by the score he or she achieves on the test. The strong push for standardized tests as the determinant for all judgments about schools from student learning to teacher quality to school report cards is completely congruent with essentialist reasoning. While Bagley wrote in the 1930s, the claims and themes of his platform have been taken up again and again in American educational texts, from the responses to the Russian launching of *Sputnik* in the 1950s and the call to go "back to the basics" in the 1970s to the Reagan administration's suggestion in the 1980s that our failing schools had put our nation at risk or the Bush administration's call in the early twenty-first century to leave no child behind in order to be able to compete in the world economy to the Obama administration's present call to race to the top or lose our competition with the rest of the world. The argument has changed very little throughout that time.

Progressivism

When Bagley wrote his 1938 essentialist platform, he presented it as a counterargument to progressivism. When Hutchins and Adler developed their perennialist philosophy, they presented it as partly a counterargument to essentialism but also as a counterargument to progressivism. Unfortunately, the term *progressivism* has many varied meanings—even when restricted to education. Educational historian Lawrence Cremin argued that there were at least four very different progressive movements in the first half of the twentieth century. This chapter will restrict its meaning to what Cremin referred to as the "pedagogical progressives." In fact, the label "pedagogical progressives" itself can be applied to two very different philosophical reasonings in education.

Romantic Progressives

One of those reasonings derives from the nineteenth-century philosophical movement referred to as romanticism. This would include well-known educational theorists such as Johann Heinrich Pestolozzi, known for his call for "learning by head, hand, and heart"; Friedrich Fröbel, often credited with the concept of "kindergarten"—German for "children's garden"; and Jean-Jacques Rousseau, author of *Émile, or, On Education,* one of the most influential books on education ever written. The "romantic progressives" are strong advocates of a form of "child-centered" pedagogy that works to allow the basic goodness and inquisitiveness of children to guide their own education. Have faith in the child, the romantics might argue, for it is the adults who have messed everything up. Or as Rousseau wrote in "The Social Contract," which has become one of the most famous opening lines in all Western literature, "Man is [i.e., humans are] born free, and everywhere he is [they are] in chains. Those who think themselves the masters of others are indeed greater slaves than they."[13] The romantic progressive reasoning has had much influence in education and still flourishes in a few small but prominent private schools.[14] But for all their influence, the romantic progressives have never had as much influence among educational philosophers as the pragmatic progressives, so this chapter will focus its attention on them.

Pragmatic Progressives

The pragmatic progressives build their argument for education based on a modern philosophy typically called pragmatism. Pragmatism and the romantic philosophy that anchors the romantic progressives are very different. Unfortunately, many critics of pedagogical progressivism make no distinction between the pragmatic and the romantic versions. Of all the philosophers associated with pragmatic progressivism, John Dewey is by far the best known and most influential; however, there are dozens of other very important educators in the pragmatic progressive tradition, such as William James, Jane Addams, George H. Mead, William Heard Kilpatrick, Francis Parker, and Boyd Henry Bode. Today we find some of the most influential philosophers of education continue to work in the pragmatic progressive tradition.

(Pragmatic) Progressivism and Epistemology

As a modern, mostly twentieth-century philosophy, pragmatic progressives tend to start with the questions of epistemology and, as described in the last chapter, argue that humans construct knowledge as they transact with the world and the world acts back. Knowledge is not something that exists outside the human experience but instead is integral to it. We create knowledge through problem solving as a member of a community that also takes the problem seriously. This social and communal approach to the construction of knowledge through problem solving is often thought to be the starting place for building an intricate web of interacting and integrated understandings that must continuously be tested against the changing world. For this reason, there is not Truth with a capital "T" but only a temporarily agreed upon truth with a little "t"—a pragmatic truth that helps us address the important problems of our day.

An epistemology that is skeptical of absolute and final Truths, or at least the capacity of humans to actually know these absolute Truths as they actually exist, is one of the primary reasons pragmatic progressives are often severely criticized by some people. Some people find fearful and threatening the idea that our schools would not teach certain facts and beliefs as undoubtable Truth. But pragmatic progressives might respond that they are more fearful of the blind commitment to "Truths" that turn out to be inaccurate when actually studied seriously or even to be little more than ethnocentric biases built into our culture's commonsense.

---

13. Jean-Jacques Rousseau, "The Social Contract," in *Internet Modern History Sourcebook,* ed. Paul Halsall, 1997, book I, chapter 1, www.fordham.edu/halsall/mod/rousseau-soccon.asp.

14. For example, see Summerhill School, www.summerhillschool.co.uk/.

(Pragmatic) Progressivism and Ontology

Because knowledge is ever-evolving as we use it to address the problems of our ever-changing world, the best we can say about a human ontology is that humans are problem-solving beings. Through problem solving we grow, our society grows, and we achieve progress. And the best kind of society is one that encourages and promotes the conditions that bring people together to solve problems, and the best kind of society for this is a democratic one. Or as Cornel West has stated, "Humans have the ability to share love, caring, and service to others."[15]

Democratic societies invite engagement of ideas; participation by all; transparency of decision making, especially the reasoning involved; and the organization and promotion of valid data collection from which to build our reasons for our collective decisions. In fact a community is not democratic because it holds elections, or because it is run by elected officials, or because it commits to the principle of majority rules. These are merely mechanisms used to try to achieve the idea of democracy. Democracy is a way of living together where everyone participates in trying to solve our problems. Democracy is the process of all of us figuring out how we can all, each and every one of us, live and work together in a common community. As John Dewey wrote, "Regarded as an idea, democracy is not an alternative to other principles of associate life. It is the idea of community life itself."[16] While all of the philosophies that have influence in American education are congruent with some idea of democracy, none places as important and central a role for democracy as (pragmatic) progressivism.

(Pragmatic) Progressivism and the Aims of Education

Given that knowledge is gained through a community of learners who study ways to address problems, and given that democracy is the best state within which such knowledge can be created, the most fundamental aim of education for progressives must be to develop in students the habits of mind to participate in democratic communities of all kinds. In his 1916 book *Democracy and Education,* Dewey wrote,

> A society which makes provision for participation in its good of all its members on equal terms and which secures flexible readjustment of its institutions through interaction of the different forms of associated life is in so far democratic. Such a society must have a type of education which gives individuals a personal interest in social relationships and control, and the habits of mind which secure social changes without introducing disorder.[17]

And also, "the aim of education is to enable individuals to continue their education—or that the object and reward of learning is continued capacity for growth."[18] Like Dewey, West

---

15. Cornel West, *Race Matters,* 2nd ed. (New York: Vintage Books, 2001), 17.

16. John Dewey, *The Public and Its Problems: An Essay in Political Inquiry* (Chicago: Gateway Books, 1946), 149.

17. John Dewey, *Democracy and Education* (New York: Macmillan Company, 1916), chapter 7, paragraph 1, www.ilt.columbia.edu/publications/dewey.html.

18. Ibid., chapter 8, paragraph 1.

focuses on the progressive commitment to freedom for all people: "Learning in school should give youth the ability to become free people by equipping children with the means to think and to stand on their own feet."[19] In all of these quotations, we see the heart of progressive purpose: to raise citizens who have the capacity and dispositions to participate in communities to the best of their abilities and to forge thriving and growing democratic communities.

(Pragmatic) Progressivism, What Should Be Taught, and How

As the fundamental aim of education is to develop problem-solvers, the content and method of education for progressives must be located in problem solving. Whether one studies language, mathematics, science, art, or physical education is less important than that one studies the subject through the process of solving real problems within the communities of the learners. This means that young children must work on problems suited to and of interest to young children, such as having children organize and run a play store, use large blocks to build a structure, or write and perform a play.

Because problems in life are rarely limited to a single subject area, interdisciplinary problems would likely predominate. Older children might rescue a vacant lot near the school, clear it, and design a park or garden in conjunction with middle school students who study the history of the neighborhood through documents and oral histories and with the aid of high school students who study the legal issues involved and work with inhabitants of the community and with the local government to obtain appropriate and proper permissions. Real problems require real learning, and real learning is meaningful and memorable.

On the other hand, pragmatic progressives do not think that learning is always "fun" or that there is no need for organized and sustained study of curricular content. But they do argue that such disciplined study must reflect and connect to the lives of the students. In a 1902 lecture, Dewey argued that the debate between those who advocated a child-centered pedagogy (e.g., romantic progressives) and those who promoted a teacher-centered pedagogy (e.g., essentialists) created a false dualism. For Dewey, any education that chose one over the other misunderstood the processes and goals of education. Education was a process that integrated the child and the curriculum together.[20] Each is found in the other, and only when brought together is education possible. And this can be done only when the student is able to find a way to connect to what is being studied. One problem with the disciplines as they were then and are still taught in schools is that they reflect the world as adults understand it. To be able to understand and study the world *as an adult* should be the goal, not the method, of education. Dewey explained (in androcentric language),

> The child's life is an integral, a total one. He passes quickly and readily from one topic to another, as from one spot to another, but is not conscious of transition or break. There is no conscious isolation, hardly conscious distinction. The things that occupy him are held together by the unity of the personal and social interests which

---

19. Cornel West, *The Cornel West Reader* (New York: Basic Civitas Books, 1999), 322.

20. John Dewey, *The Child and the Curriculum* (Chicago: University of Chicago Press, 1902), www.gutenberg.org/files/29259/29259-h/29259-h.htm.

his life carries along. Whatever is uppermost in his mind constitutes to him, for the time being, the whole universe. That universe is fluid and fluent; its contents dissolve and re-form with amazing rapidity. But, after all, it is the child's own world. It has the unity and completeness of his own life. He goes to school, and various studies divide and fractionize the world for him. Geography selects, it abstracts and analyzes one set of facts, and from one particular point of view. Arithmetic is another division, grammar another department, and so on indefinitely.[21]

So, for pragmatic progressives, educators must develop a back-and-forth method that both connects to the students' worlds and leads them into the adult world. It's a process that requires that students have a say and a role in the creation of their own education, but also requires that they have the guidance of a teacher who understands the adult world where the students will eventually take their places in a democratic community of problem-solvers.

(Pragmatic) Progressives and How We Know if Something Is Learned

In at least one way, progressives and perennialists share something: they both understand the major purpose of education to be to prepare students for continuous learning. Unlike essentialists, the acquisition of knowledge and skills is not the goal in and of itself. That is not to suggest that either progressives or perennialists think acquiring knowledge and skills is not important, but only that knowledge and skills are of importance only to the extent that they develop lifelong learners. True, progressives and perennialists do disagree strongly on what it means to learn because perennialists assume an external standard of absolute Truth whereas progressives accept the more temporal and evolving construction of pragmatic truths. But the common rejection of mastery of knowledge and skills as the primary goal of education leads both to reject a heavy reliance on tests of knowledge such as the standardized tests that now drive public schooling today.

The assumption that teachers need standardized tests to know whether students are learning sufficiently has become almost commonsense in the United States today. It was not always so, and it is not so in other places in the world. For example, in Finland, which is often cited as having the best educational system in the world, students do not take any standardized tests at all until they test for admittance to higher education.[22] When Nel Noddings was asked if a student were not tested, how can we know if a student can read, Noddings responded, "Hand her a book and ask her to read."[23] Noddings's quip captures precisely the approach that progressives advocate: evaluation of learning can only take place within contexts where the knowledge is integral to the student's purpose. This approach is often referred to as "authentic assessment." Authentic assessment locates the evaluation in a process that naturally meshes with the project being addressed: observing the students

---

21. Dewey, *Child and Curriculum*, 6.

22. See Anu Partanen, "What Americans Keep Ignoring about Finland's School Success," *The Atlantic*, December 29, 2011.

23. Nel Noddings, "Critical Lessons for Critical Thinking," public lecture, Miami University, January 29, 2009.

as they congress to plan their project, examining the work products that result from the project, asking the student to present the results of the project to classmates or to relevant outsiders. For example, in order to graduate from Harlem East High School, started by Deborah Meier, one of the most prominent of today's progressive educators, students had to complete "fourteen portfolios full of work, including seven major presentations in such areas as math, science, literature, history, the arts, community service and apprenticeship, and autobiography." The presentations were "made to a graduation committee consisting of at least two faculty members, an adult of the student's choice, and another student . . . carried out with enormous seriousness and zeal."[24] Unlike standardized tests, which "divide and fractionalize" the world, to use Dewey's language, authentic assessment examines learning within the integrated and unified and real lives of the students.

Educational Philosophy Is Neither a Salad Bar nor a Straightjacket

One of the most common inclinations of those beginning the study of educational philosophy is to want to pick and choose from among the various recommendations from different reasonings. Many students are inclined to want to combine ideas from different philosophical traditions. For example, a student might like the idea of having students solve problems (progressivism) but want to assure themselves that this pedagogy actually "works" by using standardized tests as a measure of student learning (essentialism). Or, perhaps, they cringe at the use of standardized tests (progressivism or perennialism), but like the clear organization of standards-based outcomes pedagogy (essentialism). But philosophy is not a salad bar. It is not a process of taking your plate and taking a little romaine lettuce and a little spinach and a few carrots with a dash of croutons. Philosophy is a process committed to the construction of a well-reasoned argument that requires consistency and coherency. If a teacher's method is not consistent with her/his evaluation method and neither is consistent with her/his stated aim, the classroom has no coherency, and if it has little consistency and no coherency, it cannot be justified philosophically. Of course, one does not have to commit to thinking philosophically. Plenty of teachers, perhaps most of them, simply don't worry about consistency and coherency or thinking about what they do and why they do it philosophically. For those of us who are committed to philosophical reasoning, such failure to reason philosophically results in an unreasonable and unjustified classroom.

On the other hand, just as many educators make an equally problematic mistake when they take an educational philosophy as a recipe for action or as a straightjacket that they must put on and never waiver from. One frequently hears principals and professors of education say things such as "progressives never lecture," "essentialists never utilize projects," or "perennialists never test." But such statements are absurd. Sometimes they do! Dewey, for example, only lectured in his college classes. Some have mistakenly thought that his lecturing was a contradiction of his philosophy, but that only reveals their misunderstanding of pragmatism and philosophical reasoning.

---

24. Deborah Meier, *The Power of Their Ideas: Lessons for America from a Small School in Harlem* (Boston: Beacon Press, 2002), 59–60.

What method a teacher uses to teach or assess, what book to have students read, or what curricular goals to pursue all depend on specific and concrete circumstances. What is important is not that a progressive only uses problem-based methods and only uses authentic assessment but rather that she or he reasons through the problem of that particular classroom using pragmatic reasoning: recognizing that the knowledge is constructed through a community of learners as they work through their situation together, that the ultimate purpose of the education is to develop adults who will participate in the democratic community as it works to address its problems, and that learning must arise from the student's engagement in his or her world. If through that reasoning a particular problem arises, say students do not have sufficient knowledge of educational philosophy to even begin to engage each other, then perhaps an introductory lecture or expository reading is appropriate as a way to help them begin to engage the world of education as a communal problem. In other words, philosophy does not provide us with ready-made answers to our questions but only provides us a way to reason through our problems. If he or she focuses on the reasoning process, seeks consistency and coherency, and develops arguments with strong premises, the educator may find a particular method or technique typically associated with a different philosophy might make for the best tactic for the given problem.

This chapter has presented three different approaches to philosophical reasoning about education. Perennialism, essentialism, and progressivism are well-known approaches to schooling. While there is little doubt that the vast majority of educators are primarily guided by essentialism, there are also schools (and teachers within otherwise essentialist schools) that use either perennialism or progressivism as the central philosophical foundation for their curriculum and pedagogy. The next two chapters explore two more examples of philosophical reasoning about education that share one important characteristic: they both begin their reasoning with the philosophical question of ethics.

CHAPTER SEVEN

Relations-Based Ethics

An Ethic of Care and Relational Pedagogy

The three educational philosophies discussed in Chapter 6 begin their philosophical reasoning by asking either an ontological or epistemological question and then develop a consistent and coherent argument for their particular educational philosophy. Some educators prefer to begin their educational reasoning with a question of ethics. Perhaps frustrated with educational policies and practices that seem to privilege efficacy over ethics (see Chapter 5), these educators argue that, above all else, education must be ethical. Yes, we wish our schools to be effective, but only if they are also moral. These educators argue that we must start our philosophical reasoning with a firm understanding of a public ethics that will lead to a moral public system of schooling.

In Chapter 5, I suggested that Americans' ability to discuss ethics in public space has been challenged by the belief by many that morality is a private matter. If they are correct and morality is a private matter, then there is no basis for considering ethics in public space other than to assert one group's private beliefs onto every other person. But such imposition of private interests onto everyone in public space is antidemocratic. What we need is a way to be able to engage each other regarding our shared public spaces in a manner that both respects everyone's private values but that also permits a public process for determining what is or is not ethical in public spaces. Luckily, we have 2,500 years of philosophical texts that provide us with ways to think about ethics regardless of our personal private morality. One of those approaches, an ethic of social justice, will be taken up in the next chapter. The rest of this chapter explores a second approach, relational ethics, specifically an ethic of care and relational pedagogy.

Relational Ethics

The self is a knot in a web of multiple intersecting relations;
pull relations out of the web, and find no self.
We do not have relations; relations have us.[1]

---

1. Gert Biesta et al., "Manifesto of Relational Pedagogy: Meeting to Learn, Learning to Meet," in *No Education without Relation,* ed. Charles Bingham and Alexander Sidorkin (New York: Peter Lang, 2004), 7.

The choice to build our ethics either on care or on social justice mirrors a long-standing debate in Western philosophy. An ethic of social justice is a contemporary version of the long-standing interest in ethics that center on moral principles, whereas an ethic of care is a contemporary version of those ethics that take relationships as the fundamental moral commitment. An ethic of care is a relational ethic asserting that our fundamental ethical obligations accrue to those people with whom we live. Aristotle considered *philia* (i.e., "brotherly love," the love we have for particular people) an important basis for considering ethical action. Christianity also uses the idea of *philia* but more frequently invokes *agape* (i.e., the love of God and, through God, for all people). The Jewish philosopher Martin Buber advanced a relational ethics around what he called "the dialogic principle" (i.e., the primary human relations can be described as either an I-Thou relationship or an I-It relationship).[2] The use of human relations as the foundation for ethics has been an important part of ethical thought throughout the history of philosophy. Regardless of our religious or our agnostic commitments, we can commit ourselves to an ethic based on relationships (i.e., *philia, agape,* or some other relational concept).

Not surprisingly, the 2,500-year conversation that is moral philosophy has come primarily from the experience of men. Consequently, these voices have tended to speak with a masculine perspective on the world that is revealed in its main focus on ethics of principle and virtue and only a secondary interest in relational ethics. In our contemporary moment, feminist scholars have joined the conversation and, while there is no singular "feminist ethic," one important feminist critique questions the ways that traditional Western ethics in education have centered around concepts of justice, duty, and virtue, while minimizing the moral centrality of human relationships.

Many feminist philosophers have critiqued moral philosophy for the scant attention it has paid to the "reproductive" work that is a part of many women's lives and is so important to the well-being of human beings (e.g., the caregiving of children and elders and in general the maintenance of relational networks). Those arguing for relational ethics tell us that instead of thinking of ourselves as lone individuals, we should instead understand our selves as constructed within webs of relationships because that is, in fact, the reality of most human experience. That is what is meant in the quote above: it is almost as if instead of our "having relationships," our relationships "have us" and fundamentally shape who we are.

Within these relationships, the ethic of care can serve as a guiding ideal. According to care theorists in philosophy, care is a basic foundation of human life. Philosophizing about our moral lives, as human beings, should therefore begin in the experiences of our most fundamental relationships.

An Ethic of Care

Although ethics of human relationships have existed since the beginning of moral philosophy, no one has popularized the relational ethic more than the contemporary philosopher of education Nel Noddings. Noddings was a math teacher in New Jersey for over two decades

---

2. Martin Buber, *I and Thou*, trans. Walter Arnold Kaufmann (New York: Scribner, 1970).

before studying philosophy of education in graduate school. Since becoming a professor of educational philosophy at Stanford University, she has published many books and essays on caring, educational reform, and many other topics. Her book *Caring: A Feminine Approach to Ethics and Moral Education* is the first and most noted explanation of her relational ethic.[3]

"Natural" Caring

Philosophical analysis often proceeds in its quest to clarify a concept by locating a model case. I provided an example of this technique in Chapter 3 when I presented the case of Mr. Sommers, a sixth-grade teacher, who presented his class with a lesson on the differences among *there, their,* and *they're.* In that case, I provided the model to help identify some of the necessary conditions for an event to be called teaching. Using the same technique, Noddings searched for a model case of caring to use as the starting point to help clarify what the essential elements of caring might be. She chose the mother-son relationship as that model case. In Noddings's argument, the mother-son relationship exhibits "natural caring." Of course, Noddings knows that not all mothers have caring relationships with their sons, but if we take as a model case a mother-son relationship that works naturally as we expect it to, we should find that it would possess all of the essential elements of caring. If there is something that we think is required for caring, but it is not a part of this ideal "natural" mother-son relationship, then it would not be an essential characteristic of caring.

In examining her model of "natural caring," Noddings is able to strip our idea of caring down to a few basic ideas. First, for Noddings, caring is a description of a relationship rather than a description of any individual's personal feelings or attitude toward another. For those who are new to an ethic of care, this foundational idea is essential to grasp because it rejects what most people understand caring to be. Most people think of caring as a characteristic of an individual toward others. Most people think that when "I care for someone," the caring may be *toward* him/her but it is *in* me. It is *my* "caring." I might care or I might not care, but either way it is the "I" that is key.

Noddings rejects this idea. Keep in mind the quotation that started this section. To think of care as existing in an individual alone posits that individual's self as outside of relationships. But as the above quotation tells us, "pull relations out of the web, and find no self."[4] So, to understand an ethic of care, we must think of caring as something else. Therefore, for Noddings, *caring* describes a kind of relationship between persons. It is not found in the individuals but in their relationship. To understand the essential elements of caring requires us to come up with good descriptions of what a caring *relationship* looks like regardless of the psychological attitudes of the participants. Of course, certain attitudes might lead people in a relationship to create a caring or uncaring relationship, but it is the action that occurs in the relationship that marks it as caring or not, not the attitudes.

A second essential element of caring is that the caring relationship must be between concrete people. They have to be corporeal beings, not abstractions. There has to be real

---

3. Nel Noddings, *Caring: A Feminine Approach to Ethics and Moral Education* (Berkeley: University of California Press, 1984).

4. Biesta et al., "Manifesto of Relational Pedagogy," 7.

contact between the people and not just their notions or thoughts. In our model case of natural caring, there is a real mother and a real son. A mother cannot have a caring relationship with a make-believe son. Nor can she adopt all the hungry children of the world and develop a caring relationship with all of them. While metaphorically adopting the hungry children of the world and working to provide them food is a good thing to do, according to Noddings, it is not an example of "moral caring" because moral caring requires concrete people in a concrete relationship.

So, once we have a concrete caring relationship between a mother and her son, what can we say about the essential aspects of caring? From her model, Noddings describes the caring relationship as "a connection or encounter between two human beings—a carer (or one-caring) and a recipient of care (or cared-for)."[5] In order for a relation to be a caring one, three conditions must exist.

- First, the one-caring must present *engrossment,* which is the act of being engrossed in the cared-for and attempting to experience the world as the cared-for experiences it. It requires the one-caring to be totally present to the other during the caring moment.
- Second, the one-caring must exhibit *displacement of motivation,* which substitutes the needs of the one-cared-for for her own needs. As Noddings wrote, the one-caring's "mode of response is characterized by engrossment (nonselective attention or total presence to him, the other, for the duration of the caring interval) and displacement of motivation (her motive energy flows in the direction of the other's needs and projects)."[6]
- The third essential element of a caring relationship applies to the one-cared-for. In a caring relationship, the cared-for must *recognize* and *receive* the caring in a way that signals to the one-caring that his or her efforts are understood and acknowledged in some way.

Notice that in a caring relationship modeled on the natural caring relationship of a mother and her son, the one-caring and the one-cared-for each have responsibilities to the relationship. A relationship in which a one-caring provides engrossment and motivational displacement but the one-cared-for fails to recognize and receive the one-caring's offer does not fulfill the requirements of a caring relationship. The one-caring might "care" psychologically, but the *relationship* is not a caring one.

Also notice that we need only one of the participants to be the one-caring and one person to be the one-cared-for. There is no requirement that roles reverse. We do not expect the six-month-old infant son to act as a one-caring for his mother; it is still a caring relationship if the son recognizes, receives, and acknowledges his mother's offer of care. The same is true of adults. Given the model case, adults can have a caring relationship with another individual where only one of them is the one-caring and the other is the one-cared-for. A possible example of this might be the nurse in a hospice where a caring relationship could

5. Nel Noddings, *The Challenge to Care in Schools: An Alternative Approach to Education* (New York: Teachers College Press, 1992), 15.

6. Nel Noddings, "An Ethic of Care and Its Implications for Instructional Arrangements," in *The Education Feminism Reader,* ed. Lynda Stone (New York: Routledge, 1994), 174.

develop when the nurse provides engrossment and motivational displacement to her dying charge and the one-cared-for recognizes, receives, and acknowledges that offer. On the other hand, there is also nothing incompatible with adults switching roles so that each adult in a caring relationship might sometimes act as the one-caring and at other times act as the one-cared-for. We would hope that this would be the experience of those in a romantic relationship—at times one would act as the one-caring and the other the one-cared-for, and at other times they would reverse roles.

So, for Noddings, moral caring describes a particular kind of relationship between concrete people in which there is a one-caring who exhibits engrossment and motivational displacement and a one-cared-for who presents recognition and reception. If any of those elements are missing, the relationship is not one of moral caring. Figure 7.1 provides a visual representation of a caring relationship.

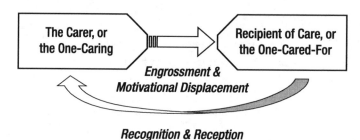

Figure 7.1 Relations between the One-Caring and the One-Cared-For in a Caring Relationship

Ethical Caring

Natural caring occurs without thought. Sometimes we just develop a caring relationship with another person, but at other times we do not. Certainly this is true of some mothers with their sons. Even though these mothers know that they are supposed to have caring relationships with their sons, such a relationship just does not arise naturally. Or the hospice nurse fails to develop a caring relationship with her charge. In these cases, in order to act ethically, we must act in such a way to create all the elements of a natural caring relationship, not because we feel like it, but because our cognitive abilities tell us that "we must." In these cases, our reason substitutes for our "natural" inclination.

Sometimes teachers are able to naturally develop a caring relationship with many of their students. But just as often, teachers just don't "feel" like acting toward some of their students in a manner required to create a caring relationship. Perhaps they become more focused on maintaining discipline over an unruly class, perhaps they have to make sure students stay on task in order to score high on their high-stakes tests, or perhaps there are just some students they do not like very much. Because there is not necessarily any "natural" caring relation between teacher and student, teachers can substitute the ethical caring ideal as a guide toward how they are morally obligated to act toward those students "in their care." Even though the "natural" condition of the classroom does not lend itself to the construction of caring relationships, teachers still know cognitively how they should act in order to create an ethical classroom.

Again, I must stress that the ethic of care describes a *relationship*, not individual attitudes. "Care" is the ideal relationship that serves as a model for teacher-student interaction, and that, argues Noddings, should be the root of all schooling experiences for children and youth. Relational ethics and relational pedagogy are based in the centrality of the human relation to the experience of teaching and learning; in what happens between two people, in this case teacher and student; and how their interactions reinforce mutual support, understanding, and growth.

The ideal of the caring relation can serve as an ethical framework for evaluating our actions as educators, but it is not a formula or a strict rule-based system. It is a moral orientation for making ethical decisions as a teacher. Moreover, Noddings is not saying that only women can be in caring relations with their students, nor is she saying that all caring relations will look exactly the same. While caring is an ideal that has characterized the historic domains and work of women—home and family nurturance—caring is the work of all people of all genders. What constitutes a caring relation will also vary by cultural context. Though Noddings insists that all human beings the world over experience the desire to be cared for, the ways that the caring relationship might be actually experienced will differ according to cultural norms, traditions, and values. While receptive attention will be characteristic of all caring encounters, how that might be performed in different cultural contexts will vary.

Relational Pedagogy

Nearly everyone agrees that American public schools are in crisis, but what they understand the nature of that crisis to be depends on several factors, including where they are positioned in relation to these schools. For example, those who are outside the public schools tend to

> state that there are serious problems of student underachievement, that there are many children whose home environments make learning difficult, that a significant number of teachers are not adequately trained to perform effectively in today's conditions, and that these problems and others are exacerbated by the changes that have been, and still are, taking place in the general society outside our schools.[7]

But those inside the schools seem to argue that such problems are the consequences of other, deeper problems in our schools, problems that largely result from students, teachers, and administrators finding themselves in situations that are not conducive to building good human relationships. As one high school student stated about school, "This place hurts my spirit."[8] A study by the Graduate School of Claremont, where researchers spent a year documenting how those inside public schools defined the problems of their schools, concluded that

> Currently, the education system in the U.S. is one in which deeply committed people inside schools feel incapable of acting on their own values. The result is that participants inside schools, from students to administrators, feel unable to meet responsibilities, expectations and goals for themselves and for others.[9]

---

7. Mary Poplin and Joseph Weeres, *Voices from the Inside: A Report on Schooling from Inside the Classroom* (Claremont, CA: The Institute for Education in Transformation at the Claremont Graduate School, 1992), 6, www.cgu.edu/PDFFiles/poplin/Voices-BW.pdf.

8. Ibid., 11.

9. Ibid., 12.

They concluded that the well-known problems of schools discussed in the media and focused on by policy-makers *follow from* the more central problem that schools are not set up to nurture good human relations. In fact, many of the most popular reforms of the present system actually exacerbate the problem.

Another factor that influences how people define the crisis of schools depends on where they locate the problems. For example, many critics of the schools believe the problem lies in poor teaching. These critics seem to believe that if we could just fire bad teachers and hire good ones, the problems of the schools would disappear. Others think that the problems lie in the students who are undisciplined, have poor attitudes and lousy home lives, and who need to be made to behave and do their work, or they should be removed from the classrooms and forced to repeat grades until they learn. But critics who make either charge clearly locate education in either the teacher (the one who teaches) or the student (the one who learns). Relational pedagogy argues that education cannot be thought of as existing either in the teachers or in the students because teaching always involves relationships; therefore, we must focus on the relations between teachers and students.[10] In other words, if we understand education correctly, any crisis that exists must emanate from inadequate relations between the teachers and the students, not from one or the other.

Relational pedagogy is a philosophy of education that begins with the claim that education occurs in human relationships. As the "Manifesto of Relational Pedagogy: Meeting to Learn, Learning to Meet" begins:

> A fog of forgetfulness is looming over education. Forgotten in the fog is that education is about human beings. And as schools are places where human beings get together, we have also forgotten that education is primarily about human beings who are in relation to one another.[11]

The manifesto clarifies this point:

> Why do schools remain? They remain because education is not mainly about the facts that students stuff into their heads. They remain because education is not mainly about developing skills. It is not about gaining knowledge. Schools remain because education is primarily about human beings who need to meet together, as a group of people, if learning is to take place.... But the fog over education has kept us from realizing that learning is primarily about human beings who meet. Meeting and learning are inseparable.[12]

This recognition that education is centrally concerned with human relations suggests the need to rethink the priorities of our schools. We must move away from thinking of schooling as primarily something that occurs in individuals (either individual teachers or individual students) and begin to focus on how to create successful relations among all members of

---

10. Gert Biesta, "'Mind the Gap!' Communication and the Educational Relation," in *No Education without Relation,* ed. Charles Bingham and Alexander M. Sidorkin (New York: Peter Lang, 2004), 12.

11. Biesta et al., "Manifesto of Relational Pedagogy," 5.

12. Ibid.

schools. Instead of focusing on test scores, course objectives, disciplining students, teachers and administrators, and the construction of attractive market-based solutions that turn education into a consumer good, we must learn to create schools where good learning relations are constructed.

And there may be no better way to think about good learning relations than to think about them as caring relations. By figuring out how to create every school as a place conducive to the construction of caring relations among teachers and students, students and students, and administrators and teachers, we create not only an ethical school, but an effective one as well. Such a school will recognize that knowledge is not something transferred from teachers to students, but that knowledge is something that is constructed in relations among students and other students and their teachers, and such learning relations are made fertile whenever those relations are caring ones.[13] Such a school will recognize that excellence is not found in objective measures such as test scores, but in positive caring relations among all members. Such a school will recognize that a focus on efficacy over ethics is futile, for schools without ethical caring will never be effective. As Bingham and Sidorkin explain, "Even the most narrowly construed 'back to basics' purposes of public schooling may become unachievable if schools lose the ability to foster human relationships that allow them to function."[14]

So, relational pedagogy requires that we focus first on creating the conditions necessary for good educational relations. But what kinds of conditions might lend themselves to good relations? We can return to Nel Noddings and her ethic of care for some guidance. Here are some of the things that Noddings suggests are necessary (though not necessarily sufficient) to create caring schools.

Schools must be small. Although small classes are also nice, the size of the school is actually more important. How small is small? Different scholars offer different suggestions, but I like Deborah Meier's rule of thumb: small enough for all the teachers to sit around a table and have a discussion about their school, its curriculum, its pedagogy, and its students.[15]

Pedagogy must be dialogical. While there are times when teachers might choose to lecture, the primary method of instruction must be conversational. If knowledge is constructed when students and teachers engage each other, then the failure of students to engage leaves them with a surfeit of the time and effort required to actually master knowledge. When students merely receive information, they may try to engage it, but without being able to vocalize their constructions, to play them off of other students, to voice and make public their understandings, the knowledge that they actually retain is likely to be incomplete and poorly understood. More important, when teaching is only one-way, it is difficult for the teacher to practice engrossment and motivational displacement.

The curriculum must provide opportunities for students to practice caring. While Noddings is clear that the seed of caring is sown when infants and young children experience caring relations as a one-cared-for, it should be obvious that learning how to be a one-caring strengthens our understanding of, our skills in practicing, and our dispositions to practice

---

13. Barbara J. Thayer-Bacon, "Personal and Social Relations in Education," in *No Education without Relation,* ed. Charles Bingham and Alexander Sidorkin (New York: Peter Lang, 2004).

14. Charles Bingham and Alexander Sidorkin, "The Pedagogy of Relation: An Introduction," in *No Education without Relation,* ed. Charles Bingham and Alexander Sidorkin (New York: Peter Lang, 2004), 3.

15. Deborah Meier, *The Power of Their Ideas: Lessons for America from a Small School in Harlem* (Boston: Beacon Press, 2002).

caring relations. Students of all ages should have places built into their curriculum that allow them, encourage them, and even require them to practice being a one-caring.

The evaluation of students (and of teachers) must be honest, personal, and confirmatory. Noddings is clear that overstating the quality of a student's work is not congruent with caring. Everyone deserves an honest judgment of the quality of his or her work. How can any student improve if uninformed about what is wrong with her or his work? Furthermore, the evaluation must be about the individual, concrete student's work, not about some mythical, abstracted norm. Albert deserves an evaluation that presents him with where he as an individual is strong and where he is weak. Finally, while evaluations must be honest, they must also be confirmatory. Just because a student has failed to learn material or has insufficient understanding to perform well on measures of learning does not mean that in revealing their shortcomings, the student needs to feel condemned. Rather, the student's lacks can be used as guidelines to lead that student forward in order for him or her to recognize real growth and learning.

According to Noddings, schools, at the very least, must be small and dialogical; have space for students to practice caring; and provide honest, personal, and confirmatory evaluation. Unfortunately, there are very few schools today that exhibit any of these conditions, let alone all of them. As the Claremont Study has shown, most participants in schools find them deadening, spiritless places and long for an environment that makes learning something meaningful to them. As one middle school student mentioned about the one teacher in her school that she appreciated, "I also like the way she talks to me like I am a human."[16]

Conclusion

One way to create ethical public spaces that does not require the imposition of some group's private ethics onto everyone else is to engage in public deliberation over the question of whether or not the public space meets the basic tests of relations-based ethics. Does the space provide for nurturance and health of the individuals and the communities in relationship with each other? In education, since good human relations are a prerequisite for learning, the primary question can be more specifically stated as, do the school and the classroom provide the space necessary for caring relationships to develop? We are in a position to argue that, at the very least, the conditions for caring schools must be put in place so that teachers and students have the potential to construct concrete, caring relationships. No one need give up their personal, private ethics to agree that the failure to provide safe and nurturing spaces to the youth of the nation is unethical: to demand that any policy, any reform movement, that undercuts this fundamental moral requisite cannot be permitted in a democratic society.

---

16. Poplin and Weeres, *Voices from the Inside*, 19.

CHAPTER EIGHT

Ethics of Social Justice

Social Reconstructionism and Critical Pedagogy

Ethics of Social Justice

Chapter 7 presented one approach to a public ethic (i.e., an ethic of care) that could be useful for considering public schooling. This chapter will present a second such ethic: an ethic of social justice. The task is to develop a well-reasoned ethic that permits people to address the ethical issues of public schools regardless of their own personal moral or religious commitments. We want to be able to engage in democratic debate without requiring the strongly religious to pretend they are atheists or the nonbelievers to pretend they believe. We want people to be able to keep their own personal moral beliefs but be able to engage those with different personal values to build a thriving democratic space for all children. We do not want to throw our hands up and say, "Ethics is merely an individual matter, and so I won't tell you what to do, and you won't tell me what to do." Nor do we want to reduce our questions to merely the efficacious; we also want to be able to ask questions of a moral kind. While an ethic of care provides one such possible ethic, many educators argue that an ethic of social justice provides a stronger argument and a more powerful guiding hand to the development of ethical schools and ethical pedagogy.

An ethic of social justice is a principle-based ethic that understands ethical action as that which is guided by a commitment to reasoned principles (or rights and responsibilities, obligations, duties, or codes). Any professional code of ethics is an example of a principle-based ethics. The National Education Association (NEA), the largest professional organization for educators in the United States, has a code of ethics for teachers with two major principles (Commitment to the Student and Commitment to the Profession), each having eight subprinciples.[1]

Ethical Reasoning

Principle-based ethics generally provide basic principles or codes that serve as warrants in normative arguments. So, as a general form, a principle-based normative argument will take

---

1. "NEA Code of Ethics," National Education Association, 1975, www.nea.org/home/30442.htm.

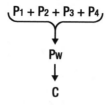

Figure 8.1 A Symbolic Representation of an Argument with a Warrant, Where P₁–P₄ Are Premises, C Is the Claim, and Pw Is the Warrant

the form shown in Figure 8.1, where *P* represents a premise, *C* represents the claim, and *Pw* represents a warrant. When a normative argument is made in the name of justice, the warrant will present an obligation to some form of justice, such as the principle often referred to as "just desserts"—people should get what they deserve. When the argument is made in the name of *social* justice, the warrant will be a principle of social justice.

We often represent the particulars of general justice to include such things as liberty, freedom, equality, equity, and fairness. But the concept of social justice privileges our obligations to those forms of justice that focus on the social and public interest, such as equality, equity, and fairness, rather than individual and private interests, such as individual liberty. It is not that those committed to social justice are against individual and private forms of justice. They *are* committed to individual liberty, but they understand that individual liberty requires social justice. Without social justice, liberty exists only for the privileged.

To explain why this might be so, I need to clarify the distinction between positive and negative forms of freedom. Most political philosophers recognize two forms of freedom (or liberty[2]). *Negative freedom* refers to the absence of constraint. Negative freedom is the situation in which there is no one, or nothing, telling an individual that they cannot do something or that they must do something. Individuals are "free" to do as they please to the extent that they have the individual capacity to do it. This is often referred to as "freedom from" because it protects us from others (especially the government) telling us what to do. For example, in the United States, parents may send their children to any school they wish to. The government does not tell parents that they have to send their children to a specific school. In fact, today, most states permit parents to keep their children at home and educate them themselves (i.e., home school). Negative freedom is probably what most Americans think of as liberty, and I will tend to use the term *liberty* in this manner when referring to negative freedom.

Positive freedom refers to people's ability to actually act as they wish. Just because the government does not require parents to send their children to a specific school does not mean that parents have the (positive) freedom to actually send them to any school they wish. They may not be able to afford to buy or rent in the districts with the best schools or be able to afford the tuition of a good private school or be able to educate their children themselves, therefore, in fact, most parents are required to send their children to the local

---

2. The two terms "liberty" and "freedom" can be used interchangeably. For most philosophers, their only difference lies in their different roots. "Liberty" comes from Latin, whereas "freedom" comes from German. However, I will tend to use the word "liberty" to be synonymous with "individual freedom" or "negative freedom."

school, regardless of whether or not they want to. Those committed to social justice argue that in order for everyone to have the maximum amount of freedom, we must commit to positive freedom as a moral good. We must privilege ideals of social justice such as equity, fairness, and equality. In other words, every child should have the right to attend a quality school regardless of where his or her parents can afford to live. To create a system of public education that allows the privileged to send their children to quality schools while requiring the poor to send their children to schools of low quality is simply not fair. Failure to privilege positive freedom results in only the few wealthy and powerful having real freedom. The rest of us must sacrifice our positive freedoms so that the powerful can take advantage of their negative freedom.

Social Reconstructionism

One of the clearest philosophies of education that is built upon a commitment to social justice developed in the 1930s in order to address the twin threats of a collapsed global economy and a troubling worldwide rise of dictatorships. During these troubled times, social reconstructionists asked whether it was possible for schools to transform a sinking nation of inequality into a vibrant democratic one. Though surely no philosopher would ever believe that schools could solve the problems of the world by themselves, social reconstructionists argued that anyone who hoped for a better future must realize that that future lay in the hands of the present-day students. Social reconstructionists have argued that rather than schools working to create a new and more democratic future, they actually work to reproduce the status quo of inequity, unfairness, and inequality. If present schools educate children to replicate today's world with all its injustice, why would we expect the future to be different? Surely, they argue, schools must be harnessed to prepare a new generation for a new world where democracy can thrive. George Counts, a professor at Teachers College, Columbia University, famously asked, "Dare the schools build a new social order?"[3] While social reconstructionists have developed into many different strands of educational thought, today this philosophy is best represented by a school philosophy referred to as critical pedagogy.

Critical Pedagogy

What if the social reconstructionists are right? What if our schools do not work to implement the values that our nation proclaims it stands for? What if, instead, the schools work against those values? What if the social reconstructionists are right, and our system of schooling actually works to reproduce unfair inequalities in our nation rather than to transform our nation so it can live up to its proclaimed values? What if, despite the best intentions of school administrators and teachers to help all the children overcome inequalities and achieve to the best of their abilities, educators' work actually increases the inequalities among students? In other words, what if our system of schooling is not ethical? And what if this unethical

---

3. George S. Counts, *Dare the School Build a New Social Order?* The John Day Pamphlets, No. 11 (New York: Day, 1932).

system is run by morally conscious, well-intended, hardworking, and caring teachers who fail to realize that their work is unjust? Would you want them to continue doing what they were told they should do? Would you want them to continue teaching the same curriculum, using the same teaching methods, and utilizing the same disciplinary techniques? Or would you want them to work to change things?

Critical pedagogy is an educational philosophy that chooses to work for change. It seeks to transform what it understands to be an unjust system of schooling in order to do its part in helping the nation live up to its proclaimed commitment to social justice. A contemporary example of social reconstructionism, *critical pedagogy* calls for curriculum and teaching to transform, rather than to reproduce, the status quo.

A Look at the Reality

Of course, to accept the idea that there is something wrong with schools reproducing the status quo requires you to think that there is something wrong with the nation as it is. I mean, if you think that things are fair and equitable as they are, then why transform it? And the truth is that most Americans seem to feel that they live in a fair and equitable society. A 2003 Gallup poll found that more than half of Americans aged eighteen to twenty-nine expected to "strike it rich" sometime in their life.[4] Even if we take the absurdly low criterion that many of them used to decide what it meant to be rich (only a worth of $120,000, which by any careful analysis does not equate to "rich"), only about a third of them will actually achieve that status. And, if we take a more realistic figure, say an income more than $320,000, only about 5 percent will ever reach that figure.[5] Surely there are going to be a lot of young Americans disappointed in their earnings when they get older. Unfortunately for most Americans, thinking that you are going to strike it rich is just wishful thinking.

And the belief that social class doesn't matter in America is also wishful thinking. For example, though we are told often enough that the United States has the "best health care in the world,"[6] statistics suggest otherwise. According to the World Health Organization (WHO), the United States ranks thirty-seventh, just behind Costa Rica and Dominica and just ahead of Slovenia and Cuba. And while there are those who suggest this WHO study is inaccurate, even the critics of the WHO ranking place the United States no higher than fifteenth.[7] Also according to the World Health Organization, the United States achieves this dismal ranking with the second highest cost. It spends more than 15 percent of its GNP on health care. France, which scored first in health care, spends only 9.6 percent of its GNP

---

4. David W. Moore, "Half of Young People Expect to Strike It Rich, but Expectations Fall Rapidly with Age," *Gallup Poll News Service*, March 11, 2003, www.gallup.com/poll/7981/Half-Young-People-Expect-Strike-Rich.aspx.

5. Thomas A. DiPrete, "Is This a Great Country? Upward Mobility and the Chance for Riches in Contemporary America," *Research in Social Stratification and Mobility* 25 (2007): 89–95.

6. For example, see minute 138, John Boehner, "Boehner on MSNBC: The American People Want No Part of Dems Govt Takeover of Health Care," MSNBC, March 12, 2010, www.youtube.com/watch?v=aYs3YRpspFY.

7. Carl Bialik, "Ill-Conceived Ranking Makes for Unhealthy Debate," *Wall Street Journal*, October 21, 2009, http://online.wsj.com/article/SB125608054324397621.html.

on health care. Furthermore, in France, 99 percent of its population receives full health care benefits while, in 2009, the United States had almost as many people without health insurance as France had population.[8]

In most developed nations, all children, even if only foreign tourists, receive free health care. In 2011, the United States had 7.6 million children without health insurance.[9] According to a study by researchers at Johns Hopkins Children's Center, between 1988 and 2005, nearly 17,000 children died in American hospitals because they lacked health insurance.[10] Critical pedagogues argue that whatever we think about the recent health care law, there is no way we can honestly argue that the United States has an equitable health care system.

One group of people who does get public health care in the United States is the incarcerated, and given that more than 3 percent of the American population is serving or has served time in prison, critical pedagogues suggest this makes for a pretty expensive way to deliver health care. Critical pedagogues might ask if you have ever wondered why the United States incarcerates more of its citizens than any other nation? The United States has 751 prisoners behind bars for every 100,000 people. That is even higher than Russia (which has 627/100,000) and far more than nations such as England (151/100,000) and Germany (88/100,000). In fact, according to Adam Liptak, "The United States has less than 5 percent of the world's population. But it has almost a quarter of the world's prisoners."[11] Critical pedagogues ask us how a nation can proclaim its commitment to social justice and yet create the conditions that lead to such a high proportion of its population being denied the most basic freedom of all?

Another area that contributes to injustice, according to critical pedagogues, is the high cost of America's military spending, which diverts taxpayer money from needed areas of equity such as schools, health care, and housing. Of all the nations of the world, the United States invests its wealth in military defense far more than any other nation. In fact, in 2012, the United States spent 39 percent of the world's military budget. Compare that with second-place China, which spends 9.5 percent of that budget.[12] According to the Federal Budget Office (FBO), 20 percent of the federal budget is spent on defense. But this figure may be misleading. Critical pedagogues point out that the FBO counting does not include costs such as the Iraq and Afghanistan wars (which were funded "off-budget"). It also does not

8. "In 2011, 48 million nonelderly Americans were uninsured, a decrease of over 1.3 million uninsured people since 2010. This change resulted from stability in private coverage and the availability of Medicaid to buffer loss of health insurance for the low-income population. While the first decrease in the number of uninsured since 2007 is promising, the number of uninsured has grown by more than 4.5 million people since the recession began in 2007." *The Uninsured: A Primer: Key Facts about Americans without Health Insurance* (Kaiser Commission on Medicaid and the Uninsured: October 2012), www.kff.org/uninsured/7451.cfm. The population of France in July 2011 was 62,814,233. Central Intelligence Agency (July 2010), www.cia.gov /library/publications/the-world-factbook/geos/sp.html.

9. *The Uninsured.*

10. Fizan Abdullah et al., "Analysis of 23 Million US Hospitalizations: Uninsured Children Have Higher All-Cause In-Hospital Mortality," *Journal of Public Health* 32, no. 2 (October 2009): 32, http://jpubhealth .oxfordjournals.org/content/32/2/236.full.pdf+html?sid=e9bb8588-ffc4-47db-bc3e-928ffddb865f.

11. Adam Liptak, "U.S. Prison Population Dwarfs That of Other Nations," *New York Times,* April 23, 2008, www.nytimes.com/2008/04/23/world/americas/23iht-23prison.12253738.html.

12. Anup Shah, "World Military Spending," July 7, 2010, www.globalissues.org/article/75 /world-military-spending.

include such things as health care, retirement, and other benefits for veterans (they are put in the budgets of the Department of Health, Education, and Welfare and the Department of Veterans Affairs). When you count these into the budget, in 2009, the United States spent more than 50 percent of its budget on defense, making the share of the world's military budget even larger than stated above.[13]

Of course, most Americans believe that such defense spending is necessary for our safety. But critical pedagogues ask if our military is actually used for defense? Many would suggest that Iraq in particular is an example of a war fought for reasons other than America's defense, and while the initial invasion of Afghanistan can arguably be counted as acting in the nation's defense, critical pedagogues argue that our presence in Afghanistan for longer than a decade moved our initial defense strategy to something other than in defense of the nation. But critical pedagogues might tell us to set these two wars aside for the moment and ask about other examples of our use of the military. For example, they ask us if we realize how many foreign military interventions the United States military has participated in since the 1890s? The answer is at least 127.[14] Were all of these interventions for our defense? Or do these interventions serve a different purpose than to defend our nation's borders?

But many will suggest that even with all of these points, America is still the most economically fair and equal nation in history. However, critical pedagogues point out that the data show otherwise. First, let us take a look at the distribution of wealth in the United States. According to Arthur Kinnickell (2009), the gap between the wealthiest and poorest in the United States grew significantly from 1984 to 2008.[15]

When you look at the data, critical pedagogues argue, one cannot reasonably argue that the United States lives up to its commitment to equity and equality. So, if we are going to hold on to the idea that the status quo in America is just fine despite these inequalities, we must believe that these inequalities are either deserved or unavoidable. In other words, to defend the inequalities as fair, we have to believe that such inequalities are "natural" and that the disadvantaged deserve their disadvantage. We have to believe that everyone has been given an equal opportunity, and if they don't succeed, it must be indicative of some individual flaw. Perhaps the poor are just not very smart, or they are just lazy, or they have poor values. After all, there is plenty of research to support such beliefs, isn't there? The children of the poor and of those assigned to racial or ethnic minority groups consistently score lower on tests than the children of the white middle class.[16] And it passes as common knowledge that poor and racial minority children are more likely to come from families that don't value education. Such statistics and assumed commonsense lead some to ask, "Doesn't that show that they are not as smart as the white middle-class kids? And doesn't that show

13. "Where Your Income Tax Money Really Goes," War Resisters League, www.warresisters.org/pages /piechart.htm.

14. Zoltan Grossman, "From Wounded Knee to Libya: A Century of U.S. Military Interventions," http:// academic.evergreen.edu/g/grossmaz/interventions.html.

15. Arthur B. Kinnickell, "Ponds and Streams: Wealth and Income in the U.S., 1989 to 2007," in *Finance and Economics Discussion Series* (Washington, DC: Federal Reserve Board, 2009–2013), www.federalreserve .gov/pubs/feds/2009/200913/200913abs.html.

16. Jennifer L. Hochschild, "Social Class in Public Schools," *Journal of Social Issues* 59, no. 4 (2003): 821–840; William T. Dickens and James R. Flynn, "Black Americans Reduce the Racial IQ Gap: Evidence from Standardization Samples," *Psychological Science* 17, no. 10 (2006): 913–920.

that they just don't work as hard as the European-American kids?" The simple answer to these questions is, "No, the data do not indicate such conclusions and what passes as commonsense in this case is simply wrong."

Critical pedagogues ask us to look critically at the data. Research that tries to get at what creates these disparities often contradicts the commonsense explanation for these findings. For example, Claude Steele's research suggests that much of the testing gap is not the result of a difference in intelligence but instead is caused by test anxiety created by psychological interference created by the social expectations that they will do poorly on such tests.[17] The Pew Research Center found that blacks and Latinos actually value a college education more than whites.[18] And research by Ronald Ferguson suggests that African American students spend just as much time on homework as their European American counterparts but that their poorer school skills prevent them from finishing their work at the same rate as their white counterparts, which counters the false belief that African American students just don't work hard in school.[19]

In other words, the data do not support the belief that the performance of the children of the poor and of non-white minorities is due to their individual personal characteristics, but instead the data show that it results from social constraints built into the social system.

Hegemony

So, how do critical pedagogues explain the fact that Americans tend to believe that we live in the most fair, most equal, and most just nation on Earth? Why is it that Americans are more likely than citizens of other nations to agree (71 percent versus 40 percent) with the statement "that the poor could escape poverty if they worked hard enough?"[20] Critical pedagogues do so by arguing that the institutions of society work to create narratives that work in the interest of the privileged and against the interests of the less privileged. This process is called *hegemony,* which is the process in which the institutions such as the legal system, the media, the churches, the health care system, the economic system, and the schools are harnessed by the powerful to work in their own interests rather than in the public's interest. Hegemony is not unique to the United States, but, according to the critical pedagogues, since the 1980s, a well-organized and well-funded coalition of forces, through a careful harnessing of the nation's institutions, has steadily worked to erode the advances made by workers following the Depression years of the 1930s. This has been a complex and elaborate process that relies less on secret conspiracies than it does on the open advantages that the American system has provided for people to work in their own interest.

---

17. Claude Steele, "Thin Ice: Stereotype Threat and Black College Students," *The Atlantic Magazine,* August 1999, www.theatlantic.com/magazine/archive/1999/08/thin-ice-stereotype-threat-and-black-college-students/4663/.

18. Paul Taylor and Rakesh Kochhar, "America's Changing Workforce: Recession Turns a Graying Office Grayer," in *Social and Demographic Trends Report,* ed. Rich Morin (Washington, DC: Pew Research Center, September 3, 2009), http://pewsocialtrends.org/files/2010/10/americas-changing-workforce.pdf.

19. For example, see Ronald F. Ferguson, Jens Ludwig, and Wilbur Rich, "A Diagnostic Analysis of Black-White GPA Disparities in Shaker Heights, Ohio," in *Brookings Papers on Education Policy* (Washington, DC: Brookings Institution, 2001).

20. Elizabeth Gudrais, "Unequal America: Causes and Consequences of the Wide—and Growing—Gap between Rich and Poor," *Harvard Magazine,* July–August 2008, 25.

Critical pedagogues will point out that when we create a system in which people work in their own individual interests rather than developing some mechanisms to look out for the public's interests, we should not be surprised when those with the most power steadily erode the resistance of those with less power. We shouldn't be surprised, they tell us, when the wealthy, working in their own individual interests, are able to bend the nation's institutions to their own interest, resulting in a redistribution of the nation's wealth from the middle classes to the wealthy. We shouldn't be surprised when the media, the churches, and the schools all work to create a commonsense that explains the status quo as "natural" and "good."

Let us look, for a moment, at the way schools contribute to this hegemony. Schools give the appearance of providing everyone a fair and equal chance. Everyone has a chance to go to school, and so it gives the appearance that those children who have the intelligence and the right values will be able to succeed and rise to the top of their class and obtain a well-paying and secure job. It appears to be a fair competition and to the victors go the spoils. If you graduate from high school and if you graduate from college and if your college is of high reputation, you will be in a position to benefit from the society's powerful economic engine. However, the hegemonic narrative suggests that if you do not do what you need to graduate from high school, you will likely not succeed and do not deserve to succeed. Again, the narrative tells us that everyone has an equal opportunity.

But, once again, critical pedagogues can point to the facts to suggest that our schools hardly present an equal opportunity to all students. Many studies show that the income of students' parents strongly influences their reading group placements in first grade, which in turn influences the whole rest of their schooling career, leading to higher school success for higher social class students.[21] Christy Lleras and Claudia Rangel have shown that ability grouping African American students in elementary schools has a large negative impact on educational achievement.[22] These are not isolated research studies. Critical pedagogues point out that these facts have been shown in the research again and again and again and again and again. The initial differences between students of different income groups increase the longer students are in school. Rather than reducing the differences between students, schools seem to increase the differential. In other words, critical pedagogues suggest that schools work to reproduce society's inequalities, but our social institutions promote a hegemonic narrative that suggests exactly the opposite. The facts on the ground do not match the narratives we tell.

The Reality of Schools

Let us return to the question that opened this section on critical pedagogy. What if the social reconstructionists are correct, and schools work against American values rather than for them? Would you advocate for teachers and administrators to continue to do what they do now—to reproduce the status quo—or would you advocate that they work to transform the school curriculum and methods?

---

21. George Farkas, "How Educational Inequality Develops," *National Poverty Center Working Paper Series*, #0609 (June 2006), www.npc.umich.edu/publications/working_papers/.

22. Christy Lleras and Claudia Rangel, "Ability Grouping Practices in Elementary School and African American/Hispanic Achievement," *American Journal of Education* 115, no. 2 (2009): 279–305.

What do schools do now?

I suspect it is not too hard to get Americans today to agree that the public schools are not doing a very good job. The main reason for the American agreement on the poor quality of their schools is not because the schools are doing a poor job (they may be, but that is not why the American people have come to think that they do), but because the media, politicians, and corporate executives have joined together to promote a hegemonic message that schools are not doing well. Parents give their own children's school good grades, but the schools of other parents' children poor grades.[23] In other words, based on their own experience with schools, parents think the public schools are doing a good job. It is only the schools with which they have no direct experience that they believe are poor. How do they come to this conclusion? How is it that their own experience tells them that their public schools are doing a good job, but they believe that everyone else's must be doing a poor job? Critical pedagogy suggests that much of the reason is the media that continue to promote a narrative about the poor quality of the public schools.

So while most Americans agree with critical pedagogues that public schools are not doing a good job, they do so for very different reasons. For more than thirty years, the media has barraged the public with the failures of the public schools. But in what way have they argued schools have failed? Do they suggest that schools have not worked to educate a citizenry capable of making wise political decisions? No. Critical pedagogues point out that the major complaint about schools is that they do not provide a well-trained workforce for corporate America. And by "well-trained," corporations mean good technical readers able to follow directions and engineer the results asked of them combined with good work habits that rarely challenge authority. They certainly do not want a workforce educated to advance the workers' economic and political interests, to challenge the authority of the corporations, or to become active citizens who advocate for their political interests in the political system. Critical pedagogues argue that these corporate executives and their politicians certainly do not want a population educated enough to see through their hegemonic discourse. They do not want an educated population capable of bringing about a more equitable and just society.

Furthermore, critical pedagogues point out the culprit in the weak education students are receiving is not progressive education, as the politicians, media, and corporate executives claim, but essentialist education. Paulo Freire refers to essentialist education as *banking education*.[24] Banking education is a metaphor that refers to the kind of pedagogy that acts as if education works by pouring knowledge and skills into the brains of children where they are stored until the children grow up to be adults when they can withdraw the knowledge and skills and apply them to their adult life. The brain is like a bank in this metaphor, a place to store and build up "human capital" to spend in the job marketplace when the graduates turn themselves into commodities and sell themselves to the highest bidder. According to

---

23. "Seventy-seven percent of America's parents gave the school their oldest child attends either an 'A' or 'B.' These are the highest grades parents have assigned to their oldest child's school since the poll began. During the past 25 years, parent grades assigned to schools have continued to improve." William J. Bushaw and Shane J. Lopez, "A Time for Change: The 42nd Annual Phi Delta Kappa/Gallup Poll of the Public's Attitudes toward the Public Schools," *Kappan,* September 2010, 13.

24. Paulo Freire, *Pedagogy of the Oppressed* (New York: Seabury Press, 1970).

Freire and other critical pedagogues, this is the essence of the essentialist education that dominates our public schools today.

Progressive education could not be the cause of poor schooling in America because there is almost no progressivism left in the public schools; essentialism has completely dominated the schools since the late 1970s. Even in the heyday of progressive education in the late 1960s and early 1970s, America's schools were still largely organized around the ideas promoted by essentialist philosophy. At that time, progressivism was growing and had found a foothold in many school districts around the country, but since the Reagan days, progressivism has been all but killed in the public schools. It simply could not be that progressive philosophy causes weak education in America's schools because, at the present time, few of America's schools practice progressive philosophy. Critical pedagogues point out that every new step in the reform movement since the mid-1970s has been to increase the logic of essentialism. President Clinton and President Obama have at least one thing in common with President George W. Bush, and that is the continued advancement of an essentialist philosophy in schools that critical pedagogues argue are "reforms" in name only. These so-called reforms simply reinforce the status quo. They move us further and further away from providing an ethical education for America's children and youth.

The hegemony of essentialism in the schools has created a commonsense about education that critical pedagogues refer to as the hidden curriculum. This *hidden curriculum* assumes that the purpose of schools is to train workers for the economy, that learning is a technical enterprise requiring clear objectives that can be measured on standardized tests, that students need to be led step-by-step through a series of tasks to master the material, that education is about knowledge and skills, that what works is more important than what is ethical, and that education is a private consumer good accruing to the individual and not a public good benefiting the society as a whole. This is the present commonsense of today, but it was not the commonsense of the 1930s, 1940s, 1950s, 1960s, and even part of the 1970s.

According to critical pedagogues, the present-day hegemony has created a system of schooling that works to maintain the hegemony of a privileged class permitting them to continue to dominate the American economic and political systems with the consent of those who are dominated. Critical pedagogues argue that it is a system that leads the poor to believe that they deserve to be poor and the rich deserve to be rich; that the powerless deserve being without power, while the powerful deserve their power. It is a system that, critical pedagogues argue, is trying to dismantle teachers' unions based on a hegemonic commonsense that it is unions and bad teachers that create bad schools rather than bad policy from the nation's politicians working in the interests of America's corporations and the super-wealthy.

Americans appear ready to believe this new commonsense even though the best educational system in the world is found in Finland, a social democracy with one of the strongest teacher unions in the world. If government can't run good schools and if teacher unions only prevent firing of lazy teachers, how is it that Finland has the best schools in the world?[25] And you don't have to go to other countries to find that unions do not create poor education. There were only five states in February 2011 where teacher unions were illegal. Where did they rank on test scores? Based on 2007 ACT/SAT composite scores, they rank as follows:

25. "OECD Programme for International Student Assessment," PISA 2009 results, www.oecd.org/edu /pisa/2009.

North Carolina, forty-seventh; Texas, forty-fifth; South Carolina, thirty-ninth; Georgia, twenty-sixth; Virginia, twenty-fifth. Such rankings hardly endorse the idea that it is the unions that are causing schools to fail.[26]

A Philosophical Response

Given the critical pedagogues' educational philosophy that places the question of ethics first, how do they suggest that we respond to this evidence of educational and social inequity and inequality? How do they respond to a system of schooling that they argue teaches a hegemonic hidden curriculum? What does this educational philosophy suggest is necessary to truly transform our schools in order to achieve democracy and social justice?

We can understand critical pedagogy better if we return to the work of Paulo Freire (mentioned above). Freire argued that educators need to begin by asking what the students do not know and why they don't know it. Freire argued that learning is a basic human ability, and if people fail to learn, then something is inhibiting them. The trick is to identify what the inhibitor is and try to remove it. Without the inhibitor, people begin to learn almost on their own. Freire has shown that illiterate rural adults can be taught to read in about ten months. From nonreaders, these rural and uneducated adults become good readers able to read sophisticated books that many an American college student stumbles over. How did he do it? By helping these illiterate, rural adults understand that their failure to be able to read resulted from their political disempowerment and their economic impoverishment. Once they began to understand that their lack of power and wealth resulted from inequality and injustice rather than from any personal qualities of their own, they began to realize that they really have intellectual abilities and something worth thinking and saying. This freed them up to learn to read with minimal instruction.

If we apply Freire's thinking to American education, we must ask what it is that American students don't know. Critical pedagogues answer that they do not realize that their current commonsense is a myth. They argue that American students do not realize that the schooling they have received has set them up to be good technical thinkers and loyal, hardworking laborers so someone else can increase their own wealth and power at their expense. Critical pedagogues argue that American students confuse democracy with capitalism rather than recognize that they are really opposites because democracy is found in public space working in the public interest while capitalism is found in private space working in private interests. Many American students have come to think that being educated means being able to perform the culture of those Americans descended from Europeans; their own culture doesn't count. Many boys learn that to be educated is to be unmasculine, while many girls learn that to be educated is to be unfeminine. They learn that all problems can be solved using good technical thinking and that any problem that requires ethical thinking, artfulness, or wisdom has no answer that can be agreed upon. Such a question cannot really ever be answered and, therefore, is not worth asking. Education students learn to ask, "Does it work?" but not to ask, "Is it ethical?"

---

26. Gus Lubin, "The Five States Where Teachers Unions Are Illegal Have the Lowest Test Scores in America," *Business Insider,* February 23, 2011, www.businessinsider.com/states-where-teachers-unions-are-illegal-2011-2.

Notice that none of the above list of American student unknowns can be addressed through better teaching methods alone. For critical pedagogues, the problem of American education is not that we have the wrong teaching methods, uncommitted teachers, or teacher unions protecting bad teachers, but that we have harnessed our schools to serve the interests of those other than the students. Although students may not be able to understand that their education is not in their own interest in an explicit and cognitive way, many do sense that their school works against them rather than for them. They may not be able to explain how or why, but they feel out of place and wronged when in school. The reason that the children of the poor and those who have been assigned minority labels perform poorly in school is not because teachers use poor methods, but because the schools do not actually serve the interests of their students, unless those students happen to be upper middle class who do gain some privilege from the system. Instead, they serve the interests of the corporations and the super-wealthy. Create a curriculum that actually respects these children, their parents, and their neighbors and cultures and that teaches these children how to participate in public life in order to gain control over their lives rather than merely being able to sell their labor to the wealthy, and then they will learn.

Hegemonic commonsense teaches that most poor and minority students do not do well in school because they don't value education. But as shown earlier in this chapter, that is a myth. Most of them do believe in education, but they don't believe they are getting an education in their schools. Just because they resist their schools does not mean they reject education. In fact, resisting their schooling may be a sign that they actually value education because so little of what they are asked to do in schools is educational. For the most part, what they gain in school is mere training to become labor for the transnational corporations, and it is being treated as merely a potential employee that many students find dehumanizing, even if they cannot explain why they feel dehumanized and disrespected.

Critical pedagogues argue that if you create a school designed to educate rather than train, one that helps people develop their full private and public humanity, remarkable learning will occur.

Do they have any evidence for this? Yes, though there certainly are not many public schools that have adopted such a purpose or curriculum. Perhaps one of the best known successes that begins to approach the goals of a critical education comes from the work of Deborah Meier, who has started several public schools in low-income urban areas across the United States. The best known of them are the Central Park East Elementary and Secondary Schools in East Harlem, New York City, and the Mission Hill School in Boston.[27] These schools build on democratic principles and have remarkable success with poor, minority inner-city students. Or look at the interesting work that Dennis Littky is doing at The MET Center in Providence, Rhode Island, whose school is also built upon democratic principles and also achieving remarkable success.[28] Or, in eastern Ohio, look at rural Federal-Hocking High school headed by George Wood, a school that has had a remarkable revival since Dr. Wood

---

27. For information on Central Park East High School, see Deborah Meier, *The Power of Their Ideas: Lessons for America from a Small School in Harlem* (Boston: Beacon Press, 2002); for information on Central Park Elementary School, see www.centralparkeastone.org/; for information on Mission Hill School, see www.missionhillschool.org/mhs/Welcome_.html.

28. For information on the MET Center, see http://metcenter.org/.

became principal and introduced critical ideas into the school.[29] Or look at the success of the Tucson High School Mexican-American Studies program before it was outlawed by the Arizona legislature in 2010. An independent study of the program showed that students who participated in the Mexican-American Studies program at Tucson High School were 51 percent more likely to graduate from high school in 2009 and 108 percent more likely in 2008 than Mexican American students who had not participated in the program.[30] That the Arizona legislature decided to shut down this program and to ban books by Paulo Freire at the same time suggests that for some politicians, improving student learning is not their primary goal.

Critical pedagogy says that teachers must start with a commitment to social justice and build an educational program consistent and congruent with that commitment. According to critical pedagogues, those who excuse inequity in our schools or who blame teachers for the failures of schools in high poverty districts are caught in hegemony. We used to do better. And today, other nations seem to be doing better than we are in developing more equity in their schools. Social reconstructionists in education, especially those who call themselves critical pedagogues, argue that the United States can do so once again. But until Americans start to tell narratives about the world that more closely match the data and until there is an honest commitment to equity in society at large, the results of American schooling will fail the public's interest in developing a thriving, vibrant democracy. According to critical pedagogues and other social reconstructionists, as long as we rely on punishment, test scores, teacher bashing, and essentialism, the American public schools will continue to fail in their purpose of creating a vibrant democratic society.

---

29. For information on Federal-Hocking High School, see George Wood, "The Lessons of a Rural Principal," *Teaching Tolerance* 38 (Fall 2010): 25–27, www.tolerance.org/magazine/number-38-fall-2010/lessons-rural-principal.

30. Nolan L. Cabrera, Jeffrey F. Milem, and Ronald W. Marx, "An Empirical Analysis of the Effects of Mexican American Studies Participation on Student Achievement within Tucson Unified School District" (Tucson: University of Arizona, 2012), www.coe.arizona.edu/sites/default/files/MAS_report_2012_0.pdf.

Part III

Ideology and Education

CHAPTER NINE

Introduction to Ideology

Philosophy and Ideology

Broadly speaking, *ideology* is a worldview that organizes the assumptions one makes about the world and constructs understandings of what constitutes "normal" and "right." If philosophy is a process of asking conceptual questions in order to arrive at reasoned answers, ideology might be thought of as the seeking of questions with which to apply ready-made answers. Whereas the good philosopher uses argument to arrive at the most reasonable answer (i.e., able to be defended through reason), ideologists use argument to win converts to their side.

On the other hand, while we are making a clear and precise distinction between philosophy and ideology, in practice we often see the two intertwined. Often the results of the reasoned process of philosophy produce a body of accepted responses that, in turn, becomes a static set of answers—in other words, an ideology. Proponents of all five of the philosophies of education addressed in the previous three chapters often use them ideologically rather than philosophically. In other words, many who commit to progressivism, essentialism, social reconstructionism, perennialism, or relational pedagogy seem to be less interested in finding out whether the reasoned exploration of their questions achieves coherency and consistency and more interested in using their claimed "philosophy" as a weapon in political wars. Considering it this way, we not only have at least five educational philosophies called essentialism, perennialism, progressivism, critical pedagogy, and relational pedagogy but we also have five educational ideologies of the same names. One of the aims of this book is to help educators recognize when one of these worldviews is being used philosophically and when it is being used ideologically.

On the surface, it may appear that by defining philosophy as "reasoned" and, by default, claiming ideology as "nonreasoned," I have defined philosophy as good and ideology as bad. I do not intend to do so. It is true that ideology is poor philosophy, but then philosophy may sometimes make for poor ideology. What really separates philosophy from ideology is its purpose. *Philosophy* is a tool for seeking scholarly and personal answers to important questions of life through reason. *Ideology* is a tool of political struggle aimed at persuading people through rhetoric and other devices of nonreason. Nonreason is not the same thing as unreason. Nonreason is merely performance based on things other than a commitment to reason. When Beth Orton sings,

> If ever that morning came again I'd take it
> If ever that morning came again I'd be there

[...]

I would light up the sky in one burning mist of flame[1]

I doubt she was trying to present a reasoned argument in the sense that I am using that term in this book. Rather, she is trying to evoke our response through nonreasoning devices such as rhetoric and, if you listen to her song, music. To use nonreason does not mean that she doesn't think, plan, or make choices. She probably did all of those while writing this song and performing it. Rather, it means that she did not try to advance a claim by providing a set of consistent and coherent premises. Could we, her listeners, take her words and build our own argument that to love and lose is better than to never have loved at all? Of course, but we don't need to, because that well-worn narrative is a comfort to nearly anyone who is reeling in the aftermath of a lost love. We don't need reason. In fact, at such times we might not appreciate anyone who is trying to comfort us with reason. Often, the nonreason of song, story, or ritual is what we really want and need.

When a person wishes to seek the answers to problems, such as "What should my goal be as I pursue my education?" or "What should be the aims of the local public schools?" then the appropriate approach is to use the tools of philosophy. But if a person's goal is to convince a school board to accept the educational aims that have been arrived at philosophically, then that person might choose to use the tools of philosophy as a way to persuade school board members, or s/he might opt to approach the problem as purely ideological, assuming that the board is not as interested in philosophy as we might be. If, for example, the board is made up of members who are ideologically committed to essentialism, while we have come to the conclusion through philosophic reasoning that progressivism has the more reasoned answers to our questions, we might choose to try to change the board members' own ideological commitments through getting them to think philosophically, hoping they will come to agree with us about the relative merits of essentialism and progressivism, or we might, instead, choose to use the weapons of ideology to be more persuasive, hoping they will make decisions without considering their own ideological commitments.

For example, if we were to become convinced by progressivism, we would find the present emphasis on high-stakes testing likely to be counterproductive and leading to a lessening in the quality of education of our district's public school students. But if the school board members are committed to essentialism, they will be predisposed to high-stakes testing. If we wished to advocate for a new reading curriculum that was congruent with progressive philosophy, we could choose to try to change the board's ideological bias against such a curriculum by presenting them with a philosophically sound progressive argument, or we could use their own ideology against them by arguing that this new curriculum should be adopted because it would achieve higher test scores. In other words, educators and those of us interested in public education have to deal with two kinds of problems. One is a problem of finding reasoned solutions, and the other is the problem of winning political struggles. Philosophy may be used for both though may be less effective for the latter problem. Ideology cannot really be used for the first problem, but sometimes may be the better approach to the second.

I believe that the educational philosophies developed in the last three chapters are too frequently used ideologically and too infrequently used philosophically. I encourage educators

---

1. Beth Orton, "Last Leaves of Autumn," *Sugaring Season*, ANTI Records, 2012, compact disc.

to use the educational philosophies philosophically and to avoid using them ideologically. By this, I mean to encourage educators to approach the educational philosophies as ways to help us ask and reason our way through the important philosophical questions in our own education and in the education of our communities' children. I encourage educators not to use the educational philosophies as mere ideologies, as ready-made answers. What is important for educators is to think and to reason about educational issues and to recognize the thinking and reasoning about education found in the culture's texts.

On the other hand, we need to be able to recognize that many authors of texts about education are not reasoning philosophically but are using the language of particular educational philosophies ideologically rather than philosophically. Much of what passes as progressive arguments or essentialist arguments, for example, does not really reason with the philosophical spirit in mind, but argues to advance a political agenda. Being able to recognize the extent to which a text is developing a reasonable argument philosophically or merely using the language of a so-called educational philosophy to win its argument helps us make a decision as to what the text is trying to accomplish.

Unfortunately, too many school administrators and professors of education demand that students or job applicants declare their "philosophy of education." When they do so, they are more likely to want a clear ideological commitment that draws on the narratives, tropes, and ideographs or one or some combination of educational ideologies rather than to read or listen to someone working to develop a reasoned argument. Such demands on students too often require students to treat progressivism, essentialism, or perennialism as an ideology that provides ready-made answers to all classroom problems. They seem to want you to go down the salad bar of ideas, build your ideological salad, and show it to them. Are you student-centered or teacher-centered, outcomes-based or process-oriented, committed to caring or to tough love? They might be suspicious of a student or applicant for a teaching job that says, "Well, it depends. As Dewey points out the choice between being student-centered or teacher-centered is a false dualism because teachers need to navigate between the two as they help guide their students from where they are to where they are going." To become the best they can be, educators need to reason in a way exactly like this, but to get that job or satisfy the examiner of the state licensure examination, educators also need a well-crafted statement of an educational ideology masquerading as philosophy. To become effective educators, they need to reason philosophically; to communicate their reasoning to others, sometimes it pays to craft a carefully worded narrative.

For this reason, we can think of perennialism, essentialism, progressivism, social reconstructionism, and relational pedagogy as either educational philosophies or educational ideologies depending on how the person is using them. If an author is asking questions in a way that seeks consistency and coherency regardless of where the questioning leads, he is developing the ideas of an educational philosophy. If, on the other hand, the author is merely using the code words of one of the educational philosophies as tropes or ideographs in order to advance a particular political agenda or as a recipe for classroom practice, she is not really appealing to an educational philosophy but to an educational ideology. Of course, in practice it is often difficult to tell the difference and, in fact, often we find a little of each in any particular text. In other words, most philosophers honestly pursuing a philosophical question using proper philosophical methods with the proper philosophical spirit probably have some bit of ideology inserted in their text. And it will also be true that even the most rabid ideologue may actually reveal some philosophical reasoning in his or her attempt to win an argument. So, while I am making a clear distinction between educational philosophy and educational ideology, such distinctions may be more sharp in theory than in practice. Still, I encourage educators to try to be self-reflective and critical of their own and others' educational arguments by recognizing to what extent the author is advancing an argument that appears to be more philosophical or that appears to be more ideological. I especially advocate that when it comes to making up their own minds about educational issues, educators attempt to adopt the spirit of philosophy and seek consistency and coherency through the use of reason.

Political-Economic Ideologies and Education

The first part of this chapter clarified some distinctions between educational philosophies and educational ideologies. But, to be a well-informed educator, there are other ideologies that may be just as important as, or more than important than, educational ideologies. Perhaps educational ideologies permeate the conversations of teachers and administrators, but the political-economic ideologies are much more important in the discourse of educational policy-makers. When state and national legislators debate education, they use political-economic ideologies. Therefore, the rest of this chapter and the two that follow will explore political-economic ideology.

Ideologies might be thought of as eyeglasses with different colored lenses. If one person is wearing a set of blue-lensed sunglasses and another is wearing a set of red-lensed sunglasses, the world will look different to each. They may be looking at exactly the same landscape, but one will see the world with a blue tinge and the other with a red tinge. But the implications are even more significant than that because when looking through blue lenses, the color blue looks neutral while the color red stands out, but when looking through red lenses, the color red looks neutral while the color blue stands out.

The same is true for ideology. When one looks at the world through an ideology, not only is everything in the world colored by that ideology, but the reflections of that ideology look neutral, normal, ordinary, and commonsensical. On the other hand, ideological representations that present a different ideological view will stand out as biased, wrong, political, and contrary to commonsense. For this reason, while it is typically easy to recognize oppositional ideologies in texts, it is often difficult for people to recognize their own ideologies. When they read a text that shares their own ideological biases, rather than seeing the text as biased, it is seen as fair and balanced—not ideological at all, but commonsense. When people call for teachers to be unbiased and objective, what they are really calling for is for those teachers to be biased and nonobjective in a manner that shares the biases and positionalities of their own ideology. *There is no such thing as a neutral teacher or unbiased classroom or objective curriculum.* They always favor some ideologies and disfavor others—though it may not always be clear right off which is being favored and which not.

The problem is not how can we make our classrooms ideologically fair and balanced (that's impossible); the problem is which ideologies will find a privileged place in our education, and which ones will be denigrated or ignored. The task of the educator is not to pretend to be neutral, objective, and balanced but rather to be fair to ideologies that contradict their own by presenting them as honestly as they can and by permitting students to opt for ideologies contrary to the teacher's as long as the student represents that ideology accurately and shows an understanding of its implications.

Some Preliminary Comments about Politics and Education

When I ask students in my undergraduate classes to raise their hands if they hate politics, I must get at least 60 to 80 percent of the students with their hands up. College students are not much different than most Americans, who seem to be sick and tired of the political shenanigans of our nation's politicians. They just want it to go away. Most think that it doesn't make any difference anyway. When campaigning, politicians, it is believed, say one thing, and then when they get into office, they do another. It appears that, in general, college students (and other Americans) dislike politics, but when it comes to education, their distaste becomes intense. "Get politics out of education!" might be the catch phrase that captures best what most Americans think about the relationship between education and politics. "Just get it out and get back to teaching!"

But the view expressed in the above paragraph shows both grave misunderstandings and dangerous dispositions if education for democracy is going to survive in America. One of the first misunderstandings that I wish to address is the one that equates politics with elections. As pointed out in the first chapter, the mechanisms of democracy, such as elections, are merely techniques we use in order to bring about democratic life. Some of these mechanisms work well, and others do not. When they don't work, we shouldn't throw out the idea of democracy itself, but we should change our mechanisms. In the same way, elections are little more than one mechanism a people can adopt to manage its politics. You can hate elections. You can think elections are meaningless. But you should never think that elections are the central element of politics. *Politics* is primarily the struggle for the legitimate use of power. Those who have legitimacy can use power as they will. Those who have legitimacy can take away people's freedom by locking them up in jail. Those who have legitimacy can take property from one group of people and give it to another group (for example, through taxation). Those who have legitimacy can kill other people (as in war and capital punishment). Those who have legitimacy can also determine whose language is "correct," and whose language is "incorrect"; who gets to be included in history, and who is ignored or demonized in history; and whose literature is considered worthy, and whose is not.

The last sentence should also help clarify why people make a big error when they think, "If we could just get politics out of education, everything would be just fine." Like it or not, education is inherently political. It *cannot* be taken out of education. *By its very nature, education is political.* Teachers are political actors whether they want to be or not—whether they realize it or not. When teachers decide whose language to correct and whose to praise; whose history to ignore and whose to tell; whose understanding of science to reject and whose to uphold; whether to teach math in a manner that leads to students who are able to calculate but not reason mathematically, or in a manner that teaches them the latter too; to decide whose style of dress is deemed immoral, and whose is acceptable; whose behavior deserves to be punished and whose rewarded—whenever they do any of those things and hundreds of other things that occur every day, teachers act politically. Just because they don't realize whose political interests are being damaged and whose favored doesn't change a thing. The very act of teaching makes teachers political. Teachers may choose not to pay attention, and they can ignore the politics of their actions, but they cannot stop being political. Don't you think that at the very least teachers ought to know in whose political interests they are working? If they are going to work that hard to connect with their students in the hopes of making their lives better, shouldn't they understand what that actually means? They may, of course, be horrified to find out that by doing what they are told to do, they actually work in a political interest that they disagree with. But putting on blinders and pretending otherwise will not make the politics go away.

If you are one of those people who doesn't pay attention to politics, you should understand that your keeping out of politics is itself a political act that works in the interests of some groups and against the interests of others. Some of the ideologies (and one in particular) described in these chapters don't mind if people turn off to politics and government. If you fail to pay attention to what is going on, you are working for that ideology whether you know it or not and whether you want to or not. Don't you think you ought to find out who is benefiting and who is hurt by your lack of paying attention? You may even be working against your own interests and don't even know it.

But another problem is that even if one pays attention, it is often difficult to figure out who is benefiting or who is being hurt. The arguments of politicians and their shills often sound like little more than kids bickering on the playground. I believe that such confusions and misunderstandings have several different causes, but here I'm only going to address one of those causes, and I choose it because it is primarily a problem of and for education. Too many Americans just don't know what is actually being argued about, and they find it difficult to find out. That's because most people get their knowledge of politics through the marketing campaigns that politicians, think tanks, newspaper columnists, and radio talk show hosts promote. It passes as "news," but it is really little more than managed messaging. People are no more likely to learn what the political struggles actually are by watching political ads on TV or reading commentaries in the newspapers or listening to talk show hosts, any more than they are likely to gain accurate information about consumer products through corporate advertising—unless they know how to read them. Somehow, Americans have to begin to learn to read these texts better. They have to be able to identify the basic ideological commitments implicit in the fog machine that is political marketing and commentary.

Luckily, understanding the political struggles is not really that confusing but instead quite straightforward. Just by learning a few basic ideologies along with the narratives spun to support them with their tropes and ideographs and heroes and villains, one can have the scales fall from one's eyes. Suddenly what appears to be confusion, lying, and squabbling can be sorted out and the real political struggle identified. What follows in the rest of this chapter and the two that follow will lay out the terrain of ideological struggle in American politics, including many of the narratives, tropes, and ideographs used. Understanding these ideologies will make clear what the real stakes might be in the politics of education, whether we are talking about a presidential election, a school board race, which textbook to adopt to teach eighth-grade science, or which methods to use to teach fifth-grade math.

Liberal Democracy as Ideology

Because ideologies organize assumptions without a strong commitment to reason, few people think very carefully about them. Instead, they simply *assume* their worldviews to be true and good and *assume* the worldviews of those they disagree with to be not true and not particularly good. But also because ideologies are not carefully considered, even people using the same ideology may not agree about what it means. For this reason, we must recognize that ideologies, like all cultural forms, are sites of contestation even while they organize our joint assumptions. For example, throughout the history of the United States, one political-economic ideology has dominated our national worldview: liberal democracy. Liberal democracy organized the worldviews of George Washington and Thomas Jefferson, Abraham Lincoln and Teddy Roosevelt, George H. W. Bush and Bill Clinton, and, now, Barack Obama. As this is the case, we can easily claim that liberal democracy is the dominant political-economic ideology of the United States.

Calling the dominant American ideology "democratic liberalism" often confuses people because in recent usage many politicians and media commentators use *liberal democrat* to describe only politicians of the Democratic Party. In this new usage, "liberal Democrats" are the opposite of "conservative Republicans." But the traditional meaning of *liberal democracy*, developed in the nineteenth century and still used today among scholars, is quite different. In this traditional usage, nearly all major American politicians have been liberal democrats. Just keep reminding yourself that Ronald Reagan was a liberal democrat even while he, more than any other politician, changed the meaning of that term by applying it only to followers of Franklin D. Roosevelt's and Lyndon Baines Johnson's political-economic agendas.

Whereas nearly all major American politicians have committed to liberal democracy, we all know that Washington, Jefferson, Lincoln, Roosevelt, Bush, Clinton, and Obama have not agreed on exactly what an ideology of liberal democracy demands from a president. In other words, while these presidents shared some underlying ideological assumptions, many of these assumptions led to different interpretations about the concrete events in everyday life. When we realize this, we appreciate that we need to recognize the struggles over ideologies in order to understand the conflicts over education policy.

Liberal democracy is the dominant political-economic ideology of the United States. Figure 9.1 shows the political economy of the United States in terms of ideal types. An *ideal type* offers a logically consistent way (as opposed to the best or most perfect way) of thinking about a social institution or belief.[2] Figure 9.1 shows a spectrum of belief systems associated with various types of political economies and suggests ways that these ideologies differ in their implications for schooling.

Under the very broad political-economic ideologies of *socialism, liberal democracy,* and *corporatism,* there exists a range of political and economic ideologies that currently help shape our society and schools. *Liberal democracy* is a form of representative democracy where elected officials make laws and policy moderated by a constitution that works to balance the interests of individuals and other private entities with the public interests of the community.

One thing must be made clear at the start: the word *liberal* does not refer to progressives or leftists. In academic language, the term *liberal* actually has two different meanings that are quite distinct from the way the term is typically used in the newspapers. One academic meaning refers to an economic ideology that favors the marketplace as the appropriate arbiter for nearly all decisions. The second meaning refers to a political ideology that argues that

---

2. As Frank Elwell puts it, "An ideal type provides the basic method for historical-comparative study. It is not meant to refer to the 'best' or to some moral ideal, but rather to typical or 'logically consistent' features of social institutions or behaviors. There can be an 'ideal type' whore house or a religious sect, ideal type dictatorship, or an ideal democracy (none of which may be 'ideal' in the colloquial sense of the term)." From Frank Elwell, "Verstehen: The Sociology of Max Weber," www.faculty.rsu.edu/~felwell/Theorists/Weber/Whome.htm.

Socialism	Liberal Democracy	Corporatism
• Nearly everything is public, therefore: • The state works in the interest of the people • All but the smallest enterprises are either owned by or heavily regulated by the state	• Some things are private, some things are public • The interests of the individual and the community must be balanced • The state works in the interests of both the people and the corporations to keep them in balance • State ownership or regulation of business is held to a minimum, but can be used to serve the interests of the public	• Nearly everything is private, therefore: • The community is subsumed to the interests of the corporations • The state works in the interest of the corporations and the state's main job is to maintain order so that the marketplace can perform unimpeded • When enterprises are either so large or complex that the state must run or regulate them, they do so to serve the interests of the corporations

Figure 9.1 The Three Major Economic-Political Ideologies

liberty is the highest political value. As mentioned above, in these two senses of the word, Ronald Reagan was a liberal and so are Mitt Romney and Barack Obama. As such, liberal democracy is an ideology that argues that the economy and the individual should be free from government interference except where the economy and individual infringe on public areas. In other words, there are two different spheres: one public and the other private. The public sphere must be organized through democratic means, but the private sphere should be organized through individual choice, and that requires a capitalist economic marketplace. Put another way, a liberal democracy is a capitalist democracy that protects the individual from the tyranny of the majority. Notice that *democracy* and *capitalism* refer to two different spheres—they are not synonyms. *Democracy* is not another word for capitalism, and *capitalism* is not another word for democracy. Under liberal democracy, the public (i.e., political) arena must be democratic, while the private (which includes the economic) sphere need not be democratic. On the other hand, the private economic sphere should be capitalist, while the public sphere should not be.

Perhaps the single most important debate within liberal democracy is where the line between the public and the private should be drawn. Those committed to liberal democracy agree that there should be a firm distinction between the private and the public, but they sometimes disagree about what is public and what is private. For example, should the nation's schooling system be public or private? Today, this is the most important debate that divides so-called liberals from so-called conservatives. Self-identified conservatives have steadily introduced measures to "privatize" public education through a combination of voucher plans, charter schools, for-profit schools, and outsourcing everything from busing to testing. These measures are based on the assumption that schooling is not a public good but a private one accruing to individuals rather than to the commonweal.

In another example, is war a public or a private action? Apparently, today many Americans seem to think that it is more of a private than a public act, for we find estimates that 60 percent of the roles filled by the military personnel in the first Gulf War (1990–1991) were in the recent Iraq and Afghan wars being filled by private corporate personnel. In July 2007, the United States had 160,000 troops in Iraq, but contracted more than 180,000 private agents.[3] The protection of America's ambassador to Iraq is not carried out by the military or the secret service or any other government organization but by a private firm hired to protect him. The question under debate might be understood as follows: is the conduct of a war in the public or the private realm? Or, is the protection of the nation's ambassadors a public or a private good?

As used in this book, *socialism* is an ideology with the core belief that a society should exist in which citizens control the means of power, and therefore they should control not only the institutions of government but also the means of production. Socialism argues that if democracy is good in the public sector, it is also good in the private sector. In some ways, socialism can be understood to be radical democracy because it argues that not only should we consider the political sphere public and, therefore, democratic, but we should also consider the economic sphere public and, therefore, democratic. Notice that the focus is on a democratic public sphere, not government.

While it is true that the predominant form of socialism known in the twentieth century put faith in central governments to administer the democratic spheres, newer approaches seek a way to decentralize the administration of public space, placing the administration of public space into smaller agencies and directly into the hands of the members of local communities. These newer forms tend to focus on socializing local governments, creating community cooperatives, and encouraging worker-owned and worker-managed businesses.[4] For example, some American socialists point to the desirability of merging the interests of indigenous people with socialism, as found in Ecuador.[5] An ideology opposing great inequalities between rich and poor, the goal of socialism is to minimize the disparity of class and other structured privileges (such as race, ethnicity, and gender) in society. There has been a growing interest in socialism by American youth. A 2011 Pew Foundation Poll found that people aged eighteen to twenty-nine had a more favorable opinion of socialism than of capitalism (49 percent favorable for socialism, 46 percent favorable for capitalism).[6]

In this book, *corporatism* advocates for government to serve the interests of corporations. Corporatism argues that almost everything except the government, military, police, and courts are in the private realm and that the primary interest of the public realm is to serve the private interests of corporations by maintaining order. If socialism is the expansion of the public realm to what we often consider private so that socialism becomes radically democratic, then corporatism might be understood as the expansion of the private realm to what we often consider public, so that corporatism should be considered radically capitalist. Keep in mind that the three ideologies presented here—socialism, liberal democracy, and corporatism—are "ideal types," constructed to be logically consistent, and, therefore, located

---

3. T. Christian Miller, "Contractors Outnumber Troops in Iraq," *Los Angeles Times,* July 4, 2007, http://articles.latimes.com/2007/jul/04/nation/na-private4.

4. See Gar Alperovitz, "The Question of Socialism (and beyond!) Is about to Open Up in These United States," in *Truthout,* ed. Dina Rasor, www.truth-out.org/news/item/15680-the-question-of-socialism-and-beyond-is-about-to-open-up-in-these-united-states.

5. For example, see Marc Becker, *Indians and Leftists in the Making of Ecuador's Modern Indigenous Movements* (Durham: Duke University Press, 2008).

6. "Little Change in Public's Response to 'Capitalism,' 'Socialism': A Political Rhetoric Test," Pew Research Center for the People and the Press, December 28, 2011, www.people-press.org/2011/12/28/little-change-in-publics-response-to-capitalism-socialism/?src=prc-number.

in the realm of ideas. They are abstractions that are unlikely to ever be found fully realized in practice. But they are "ideas" from which "ideologies" build their narratives complete with plots, themes, heroes, villains, tropes, and ideographs.[7]

Historically, both socialism and corporatism are publicly distrusted in the United States. Although we can construct a continuum with socialism on the left and corporatism on the right, in the United States few public figures are willing to accept the label of "socialist" or "corporatist" even if they advocate such ideologies. But the truth is that in the United States nearly all political discourse takes place between the two poles of socialism and corporatism in the ideological region of liberal democracy. While there may be some strong voices advocating socialism in the scholarly literature, even at universities their number is few. And while there are a growing number of voices that seem to be advocating what I am calling corporatism, you won't find any such spokespersons claiming that identity. That is not to say that there are not vigorous criticisms from socialists or that there are not strong corporatist voices in the United States, but only that the major politicians, their political parties, and the mainstream media outlets (including cable television news) rarely have an articulate spokesperson for ideologies outside of liberal democracy. Because this book aims at explicating how to read texts about education in the United States, it will focus on clarifying the debate *within* liberal democracy rather than address ideologies that fall outside of it.

The health care debate is a clear example of the traditional and standard and age-old debate in America's liberal democracy as to where the line between the public and the private should be drawn rather than a debate between socialism (or corporatism) and liberal democracy. The health care law that was finally passed does not come close to socialized medicine; instead, it is simply the extension and expansion of government regulation over the commerce of medical insurance. It leaves medical care and the means for paying for it squarely in the private realm.

Part of the confusion lies in the way in which the United States conducts elections in its two-party system. Just as Coke and Pepsi compete in the public market by contrasting themselves with each other, so too, America's politicians focus much more on the differences between them than in their similarities—even if they have to create and exaggerate differences. If we were to believe the political rhetoric of the last presidential election, we would believe that President Obama and Governor Romney were on opposite ends of the economic ideological spectrum, but as Adam Davidson pointed out in a *New York Times Sunday Magazine* commentary, the Democratic and Republican presidential candidates actually agreed on much more than they disagreed. According to Davidson, their disagreements were little more than relatively minor differences in quantities of cuts or additions and, at

---

7. On Thom Hartmann's blog, lycanthropist posts an excellent discussion of the concept of corporatism as it was conceived in fascist Italy under Mussolini that clarifies how it is distinct from the idea of corporatism as developed in this chapter. I agree with lycanthropist that one should not equate today's concept of corporatism with that of Mussolini's. They are two different things. However, I disagree with lycanthropist's assumption that today's fascists would be unable or lack the desire to suture their commitment to fascism with today's concept of corporatism. Although the twentieth-century corporatism is distinct from twenty-first-century corporatism in several essential ways, they are similar in their ability for fascists to use either as an idea upon which to build their own fascist narratives. But to be completely clear, the usage of the term "corporatism" in this book does not require, or assume, that its advocates also commit to fascism. See www.thomhartmann.com/users/lycanthropist/blog/2012/06/corporatism-and-fascism-some-clarity-needed.

least *ideologically* speaking, were really cut from the same cloth.[8] How it is that President Obama and Governor Romney may actually share the same economic ideology will become clear in the next two chapters.

Conclusion

Often people confuse ideology for philosophy because both claim to have answers to life's big questions, and both can be used to organize individual and societal strategies for dealing with problems. But this chapter has argued that there are some very important distinctions between philosophy and ideology. Philosophy aims to use reason to arrive at the best consistent and coherent answers regardless of what answers the reasoning produces. Ideology aims to use given answers to find questions and problems to address. This confusion leads many educators to treat educational philosophies, such as essentialism and progressivism, as ready-made answers to be applied to classrooms and schools. Many teachers think that a progressive teacher never lectures or that an essentialist teacher never provides students with hands-on experiences, but progressivism and essentialism each provide space for lecturing and student-based problem solving. The difference lies in when and why a teacher might choose to lecture or to provide students active learning experiences. Just because you observe a teacher giving a lecture does not mean that the teacher is an essentialist, nor does a single observation of a teacher having students work in groups to solve a problem mean that the teacher is a progressive. One needs to look for continuous, ongoing patterns in the classrooms or interview the teachers to find out why they may be lecturing or providing hands-on experiences before one could comfortably conclude what philosophy the teacher is using.

On the other hand, when used as an ideology, teachers simply apply given methods as if they are the answer. An unphilosophical but ideologically progressive teacher might have students continuously using problem-based, student-centered techniques even in those moments when a progressive philosopher might suggest an alternative method, just as an unphilosophical but ideologically essentialist teacher might use lecture exclusively even when the use of a student activity might serve the goals of essentialism better. I suggest that educators pay attention to both philosophy and ideology. I argue that educators must learn how to recognize when an argument is actually philosophical and when it is primarily ideological.

While *educational* ideologies are obviously important for schools, the *economic-political* ideologies used by America's policy-makers may actually be more important because they are the ones who set the bigger policies that govern our public schools. This chapter has argued that, unlike many other nations in the world, there is really only one viable economic-political ideology found in the American political debate and in the major media outlets—liberal democracy. But it has also argued that just because policy-makers are committed to liberal democracy does not mean that they agree on all aspects of what a liberal democracy demands of them. A few of them do come very close to socialism, and many come very close to corporatism, but overwhelmingly the nation's politicians, news editorialists, and policy-makers easily fit into liberal democracy. Therefore, unlike many other nations whose ideological

8. Adam Davidson, "Vote Obamney!" *New York Times Magazine,* October 9, 2012, www.nytimes.com/2012/10/14/magazine/mitt-romney-barack-obama-economy.html?ref=itstheeconomy.

struggles span a much greater ideological territory, in the United States our ideological contestations are limited to a rather narrow distance. Perhaps the most central issue at debate in the United States today is where the border between the public sphere and the private sphere ought to be drawn within a liberal democracy. Where one draws that line is a strong indicator as to what economic-political ideology is being used in an effort to win the argument. The next two chapters will explore the range of ideologies *within* liberal democracy to present a clearer understanding of what is really at stake in today's debate over education.

CHAPTER TEN

Political-Economic Ideologies

The Conservative Coalition

Ideologies within Liberal Democracy

Chapter 9 argued that the range of political ideologies found among major American politicians and media is narrowly restricted to liberal democracy. While many other nations in the world see a range that extends to corporatism on the right and to socialism on the left, in the United States very few major politicians or news media personalities advocate anything that does not fit nicely within liberal democracy.

On the other hand, clearly there are some sharp distinctions among liberal democrats, or there would be no vigorous debate at all. It is one thing for those committed to liberal democracy to agree that there needs to be a firm line between the public and the private and another thing to agree where that line should be drawn. It is one thing for everyone to agree that there needs to be a balance between the interests of the individual and that of the community and another to agree what constitutes a "balance." It is one thing to agree that the state should work in both the interests of the people and those of the corporations, but what do we do when those interests are in conflict? Surely it is obvious that American politics are riddled with ideological struggle. In fact, most Americans are more surprised that there is ideological agreement on anything in American politics, rather than that there is ideological disagreement. But while most Americans know that there is ideological disagreement among politicians, few really have much understanding of what those disagreements are and why they are important. In fact, to many Americans, the competing ideological struggles appear to be mere "bickering" and "shouting." To these Americans, politics is something to avoid. To these Americans, politicians "are all alike"; and so, many Americans just want to be left alone. Unfortunately, they will not be left alone and to seek to be left alone is itself working in the interests of one ideology over others. But more importantly, the political disagreements are not mere bickering. They mean something quite significant and depending on how the nation responds, these disagreements will impact their lives significantly—for better or for worse.

Chapters 10 and 11 map the terrain of the ideological debates in the most available educational texts found within the United States. While they will not cover all of the ideologies drawn upon in those texts, they will address six of the most commonly used. Three of these ideologies are often referred to as *conservative,* and three are often referred to as *liberal* or progressive.

One thing to keep in mind as you read through these different ideological positions: While some adherents to some of these ideologies are committed to ideologies other than liberal democracy, each of the ideologies can fit easily into liberal democracy. Each ideology shows commitments to typical liberal democratic values such as freedom, liberty, equality, equity, fairness, protection of minorities, and social and individual justice. Each ideology has adherents committed to a balance of public and private interests and to using the state to protect the interests of individuals and the community and the corporations. Much of the confusion lies in the fact that each ideology will claim to be in favor of democracy or equality or liberty or social justice. And they will vehemently argue for their side in the name of those values and argue that the other side is opposed to democracy or equality or liberty or social justice, and this is why they seem to be "merely bickering." But, don't make that mistake. Just because they use the same words, does not mean that they are committed to the same things. One person's freedom is another's tyranny. One person's democracy is another's oppression. Knowing what each means by these terms becomes important in understanding what their rhetoric really signifies. And it might help clarify why a politician may not be "lying," when she runs for office promising a commitment to freedom and justice and then adopts a policy that the voter thinks is the opposite of those values. The politician probably was not lying, she was more likely just not precise in what she meant by the term and left it to the voter to be savvy enough to recognize which meaning she intended. Or, perhaps, she hoped the voter would treat the term as an ideograph that evoked strong emotion without having any precise meaning at all. The rest of this chapter will focus on the ideologies found within the so-called conservative coalition.

A Coalition of (So-Called) Conservative Ideologies

In ordinary usage the terms *liberal* and *conservative* have widely varying meanings. They are not precise terms, but vague references to broad and varying ideas. Perhaps the best way to understand these differences is to focus on where proponents of these ideologies think the line is to be drawn between the public and private spheres. In the United States, because both so-called liberals and so-called conservatives are, for the most part, subsets of the broader liberal democracy, they both believe in a strong line between public and private spheres. They just differ as to where that line should be drawn. Those ideologies that are normally referred to as conservative in today's politics tend to argue for a reduction of the public sphere (at least in some areas) and an expansion of the private sphere. But, in truth, some self-identified conservatives actually wish to expand the public sphere in areas that liberals wish to shrink it. While recognizing that the distinction between conservative and liberal has much to do with where the line is to be drawn, it is also important to realize that there is also disagreement within each ideology as to where that line should be drawn (see Figure 10.1).

Ronald Reagan is often credited with creating the contemporary coalition of conservative ideologies by bringing together under one rubric (i.e., conservatism) three ideologies that have some very strong differences. Reagan is often thought to have made popular the narratives necessary to have these different ideologies ignore each other's differences and

PUBLIC	PRIVATE

Figure 10.1 In General, Conservative Ideologies Claim to Favor a Wider Private Sphere

emphasize their commonalities in order to build a winning political coalition. That the rhetoric erases differences, however, does not mean that those differences don't continually and regularly raise their heads in a struggle within the conservative coalition. For example, consider the 2012 Republican presidential primary in which Mitt Romney and Ron Paul represented the classical liberal/neoliberal wing of the party; candidates such as Michele Bachmann, Rick Perry, and Rick Santorum represented the social conservative wing of the party; while Newt Gingrich represented the neoconservative wing of the party. If one does not understand this division within the Republican Party's coalition of ideologies, then the primary struggle made little sense beyond a contest of personalities. This chapter describes how the three so-called conservative ideologies (classical liberalism/neoliberalism, social conservatism, and neoconservatism) differ on the division between the public/private, the meaning of democracy, the meaning of freedom and liberty, and the requirements of justice. The chapter will also explore some of the rhetorical devices such as narratives, tropes, and ideographs favored by each of the ideologies.

Classical Liberalism/Neoliberalism

Most advocates of this ideology refer to it as *classical liberalism* while most opponents of this ideology refer to it as *neoliberalism*. In an attempt to honor both advocates and critics, I will typically use both terms separated by a slash. Readers should feel free to choose one or the other in your own usage. One might be tempted to refer to classical liberals/neoliberals as "economic conservatives," but an economic conservative is primarily a person interested in keeping government books balanced and while it is true that most classical liberals/neoliberals advocate balanced books, they nearly always want to balance the books by cutting government spending, almost never by raising taxes. So, while classical liberals/neoliberals are typically economic conservatives, there are many economic conservatives who are not classical liberals/neoliberals. But whether we use the term classical liberal or neoliberal, most everyone will agree that this ideology is the driver of the so-called conservatives in American politics. *Classical liberalism* or *neoliberalism* (whichever term you choose to name it) is a form of liberal democracy strongly influenced by the work of Austrian economist and political theorist Friedrich von Hayek that argues that individuals pursuing their own individual private interests in an unregulated marketplace results in the greatest liberty for all.

Public/Private

Hayek worked in a period when the Soviet Union, with its "dictatorship of the proletariat," dominated Eastern Europe. One might not be surprised to find that Hayek opposed left-wing governments and their economics. His economic-political writings make a few foundational assumptions. First among those assumptions is that any injection of government into society, except to maintain basic order, will *inevitably* lead to tyranny. A second assumption is that every person is an individual, first; and a member of a community, second. A third assumption is that every person engages with others in a zero-sum economic game in which the actor will act rationally in his/her own self-interest. These assumptions lead Hayek and his classical liberal/neoliberal followers to conclude that a market, if left on its own where every individual is free to act in his/her own self-interest, will eventually lead to the fairest balance of wealth and power. As a result, classical liberalism/neoliberalism advocates for a government whose only legitimate role is to maintain order and, therefore, calls for small government and unregulated markets. In other words, classical liberalism/neoliberalism wishes to shrink the public sphere to as small a space as possible and expand the private space as far as it can.[1] Of all the ideologies discussed in this chapter, classical liberals/neoliberals come closest to the right-wing ideological line of liberal democracy and while most classical liberals/neoliberals accept the basic tenets of liberal democracy, some seem to cross the line into corporatism, or come very close to doing so.

Because many people refer to this ideology as classical liberalism or neoliberalism, some people do not realize that it is understood to be a conservative ideology. Ronald Reagan is probably the best known classical liberal (or neoliberal) politician. When Reagan proclaimed that government is not the solution to our problems, it is the problem, he was advocating a classical liberal ideology. Those politicians and media commentators who champion charter schools and voucher plans, advocate for less government regulation of industry, and work to lower taxes (in order to force government to shrink) and eliminate workers' unions advocate a classical liberal/neoliberal position—but they call themselves "conservatives." The 2012 Republican nominee for president, Mitt Romney, represented the classical liberal wing of the Republican Party and his vice presidential running mate, Paul Ryan, presented himself as a true believer of classical liberalism. If you understand the Republican coalition, you understand that the decision to put two classical liberals/neoliberals at the head of the national ticket was a signal that the classical liberals had taken control of their party from the neoconservatives and the social conservatives. Certainly, if elected Mr. Romney and Mr. Ryan would have tried to find ways to placate the social conservatives and neoconservatives in order to keep them in their coalition, but we should all have expected that a Romney-Ryan administration would have moved full steam ahead with the classical liberal/neoliberal agenda of deregulation and privatization and any rhetoric we heard during this presidential campaign that sounded like they were interested in anything else should have been taken skeptically.

Democracy

When classical liberals/neoliberals think of democracy, they think of the autonomous individual acting in his/her own interests in the marketplace. In other words, for classical liberals/neoliberals, democracy is a system of government that promotes free markets. Democracy protects the individual's right to act in his or her own interests in the market. According to classical liberals/neoliberals, a democratic society will free up individuals to

---

1. For a full presentation of Hayek's theory, see Friedrich A. von Hayek, *The Constitution of Liberty* (Chicago: University of Chicago Press, 1960), and Friedrich A. von Hayek, *The Road to Serfdom* (Chicago: University of Chicago Press, 1944).

earn as much money as possible and to use that wealth for their own interests. It will keep the state small and require the individual to cede money and power to the state only for purposes to maintain order. People earn their money and should be allowed to keep it; they will spend it more wisely than the state can. Classical liberals/neoliberals argue that when millions of individuals act in their own individual interests, the sum total of their decisions will lead to the most fair, most equitable, and most democratic society possible.

Freedom and Liberty

What American is not in favor of liberty and justice for all? But do we mean the same thing when we so pledge our allegiance to these values? Probably not. The terms *freedom* and *liberty* are often used interchangeably in both ordinary and philosophical usage. For most people, most of the time, freedom and liberty refer to the *absence of constraint*. In this sense, it means that there is nobody restraining or prohibiting a person from thinking, saying, or doing what she or he would like to think, say, or do. But, as discussed in Chapter 8, there is another sense of freedom and liberty: one that recognizes that there is a difference between absence of constraint on the individual (sometimes called liberty) and the individual's actually having the power to act when unconstrained.

For classical liberals/neoliberals, the one major role that the state must play in a democracy is to insure individual liberty (i.e., negative freedom). When classical liberals/neoliberals speak of freedom, they mean the government "staying out of people's lives." As long as you are not disrupting the order necessary for the stability of the market or harming other people's property or person, you should be permitted to do whatever you wish. This is what led candidate Rand Paul (the son of presidential candidate Ron Paul and the junior senator from Kentucky and a likely contender in the 2016 Republican presidential primary) to state his belief that the 1965 Civil Rights Law erred when it required restaurants and motels to serve African Americans. From his classical liberal/neoliberal position, the law interjected government into the orderly process of the market. Paul believes that such interference is tyranny because it interferes with merchants' individual liberty (i.e., negative freedom). He is not concerned with making sure that the African Americans, who might not be permitted to eat at these establishments, did not have the positive freedom to eat wherever they wanted to. As long as the government was not the one telling them they could not eat at those restaurants or stay in those motels, Paul is fine with it. Paul's thinking is that in the long run, these merchants would act on their own to racially integrate their establishments because it was in their economic interests to do so and Hayekian economics assumes that people will act in their own rational self-interest. No government interference was necessary, he insists. Listen to or read this interview with candidate Rand Paul (www.npr.org/templates/story /story.php?storyId=126985068) and notice how he makes a distinction between what he calls "institutional racism" (by which he means racism in government—later in this book I will define this term quite differently), which is the part of the civil rights act he supports, and his attempt to avoid admitting in his belief that the 1964 Civil Rights Act should not have also applied to private businesses. In the same interview you can hear him advocating against the Americans with Disabilities Act (ADA) and the Environmental Protection Agency (EPA) using the same reasoning. In May 2011, once again showing clearly his classical liberal/neoliberal ideology, Senator Paul argued that requiring emergency rooms to provide service to those who could not pay was equivalent to turning doctors into slaves. He argued that doctors would not need the government requiring them to do so because doctors' Hippocratic oath would lead them to freely choose to serve these patients.[2] In these examples we can see how classical liberals/neoliberals understand liberty (and freedom) to refer mostly to protection against government constraint on the individual and show their understanding that the freedom that they are concerned about is of the negative kind.

Justice

The above discussion should make it clear that while Americans are likely to commit to the idea of liberty, they can mean quite different things when they do so. This is also true of justice. The idea of justice is actually even more complex than the idea of liberty. In the modern history of Western ethics, justice has typically been asserted as the fundamental moral principle preceding other moral principles such as benevolence and love. While it is certainly true that history has presented many who disagree with the preeminence of justice, it is also true that there are many more advocates of an ethics based on justice than on all other foundations combined. Given that 2,500-year history, you should not be surprised to learn that there are dozens of different concepts as to what "justice" might actually mean, so any attempt to reduce this complex philosophical debate to a simple typology may actually be oversimplifying. But one way to simplify in order to clarify distinctions between these ideologies is to see to what extent an ideology commits to individual justice or to social justice. While it is important to realize that all of the major American liberal democratic ideologies believe in both individual and social justice, just as they believe in both a public and a private sphere, nonetheless, some ideologies seem more interested in one than the other.

Because of the classical liberal/neoliberal support for a larger private than public sphere, we should not be surprised to find that classical liberals/neoliberals tend to emphasize individual justice over social justice. Just to be clear, however, classical liberals/neoliberals do support social justice in the public sphere; it is just that they shrink the public sphere to as small a space as possible resulting in a greater interest in individual justice because it is primarily in the private sphere. Return to the interview with Rand Paul mentioned above. In his discussion of the 1964 Civil Rights Law, Paul repeatedly explains that he is opposed to institutional racism. Paul's use of this term is unique and idiosyncratic, but it is clear from his usage that he means "government-supported racism" and it is equally clear that Paul is firmly opposed to such racism in the public sphere. Wherever government has a legitimate concern (where it is, in Paul's mind, legitimately "public" and not "private"), Paul considers social justice to be relevant. But, when we enter into private space, Paul privileges individual justice.

While there are many approaches to individual justice, one of the most prevalent approaches made by classical liberals/neoliberals is to focus on what is referred to as "just desserts." This ethic basically argues that the goods of society (power, wealth, status) should be distributed to people based on their worth. The more a person contributes, the more she/he deserves. How do we determine what a person is worth to society? According to classical liberals/neoliberals, we let the market decide. Your wealth represents your worth to society.

---

2. www.politico.com/news/stories/0511/54769.html.

The more you are worth to society, the more your individual worth as measured in wealth; the less you are worth to society, the less your individual worth as measured in wealth.

Classical Liberal/Neoliberal Rhetoric

Ideologies are promoted less by philosophical reasoning and more through persuasive rhetoric. Being able to recognize the rhetorical devices that ideologies use can help the reader of texts grasp more fully what an author might be advocating, but getting hold of the relevant indicators can be difficult. Once again keep in mind that all of the major ideologies will claim to advocate for liberty, justice, equality, equity, and democracy, so when a text uses one of these words, the careful reader will dig underneath to figure out what is really meant.

Classical Liberal/Neoliberal Narratives. Hopefully, the reader of this text has been able to recognize some of the rhetorical devices utilized by classical liberals/neoliberals. Perhaps the most obvious cultural narrative is Market Fundamentalism (see Chapter 4). Market fundamentalism tells a story of an America built on the competition of free-market capitalism leading to the richest, most advanced, and most powerful nation in history. This narrative suggests that the success that the United States has had historically is primarily due to its economic traditions rather than to its democratic traditions. Or, perhaps more accurately, that the democratic traditions of the United States are primarily about creating free-market competition and growing wealth, so to the extent that the historic success of the United States is due to its democracy, it is because its democracy was limited to making sure that private rights and marketplace freedom were its highest concerns. The good guys are the entrepreneurs and the hardworking business leaders who create jobs and capital. The bad guys are the government bureaucrats who spend other people's money and get a fat paycheck and unfair pension with unions that protect uncaring and lazy government workers such as teachers.

Warning: Don't confuse all criticisms of government as invoking market fundamentalism. Market fundamentalism blames government for problems because it assumes that government is *inherently* unable to solve problems well. Others may argue that government officials may be creating a problem or may not be solving a problem but not just because they work for government but because they are misusing the government apparatus to serve the interests of the very wealthy or the corporations. This is a different narrative, which does not blame government itself, but those who control government. This other narrative assumes that if we put a different set of hands in control, the government will be part of the solution and no longer the problem.

While market fundamentalism is a prominent contemporary narrative, its ascendance is relatively recent. This is the basic narrative that Barry Goldwater used in his unsuccessful bid for president in 1964 when Lyndon Johnson won in a landslide rejection of this rhetoric. Even among whites in the American South, who were still feeling the bite of the federal government's injection into schooling through *Brown v. Topeka Board of Education,* the antigovernment narrative did not find legs. While this story was not particularly persuasive in 1964, the 2010 midterm elections were centered primarily around this narrative and swept classical liberals/neoliberals into Congress and into state legislatures and governors' offices.

There is, however, another important cultural narrative utilized in the rhetoric of classical liberalism/neoliberalism, one that might go unnoticed if the reader is not attuned to it and one that has been a strong part of American culture since its beginning. This more subtle narrative is Individualism (see Chapter 4). This narrative suggests that people are both capable and obligated to be autonomous, to make up their own minds without influence from family and cultural groups, to make their own decisions, to stand on their own two feet and take the consequences of their choices. If a person has talent, works hard, and has good morals, he or she will succeed. In this narrative, anyone in America can make it, and those who don't succeed have only themselves to blame. The heroes of this narrative are the "self-made man," especially the business tycoons, like Bill Gates and Oprah Winfrey. The villains in this story are those people on welfare and Medicaid who are like leeches sucking the blood from their host. The narrative of Individualism is implicit in the classical liberal/neoliberal assumption that government should not provide support for those in need (except temporarily in emergencies). The basic thought is that programs such as welfare, affirmative action, and antihate laws only work to encourage the lazy to not do what they should be doing—that is, what they should do is to shut up and work hard and be grateful for the opportunity.

Classical Liberal/Neoliberal Tropes and Narratives.   The narratives of Market Fundamentalism and Individualism are evoked in the ideographs and tropes of classical liberalism/neoliberalism. Back in Lyndon Johnson's day, to speak of government was to speak of the good guys, the ones who are there to work in the interest of the people against the special interests of greedy corporations. Today the term *government* is invoked as an ideograph by classical liberals/neoliberals to represent all that is wrong with America. This is why many advocates of classical liberalism/neoliberalism will speak of "government schools" rather than "public schools." By replacing the word *public* with *government,* classical liberals/neoliberals can substitute a negative ideograph for a more neutral term and evoke the whole Market Fundamentalism narrative.[3] They also use the ideograph "bureaucrat," which always refers to a "government bureaucrat" even though there are at least as many corporate bureaucrats as government bureaucrats. During the recent health care debates, classical liberals/neoliberals railed against government bureaucrats getting between you and your doctor. The possibility of insurance company bureaucrats getting between you and your doctor was not seen as a concern.

Another ideograph frequently appealed to is "choice," but, for classical liberals/neoliberals, choice always means market choice—consumer choice. Everything is assumed to be a consumer product and, therefore, the market is the best place to allow consumers to choose.

We can see many of these rhetorical devices picked up and used by classical liberals/neoliberals in their texts on education. Think about their problem for a minute. Given that a record number (nearly 80 percent) of parents of public school students believe that their children are getting a good education in their school, how do you convince them to dismantle public schools and turn them over to the private sector?[4] One way is to continually tell the story of failing schools with poor lazy teachers (i.e., government workers) who are

---

3. For a good exemplar of classical liberal/neoliberal rhetoric, see Jonah Goldberg, "Do Away with Public Schools," *Los Angeles Times,* June 12, 2007, www.latimes.com/news/opinion/commentary/la-oe -goldberg12jun12,0,6103226.column.

4. William J. Bushaw and Shane J. Lopez, "A Time for Change: The 42nd Annual Phi Delta Kappa/ Gallup Poll of the Public's Attitudes toward the Public Schools," *Kappan* 92, no. 1 (2010): 9–26, www.pdkintl .org/kappan/docs/2010_Poll_Report.pdf.

overpaid and underworked and are protected by their unions so that tenure protects these lazy, uncaring teachers and prevents school administrators (i.e., management) from hiring good, enthusiastic young teachers. How do we solve the problem? We get rid of unions, give top administrators the power to fire anyone they think might not be doing a good job, and test students to collect data to make those decisions. You create charter schools (still public but they can be for-profit) to create market-based competition. You claim all of this is necessary to promote democracy and fairness and equality since those terms mean private-sector markets, negative liberty, and individual just desserts.

Classical liberalism/neoliberalism peppers its rhetoric with business tropes so that schools are businesses, and students are consumers, and test scores are "the bottom line" (itself a metonymy for profit). In the eyes of classical liberalism/neoliberalism, turning education into a consumer product and turning public schools over to the private sector as quickly as possible is the best way to build a strong education system.

Social Conservatism (aka the Religious Right)

Whereas classical liberalism/neoliberalism has a clear intellectual lineage, social conservatism has developed as an ideology from many different sources, but those who think of themselves as "conservative" on social issues do share certain values and rhetoric even when they differ in other areas.

Public/Private

Like classical liberals/neoliberals, social conservatives are also generally skeptical of government influence in the economic sphere, but they tend to pick and choose where government should and should not be involved in the private sphere. Essentially, social conservatives believe that government should be involved in imposing socially conservative beliefs in the public sphere, but should not impose what they would see as liberal beliefs. By "socially conservative," they generally mean what they consider to be *traditional values, wholesome values, family values,* or *American values.* Of course, each of these terms is really an ideograph that picks and chooses what is traditional, wholesome, family, American, and what is not. But you could probably name many of the values that they advocate. They typically oppose abortion, sex education, premarital sex, gay marriage, gay adoption, drug culture, highly sexualized media, and any presentation of self that seems to challenge the norm such as outlandish tattoos, piercings, and haircuts. If we can take the public utterances of the 2012 Republican primary candidates as an indicator, social conservatives have moved beyond advocating against abortion and are now advocating against birth control, since all major Republican presidential candidates signed or publicly supported the "personhood" pledge, which, by defining life to be at conception, means that anyone using birth control that prevents a fertilized egg from becoming implanted in the uterus would be guilty of murder. Social conservatives tend to advocate for abstinence education, church attendance, prayer in school, public Christmas displays, patriotism, the military, and gun rights. While many people question whether or not these positions are "traditional," "wholesome," "family-friendly," or "American," social conservatives appear to have little doubt that such is the case.

The issue as to the relationship between public and private is a bit more confusing with social conservatism. Whereas religion is considered to be in the private realm, social conservatives often argue that the cultural history of the United States makes it perfectly legal to allow some aspects of religion to move into the public sphere. Primarily they advocate the public space be open to the display and expectations of broad Judaic-Christian traditions and often specifically Christian traditions. While they agree that the government has no right to require people to practice any particular religion in their private spheres, they do think, that in public space, Americans should be expected to honor Christian religious traditions. Public schools should have Christian holidays off everywhere and they should be named after the holiday: not Winter Break, but Christmas Vacation; not Spring Break, but Easter Vacation (and it should be over Easter). If there are large numbers of students from a non-Christian church at a particular school then it might be permissible to have those Jewish or those Hindi days off from school as well; but generally, social conservatives tend to argue that there are common Christian traditions that ought to be honored in public.

In addition, they argue that many traditionally Christian beliefs and values form the basis of American culture. For example, many argue that the Ten Commandments are the basis of American law and, therefore, should be displayed in all public buildings especially court houses, legislative buildings, and schools. Their belief that certain specifically Christian beliefs have a legitimate place in public space requires them to advocate for legislatures to oppose the imposition of the beliefs of other religions in public space. For example, some social conservatives have argued that Sharia law should be illegal in the United States. Of course, progressives argue no such law is necessary because the American Constitution already bans such practices—even of Christian beliefs.[5]

Social conservatives also wish to enforce their understanding of decency and morality in public spaces; so, for example, in 2012, the state of Florida passed a bill making illegal the inappropriate display of underwear (apparently to discourage "sagging"). Texas prohibits sex education in the public schools unless it is abstinence only. Some Missouri State Representatives have proposed a bill that "Prohibits the discussion of sexual orientation in public school instruction, material, or extracurricular activity except in scientific instruction on human reproduction" therefore banning any discussion of sexuality beyond reproduction including the likely banning of words such as homosexuality, gay, and lesbian.[6]

While having much sympathy with the classical liberals/neoliberals about shrinking government in general, when it comes to social issues, social conservatives often argue that it is desirable for religious beliefs to be inserted into public space, if there are large numbers of adherents and if the traditions of the country support such beliefs. But on the other hand, they also argue that it is inappropriate for the state to insert itself into the private lives of individuals. So, according to social conservatives it is acceptable for Christian organizations to enter public schools to teach abstinence education, but it is not acceptable for people to be

---

5. Andy Barr, "Oklahoma Bans Sharia Law," *Politico*, November 3, 2010, www.politico.com/news /stories/1110/44630.html.

6. Barbara Liston, "Florida Lawmaker Hands out Belts under Saggy Pants Ban," Reuters, August 30, 2011, www.reuters.com/article/2011/08/30/us-florida-saggypants-idUSTRE77T60Y20110830; Mark Agee, "Texas Teens Most Likely to Learn Abstinence in Schools, Become Young Mothers," *Star-Telegram*, September 22, 2008, www.star-telegram.com/2008/09/22/925604/texas-teens-most-likely-to-learn.html; HB 2051, Missouri House of Representatives, http://house.mo.gov/billsummary.aspx?bill=HB2051&year=2012&code=R.

forced to accept Christian organizations into their homes. In the same way, the government should not insert itself into people's economic lives except to regulate sin such as Sunday sale of liquor and control of pornography. Taxes should be low. People should be permitted to own and carry guns.[7]

Religion

As a group, social conservatives tend to be more highly religious than others. They attend church more and they are more likely to attend an "orthodox" church. This would include many (though not all) evangelical fundamentalist Protestant Christians, traditional Roman Catholic and Eastern Orthodox Christians, orthodox Jews, and orthodox Muslims. Probably the most influential of these groups are the large conservative evangelical fundamentalist Protestants who argue that the United States was "founded as a Christian nation" and that the Ten Commandments should be displayed in all schools and public buildings; but social conservatives also include a high number of conservative Catholics in their number particularly around the issues of abortion and gay marriage and they are less likely to appreciate the Ten Commandments being displayed in public buildings because they fear that it would be the Protestant version of the Commandments that would be posted rather than the Catholic version.[8]

But just because the largest supporters of the ideological social conservatism are Christian adherents does not mean that all Christian believers are social conservatives. Certainly the still large mainstream Protestant and Catholic parishes promote many socially progressive policies, particularly those that work to take care of the poor. Not even all evangelical Protestant churches support the social conservative ideology as described here. There is a large and growing progressive evangelical movement that advocates the direct teachings of Jesus as the primary basis of their religion, which, they believe, require them to work in the interests of the poor, for peace, for the protection of the environment, and against the death penalty, and make them more inclined to sympathize with the plight of oppressed people including gays and lesbians who wish to marry (all issues associated with liberals). So, while the social conservative movement is fueled by conservative religions, don't make the mistake of assuming all religious people are social conservatives. There is a long history of progressivism in America's religions as well.

Still, while many religious Americans are liberal in their ideological commitments, the social conservatives have been the group most closely associated with an evangelical and fundamentalist Christian Protestantism. It is this ideological group that has brought a new focus on politicians' religious beliefs so that we find most major politicians compelled to swear their moral rectitude is based on a Judaic-Christian morality. This group tirelessly advances as "family-friendly" issues that are consistent with their religious beliefs. They are the group most likely to demand prayer in school, the posting of the Ten Commandments in all public buildings, and the continued inclusion of "under God" in the American Pledge of Allegiance.

---

7. SB 17, State of Ohio 129th General Assembly, www.lsc.state.oh.us/analyses129/11-sb17-129.pdf; Hannah C. Bealer, "Bill Would Allow Guns on Campus, in Church," *Springfield News-Sun*, June 22, 2011, www.springfieldnewssun.com/news/news/local/bill-would-allow-guns-on-campus-in-church-1/nMsNZ/.

8. To compare the Protestant and Catholic versions of the Ten Commandments, see "The Ten Commandments," *The Catholic Bible*, www.catholicbible101.com/thetencommandments.htm.

Democracy

When social conservatives appeal to democracy, they are likely to be speaking to their right to worship as they see fit and what they see as their right to not have to witness in public spaces behavior that is incongruent with their conservative values or to have to allow their children to hear views counter to their parents' views. And they should never have to tolerate their children being required to experience spaces that are not consistent with what they consider to have good family values. Social conservatives also advocate the advancement of democracy outside the United States and their strong patriotism leads them to believe that a strong military is necessary to defend democracy.

Freedom and Liberty

Social conservatives tend to favor liberty (i.e., negative freedom) except when the failure to intervene might lead to inappropriate moral license. They are likely to argue that the government has no right to constrain a person's behavior unless that behavior is so morally inappropriate as to offend public propriety. At one time, of course, this meant any kind of sexual activity outside the mainstream practices, but today social conservatives are much more likely to accept such unusual sexual activity as long as it is behind closed doors and windows and is not presented in public space such as the media. Evangelical Protestant Christian social conservatives might support a kind of positive freedom in what many believe is their Christian duty to bring the teachings of Jesus to those who are not believers. Without having been exposed to these teachings, many believe, a person does not have the positive freedom necessary to live a moral life. But beyond this form of positive freedom, most social conservatives focus more on negative liberty than positive freedom. Internationally, social conservatives are often strong advocates of advancing democracy in non-Christian nations in order to permit the minority Christians within those nations the religious liberties they have in the United States.

Justice

Social conservatives tend to think of justice in terms of the individual's right to worship and practice their faith. They have been active in demanding the right for prayer in school and other public venues. They strongly wish to maintain "under God" in the Pledge of Allegiance. Foreign policy is often formed around addressing religious tyranny in other nations. Perhaps the primary issue of justice for social conservatives is what they define as "the right to life." Social conservatives often assert that "life begins at conception," which means that a human zygote should be considered a human being with all of the rights of a human being. This is contrary to the decision of the US Supreme Court, which ruled that such recognition of human rights does not begin until "viability" (the ability of a fetus to survive outside its mother's womb).[9] Social conservatives argue that the Court was guilty of placing a woman's "right to choose" above a fetus's "right to life."

---

9. For a full discussion of viability and other aspects of *Roe v. Wade*, see William R. Hopkin Jr., "*Roe v. Wade* and the Traditional Legal Standards Concerning Pregnancy," *Temple Law Review* 47 (1974): 715–738.

Social Conservative Rhetoric

As with the above discussion of classical liberalism/neoliberalism, the rhetoric of social conservatism has already shown its colors in this chapter. Ideographs such as "right to life," "freedom to worship," and "family values" should be obvious. But social conservatives also use the term *conservative* itself as an ideograph. In the name of conservatism, they frequently claim things that have not been considered conservative in the past. For example, American conservatism used to be known for its commitment to stay out of foreign entanglements, especially wars. This is one reason World War I began in 1914, but the United States did not enter until 1917, only one year before its conclusion. And while World War II began in 1939, the United States did not enter until the 1941 invasion of Pearl Harbor. While the war in Iraq was clearly promoted by neoconservatives (the next ideology to be discussed in this chapter), the rhetoric that was used to convince the American public to go to war evoked many social conservative ideographs. Clearly the images and words that promoted fear of terrorism particularly when attached to radical Islam appealed to social conservatives. So too was the basic patriotic appeal to defend our nation after September 11, 2001. Much of this rhetoric was used to convince social conservatives that the invasion of Iraq was a "conservative" act. More than either of the other two conservative ideologies, social conservatives claim the term *conservative* as their own.

In the same way, social conservatives have turned the term *liberal* into a negative ideograph. To accuse one's opponent of being a "liberal" is one of the major ideographs used by self-proclaimed conservative politicians. Part of the strategies found in Republican primaries and by Republican candidates in general elections is to find ways to claim that they are the "conservative" candidate, and their opponent is "liberal." Simply attaching those words to candidates apparently sways some social conservative (and, perhaps social liberal) voters. And, of course, social conservatives regularly claim that there is a "liberal bias" in the press.

Not surprisingly social conservatives draw upon a number of traditional narratives. Some of the prominent narratives presented in Chapter 4 used in social conservative rhetoric include American Exceptionalism, the American Jeremiad, and the Good Wholesome Middle-Class [Family]. We also find social conservatives take up the Minority as Victim narrative by pointing to what they consider "angry blacks" or "angry feminists," but also by turning it around and claiming that they, the numerical majority Christians, are the oppressed minority. Some important narratives appealed to by social conservatives that were not mentioned in Chapter 4 include the America Is a Christian Nation narrative discussed earlier; the God Created Man as Head of the Family and any other traditional family narrative, such as the Evils of Drugs and the Evils of Sex narratives; and any of the narratives found in the Bible, especially the Genesis, Jesus Son of God, and the Apocalypse narratives.

While most social conservatives are strongly offended when accused of being racists, their critics claim that their rhetoric is filled with "code words," (i.e., ideographs) and narratives that appeal to those with racial and ethnic prejudices. Think of the continuing promotion of the birther narrative that claims that Stanley Anne Dunham gave birth to her son, Barack Obama, in Kenya while her parents dishonestly published a birth announcement in the Hawaiian newspapers in order to make it possible to claim her son to be an American citizen. Forget the fact that a child born of an American mother anywhere in the world can claim American citizenship, the fact that such a story has been promoted about the only

African American to be president appears to many to be appealing to racist beliefs. We hear claims that President Obama is a Muslim, that he has sympathies with his father's attraction to the Mau-Mau rebellion against the British, and that he is really a secret socialist-fascist. These are all rhetorical devices likely to appeal to racists and since their logic has no basis, critics argue that we must assume that this kind of rhetoric is promoted to appeal to the racist beliefs that many people still hold.

Look at the rhetoric that some of the major social conservative politicians have used to address the issue of immigration. First of all, should we call the people "illegal immigrants" or "undocumented workers"? Progressives argue that the term *illegal* is inappropriate because these workers have not actually broken laws, but rather they have violated administrative rules put into place by the government bureaucracies charged with enforcing the laws. Social conservatives are having none of that. They consider such nuance irrelevant and choose to call the immigrants "illegal" rather than "undocumented."

Also, notice the way social conservatives label any program as "amnesty" that is designed to help these illegal or undocumented immigrants obtain legal status. Listen to some of the rhetoric used to describe these illegal or undocumented immigrants that accuse them of a disproportionate percentage of crime. Arizona's Governor Jan Brewer and Senator John McCain have publicly promoted the narrative that immigrants are engaging in violent crime. On television Brewer told Arizonans, "Our law enforcement agencies have found bodies in the desert either buried or just lying out there that have been beheaded." And on the floor of the US Senate, McCain claimed, "The government's failure to secure the border has led to violence—the worst I have ever seen." These narratives are promoted even though there is no evidence to support them.[10] Whether the individuals using this rhetoric are themselves prejudiced or not is not the point because their rhetoric appeals to the prejudiced among us while appearing to be neutral to those who are not prejudiced. Such rhetoric makes those who use it vulnerable to the kinds of criticism leveled against them, but it is important to remember that prejudice and racism are not inherent in social conservatism. Those who are socially conservative need to distance themselves from such rhetoric, or they may find themselves criticized for their failure to do so. Many suggest that President Obama's reelection and the gain of Democrats in the Senate in the 2012 election was a direct result of people being disturbed by this kind of rhetoric.

Neoconservatism (aka Foreign-Policy Conservatives)

Neoconservatism is a narrow but influential part of the conservative coalition. It is primarily interested in foreign policy, but it does speak to important domestic issues including education. Neoconservatives differ from classical liberals/neoliberals in that neoconservatives believe in a strong government presence—particularly in the use of the military and surveillance. Whereas classical liberals/neoliberals wish foreign policy to be led by economic interests, neoconservatives advocate a foreign policy led by military strength (and action when necessary). Historically neoconservatives have differed from social conservatives in that they

---

10.   Karina Salazar, "Nogales Border Safe, Open for Business, Residents Say," *Arizona Daily Sun*, April 18, 2011, http://azdailysun.com/news/state-and-regional/article_3525eaea-ddc2-5dfa-bfe8-416f62666692.html.

are often quite progressive on many social issues. They are particularly uncomfortable with the social conservative focus on orthodox religions and its heavy Christian emphasis (many prominent promoters of neoconservatism are Jewish); however, they are often dismayed by what they see as an increase in the "vulgar" in society, which leads them to sometimes form an alliance with religious conservatives. Neoconservatives sometimes differentiate themselves from classical liberals/neoliberals and from progressive liberals by suggesting that neoconservatives like "strong government," not small government or big government. The influential neoconservative, Irving Kristol, wrote, "People have always preferred strong government to weak government, although they certainly have no liking for anything that smacks of overly intrusive government."[11]

Neoconservatives represent the military-industrial complex in America and, as a result, have great power in Washington, DC. Some of the best known political advocates of neoconservatism are former Republican presidential nominee Senator John McCain, former Democratic vice presidential nominee Senator Joseph Lieberman, and former vice president Dick Cheney. According to Ari Berman, a contributing writer to several progressive magazines and blogs, there were no natural neoconservatives in the 2012 Republican presidential primary, which apparently suggested to the candidates that the neoconservative votes were there to be taken by the candidate who showed himself or herself most willing to aggressively employ America's military. Berman pointed out that prominent neoconservative John Bolton was one of Romney's major advisers and suggested that Bolton would have been a top candidate for secretary of state if Romney had won. Berman wrote, "Bolton is one of eight Romney advisers who signed letters drafted by the Project for a New American Century, an influential neoconservative advocacy group founded in the 1990s, urging the Clinton and Bush administrations to attack Iraq."[12] Given the prominence of the neoconservative advisers combined with Romney's own statements on foreign policy, there is every reason to believe that neoconservatives would have had as much influence in a Romney administration as they did in the George W. Bush presidency. As Berman stated it,

> If we take the candidate at his word, a Romney presidency would move toward war against Iran; closely align Washington with the Israeli right; leave troops in Afghanistan at least until 2014 and refuse to negotiate with the Taliban; reset the Obama administration's "reset" with Russia; and pursue a Reagan-like military buildup at home. The *Washington Monthly* dubbed Romney's foreign policy vision the "more enemies, fewer friends" doctrine, which is chillingly reminiscent of the world Obama inherited from Bush.[13]

But neoconservatives still believe that we are in a unique period of world history in which the United States is the only remaining superpower and if we fail to take advantage of this power imbalance to advance our interests and the interests of democracy, we do so at our own peril.[14]

---

11. Irving Kristol, "The Neoconservative Persuasion," *The Weekly Standard* 8, no. 47 (August 25, 2003), www.weeklystandard.com/Content/Public/Articles/000/000/003/000tzmlw.asp?nopager=1.

12. Ari Berman, "Mitt Romney's Neocon War Cabinet," *The Nation*, May 2, 2012, www.thenation.com /article/167683/mitt-romneys-neocon-war-cabinet#axzz2dYnzIDvs.

13. Ibid.

14. Kristol, "The Neoconservative Persuasion."

Whereas today, neoconservatives are more likely to identify with the Republican Party, their roots are in the Democratic Party. In the early 1970s, when the Democratic Party was taken over by the antiwar faction of the party led by George McGovern, the pro-defense wing felt pushed out. Known then as "Scoop Jackson Democrats," named after the senator from Washington who was their most important advocate, these pro-military Democrats believed that America's foreign policy had to be led by a strong military. They argued (and still argue today) that the world is a dangerous place and the spoils will go to the victor. There is no place for weakness. Strongly anticommunist in the 1960s and 1970s, they were (and are) strongly pro-Israel. Today they remain equally vigilant against any potential military threat against American interests with a focus on the Middle East and Islamic terrorism. Having felt abandoned by the Democratic Party under McGovern, many eventually found a home in the Republican Party of Ronald Reagan.

Domestically, neoconservatives tend to be supportive of cutting taxes to create economic growth but their hearts do not lie in these issues.[15] In education, they advocate for a national curriculum to standardize and promote a common culture. They are particularly interested in the teaching of history and are often in the forefront of battles over social studies curriculums and textbooks. Their best known domestic advocate is former vice president Cheney's wife, Lynn Cheney, who was the chair of the National Endowment for the Humanities from 1986 to 1993, which gave her a powerful position from which to influence the teaching of history in American schools.

Earlier I mentioned that in 1964 the American voters soundly rejected the classical liberalism/neoliberalism of Republican Barry Goldwater. What changed from then until now that has brought classical liberalism/neoliberalism to its present prominence? Well, one thing was the work of Ronald Reagan, who forged a successful coalition of three very different ideologies under the umbrella of "Conservatism" and the Republican Party. Despite some very real and significant differences among classical liberals/neoliberals, social conservatives, and neoconservatives, they have forged a relatively successful coalition. Republicans have had problems getting elected when that coalition breaks down. For example, it can be argued that George H. W. Bush failed in his reelection bid because, as a classical liberal/neoliberal, he failed to connect with social conservatives. His son, George W. Bush, was able to solve that problem by becoming a born-again Christian and loudly proclaiming it. Combined with his classical liberal/neoliberal roots, he embodied two of the three ideologies in his own being. In selecting neoconservative Dick Cheney as his vice presidential running mate, Bush was able to secure the third ideological group. After assuming the presidency, Bush charged Cheney with staffing the departments of the federal government and Cheney filled the Department of Defense with neoconservatives. Men like Donald Rumsfeld, Richard Perle, and Paul Wolfowitz ran the Department of Defense with a neoconservative ideological strategy. Some claim that they engineered the war on Iraq as a way to bring democracy to the Middle East and, hopefully, create a friendly neighbor for Israel. They were important architects of the Bush administration's "War on Terror," including the 2001 Patriot Act that led to expansion of the surveillance of Americans including the legal right to obtain library records, new rules on wiretapping and tracking banking transactions leading to the expansion of the National Security Agency (NSA). The act also permitted indefinite detention of American citizens, enhanced border security,

---

15. Ibid.

and a host of other antiterror tactics. This act also required all schools to share their student records with military recruiters and to permit recruiters onto their campuses.

Public/Private

One of the important differences between neoconservatives and classical liberals/neoliberals is that neoconservatives argue that there is a public interest in maintaining defense to such an extent that it is acceptable to violate the private rights of individuals whenever there is a compelling reason to do so. The Patriot Act and its subsequent renewals have provided for unprecedented government intrusion into formally private space. The tracking of library records, monitoring of bank transactions, mining electronic communications, indefinite detention and the suspension of the right of habeas corpus (one of the original rights incorporated in the Magna Carta), assassination of Americans without the benefit of trial, all reflect the neoconservative belief that public interest for safety outweighs any private interest. The flap in 2012 when airport security began full-body x-rays is an example of how neoconservatism belies the more traditional conservative value of limited government by advocating the right of security officers to either x-ray you or give you a full-body frisk. That so many people saw this as an example of "liberal" intrusion of government shows just how confused many people are. This intrusion of the state on our bodies is congruent with neoconservatism, not any of the so-called liberal ideologies. Representative Ron Paul, a classical liberal/neoliberal and candidate in the last several Republican presidential primaries, soundly attacked the neoconservative agenda of foreign wars[16] and domestic surveillance[17] clarifying the ideological differences between the two ideologies' positions on the relative importance of the public and the private.

Democracy

Neoconservatives advocate for the creation and protection of democracies in other nations through military intervention if necessary, though covert military options are generally preferred. Neoconservatives often equate democracy with capitalism, so when they advocate for democracy in other nations, it means that they are advocating for capitalism as well. The United States has admittedly forcefully removed at least fifteen heads of state since 1890.[18] Neoconservatives generally understand these covert actions as unfortunate, but necessary in a dangerous world. The heart of the neoconservative ideology is their strong advocacy of military intervention in the Middle East as a way to bring capitalist democracy and, therefore, peace to that region and the world.

Freedom and Liberty

A neoconservative concept of freedom or liberty is more difficult to squeeze into our positive/negative concepts of liberty. Neoconservatives will argue vehemently in favor of negative

---

16. See www.youtube.com/watch?v=DGeC5fjpHUo.

17. See www.lewrockwell.com/paul/paul295.html.

18. Stephen Kinzer, *Overthrow: America's Century of Regime Change from Hawaii to Iraq* (New York: Times Books, 2006).

freedom. Individuals and nations must be free of coercion from others, but to achieve that, negative freedom will require the coercion of undemocratic states to bring them into a democratic freedom. Perhaps in a similar way to social conservatives who favor negative freedom except when issues of public morality are concerned, neoconservatives favor negative freedom except when matters of defense of democracy and capitalism are concerned. As mentioned above, neoconservatives are also quite willing to use the government to advance certain domestic cultural interests such as fighting against pornography and the drug culture and, so, on some domestic issues we find the neoconservatives and the social conservatives calling for strong government action in ways that many classical liberals/neoliberals may consider inappropriate.

Justice

As with liberty, a neoconservative understanding of justice may not be easily captured in the dichotomy between individual and social justice. With a strong commitment to the right of Israel to exist in peace, one could argue that neoconservatives are primarily interested in social justice. But, their primary goals for military intervention in the Middle East and elsewhere seem to be aimed more at creating stable democracies where individual justice can flourish; and so, it could be argued that their true commitment is to individual justice. Like many other issues, neoconservatives take a pragmatic approach to complicated issues and recognize the need to walk a fine line between social and individual justice.

Neoconservative Rhetoric

The Sylvester Stallone *Rocky* movies are an excellent example of one of the primary narratives utilized by neoconservatives. The first *Rocky* movie centered on a once-promising, now down-on-his-luck and over-the-hill boxer named Rocky Balboa who is plucked out of obscurity for a fight with the reigning heavyweight champion in order to give the champ an easy, big box office. Many of us love these kinds of underdog stories that *Rocky* taps into. Despite having everything against him, through shear willpower, Rocky wins and becomes champion of the world and a Hollywood franchise is born. Through six movies we see the same cultural narrative told with only the surface narrative changed. Of particular interest for us is the way in which the storyline is so easily translated into the patriotic 1985 *Rocky IV*, in which we see Rocky, who represents the United States, battling Ivan Drago, who represents the Soviet Union. Filled with patriotic tropes, we demonize "Communist Russia" while cheering on the "good ol' USA" to victory. Of course this narrative also appeals to social conservatives with their strong patriotic commitment, but the neoconservative ideology is not only patriotic, it celebrates the destruction of our enemy through physical force. In fact, this narrative of the lone, misunderstood, silent, but strong and good hero who goes after the bad guys even if he has to cut corners while everyone else just pussyfoots around is the stock of many Hollywood movies. Think Harry Callahan (*Dirty Harry*), John McClane (*Die Hard*), Jack Bauer (*24*), John Hartigan (*Sin City*), and half the detectives on the screen or on television. These are tough guys who stand between the evil of the world with all its dirty "realness" and the illusion of goodness that ordinary people assume makes up the world. Our heroes are the men ("real men") who take a beating and keep on going back for more, who fight evil with justified violence to make life safe and good for the rest of us. Obviously without these heroes willing to violate social niceties, there would be no civilization left. It would collapse into the chaos of evil.

Of the narratives discussed in Chapter 4, neoconservatives often use American Exceptionalism and Balkanization as the cultural narratives that underpin their texts. American Exceptionalism tells the story of the United States as the best, the most moral, and the greatest nation in the history of the world. We are the exception. While they may argue that the United States becoming the most powerful and only superpower in the world was an accident of history, it was an accident that we should take advantage of.[19] We should be allowed to invade other countries because we only do so for good reasons. (Since the 1890s the United States military has been involved in at least 131 foreign military interventions and, as mentioned above, has been involved in, at least, fifteen successful removals of heads of state.)[20] American Exceptionalism tells us that our federal constitutional republicanism with its three branches of government and its two-party system is the best in the world, much superior to the parliamentary systems of other democratic nations. Our sports and athletes are the best in the world. Our culture is superior to all others. At one time, our public schools were the best in the world and that their superiority is no longer the case is a shame that we must erase, or, according to neoconservatives, the rest of the world will crush us.

In order to avoid this last event from occurring we must do what it takes to compete with the world in education, and this can only occur if we get those test scores up above those of the students in China, Japan, Germany, and all the other nations whose students outperform ours on international tests and who someday might use all of that learning to defeat us.

The other narrative assumed by neoconservative texts, Balkanization, accepts as fact the idea that diversity brings weakness. By permitting differences to remain, we will allow a cleavage that can be used against us and make us weak. As Abraham Lincoln stated, "A nation divided amongst itself cannot stand."[21] This narrative and its ideographs and tropes are picked up and used by neoconservatives as they argue against multicultural education and against any social studies curriculum that they believe promotes a multicultural narrative, especially in the US history textbooks and state curriculums.

A Couple of Other Conservative Economic-Political Ideologies

Since Reagan, there has been a concerted effort to create the illusion of a single Conservatism, but, in reality, it is an uneasy coalition of at least three different ideologies. John McCain, a neoconservative, selected Sarah Palin, a social conservative, as his running mate in an attempt to bring those two wings of the coalition together. Unfortunately for McCain, Palin upset the classical liberal/neoliberal wing of the party to such an extent it led many of them to vote for Barack Obama. The Tea Party is a loose and ever-evolving movement that has been known primarily for advocating for the reduction of the federal debt by cutting taxes and reducing

19. Kristol, "The Neoconservative Persuasion."

20. Zoltan Grossman, "From Wounded Knee to Libya: A Century of U.S. Military Interventions," http://academic.evergreen.edu/g/grossmaz/interventions.html; see also Kinzer, *Overthrow*.

21. Abraham Lincoln, "A House Divided against Itself Cannot Stand," June 1858, www.nationalcenter.org/HouseDivided.html.

government spending. Many people claim credit (and are assigned blame) for starting the movement, including followers of the conservative libertarian Ron Paul, the wealthy Koch brothers, conservative bloggers, longtime antitax activists, and even the tobacco industry. Whoever got the movement started, it was originally designed to harness the true believers to work in the interest of classical liberalism/neoliberalism in order to take back the Republican Party from the neoconservative/social conservative coalition that they believed had led to the loss of the presidency to Obama. In a very surprising move, social conservatives, led by the power of FOX News, conservative talk radio champions such as Glenn Beck and Michelle Malkin, and social conservative politicians such as Sarah Palin and Michele Bachmann, infused the movement with social conservatism leading us to an uneasy coalition of strong supporters of social conservatism and classical liberalism/neoliberalism but *not* particularly wedded to neoconservative ideas. After the 2012 Republican Party debacle at the national level, we began to see a split within the Republican Party between the true-believer Tea Party Republicans and the more pragmatic Republicans, who are willing to compromise their ideological commitments for some real material successes. The Tea Party shutdown of the federal government in the fall of 2013 appeared to have support from both factions within the Tea Party and with the rest of the Republicans in Congress until the possibility of government default became real. While the social conservatives within the Tea Party were apparently okay with the possibility that an American default on its loans might send the world economy into free fall, the classical liberals/neoliberals within the Republican Party, including those within the Tea Party, appeared less sanguine about such an action. Classical liberalism/neoliberalism maintains that government should be small, but those small roles are crucial. A government default would violate one central principle of classical liberalism: the maintenance of a stable and well-functioning free market. Whether the Tea Party coalition within the Republican Party of true-believer classical liberals/neoliberals and social conservatives can survive will be interesting to see.

One also hears a lot about an ideology called *libertarianism*. At the present time, libertarians tend to be seen as conservative and align very closely with classical liberalism/ neoliberalism. Libertarians have a strong commitment to radically small government. Like classical liberals/neoliberals, they wish to get government out of the economy and turn as much as possible over to the market. In fact, as mentioned above, some argue that the Tea Party was started by followers of libertarian Ron Paul. However, unlike classical liberals/ neoliberals, many libertarians are interested in getting government out of people's personal lives too, especially around social issues. These are sometimes referred to as liberal libertarians and have been the primary support for legalizing marijuana and other issues around lifestyle. So, there is a large overlap between libertarians and classical liberals/neoliberals, but the two ideologies are not exactly the same.

CHAPTER ELEVEN
Political-Economic Ideologies
The Progressive Coalition

A Coalition of Progressive Ideologies

Whereas the conservative ideologies focus (with some exceptions) on narrowing the public sphere and expanding the private sphere, progressives (with some exceptions) focus on expanding the public sphere and narrowing the private sphere (see Figure 11.1). In other words, whereas conservative ideologies typically favor capitalism over democracy and the right of the dominant religions and dominant concepts of family to organize public space, such as advocating prayer in school and opposing gay marriage, progressives favor democracy over capitalism and the protection of minorities from the imposition of majority doctrines through religious-based decisions in schools, such as prayer in school, abstinence-only sex education, or the teaching of "intelligent design" in science classes.

One important reminder: both conservative and progressive ideologies are committed to having both public and private spheres. Once advocates of a conservative ideology reduce the public sphere to little more than support for a free marketplace, they have moved beyond the traditional American commitment to liberal democracy and can be called corporatists. In other words, for conservatives to remain within the historical American commitment to liberal democracy, there must be room for a public sphere that goes beyond merely serving the interests of the corporations. In a similar manner, once advocates of a liberal ideology advocate reducing the private sphere to little more than serving the public interest, they have also moved beyond the traditional American commitment to liberal democracy and can be called socialists. On the other hand, today the American ideological continuum (at least among public figures) is more heavily weighted to the right side than the left. It is true that today's American politicians have quite a few among them who come pretty close to corporatist ideological positions but their counterparts on the left barely exist in elected office. Even Bernie Sanders, the Independent Senator from Vermont, who calls himself a "socialist," doesn't come close to socialism as defined here. He is really a "social democrat" and fits squarely within the liberal-democratic middle. The difference between liberals and

PUBLIC	PRIVATE

Figure 11.1 In General, Liberal Ideologies Claim to Favor a Wider Public Sphere

conservatives in the United States lies primarily in which side is stressed—the public or the private—not which is eliminated. This makes politics in America much more centrist and narrow than politics in other nations around the world, which nearly all have a wider band of ideological influence in their politics.

The differences that exist among the so-called liberal or progressive ideologies lie either in how narrow to make the private sphere or what particular aspects of the private need to be made public. The three progressive ideologies to be discussed in this section include progressive democracy, the New Democrats, and social democracy.

Each will be discussed in terms of public/private, the meaning of democracy, the meaning of freedom and liberty, and the requirements of justice. As with the last chapter, this one will also explore some of the rhetorical devices such as narratives, tropes, and ideographs favored by each of the ideologies.

Progressive Democracy

When most Americans use the term *liberal*, they are referring to what in this book I call "progressive democracy." Progressive democracy promotes the interests of minority social groups and identity issues combined with Keynesian economics. Others might call this "liberal democracy," but since that is the term that I use for all major American economic-political ideologies, using it for this particular ideology would be too confusing, so I have opted for the term "progressive democracy."

Public/Private

Progressive democrats advocate an increase in the public sphere and a decrease in the private sphere in certain areas, while arguing for strong protection of the private sphere in other areas. Progressive democrats are best known for their advocacy of culturally "liberal values." These so-called liberal values are promoted as the mirror opposite of what social conservatives call family values.

In the areas of *cultural norms,* the two ideologies, progressive democrats and social conservatives, both seem to advocate for an increase in the public sphere on some issues and an increase in the private sphere in other areas—they just reverse those areas.

Whereas social conservatives advocate for *expanding the public sphere* in such issues as legally restricting the concept of marriage to a contract between "one man and one woman," progressive democrats advocate for allowing marriage to *remain a private matter* between couples and, therefore, permitting marriage between couples of any sex. Whereas social conservatives wish to expand the public sphere through advocating for a "traditional family" therefore advocating to prohibit gays and lesbians from adopting children, progressive democrats advocate for increasing the private sphere by permitting families to define themselves and, therefore, permitting gays and lesbians to adopt. Whereas social conservatives wish to expand the public interest to include individual behaviors by forbidding individuals to engage in certain practices such as certain sexual acts, nudity, pornography, prostitution, doctor-assisted suicide, and medical marijuana, progressive democrats wish to defend the private rights of adults to smoke pot, engage in whatever sex they choose to, watch what they desire, and have the right to choose to die.

On the other hand, social conservatives wish to expand the private sphere to permit the practice of religion in public schools including the reading of the Bible, the saying of prayers, and the posting of the Ten Commandments, while progressive democrats wish to restrict the practice of private religion in public spaces. Social conservatives also wish to expand the private right for people to own guns of any sort and for them to use guns as they see fit. The 2011 Ohio law that permits people to carry guns into bars and other locals that serve alcohol such as bowling alleys and football stadiums is an example of this social conservative ideological expansion of the private sphere.[1] Progressive democrats, however, argue that there is a line that is crossed from private to public under some circumstances. At the moment, for example, progressive democrats wish to maintain the prohibition to carry guns into college classrooms, which promises to be the one area that the social conservative gun lobby is likely to attempt to expand gun rights.[2]

At other times, social conservatives and progressive democrats merely assert different private rights to be protected. For example, social conservatives have claimed that the "right to life" is a private right that belongs to fetuses and that must be protected from the public law as interpreted by the US Supreme Court (which defines personhood—the recognition of being a person under the Constitution—as beginning at viability rather than conception); while progressive democrats advance the idea that a woman's "right to choose" what happens to her own body is a private right that must not be infringed upon. Notice in this case, both sides claim to be defending a private right from the encroachment of the public. Most recently some social conservatives, such as Rick Santorum—a candidate in the 2012 Republican presidential primary—advocate amending the Constitution to declare life and citizenship to begin at conception, thereby turning abortion for any purpose at all into murder. The legislature of the state of South Dakota recently declared life to begin at conception by proposing a state constitutional amendment to be voted on in 2014.[3] In fact, since some birth control pills work by preventing the implanting of the conceived zygote to the uterus, such a "personhood amendment" would appear to turn certain forms of contraception into murder as well. It would also appear to outlaw in vitro fertilization since after conception, only some of the zygotes are implanted in the mother and the rest are "discarded."

While social conservatives argue that the health of a fetus is a matter for the public, they tend to argue that the issue of health for children is a private matter left to parents. Some progressive democrats, on the other hand, while insisting on a woman's right to choose an abortion, claim that children have the right to health care and protest against capital punishment. (This is one of the major dilemmas for many Catholics because while the Catholic

---

1. "Ohio Governor Signs Law Allowing Guns in Bars," Reuters, June 30, 2011, www.reuters.com /article/2011/06/30/us-ohio-guns-idUSTRE75T7BX20110630.

2. Hannah C. Bealer, "Bill Would Allow Guns on Campus, in Church," *Springfield News-Sun,* June 22, 2011, www.springfieldnewssun.com/news/news/local/bill-would-allow-guns-on-campus-in-church-1 /nMsNZ/; also see John Eligon, "A State Backs Guns in Class for Teachers," *New York Times,* March 8, 2013, www.nytimes.com/2013/03/09/us/south-dakota-gun-law-classrooms.html?src=rechp&_r=0&gwh=C1C25 D9FAFE19C4CF086A1AF54E6F06A.

3. "North Dakota Lawmakers Approve Measure That Could Ban Abortion," Reuters, March 22, 2013, www.reuters.com/article/2013/03/22/us-usa-abortion-northdakota-idUSBRE92L19Z20130322.

Church speaks very strongly against abortion—a social conservative position—it also speaks very strongly for the caring of the poor and the abolition of the death penalty—a progressive democrat position.)

Progressive democrats may be best known for their advocacy of minority rights. They support the expansion of public rules that prohibit discrimination on the basis of race, ethnicity, gender, sexuality, and disabilities. They advocate for finding a way to permit immigrants who are in the country without proper documents to be treated in a manner that makes it possible for them to remain in this country, if they serve some kind of penalty first for their improper immigration. This is particularly so for parents who have children who were born in this country and have grown up in this country, and for children who were brought to this country by their parents and have grown up in the United States and know nothing of the land of their birth. The so-called Dream Act, a bipartisan bill introduced to Congress in 2011, would

> permit certain immigrant students who have grown up in the U.S. to apply for temporary legal status and to eventually obtain permanent legal status and become eligible for U.S. citizenship if they go to college or serve in the U.S. military; and would eliminate a federal provision that penalizes states that provide in-state tuition without regard to immigration status.[4]

Progressive democrats are skeptical of turning over public institutions to the private sphere in the name of efficiency and competition. Progressive democrats are likely to suggest that the private sphere is interested in meeting their private interests and whenever their private interests conflict with the public interest, private firms will serve their own private interests and abandon those of the public. Private corporations should not be given public entities such as public schools, prisons, waterworks, military operations, and highways because as private entities, they assume that they are required to maximize profit rather than to serve the interests of the public.[5]

Religion

Even though social conservatism is better known for its religious adherents, in fact, progressive democrats have long attracted committed churchgoers as well. For example, religious leaders played a large part in the civil rights movement of the 1960s and the antiwar movement of the 1960s and 1970s. While mostly associated with mainstream Christian churches and reform Jews, there is a strong and growing progressive movement within fundamentalist Christian churches as well. As mentioned in the last chapter, progressive fundamentalist Christians tend to speak to the teachings of Jesus, as reported in the Bible, as the highest

---

4. "Dream Act: Summary," National Immigration Law Center, May 2011, http://nilc.org/dreamsummary .html.

5. Maxwell S. Kennerly, "*Ebay v. Newmark*: Al Franken Was Right, Corporations Are Legally Required to Maximize Profits," *Litigation & Trial*, September 13, 2010, www.litigationandtrial.com/2010/09/articles/series /special-comment/ebay-v-newmark-al-franken-was-right-corporations-are-legally-required-to-maximize-profits/.

statement of their moral foundation and these teachings, they argue, call for the need to take care of the poor and the sick and the forsaken. They teach people to turn their cheek when struck by their enemy and require the rich to give away their wealth to those in need. They require that we love our neighbor. For a growing number of evangelical Christians, the teachings of Jesus require them to support progressive democracy.

Democracy

When progressive democrats talk of democracy, they imagine a public arena where a wide variety of interests is fairly represented. Progressive democrats are "big-tent democrats." They believe that democracy demands that minorities have their rights protected; but more than just having their rights protected, they must also have a place at the table. Even well intended people are blind to their own prejudices and privileges and so, in order to guarantee fair decision-making, progressive democrats argue that we must make sure that there is a fair representation of different groups among those empowered to make the decisions. Anytime those making public decisions appear to represent a narrow part of the population, progressive democrats are skeptical. For this reason, progressive democrats tend to support some form of affirmative action for members of minority groups. Democracy works best when its leaders represent the wide range of interests.

Progressive democrats are also committed to transparency in decision-making. Open meetings and open records are an important mechanism for maintaining that transparency. While recognizing that there are times in which decisions and acts must be kept secret, many progressive democrats believe that there is far too much secrecy in government. While they might not all be supportive of the vast and indiscriminate release of classified documents that WikiLeaks (www.wikileaks.ch/) has produced, one thing is clear to progressive democrats: much of what is classified top secret is merely being kept secret from the voters and protecting the personal interests of the politicians, military, public bureaucrats, and corporate leaders, and are not really serving the public's interest.

For progressive democrats, democracy requires that the strong and the successful nurture the needy and protect the weak. Progressive democrats seem to take seriously the oft-stated idea that the strength and quality of a democratic society can be found in how the society treats the least amongst them. They tend to be appalled that the United States permits more than 50 million of its citizens to remain without health insurance[6] (which is greater than the total population of Spain[7]). To progressive democrats, that the richest nation on earth has a higher child mortality rate than at least forty-nine other nations is evidence that democracy is far from being achieved in the United States.[8]

---

6. "Income, Poverty and Health Insurance Coverage in the United States: 2009," United States Census Bureau, September 16, 2010, www.census.gov/newsroom/releases/archives/income_wealth/cb10-144.html.

7. "Spain," *The World Fact Book 2013–2014* (Washington, DC: Central Intelligence Agency, 2013), www.cia.gov/library/publications/the-world-factbook/geos/sp.html.

8. "Infant Mortality Rate," *The World Fact Book 2013–2014* (Washington, DC: Central Intelligence Agency, 2013), www.cia.gov/library/publications/the-world-factbook/rankorder/2091rank.html.

Freedom and Liberty

While progressive democrats do favor the protection of many negative freedoms (see the above discussion on public/private), they are also strong advocates of assuring positive freedoms. Typically, progressive democrats advocate for forms of affirmative action that require public organizations to take steps to make sure that women and racial and ethnic minorities are given a fair chance to get a job or promotion and to gain acceptance to good public schools. From the progressive democrat perspective, affirmative action has been misrepresented in the popular press. Affirmative action, they argue, has never been intended to give unfair advantage to minorities, only to make sure that the playing field is fair and that organizations engage in outreach and procedures that guarantee such fairness.

One of the clear areas of distinction between progressive democrats and classical liberals/neoliberals and their social conservative coalition colleagues lies in the understanding of what it means to advocate for freedom in education. In order for the poor to achieve the freedom they deserve, the conservative ideologies advocate an understanding of liberty that turns public schools over to private entities such as charter schools and voucher plans. In other words, the conservative ideologies argue that the way for the poor to have freedom is for them to be given the chance to choose a charter school or given a voucher to help them afford to pay for their children to attend a private school. For the conservatives, positive freedom requires us to give economic support to those with less economic means so they can participate in the private sphere. For progressive democrats, however, such an attempt will never work because charters and vouchers always favor those with more money and more education to take advantage of these programs. Instead, progressive democrats advocate equal funding of public schools. Progressive democrats are the ones to bring court challenges in many states to require the state to live up to what they believe is the state's constitutional requirement to provide for equal education. For example, in 2002, for the fourth time, the Ohio State Supreme Court ruled unconstitutional the way in which Ohio public schools were funded, yet the state legislature all but ignored its state's court and changed its funding very little, leaving a wide disparity in school spending across the state.[9] In fact, in Spring 2013, Ohio Governor Kasich introduced a new school funding formula that increases the state support for the wealthier districts and reduces it for the poorer districts.[10] In a similar manner to Ohio, in 2012 the Washington State Supreme Court declared that the state's funding of public schools was unconstitutional.[11] In 2014 we are still waiting to find out how the Washington State legislature will respond.

---

9. Jim Siegel and Joe Vardon, "15 Years—No School Funding Fix," *Columbus Dispatch,* March 25, 2012, www.dispatch.com/content/stories/local/2012/03/25/15-years—no-school-funding-fix.html.

10. Nolan Rosenkrans, "Kasich Funding Formula Favors Suburban Schools; TPS, Other Urban Districts, Mostly Flat under Governor's Plan," *The Blade,* February 8, 2013, www.toledoblade.com /Education/2013/02/07/Kasich-funding-formula-favors-suburban-schools-TPS-other-urban-districts-mostly -flat-under-governor-s-plan.html.

11. "*Mcleary v. State of Washington,*" *Hot Topics: Current Education Issues in Plain Language,* Office of Superintendent of Public Instruction, 2013, www.k12.wa.us/Communications/HotTopics/HotTopic-McCleary .pdf.

Justice

Progressive democrats do favor equal opportunity, but believe that a true democracy will result in a fair distribution of goods and power and so point out that one way to know if we have real equality in opportunity is if there is evidence of equality in results. For example, conservatives may claim that in the United States every child has the equal opportunity to an education. After all, they argue, every child can attend a public school and if they work hard and have the ability, they will succeed in school and be able to find a good job and succeed in life. But progressive democrats have for decades pointed out that the children of the poor are not well served by the public schools and so there must not be real equality of opportunity because if there were, then the outcomes would be more equal. Part of the reason for the bipartisan support of President Bush's "No Child Left Behind" act was its emphasis on outcomes as a measure of success of schooling for the poor combined with a promised massive increase in funding of schools for children living in poverty. Unfortunately, from the progressive democrat view, NCLB never really provided the funding promised and figuring out how to determine educational outcomes has proven difficult.

Of course, conservatives (especially classical liberals/neoliberals) have argued that the solution to this problem is to turn education over to the private marketplace and let the consumer decide what works and what does not. But, as has already been pointed out, progressive democrats argue that such privatization of education does not serve justice because it will only lead to the increase in wealth of the corporations who make a profit off of these schools while not improving education for the poor. Instead, progressive democrats argue that the solution is to provide equal funding and equal education in public schools that serve the interests of the public rather than corporate profits.

Keynesian Economics

While progressive democrats are best known for their commitment to "liberal values," equally important to their ideology is their commitment to Keynesian economics, an economic approach they believe is more fair and more just than the approach advocated by classical liberals/neoliberals. From the presidency of Franklin D. Roosevelt until that of Ronald Reagan, Keynesian economics was the dominant economic ideology in the United States. Progressive democrats point out that during this time the United States had the longest period of economic expansion in its history while dramatically expanding the middle class and reducing poverty. During this time, the United States achieved the greatest equality in its history. Since the abandonment of Keynesian economics, they also point out, the United States has surpassed its past record of greatest inequality and it has seen two enormous economic collapses (the savings and loan crises of the 1980s and 1990s and "The Great Recession" of today).

Keynesian economics argues that left unregulated, as classical liberalism/neoliberalism demands, the market will lead to greater inequality and it will also eventually lead to great economic crises. Progressive democrats argue that economic bad times such as the ones mentioned in the last paragraph, as well as the Great Depression of the 1930s, followed from the laissez-faire, hands-off economic policies that preceded all three collapses. Progressive democrats argue that the present collapse of our economic system results from thirty years of economic policy that favored classical liberalism/neoliberalism.

Of course, the United States did not switch overnight from Keynesian to classical liberalism/neoliberalism. As mentioned above, the last administration that was clearly guided by Keynesian economics was that of President Jimmy Carter, but it is also in his administration that we see the start of the return to classical liberalism/neoliberalism as economic policy. Progressive democrats might also point out that it was during the Carter administration that economic inequality reached its lowest point in American history. In other words, it was during the Carter administration that economic equality was greatest. So, in response to the classical liberal/neoliberal claim that their economic policies lead to the greatest equality, Keynesians simply point to the data, which, they claim, show that classical liberalism/neoliberalism really leads to the greatest inequality.

Beginning with the Reagan administration, the government swung strongly toward classical liberal/neoliberal economic policies and away from Keynesian policies. During the Reagan years, Congress began to change the tax structure and deregulate many businesses. As mentioned, there had been some deregulation under Carter—namely, transportation—but it was not until Reagan that deregulation became a prime goal of economic policy. From Reagan through the last Bush administration, this deregulation and change in tax policy accelerated, so that what was the greatest economic equality in American history during the Carter administration became the greatest inequality in American history during the George W. Bush administration and this inequality has continued to increase during the Obama administration.[12] According to progressive liberals, while the policies of classical liberalism/neoliberalism lead to accelerated economic growth (as occurred during most of the Bush administration) and that makes some individuals quite wealthy, these policies cannot be sustained, and they lead to eventual economic collapse to "correct" the economy. This is, according to Keynesians, what happened at the end of the Bush administration leaving the Obama administration to try to correct the great economic stress that classical liberal/neoliberal policies created. According to the Keynesian progressive democrats, we are still trying to correct for the bubble created in the hot economy of the George W. Bush administration.[13]

Progressive democrats also argue that rather than working to create more equality, classical liberalism/neoliberalism works to redistribute wealth upward, taking money from the poor and middle classes and giving it to the wealthy, therefore creating even greater inequality. This occurs because without regulation of the market by government, those who have the most power in the market are those with the most wealth and they begin to fix the game in their own interest. Government is needed, according to Keynesian economics, to balance the power. With government used to oversee and regulate the market, we can provide some protection against the wealthy taking everything. Progressive democrats point out that these predictions of Keynesian economics have been shown to be correct: without regulation, we get wild swings in the economy that lead to greater inequality. According to Keynesian progressive democrats, every period of strong laissez-faire, hands-off-the-economy government

---

12. Carol Higgs, "Plutocracy Reborn: Re-Creating the Gap That Gave Us the Great Depression," (Washington, DC: Institute for Policy Studies and the Public Good), reproduced in *The Nation*, June 30, 2008.

13. For the source of the national deficit broken down between Presidents Bush and Obama, see Teresa Tritch, "How the Deficit Got This Big," *New York Times Sunday Review*, July 23, 2011, www.nytimes.com/2011/07/24/opinion/sunday/24sun4.html?_r=2&partner=rssnyt&emc=rss.

has led to great accumulation of wealth by a few and great impoverishment of the many and eventual severe economic crises.

Progressive democrats generally support Keynesian economics and argue that government should be used to counter these big boom and bust cycles and smooth out the bumps and valleys by countering the direction of the economy. During boom times, government should promote monetary policy that slows growth down (such as putting the mechanisms in place to raise interest rates) and during bust times, government should promote policies that speed growth up (such as spending money even if it means borrowing it). The failure to follow such regular government regulation leads to the need for very large, massive government spending that even progressive democrats don't wish to spend—but they argue that in difficult economic times, such as now, such large government spending is necessary when laissez-faire policies have created such massive economic problems. In other words, progressive democrats argue that the reason the Obama administration and Congress must pour massive amounts of money into the economy now is because for the past thirty years and especially during the Bush administration, monetary policy did nothing to temper economic growth and that led to a boom economy with its inevitable financial collapse.

So, progressive democrats will argue that it is the classical liberal/neoliberal economic policies of the last thirty years that led to present economic problems. Beginning in the fall of 2008, even the extreme classical liberals of the Bush administration decided that massive intervention by the government was necessary to avoid a collapse so devastating that it would have been deeper and longer lasting than the Depression of the 1930s and, as a result, they pumped money into the economy as Keynesians argue must be done. Progressive democrats argue that the massive investment of government in the economy worked and prevented what would have been the most severe economic collapse in world history. Until recently, the government has been spending money and planning to spend more money to keep the economy from total collapse and a slow and mild recovery is in process. Progressive democrats would prefer to see even more government spending. The classical liberals/neoliberals of the Republican Party have argued vigorously for the opposite policy—which they call "austerity." In other words, they wish to balance the budget by cutting government spending.

Progressive democrats favor government intervention in the economy supported with strong oversight and regulation. *This is not socialism.* Socialism argues that government should own the companies and is less concerned about a distinction between good times and bad arguing that the market always works in the interest of the wealthy against those of the average person. Keynesians advocate that the government spend money when times are bad, but remain tight when times are good. And while they may support temporary government ownership of private companies in bad economic times, this ownership should only be temporary. As soon as the company and the economy are sound, the government should withdraw from any ownership of such companies. This is what the government has done recently with the automobile industry. They "bought" into Chrysler and General Motors to keep them from collapsing; but when the economy recovered sufficiently, the government began to sell its stock and actually made a profit while saving one million jobs and, according to progressive democrats, keeping the Midwest economy from total collapse.[14]

---

14. Jonathan Cohn, "The Bailout That Worked," Newrepublic.com, October 30, 2010, www.tnr.com /blog/jonathan-cohn/78781/obama-gm-detroit-auto-bailout-worked.

On the other hand, even in good times, progressive democrats will not want to go back to the hands-off, deregulation policies of classical liberalism/neoliberalism that they believe got us into this bad economic situation. Regulation allows the government to tamp down excessive economic growth to keep the ups and downs of the economy more steady and predictable. Progressive democrats will argue that today's government has to spend this massive amount of money to clean up the mess that was made by the classical liberal/neoliberal policies.

One other thing, progressive democrats also commit to a social liberalism that supports taking care of people whom the system excludes. They often argue that we all owe some support to people who are not employed or who are underemployed since we all benefit from their situation. Capitalism requires unemployed workers—it cannot survive full employment. Most economists think some unemployment is desirable.[15] For that reason, progressive liberals argue that we should support these people through the public sector (i.e., through government) with things such as schools, mass transit, health care, and welfare. This is especially true for children who have no responsibility for their poor economic situation. Furthermore, they also argue that certain groups have been systematically left out of the system and so the government must step in where the market fails to correct its exclusions such as in the areas of race, gender, sexuality, and disability.[16]

Finally, while progressive democrats advocate a free marketplace, they do not include the labor force as being just another consumer product in that market. Progressive democrats argue for strong protections for workers' rights including the right to unionize. Without strong unions, they argue, laborers are reduced to individuals in the market competing over who will work the most for the least pay, which results in no workers earning a living wage. The lack of workers earning a living wage not only hurts the worker and his/her family, it also hurts the economy because exploited workers do not have enough money with which to participate in the economy, which creates a downward spiral leading to economic collapse. According to progressive democrats, this is one of the problems with the present economy. As a result of thirty years of classical liberal/neoliberal policies, workers in the United States have lost their ability to influence their pay as a collective. The result has been that American workers have less money to spend in the marketplace, which has resulted in a slowing of the economy, which has dragged the economy downward for everyone. The only way out of this situation is to get money into the pockets of ordinary people so that they have enough money to spend and get the economy moving again and the best way to do that, according to social democrats, is to provide protections for workers to organize in their collective interests.

Progressive Democratic Rhetoric

Progressives, like conservatives, utilize rhetoric to try to win people's support. One major cultural narrative used by progressive democrats might be called There Is More to Life Than Money, in which it is told that "money doesn't buy happiness." In this story, those

---

15. To understand why, see Mike Moffatt, "Would 0% Unemployment Be a Good Thing?" About.com, http://economics.about.com/od/helpforeconomicsstudents/f/unemployment.htm.

16. For more information on Keynesian economics, see "What Is Keynesian Economics?" *WiseGEEK,* www.wisegeek.com/what-is-keynesian-economics.htm.

who pursue wealth become miserable people, while those who pursue relationships with others find happiness. If classical liberals/neoliberals ask everyone to act selfishly in their own self-interest in a free marketplace, the progressive democrats counter with the There Is More to Life Than Money narrative, whose theme asks everyone to act unselfishly and to "treat your neighbor as yourself."

We also find the use of a cultural narrative that we might call It Takes a Village. Understood to be an African aphorism, "It Takes a Village" was used by Hillary Clinton as the title of her book on the need for society to take joint responsibility for raising children.[17] The main plotline of this cultural narrative builds around the ways in which multiple persons play an important part in any individual's life. In this story, we are not islands of individuals, but are all in it together, and it will take us working together to get us out. We can see President Obama using this narrative in this excerpt from a campaign speech:

> There are no Democrats or Republicans during a storm, there are just fellow Americans: leaders of different parties working to fix what's broken; neighbors helping neighbors cope with tragedy; communities rallying to rebuild. A spirit that says, in the end, we're all in this together: that we rise or fall as one Nation, as one people.[18]

And former president Bill Clinton also drew on this cultural narrative during his speech at the 2012 Democratic Party Convention when he compared the Democratic Party with the Republican Party by saying, "We [Democrats] think 'we're all in this together' is a better philosophy than 'you're on your own.'"[19] The theme suggests we have a moral responsibility to take care of each other and especially of those who are most vulnerable and in need. As told in the It Takes a Village narrative, no one makes it solely on their own two feet. Everyone depends on others.

This is true of raising our children, but it can be true of anyone, including those who are quite different from ourselves. Rodney King's lament, "Can we all get along?" (expressed following the not guilty verdict of the police officers videoed beating him in 1992) expresses this idea well.[20] King's cry has become an ideograph for progressive democrats that appeals to their commitment to promote peace and to oppose war, racism, sexism, homophobia, and any action that treats violence as a solution to problems of human relations—including zero tolerance rules in schools. While most progressive democrats acknowledge that there are surely times when war and state-based violence are necessary, most appeal to their belief that people are basically good and so we must always be hesitant to use violence even against our enemies; and we must question carefully, and in fact be skeptical of, those who advocate the use of violence to advance their positions.

---

17. Hillary Rodham Clinton, *It Takes a Village: And Other Lessons Children Teach Us* (New York: Simon & Schuster, 1996).

18. Barack Obama, "Remarks at a Campaign Rally in Green Bay, Wisconsin," The American Presidency Project, 2012, www.presidency.ucsb.edu/ws/index.php?pid=102560.

19. Bill Clinton, "Transcript: Bill Clinton's Democratic Convention Speech," September 5, 2012, http://abcnews.go.com/Politics/OTUS/transcript-bill-clintons-democratic-convention-speech/story?id=17164662#.UNXPMY5Fu0s.

20. Rodney King, "Can We All Just Get Along?" YouTube video, 1992, www.youtube.com/watch?v=1sONfxPCTU0.

If conservative ideologies tend to evoke the Balkanization narrative discussed in the last chapter, progressive democrats utilize the Cultural Pluralism narrative and use the salad bowl trope to counter the melting pot metaphor of conservatives. Unlike a melting pot in which everything is melted together to become indistinguishable from each other, the contents of a salad bowl maintain their unique integrity while contributing to the goodness of the whole. The Cultural Pluralism narrative's theme embraces the idea that diversity is good and must be embraced and that everyone has a right to maintain and be proud of their own culture, including languages other than English and English dialects other than standard school English.

Progressive democrats have faith that humans are capable of creating a better future built upon new ideas, science, and discovery. Not surprisingly, progressive democrats often evoke the Progressive narrative (see Chapter 4) to appeal to the hope that all of us have for improving ourselves and our societies. For progressive democrats, science is an ideograph that is difficult to challenge. If scientists tell us that eating too much saturated fat is likely to lead to heart disease or that permitting the over consumption of soft drinks by children leads to diabetes or that second-hand smoke leads to cancer or that global warming is caused by hydrocarbons put into the air by human activity, who are they to question it? Such findings by professional experts are to be followed and used to improve our personal and social lives. It might mean banning all smoking in restaurants or banning Coke machines in schools or forcing restaurants to post the fat content of their meals, but since experts tell us that this is what must be done, progressive democrats are likely to take this as an ideograph and follow their directions, even if they never read or understand the basic research itself.

Progressive democrats evoke "corporate fat-cats" and "Wall Street" as metaphors for the villains in the growing economic inequality in the nation. The oft-quoted statement by Gordon Gekko that "greed, for lack of a better word, is good" might serve as an ideograph for progressive democrats and classical liberals/neoliberals alike except that for progressive democrats, the ideograph evokes strong negative emotions, whereas for classical liberals/neoliberals, it evokes commonsense.[21]

The New Democrats (Pragmatic Liberals, Moderate Liberals, Progressive Neoliberals, or Neoliberal Democrats)

Trying to come up with the best term to name this ideological group is the most difficult of these chapters because members of this group tend not to refer to themselves with an ideological label, but simply as "socially liberal and economically conservative," as "pragmatic," or as "nonideological." To the extent that they do use a label, it is frequently the New Democrats. The problem with New Democrat as a term is that it refers specifically to the Democratic Party and not clearly naming an ideology. I think perhaps the best term that could be used might be "pragmatic liberals" because the New Democrats often claim that they are just being pragmatic. We often hear President Obama say things like he doesn't really care how

---

21. For example, note this quotation from noted neoclassical ideologue Michael Novak: "Capitalism is a system built on belief in human selfishness; given checks and balances, it is nearly always a smashing scandalous success," in "A Closet Capitalist Confesses," *Washington Post,* March 14, 1976.

a goal is met as long as that goal is met. Some progressive democrats complain that the New Democrats seem willing to give up Keynesian economic principles and embrace neoliberal economics in the name of being pragmatic and moderate. The New Democrats' seeming embrace of a progressive democrat cultural agenda combined with classical liberal/neoliberal economic policies suggests that the term *progressive neoliberal* might most accurately describe their ideology. Unfortunately, no one actually uses that term and so while it might be the most accurate description of their ideology, its lack of use makes it less desirable as a label. Despite its shortcomings, in this chapter, I have reluctantly decided to use the most frequently used term, New Democrats, to name this ideological group for lack of a better alternative.

When George W. Bush first ran for president, he referred to his politics as conservatism with a heart. This ideograph was intended to counter the sense that classical liberalism/neoliberalism's focus on self-interest meant that conservatives didn't care about people. In a way, we might call the New Democrats as "liberalism with business sense" as a way to counter the idea that liberals don't care about business. Bill Clinton, the prototype New Democrat, was the one who made popular the term New Democrat. Tony Blair, who was the United Kingdom's version of Bill Clinton, called it the Third Way.

While clearly one of the important ideological wings of the Republican Party, classical liberalism/neoliberalism became an important ideological position within the Democratic Party with the founding of the Democratic Leadership Council (DLC) in 1985. Former president Bill Clinton is generally held out as the quintessential DLC New Democrat or "third-way democrat." These *moderate liberals* combine an economic classical liberalism/neoliberalism with some aspects of progressive democracy. Primarily, the New Democrats share the progressive democrats' concepts of democracy with their commitment to equity, fairness, and protection of minorities; but they also support the economic policies normally associated with the ideology of classical liberalism/neoliberalism that argues that markets should be as free as possible, the government should be as small as possible, and market solutions are always better than government solutions when possible. Simply stated, the New Democratic ideology combines the cultural values of the progressive democrats and the economic ideology of the classical liberals/neoliberals.

We see the influence of the New Democrats in the Obama health care law, which addresses the health care crisis without the government-funded, single-payer health care systems of countries like Canada, France, and Germany, which would be favored by progressive democrats. Instead, Obama picked up a health care plan advocated by the classical liberal/neoliberal think tank, The Heritage Foundation, and supported by Republicans as a classical liberal/neoliberal response to the health care problems of the nation. The Heritage Foundation's classical liberal/neoliberal response provides minimal regulations of the health insurance companies (such as requiring that they offer a plan for those with chronic illnesses and the ban against dropping people from their health care when they get sick) and, in turn, it created an individual mandate requiring all Americans to purchase health insurance from a private company creating an economic bonanza for the American health insurance industry. This plan was originally conceived by The Heritage Foundation as a conservative Republican response to the Clinton health care plan that failed to pass Congress during Clinton's first term. It is the same basic plan that Republican Mitt Romney, when he was governor of Massachusetts, pushed into law. That today's conservative rhetoric equates a classical liberal/neoliberal health care plan with socialism shows just how far rhetoric can distance itself from argument. And while the Obama administration legitimately points out that the health care plan has nothing to do with socialism, it has been less forthcoming in acknowledging that its plan is not really in line with progressive values either but instead reflects the same conservative economic values that were drawn upon by The Heritage Foundation in its creation.

We also see the influence of the New Democrats in the Obama administration's continuation of the educational reforms of the Bush administration that treat education as a consumer good. The Obama administration's embrace of the idea of education as a consumer good has led to their conclusion that the solution to education's problems is free-market competition. For this reason, Obama's Race to the Top education policy stresses evaluation of teachers using test scores and favoring charter schools, which are a mechanism for the privatization of public schools. Where the Obama education plan differs from the conservative alternatives promoted by the Republicans is that the Obama plan does not support vouchers that can be used to promote a religious education in parochial schools.

We also see that the Obama administration's economic policy has been placed in the hands of the same people that the Bush administration trusted. Like the Bush administration, the Obama financial team consists of Wall Street heavy hitters who believe that the primary goal of government is to take care of corporate interests in order for the economy to continue to provide the needed jobs and wealth of our liberal democratic society. The apparent use of Keynesian economic policies to bolster the economy during this recession is precisely the same steps taken by the Bush administration. Even the rabid classical liberal/neoliberal policy-makers in the Bush administration understood that in a period when the world's economic system was on the verge of collapse, government must do something to prop it up. We can be assured, however, that when, and if, the economy returns to a more stable growth, the Obama administration's financial team will argue for a market almost as free from regulation as the Bush administration sought.

The New Democrat Rhetoric

New Democrats tend to use the rhetoric both of progressive democrats and that of classical liberals/neoliberals. They promise equity for and protection of members of minority groups at the same time that they promote policies that make sure that the marketplace is allowed to operate with minimal regulation. New Democrats are likely to use progressive democratic rhetoric on cultural issues *and* classical liberal/neoliberal rhetoric on economic issues. For this reason it is easy to confuse them with one or the other side. Typically, social democrats consider New Democrats as simply "neoliberal," while classical liberals/neoliberals tend to view them as classic progressive democrats often leading to much confusion among the electorate who have come to believe, for example, that Bill Clinton was a classic progressive democrat, when it is clear from his record and his words that he shared the ideas of progressive democrats only on cultural issues, siding with classical liberals/neoliberals on economic issues such as the deregulation of industry, the elimination of welfare, and the promotion of free trade zones. It is this combination of progressive commitments in cultural issues and conservative commitments on economic issues that led many to consider the New Democrats as the middle-of-the-road ideology. For this reason, many consider the policies of President Obama to already be a compromise between the progressive and conservative interests of the American people. Any further compromise between the New Democrats and the Conservative coalition is, in their mind, not seeking a balance between progressives and conservatives, but tilting the field to the conservative side. Of all of the ideologies discussed in this book, the New Democrats may be the most difficult to identify.

Social Democracy

Social democracy is a form of liberal democracy strongly influenced by the extensive worker rights found in socialist ideals, but still advocating for a capitalist economy that is primarily in the private sector, with some important exceptions such as education and health care and some large industries. While social democracy is quite prevalent in European political dialogue, it hardly exists outside of a small group of scholars and activists in the United States. Only a few American politicians would fit into this category. Among national politicians, only Bernie Sanders, the Independent senator from Vermont, fits comfortably into this category. Not even former presidential candidate Dennis Kucinich seemed to represent a social democratic ideology when he was representing Cleveland in Congress. In other words, while social democracy contributes a strong voice in the political dialogue in the rest of the world, it is just a quiet whisper in American political discourse. The result is that to the rest of the world, the United States does not really have a "left wing" at all. From their view, our politics is decidedly conservative—even our liberals appear conservative to them. But, there is a growing social democratic voice and it is primarily found in the blogosphere where the social democrats have not been locked out as they have been by the newspapers and television and radio news. That voice is also heard on college campuses where a small, but vocal, set of professors is comfortable with social democracy.

Democracy

When social democrats speak of democracy, they focus on the need for all citizens to actually participate in decisions affecting the public realm. The emphasis on "participatory democracy" suggests that people ought to be making more decisions while lobbyists who represent corporate interests and the politicians they influence should be making fewer. When social democrats speak of free markets, they mean markets in which there are a large number of competing firms whose competition works in the interest of the consumer. When markets are reduced to just a few real players, then the market is no longer "free"; it is an oligopoly controlled by a few who make decisions that essentially work in their collective interests and against the interests of consumers and workers. When the sellers in a market become reduced to so few in number as to be oligopolistic, social democrats argue that the market should be broken up into smaller units creating more sellers, or the government should step in with regulations to protect consumers and workers, or, if necessary, the government should actually take over the industry, such as the Airbus consortium of European nations created to ensure that Europe maintains the capacity to build airplanes. Social democrats also argue that industries that are themselves fundamental to the public interest, such as education and health, should be either run by the government or the government should enter into the market with a subsidized product that works in the public interest of the community and individual rather than in the private interest of corporate profit (such as public broadcasting).

If classical liberals/neoliberals tend to define democracy in terms of free-market capitalism, social democrats tend to define capitalist markets in terms of democracy. While social democrats recognize the right of corporations, as private companies, to make the bulk of decisions about their business, they also recognize that corporations exist only through the people's will. Without the people represented by the government providing the charter to incorporate a company with some of the rights of individuals, no corporations would exist. While corporations enjoy the status of individuals in order to distribute the jeopardy of high-risk and expensive enterprises and encourage industries important to the nation, they are not people and do not have the moral conscience of people. For this reason, corporate charters tend to include a clause requiring corporations to work in the public's interest. Social democrats wish this clause to be enforced and argue that government or citizens should have a role in important decisions that affect the community. Since corporations are a quasi-public entity, they must be a quasi-democratic entity as well and, therefore, they must submit themselves to some form of democratic governance or oversight to protect the public's interest.

Freedom and Liberty

Social democrats tend to emphasize positive freedom whenever positive and negative forms come into conflict, at least, when referring to the protection of minorities and the promotion of participatory democracy. For example, in order to have a viable participatory democracy, individuals must be able to read, write, and analyze arguments. They must have the ability to articulate their own arguments and the courage to stand up and speak. They must also have the leisure time and the income necessary to make such public participation possible. If someone must work eighty hours a week at minimum wage just to make ends meet, we cannot expect that person to spend time gathering the information needed to understand basic public issues, let alone the energy to go to public events and make their position known. They may have negative liberty, but they do not have much positive freedom.

In today's world, social democrats suggest that positive power has been handed over to those with wealth. Social democrats point to the 2010 US Supreme Court 5–4 decision in *Citizens United v. Federal Election Commission* that held that corporations cannot have their spending limited in the independent funding of broadcasts in political campaigns. The court argued that corporations have been given the status of individuals and as individuals are protected by the first amendment, so, restricting the amount of money they spend on political campaigns violates their First Amendment rights. Social democrats see such reasoning as one more way in which individuals lack positive freedom in American elections unless they are wealthy. After all, no one is telling anyone that they may not contribute to political broadcasts for their favorite candidates; they, therefore, have negative freedom. But how many of us except for the very wealthy and corporations have enough money to produce a television ad and then to buy time for it on television? Social democrats are likely to argue that the Court went too far to the side of negative freedom. In order to guarantee corporations the negative freedom to speak, they have essentially eliminated individual human beings' exercising the positive freedom to speak.

Public/Private

Social democracy advocates the expansion of the public sphere and the shrinking of the private sphere. Unlike socialism, social democracy does believe in developing and maintaining a vibrant capitalist market economy, but it also believes that the mere regulation and monetary policies of Keynesian economics do not go far enough to keep the promise of equality and equity that a democracy requires.

Social democrats reject both classical liberalism/neoliberalism and Keynesian economics, although they are more sympathetic with the Keynesians than with the classical liberals/neoliberals. Social democracy advocates that government go further in intervening in the economic sphere than Keynesians, but not as far as socialists. As I am using the term, socialists argue for all but eliminating the capitalist economic sphere and replacing it with a socialist one in which the government controls nearly every aspect of the economy except for small, local markets (e.g., farmers markets and flea markets). Social democrats want to maintain a vibrant capitalist market where possible, but to socialize aspects of the economy where the capitalist market fails to self-regulate sufficiently to maximize equity and equality. For example, the public schools were created and are maintained and "owned" by the government because the private capitalist marketplace cannot, they argue, provide appropriate education for all children; and yet, democracy depends on a well-educated citizenry. According to the social democrats, the privatization movement promoted in the United States over the last forty years is a good way to guarantee that democracy is diminished. If we want a strong democracy, they argue, the schools must remain public.

Likewise, social democrats argue that the private capitalist health care system does not work for many people and it is just too expensive to maintain. Furthermore, the United States spends a higher proportion of its GDP on health care than any other nation, but has a poor record. In 2011, the United States spent 17.9 percent of its GDP on health care. France, which scores first in health care, spends only 11.6 percent of its GDP on it.[22] Social democrats argue that these data show that a government health care system is both better and less expensive than the US private, market-based system. As explained earlier in this chapter, President Obama's health care plan is a classical liberal/neoliberal marketplace solution and is, therefore, a private model and not a public model. Social democrats may have supported the plan, but only because it was better than no plan at all. As far as they are concerned, a single-payer, government-run plan is what is needed.

Social democrats demand a strong presence of the state in the economy, when it is necessary for the economy to promote steady and fair growth. For example, social democrats criticize the classical liberals/neoliberals who argued in the early days of this recession that we should just let the automobile companies and the banks fail. Like the Keynesians, social democrats argue that such a complete economic collapse would have had devastating effects

---

22. "Health Expenditure, Total (% of GDP)," The World Bank Group, 2014, http://data.worldbank.org/indicator/SH.XPD.TOTL.ZS.

on the economy for decades, let alone the unfair price it would place on individuals who had absolutely nothing to do with the unfair and unstable financial practices of the banks that the unregulated banking system created. But unlike the Keynesians, social democrats wonder why the government only steps in to protect the economy when a business is "too big to fail." They argue that if a business is too big to fail so that the people must step in whenever they are in financial problems and pick up their losses, the people should have a part in getting the profits of these companies when times are good. Social democrats ask why it is that the public should pick up the costs and private individuals get the profits? Social democrats argue that any company that is too big to fail should be owned by the public or the public should share in the ownership and have a place in the boardroom. On the other hand, businesses that are not so big that their failure would bring down the whole economy or whose business is not essential to the national interest should remain in a true, competitive, though regulated, marketplace. As it is now, with corporations as large as they are, social democrats argue, there is no real marketplace where different individuals compete, but rather a fixed game in which a few companies get all of the benefits while the rest of us take all the risks.

In this period of difficult economic times, social democrats point out that many of the strongest economies in the world, including Norway and Sweden, have long been influenced by social democratic ideology. In South America, social democrats point out, the only economies that seem to be growing (such as Argentina, Bolivia, Brazil, and Venezuela) are those that have abandoned the classical liberal/neoliberal policies thrust upon them by the World Bank, International Monetary Fund, and the World Trade Organization during the 1980s, 1990s, and early twenty-first century and that have moved toward social democracy instead. According to social democrats, the failure of the classical liberal/neoliberal economic policies in Latin America and the success of democratic socialism are one of the clearest examples of just how wrong classical liberal/neoliberal claims are.[23] In the United States, very few social democrats have risen to influential positions in government. Today only Senator Bernie Sanders of Vermont is a clear advocate of social democracy.

In the area of education, social democrats argue that if we ever wish to develop both a vibrant democracy and strong economy, the nation must return to the days following World War II through the early 1970s when it invested heavily in its public schools. To do this requires that the super-wealthy and the corporations pay taxes at a rate similar to what they paid in the 1960s, when our schools were providing a more equitable education than appears to be the case today. They suggest that if we were to return to the tax structure of the early 1960s, the nation's deficit would be retired in two years and then the nation could invest once again in good schools, affordable higher education, alternative energy, and upgraded infrastructure.

Justice

Social democrats advocate "social justice" as opposed to the "individual justice" advocated by some other ideologies. The *Citizens United v. Federal Election Commission* Supreme Court

---

23. Rajesh Makwana, "Neoliberalism and Economic Globalization," in *Share the World's Resources: Sustainable Economics to End Global Poverty* (London: Share the World's Resources, November 6, 2006), www.stwr.org/globalization/neoliberalism-and-economic-globalization.html.

decision discussed above is a good example of the conservative bias toward individual justice at the expense of social justice. The logic that a corporation is "an individual" and, therefore, must be protected from violation of their individual rights makes little sense to social democrats. Rather than protecting the individual rights of corporations, the Constitution should be interpreted as protecting the interests of the society and the individual rights of real people. The Court's decision essentially privileges one set of citizens (i.e., the super-wealthy) over another set of citizens (i.e., the rest of us). According to social democrats, that is an act of social injustice.

Social democrats advocate state legislatures adopt more equitable funding formulas so that children of the poor and the wealthy will be able to attend schools with a more equitable per pupil expenditure. They insist that schools must be funded in such a way that the children of the well-to-do are not given more educational privilege than the children of the less well-to-do. They point to the social democratic education system of Finland as the best example of how to provide socially just schools. To do anything else, they argue, is unjust.

Social Democratic Rhetoric

Unlike the other economic-political ideologies, Americans seldom fail to recognize the rhetorical devices of social democrats. This is probably because social democracy is not part of the commonsense of American conversation, and so the narratives, tropes, and ideographs stand out as "biased" and "political" even while the rhetoric of more accepted American ideologies often go unnoticed appearing to be "fair," "balanced," and "objective." This does not mean that social democrats are more biased than any of the others, but only that many of the other ideologies have been more successful in convincing the American public that their narratives represent the natural, commonsense way of the world. When an ideology looks neutral or unbiased to the majority, it may only indicate that it uses the biased language of the majority who fail to think their own stories are biased.

One of the major cultural narratives utilized by social democrats might be called Fragility of Democracy. This narrative suggests that the once strong democratic practices of the American experiment are dangerously close to extinction to be replaced by a corporatocracy that uses government to work in the interests of corporations and against the interests of the people. This corporatocracy uses the nation's military to fight wars to serve the interests of corporations (Chiquita and Dole in Central America, and the oil industry in the Middle East). It uses the patent system to protect large corporations against ordinary individuals such as agribusiness giant Monsanto who legally forbids family farmers to plant soybeans they raise instead of selling them for feed or food.[24] The rapidly growing corporatocracy, according to the Fragility of Democracy narrative, uses the schools to promote their products and requires schools to purchase their textbooks and tests.[25] Corporatism has taken

---

24. Suzanne Goldenberg, "US Supreme Court Rules for Monsanto in Indiana Farmer's GM Seeds Case," *The Guardian*, May 13, 2013, www.theguardian.com/environment/2013/may/13/supreme-court-monsanto-indiana-soybean-seeds.

25. For example, see Alex Molnar, *Giving Kids the Business: The Commercialization of America's Schools* (Boulder: Westview Press, 1996); see also Deron Boyles, *American Education and Corporations: The Free Market Goes to School*, Garland Reference Library of Social Science (New York: Garland, 1998).

over universities by imposing the "logic of neoliberalism" leading to the reduction of quality faculty (nationwide nearly 50 percent of all university courses are now taught by adjuncts) and the skewing of research to serve the interests of corporations (through the need to attract corporate sponsorship to make up for the reduction in state funding) and giving those corporations a say in who universities hire.[26] All of these examples help to keep the Fragility of Democracy narrative believable and an effective rhetorical device.

Social democrats frequently appeal to democracy and to social justice and to equity in a manner that may be as much the use of ideographs as rationally constructed concepts. *Democracy* (which means "participatory democracy") is always good. *Justice* (which means "social justice") is always desirable. *Equity* (which means fair distribution of wealth and power) always requires the wealthy and the corporations to give way to the ordinary people and the workers.

A Word about Socialism

Since the intent of this book is to help students learn to read educational texts that appear in the main outlets of American media and in the words and arguments of American politicians and educational policy-makers, the last two chapters have focused on conservative and progressive liberal democratic ideologies. As already mentioned, the American conversation in these outlets is narrowly limited to the ideological center and even leans heavily to the right. Many who advance the ideas of classical liberalism/neoliberalism come very, very close to crossing the line into corporatism, but among the American politicians, the popular press and other media outlets, there are few texts found that even come close to crossing the line into socialism. If we look at the main media outlets and at the words and narratives of politicians and policy-makers, the conversation about American education is decidedly to the right of center. On the other hand, on university campuses and other outlets of the academy, we can find a clear, vibrant, cogent, and regularly produced set of texts that advance socialism. To be clear, this contemporary American socialist movement is a radically democratic ideology. The authors of these texts are passionately interested in advancing social justice and its commitments to equality, equity, and fairness. If classical liberal/neoliberal advocates take as a fundamental principle that government inherently leads to tyranny, these democratic socialists argue just as strongly that capitalism leads inherently to oppression. As long as the economic sector permits the accumulation of very large concentrations of wealth in the hands of private individuals and corporations, these very wealthy people and corporations will use that wealth to accumulate more wealth even if that means the subversion of the public interest. According to these democratic socialists, the privatization of the public sphere, such as is being seen with the turn to for-profit charter schools and the defunding of public universities, can only lead to the increase of inequality and decrease of democracy. Perhaps the strongest American voices contributing to a socialist

---

26. Kris Hundley, "Billionaire's Role in Hiring Decisions at Florida State University Raises Questions," *Tampa Bay Times,* May 9, 2011, www.tampabay.com/news/business/billionaires-role-in-hiring-decisions -at-florida-state-university-raises/1168680.

conversation on education belong to Peter McLaren and Antonia Darder.[27] Both authors provide an excellent entry into this literature.

Conclusion

The coalition of so-called progressive ideologies is no more cohesive than that of the so-called conservative ideologies. If nothing else, the last three chapters make it clear that there is no such thing as a liberal or a conservative. Instead, these terms are used to represent several different ideologies. It is a mistake to think all Republicans are conservative in the same way for, in fact, there are some very important differences among them. It would also be a mistake to think that Democrats are all progressives in the same way. In fact, the most influential wing of the Democratic Party is economically nearly as conservative as those in the Republican Party and the other two have very important differences between them.

One important advantage that the progressive coalition has over the conservative coalition is that the progressives are more aligned on social issues than the conservatives. There are distinctions among the three progressive ideologies on social issues, but for the most part, when it comes to issues related to minority groups, identity issues, and moral questions, progressives are in more agreement than the conservative coalition. The conservative coalition has the social conservatives, whose name correctly suggests they are strongly conservative on social issues. It is also true that the moderate Republicans who were economically conservative and committed to classical liberal/neoliberal policies, but socially progressive, feel less and less at home in the Republican Party. Given the growing power of the New Democrats, many of these former Republicans have stopped identifying with the Republican Party and have started to vote for Democrats. The neoconservatives have generally been progressive on social issues since the days they were primarily in the Democratic Party. Other than issues related to immigration and multiculturalism/bilingualism, neoconservatives often side with positions more likely associated with progressives. Consider, for example, former vice president Dick Cheney, arguably the most influential neoconservative, has publicly supported gay rights.

To summarize, all six economic-political ideologies discussed in this book are committed to a strong and vibrant capitalist society (see Table 11.1). In American politics, few advocate

Table 11.1 Summary of Economic-Political Ideologies

	Ideology	Economic Policy	Sociocultural Politics
conservative coalition	social conservative	Hayekian	strongly conservative
	neoconservative	Hayekian	mixed
	classical liberal/neoliberal	Hayekian	moderately conservative
progressive coalition	New Democrats	Hayekian	moderately progressive
	progressive democrats	Keynesian	strongly progressive
	social democrats	moderate economic democracy	strongly progressive

27. For an example of McLaren's work, see Peter McLaren and Ramin Farahmandpur, *Teaching against Global Capitalism and the New Imperialism: A Critical Pedagogy* (Lanham, MD: Rowman & Littlefield, 2005); for an example of Darder's work, see Antonia Darder, *A Dissident Voice: Essays on Culture, Pedagogy, and Power*, Counterpoints: Studies in the Postmodern Theory of Education (New York: Peter Lang, 2011).

something other than capitalism. So, if you find yourself strongly committed to capitalism, you can comfortably support any one of the six ideologies. If you reject the idea of a strong capitalist economy, then you need to look at one of the ideologies not discussed in this book.

Next, keep in mind that there are only three basic economic ideologies: Hayekian economics, Keynesian economics, social democratic economics.

Hayekian economics argues that every person is an autonomous individual who is responsible for his or her own way in life and must act in his or her own individual self-interest. Hayekians believe that the result of an economy based on that assumption will be the most fair society possible. Any attempt to manage the economy through government intervention inevitably leads to tyranny. Hayekian economics always prefers a market-based solution to public issues. It turns the public over to the private whenever possible. Hayekian economics is most strongly advanced by classical liberals/neoliberals (and so is most often called classical liberal economics or neoliberal economics). Classical liberals/neoliberals are the "true believers" of Hayekian economics and everything about their political-economic ideology follows from this. But social conservatives, neoconservatives, and New Democrats also support Hayekian economics, though they temper their economic ideology with other interests. Social conservatives support Hayekian economics, but they often are more concerned with advancing socially conservative values than with economics. Neoconservatives tend to support Hayekian economics, but are not really that interested in economics itself, believing that taking care of security is more important than the economy because without security, there would be no economy. New Democrats tend to support Hayekian economics but in a mirror opposite way to social conservatives in that the New Democrats often are more concerned with culturally progressive issues than with economics.

Keynesian economics argues that in order for capitalism to succeed and to work well and not collapse, government needs to intervene where it can to manage the natural cycles of a capitalist economy. Failure to do so will inevitably lead to the collapse of the capitalist economy and the democracy necessary to maintain it. Through regulatory policy such as how much money is printed, what the government lending rate is, how much taxation is levied, and how much government buys in the market, government is able to minimize the problems that a freewheeling market economy inevitably brings and protect the capitalist system. Keynesian economics is the economics that governed our economy from President Franklin Roosevelt through President Jimmy Carter and is the economic ideology progressive democrats support.

Social democracy argues that for capitalism to succeed and work in balance with a fair and democratic society, the government must intervene to make sure that the market does, in fact, remain free. Right now, they argue, there is not much of a free market, since only a couple of massive corporations control each market. Without real competition, there is no free market. Government must step in either to break up monopolies and oligopolies or it must enter into the market itself to guarantee an equitable democratic society. Failure to do so will inevitably lead not only to the loss of a true free market, but to the loss of democracy as well—the rich will use the system to increase their power and turn the system to their own advantage. If classical liberals/neoliberals fear that government intervention will lead to tyranny, then social democrats believe that the refusal of government to intervene will lead to oligopoly and monopoly controlling the government and rather than democracy, we will become a corporatocracy.

Notice that all three of these economic ideologies (Hayekian, Keynesian, and social democrat) are committed to capitalism. They just differ on what it takes to make capitalism strong and vibrant.

On social issues, only the social conservatives are consistently and vehemently advocates of socially conservative "family values." Classical liberals/neoliberals tend also to favor such social conservatism, but not if it interferes with their major concerns with keeping government small and out of the market. Historically, neoconservatives actually supported progressive social values. Today many continue to be committed to progressive social values, but many also seem to be quite content to not worry about social values at all as long as the security apparatus remains strong.

On the other hand, all three of the progressive ideologies (New Democrats, progressive democrats, and social democrats) support progressive social values, which leads them to have more agreement on social issues. The progressive democrats and social democrats do, however, strongly disagree with the New Democrats' turning to the market for solutions, which sometimes puts them in bed with the conservatives, while the progressive democrats and social democrats are more interested in using the power of government to help balance the power of the wealthy and the corporations.

The problem of identifying ideologies is hard enough when the speaker communicates in a straightforward manner, but most politicians and media personalities and think tank scholars hide their true ideological commitments behind words that have been carefully tested by marketing firms. I mean this literally. The political parties and the ideological interests actually hire marketing firms to test their words and phrases to try to hide those aspects of their ideology that are not popular and to present those elements that have the potential of being supported. These firms develop rhetoric to use merely to sway people to their side—even if the people misunderstand what they are supporting. It is not that these politicians "lie" as much as they carefully craft their language in a way that misleads in exactly the same way as corporations sell their products through advertising. The wise reader of educational texts will carefully analyze the texts to discern what the actual rhetoric being used is, and they will interpret these devices by connecting them to the major ideologies found in the American economic and political conversation.

Part IV

Educational Narratives in Sociocultural Context

CHAPTER TWELVE

Narratives of Education in Historical Context

Introduction

Parts II and III developed two important contexts for interpreting educational texts: philosophy of education and economic-political ideology. Part IV explores sociocultural contexts that are equally useful for interpreting texts. Among the most important of these contexts are social class, race, racism, gender, and sexuality. Each of these will be developed individually in later chapters, but, unfortunately, due to space, other important contexts will not be covered. For example, this book will not individually address religion, ability differences, language, sustainability, or geographic region as contexts, though each can potentially deepen our understanding of any text. History can also be understood as an important sociocultural context in itself but also as it intersects each of the other contexts. The remainder of this chapter will explore history and, in doing so, help locate certain cultural narratives in time.

History is more than a chronological narrative of events that happened in the past. It is also a method of analyzing historical narratives. One way to rethink history is to recognize that history is less "what actually happened in the past" and more "how we tell stories of what happened in the past." There are three points to make about how history is written. First, history is more than the stringing together of facts. Second, historical narrative is driven by the questions asked by the historian, the theory relied upon, and the argument created. Third, the nature of the historical data that are used drives the interpretation. In other words, there is not one true historical story out there waiting to be told if only the correct facts could be pulled together. Rather, history is interpretation of the past by historians, drawing on available sources. In a very real sense, there is no history until historians tell it, and it is the way in which they tell it that becomes what we know of as "history."

If we think about it for a moment, history cannot be merely a description of what happened in the past, or there would not be the need for more books written about George Washington, the Battle of 1812, or the Trail of Tears. It is true that once in a while a historian will discover new facts about our first president, but for the most part, new books on Washington are less about new facts and more about making new meaning out of the facts already known. In other words, histories, like other texts, include argument and rhetoric as mechanisms to convince and persuade readers to accept an author's claim.

For example, a text that presents a history of education in colonial America will make an argument that, like all arguments, includes a claim, premises, and a warrant, and it will use rhetorical devices to persuade the reader to accept the essay's claims as legitimate. The techniques developed in this book to analyze and interpret contemporary texts can be used to analyze and interpret texts written *about* the past and those written *in* the past. Like all other texts, historical texts need to be read critically in order to gain a deeper understanding and appreciation of what they mean.

Here's an example. I suppose everyone knows that at one time not every American child went to school. But I wonder how many know when it was that schooling in America became universal. When was it that every child (or nearly every child) attended an elementary school and their older siblings attended a high school? Might it have been by 1900? 1920? 1950? 2000?

In fact, schooling never has been universal. Even today, not 100 percent of children attend elementary school, let alone high school. Table 12.1 presents some of the relevant statistics.

If you look at Table 12.1, you will notice that by 1800 half of eligible white students attended elementary school but that by 1900 the percentage had only increased by 10 percent. Also notice that in 1800 only 2 percent of black children attended elementary school, but by 1900 that percentage had increased to 30 percent, which was a significant increase but still far below the percentage of white children at the time. So, what happened during the nineteenth century that might explain the increase? One obvious possible cause was that the end of slavery led to an increase in black students' attendance in school. But there had to be something else beyond the end of slavery going on because if it were merely that, why were black children still half as likely to attend elementary school in 1900 as white children? The end of slavery may have created new opportunities for black children, but there had to have been some other factors inhibiting their attendance. Perhaps the institutionalization of Jim Crow laws that created legal segregation in schools depressed their attendance? Or, perhaps the fact that a high percentage of blacks compared with whites lived in rural areas where school attendance was far below that of urban areas was the key factor? One thing the table tells us is that the facts are there for all of us to see, but the narratives we tell to explain these facts are less obvious and more numerous.

The point is that we have some facts here, but we don't know the story until a historian draws the facts together and interprets them. Historians do not just present us with the facts;

Table 12.1 Elementary School Enrollment (% of eligible age group) by Race

	White	Black	Notes to consider
1700	10%	2%	These percentages actually refer to literacy, not enrollment in schools.
1800	50%	2%	Even though these are school enrollment percentages, we need to remember that the literacy rate was actually higher because many children, especially those of the wealthy, were taught at home.
1900	60%	30%	By 1918, every state required students to complete elementary school even though not all eligible children actually did so.
1950	80%	40%	Before the civil rights actions in the 1950s, less than half of the black population enrolled in elementary schools.
2000	95%	94%	By the turn of this last century, we approach universal education.

Source: Kate Rousmaniere, "The Forging of Common Public Schools" (lecture, Miami University, Oxford, OH, March 12, 2012).

they also present us with the narratives that help us make sense of the facts. The facts are part of history, but so are the stories we tell to explain those facts. In this book, I am interested in the facts, but I am just as interested in understanding the stories that interpret the facts.

A second way to rethink history is to think of it as not merely "the things that happened in the past," nor even as "the stories we tell of what happened in the past," but as "the process of placing things in time." There is a long tradition in the academy (i.e., the world of academics) to abstract things out of history, to treat what is being discussed as outside of time. When we read a textbook on chemistry, algebra, or aural rehabilitation, for example, we rarely see time markers included in the text. Instead, the authors write as if what they are telling us is true now as well as in the past and into the future. But when we abstract our arguments or our facts outside of time, we have merely chosen a particular rhetorical strategy that we adopt because we think it will be more convincing. Let's take a look at a sample taken from a textbook on aural rehabilitation (with the citations removed for readability):

> Hearing loss is more common than people may think. Prevalence is the number of individuals per segment of the populations that have a particular condition. It has been estimated that 32 million individuals in the United States have hearing loss or about 10% of the population. Prevalence of hearing loss is greater for about 30% for those individuals over 60 years of age.[1]

If we readers didn't look at the copyright of the text or the cited resources, we wouldn't know whether this was talking about today, 1990, or 1960. The time markers have been stripped from the text. It has been written as if it were outside of history. This is so common in academic writing that to insert time markers might even seem strange to some. But, good readers will insert their own time markers in order to interpret the text better. For example, knowing that the above quotation was taken from a 2012 textbook on auditory rehabilitation, a careful reader might read the text as follows:

> Hearing loss is more common than [twenty-first-century] people may think. [Today, auditory specialists agree that] Prevalence is the number of individuals per segment of the populations that have a particular condition. It has been estimated that [at the beginning of the twenty-first century] 32 million individuals in the United States have hearing loss or about 10% of the population [at this time]. [At the beginning of the twenty-first century] Prevalence of hearing loss is greater for about 30% for those individuals over 60 years of age.

Clearly inserting time markers for every statement can become cumbersome, but failure to include any time markers creates a rhetorical illusion that the statement is outside of time, outside of history. For that reason, good readers need to insert their own time markers as they read to help clarify the possible meaning of the text.

There are always at least two time markers a reader can insert in order to interpret a text: when the text was written and when the text is being read. Sometimes the difference

---

1. Carole E. Johnson, *Introduction to Auditory Rehabilitation: A Contemporary Issues Approach,* The Allyn & Bacon Communication Sciences and Disorders Series (Boston: Pearson, 2012).

between the two is so short that it doesn't make a difference. These days a person could read a blog entry or a newspaper story online only minutes after it was published. In such cases it would be rare that things had changed enough that the reader would need to treat the two moments differently (rare, but not unheard of). On the other hand, a text written by Thomas Jefferson and read today requires us to recognize that the meaning of the text when written could have been quite different than its meaning today. The words could have completely different denotations as well as connotations.

For example, one of the most famous lines of the American Declaration of Independence refers to our "unalienable right to life, liberty, and the pursuit of happiness." Placing this phrase into the historical context of its writing helps us understand at least two interesting ideas. One is that this phrase is obviously a paraphrase of the well-known work of English philosopher John Locke. Locke wrote of the rights of "life, liberty, and property." But why did Jefferson change the word "property" to "pursuit of happiness" in this trilogy of rights? What is wrong with claiming the right to property? We know that the congress that approved the declaration was made up of a privileged group of landowners in a country where most people were without land. Might this fact have anything to do with their decision to not claim property as an unalienable right? Would they have been able to persuade the majority of landless colonists to fight a war of rebellion against their king if they were fighting for the right of the wealthy minority to keep their land? Perhaps it just made sense to the wealthy landowners not to wave the flag of property in front of their landless neighbors. But if removing "property" was seen as important, why replace it with "pursuit of happiness"? Today, most Americans equate "happiness" with "pleasure." Did John Adams and Thomas Jefferson mean to suggest that all people have the right to pursue pleasure? Probably not.

Most of the men who signed the Declaration had been classically educated. "Happiness" is the popular English translation of one of Aristotle's central ethical and political concepts: *eudemonia*. To Aristotle, *eudemonia*, or "happiness," is the highest good and is attained through the successful pursuit of all other goods such as health, wealth, pleasure, friendship, wisdom, civic participation, and family. In other words, given the familiarity with Aristotle of the signers of the declaration, it seems reasonable to assume that the "pursuit of happiness" probably referred to the right to seek all the goods a society can provide necessary to achieve a "full and good life" and should never be confused with the simple pursuit of pleasure. By being able to place the Declaration of Independence into its historical context, we are able to understand some important new aspects to its meaning.

But historical contexts do not mean that we merely look at the past: they also require that we place something into time, even our own time. For example, in discussing the meaning of the Declaration of Independence, we might also want to point out that if Jefferson were writing it today, he would have been more likely to speak of "life, liberty, and the pursuit of a good life." In this way, we take the declaration out of the historical moment in which it was written and insert it into the present moment.

A good reader would want to interpret a text by Jefferson, John Dewey, or Jane Addams by placing it into at least two different historical moments. What do we know about the time in which it was written that might help us better understand what the text might have meant to those reading it then? What do we know about the time in which we are reading it that might help us better understand what the text might mean to us today?

So, to analyze a historical text we must use the techniques of argument and rhetoric analysis. To interpret a text historically we must place that text into time, and there are always at least two moments of time that we can place a text: when it was written and when it was read. Of course, to place a text into two historical moments requires that we know something about those different moments of time. The rest of this chapter will present a history of people, events, ideas, and narratives that can help us place many educational texts into time in order to better interpret them.

The Forging of the American Public Schools

Throughout our history, Americans have engaged in public discussion about education: Why should we have schools? Who should go to school? Who benefits from public schools? How should they be organized and paid for? As these questions are taken up during different moments in our history, we find some recurring cultural narratives that are often used in different ways at different times. We also find that at certain times, some of these narratives are more influential than others. The rest of this chapter will address four different moments of American history in which the discussion about education was particularly intense:

Colonial period (1640s–1770);
Early National period (1770–1820);
Mid-nineteenth century—Common School reform movement (1820–1880);
combined with the Progressive era (1880–1920)

In exploring these periods, cultural narratives familiar to us today and still used as prominent aspects of our educational rhetoric will become apparent.

Colonial Period (1640s–1770)

While the indigenous people of the Americas had created a well-developed, highly successful social and political organization that served, nurtured, and maintained social life, the European colonialists found themselves in an unfamiliar land where their cultural assumptions and practices, which had been developed in a different social and physical environment, were not as rooted in the local environment as the native peoples'. To a European settling down in the forests of New England, survival was always a questionable achievement. To ensure existence required the small contingent of exiles to stick together and work toward mutual interest. But mere physical survival was not sufficient for the New Englanders due to their strong commitment to a particular religious belief—Puritanism, a particularly strict sect of English Protestants who rejected hedonism and embraced a life of modest display. They were fiercely anti-Catholic and understood the Catholic Church to be the "Church of Satan." Besides the need to physically survive the New England winters and wilderness, the New England colonists had the need to make sure that their religion and their social ways also survived the stresses of the "new world."

One of the important particular beliefs of Protestants in contradistinction to Catholics, at this time, was a belief that God spoke directly to, in, and through individuals. As a result, individuals had the responsibility to speak directly to God—no priest need act as a go-between. But for every person to be able to speak and hear God required every individual to be familiar with "God's Word," which was believed to exist in the Bible. This then is the impetus for teaching children to read in colonial New England: if they can read, they can read the Bible. If they can read the Bible, they can read God's Word directly and know God in an unmediated way. If they can know God, the Puritan way of life will be continued from generation to generation. Reading then became a central characteristic of Protestant, and especially Puritan, communities.

In order to help maintain the solidarity to survive both physically and culturally, the New England colonists insisted that parents either teach their children to read or arrange for someone else to teach them. They also insisted that the community make available mechanisms to help children of the illiterate learn to read. As a result, many historians credit the New England colonists with the first public education system. We find it encoded in Massachusetts School Law of 1647, which has come to be colorfully known as "The Old Deluder Act":

> It being one chief project of that old deluder, Satan, to keep men from the knowledge of the Scriptures.... It is therefore ordered that every township in this jurisdiction, after the Lord hath increased them to fifty households shall forthwith appoint one within their town to teach all such children as shall resort to him to write and read....[2]

The law required that (1) all communities pay for a school teacher, and (2) the attendance of boys and girls for preliminary literacy.

In other words, in colonial New England, the cultural narratives reinforced the idea that in order to survive as a Puritan community, all children had to learn to read. Education, especially reading, became a mechanism for creating the solidarity necessary for spiritual and cultural survival in the harsh, unfamiliar, un-European land. While the primary responsibility of education lay with the parents, when parents were unable to meet those obligations, the whole community had to bear the responsibility and the cost because ultimately education was for the good of the whole community.

Although many historians tell and retell a story that places the beginning of public education in colonial New England, we must keep in mind that not all the colonies in America were Puritan. They weren't even all Protestant. By the eighteenth century, Maryland was officially Church of England, but it had been founded by Catholics, and Catholics still maintained a relatively large presence there. Pennsylvania included many Quakers. Virginia, the Carolinas, and Georgia were committed to the traditional Protestant Church of England, and throughout all of the colonies myriad religious sects thrived. While the early

---

2. "The Old Deluder Act (1647)," from *Records of the Governor and Company of the Massachusetts Bay in New England* (1853), II: 203 (Austin, TX: Constitution Society), www.constitution.org/primarysources /deluder.html.

New Englanders certainly did build a system of education for their children, education both lapsed and took different forms in other parts of the colonies.

The rapidly growing urban areas especially in the mid-Atlantic colonies relied on the apprenticeship system for their education. Some of those apprentices learned reading and writing and bookkeeping from their masters, but others did not.

In the mostly rural South, reading and writing primarily occurred on the plantations and were restricted to the children of the wealthy landowners; typically their sons received reading and writing and education in the classics while their daughters received education in the arts.

So, while we find a beginning of what might be called public education in a couple of the New England colonies, throughout the rest of the colonies different cultural narratives formed different bases for a variety of American stories of education and its purpose. For a few, education was a public good serving the whole community. For some, it was a private matter connected to vocations. For others, it was only something for the "gentility." In other words, while we tend to acclaim the American colonies as the moment of birth of public education, we must keep in mind that like all moments of history, there was a wide range of narratives circulating that created a vibrant debate about the purposes, needs, and forms of education.

Early National Period (1770–1820)

If the primary problem of the New England colonialists was physical and spiritual survival, the primary problem of the period following the successful American revolution was how to forge a common and democratic nation out of thirteen former colonies of the British Crown. The Americans' embracing of democracy placed similar demands on the whole country that had, in colonial times, been primarily found only in New England. Repudiating the English king and picking up the responsibility of joint governing was quite similar to the Protestant rejection of the Pope and the demand that individuals take responsibility in conjunction with their neighbors for determining what was right and wrong. Just as the Protestants believed that their children needed to learn to read in order to know God's word, citizens of a democracy, regardless of their religion, needed an education in order to perform their responsibilities in a democracy. And, just as the Puritans needed to develop a form of socialization to maintain community in a hostile land in order to guarantee survival, the citizens of the new republic needed mechanisms of socialization in order to forge a new national unity out of past colonial divisions.

But unlike the Puritans of the old New England colonies, the new republic had to find a way to construct a democratic public space that welcomed members of all faiths. In colonial New England, public space could be Puritan, for, in matters of religion, there was no distinction between the private and the public, but in the new nation consisting of people of many faiths, a new religiously pluralistic public space had to be nurtured and maintained. For at least some prominent Americans, the new mechanisms to accomplish this were best found in a system of schooling designed to develop citizens who could read, write, think, and dispute as well as who had developed a commitment of solidarity to their new fellow citizens and pride in their new nation.

Thomas Jefferson and the Bill for the More General Diffusion of Knowledge

Perhaps the most eloquent and perspicacious of the new American leaders was Thomas Jefferson, who wrote in a letter to a friend, "If a nation expects to be ignorant and free ... it expects what never was and never will be."[3] Jefferson might be credited with advocating the first true system of public schooling when he wrote and promoted the "Bill for the More General Diffusion of Knowledge" (1779).

As seen in the last section in this chapter, how you were educated during the colonial period depended upon which region of the continent you lived in. The environment in the southern colonies like Virginia, both economically and politically speaking, was quite distinct from that of New England.

Whereas the New England colonies made little distinction between the private and public interests of schooling, in the South education was seen largely as a private matter. The children of wealthy farmers were tutored: the boys learning reading and writing and then going on to a grammar school, the girls receiving basic literacy and then instruction in music, dancing, and French. The very few village or town schools serving a public function in the southern colonies served the small middle class, but there were no laws on the books requiring communities to form schools to educate their children as there had been in New England. Education was largely seen as a private matter, the domain of the home, and politically and economically wealthy farm owners did not see the point in spending their money to educate the children of others. Thomas Jefferson was one of the first prominent Americans to recognize the need for a public and secular public education and he battled the entrenched cultural attitudes of Virginians when he proposed a limited form of common schooling in the state of Virginia in 1779.

Jefferson's proposal, the "Bill for the More General Diffusion of Knowledge," presented the Virginia Assembly with a pyramidal approach to schooling. In his plan, each county would be divided into 100 wards, and each ward would run its own primary school open to all free girls and boys. The curriculum would consist of reading, writing, basic math, and "books which shall be used therein for instructing the children to read shall be such as will at the same time make them acquainted with Graecian, Roman, English, and American history."[4] After three years in the primary school, families who wanted their children to stay would pay tuition. The very best scholars would be sent to the next level of schooling for free.

Children (almost always male) who wanted to continue their education would move to grammar schools. Jefferson proposed that these institutions be established, one in every three counties, as secondary education. These would be boarding schools with a curriculum of Latin and Greek languages, geography, English grammar, and higher math. The very best scholars of these schools would, after four to five years, be sent to the College of William and Mary for three years at public expense.

One important detail to note about Jefferson's bill is that the Bible—a staple in most school and university curricula of the day—was purposefully excluded from the public school curriculum. Another point to note is that Jefferson's proposal did provide for a basic

---

3. Quoted from a letter from Thomas Jefferson, "To Colonel Charles Yancey, January 6, 1816," in *The Works of Thomas Jefferson,* Federal Edition, Vol. 11 (New York: G. P. Putnam's Sons, 1904–1905), 497.

4. Thomas Jefferson, "A Bill for the More General Diffusion of Knowledge," in *The Works of Thomas Jefferson 1771–1779,* Vol. 2, ed. Paul Leicester Ford (New York: G. P. Putnam's Sons, 1905), http://oll.libertyfund.org/title/755/86186.

three years of education for girls, but not for people held as slaves. And finally, we should note that his proposal provided at least some continued schooling for those of promising scholarship whose families could not pay.

Jefferson's proposal, though not passed in the Virginia legislature in any form during his lifetime, points to one of the first important links made between democracy and schooling. As in other emerging democratic societies at this time in history, leaders were conceptualizing the proper education for free citizens, even as some of them, like Jefferson, enslaved people and benefited from the slave economies of the time. While clearly insufficient and, in fact, immoral by today's standards, Jefferson's proposal added some important new purposes into the discussion of education creating a new narrative emphasis.

Jefferson's Narrative. Jefferson's proposal focused on the important purposes of schooling for citizenship. *Citizenship* refers to the knowledge, skills, and values needed by citizens, and *democratic citizenship* refers to the particular set of knowledge, skills, and values citizens need in order to participate in shaping their own government. According to Jefferson and others who advocated for public education, for a democratic society, citizens need to have both literacy and a narrative that constructs a common history, language, culture, and nation. This democratic narrative also suggests that citizens need to be able to intelligently elect, monitor, and evaluate their political representatives and leaders. Jefferson wrote, "History, by apprising them of the past, will enable them to judge of the future; it will avail them of the experience of other times and other nations; it will qualify them as judges of the actions and designs of men."[5] By choosing history rather than the Bible to teach democracy and moral conduct, Jefferson also made an important initial step in conceiving of common schooling as secular, not religious; one that could include those children whose parents were loyal to the new American version of the Church of England (Episcopalians), as well as those children whose parents committed to one of the wide variety of other less-influential (in Virginia) churches including Methodists and Puritans, and non-Protestant religions such as Catholics and Jews.

Jefferson's proposal also picks up the emerging ideas of meritocracy and includes them in his narrative. Compared with an aristocracy, where power and position are gained through birth and social status, a *meritocracy* refers to a social system where ability, or native intelligence, plus effort yield achievement. In throwing off the aristocracy of old England, the new American society embraced the idea of meritocracy. Jefferson's bill creates a new educational narrative based on meritocracy where individual merit and not birth would establish leadership in the new democratic society.

The Northwest Ordinances

Perhaps the first mechanism for the institutionalization of public education as a national interest can be found in the Land Ordinance of 1785, which created a method for paying for public schools in the expanded territories given to the United States by the Treaty of Paris (1783), the treaty that ended the Revolutionary War. This new territory west of the Appalachians, north of the Ohio River, and East of the Mississippi River was to be divided into ten states and the Land Ordinance of 1785 provided a mechanism for mapping and

---

5. Thomas Jefferson, "Notes on the State of Virginia," quoted in Joel Spring, *The American School, 1642–1993*, 3rd ed. (New York: McGraw-Hill, 1994), 39.

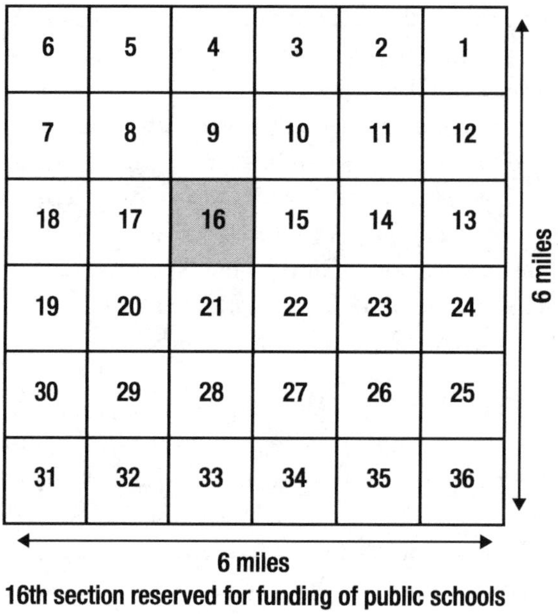

6 miles
16th section reserved for funding of public schools

Figure 12.1 The Township System under the Land Ordinance of 1785 Showing the Sixteenth Section Reserved for the Funding of Public Education

organizing the new land into townships (see Figure 12.1). For our interests in this chapter, the importance of this ordinance was its mechanism for providing a way to fund public schools. The Land Ordinance of 1785 called for the surveying of the new territories into six square mile–sized townships. Each township was divided into thirty-six one-square-mile sections with the sixteenth section reserved for the funding of public schools either by using their taxes to fund schools for the whole township or to actually physically locate schools in this part of the township. But while the federal government under the Articles of Confederation was willing to create a mechanism for public schools in their new territories, it had no power to do so in the thirteen states. The effect was that public education came to the Midwestern territories and states before it came to most of the original thirteen states.

Common School Reform Movement (1820–1880) and Its Survival into the Early Progressive Era (1880–1920)

Public education grew first slowly and then rapidly during the middle part of the nineteenth century in what has come to be known as the Common School Movement. Pennsylvania had provided for public schools for poor children in the 1790s. New York provided free schools funded by wealthy businessmen for poor children at the beginning of the nineteenth century. While there is a lengthy list of claimed "public" high schools beginning with Boston Latin (1635), these schools were primarily created for and attended by the children of the elite. It was not until the 1820s that we begin to see high schools created for the children of the poor. One of those first schools, Boston English, was created in 1921 specifically for working-class boys, including free blacks (but no girls were admitted).

Three Narratives of the Common School Movement

In the 1800s and especially after 1830, we see the gradual development of the system that we now understand as the public schools supported by three separate, but often intertwined, cultural narratives: "Education for Nationalism," "Education for Protestant Christian Morality," and "Education for Capitalism."

Education for Nationalism. Among free people and among the political leaders of the eighteenth century in the United States, there was an acute consciousness that their nation-state was immature and potentially volatile. Several leaders of the early nationalist period advocated schooling to promote a consciousness of and loyalty to the emerging republic. While in today's ordinary language the word "nation" is a synonym for "state" or "country," the term actually refers to something other than the geographic boundaries of a country. A *nation* is a community of people who understand themselves to share a common ethnicity, history, culture, and language and implies a right to self-rule and often a right to a geographic locality. Therefore a nation-state is a country whose geographic and political boundaries are tied to a *people as a nation* with a sense of common peoplehood. One of the problems of forging the new United States of America was the fact that until the late eighteenth century, the thirteen colonies did not think of themselves as being a common people. At the beginning of the new republic, it had not yet forged a common set of peoplehood with a common culture and common language. Recognizing this lack of commonality, many leaders advocated a commitment to nationalism be forged in a common school experience. *Nationalism* refers to the feelings of identification, solidarity, and loyalty to the nation. It requires the forging of a commonsense of ethnicity, history, culture, and language. Both in terms of a loyal population and for the training of future political leaders, early educational commentators stressed the importance of schools teaching a narrative of common identity, culture, and language embedded in the nation. For example, Noah Webster (1758–1843) moved from country schoolmaster in Connecticut; to author of a series of spelling books, grammar books, and a reader; and then salesman of his books all across the new states. In an effort to create a uniquely American language and identity, these books laid down an American lexicon, distinct from British and other English usages of the times. Many of the uniquely American spellings of English words were created consciously by Webster to distinguish the American language from that of England. Webster would, in later years, work on behalf of a state school fund to start common schools.

Education for Protestant Christian Morality. A second narrative comes out of the powerful influence of Anglo-Saxon Protestantism, a form of Christian ideology that translated into the pedagogical virtues of obedience, self-sacrifice, self-control, self-restraint, and the teaching of the Protestant Bible. This Christian narrative promoted a social "consensus"[6] regarding the religious, moral, and social virtues among powerful leaders.

For example, Webster, who, as stated above, worked to create a common American lexicon through his dictionaries and other writings, embedded a religious morality into his

---

6. Even during the 1700s and early 1800s, the nation was diverse, and thus a true religious, let alone political, consensus would not be possible. Almost all political leaders were of Anglo-Saxon Protestant descent, and only white men had the right to vote. This preceded the more diverse immigrant waves in the 1800s and 1900s, including the Irish-Catholic waves starting in the 1830s.

narrative of the unified American spirit. His story was that an inspiring and conforming kind of patriotism would teach the poor and newly arrived immigrants, who he assumed were largely ignorant and immoral. In the quotation below, notice how Webster alludes to a narrative of religious duty as a solution to what he considered to be the immorality found in too many youth:

> More pains [should be] taken to discipline our youth in early life to the sound maxims of moral, political, and religious duties. I believe more than is commonly believed may be done in this way towards correcting the vices and disorders of society.[7]

Despite the existence of large numbers of Catholics, this Protestant "consensus narrative" was translated into the development of the common schools' *formal curricula* (i.e., that which is intentionally taught from books or by teachers) as well as the covert or *hidden curricula* (i.e., that which is taught through the routines, rituals, and organization of schools themselves). There was strong Protestant religious content in the school texts such as the *New England Primer*[8] and McGuffey Readers. Unlike Jefferson's desire to keep the Bible out of public education, during the middle nineteenth century, the Protestant Bible was used as a text for teaching basic literacy and scripture in public space. The Protestant virtues of obedience and self-control were inculcated through pedagogy and school structures that emphasized the authority of the teacher, such as rote memorization and corporal punishment. Not only was Protestantism taught, but an anti-Catholic narrative permeated many schools. As more Catholics became citizens through the 1800s, these Protestant narratives with their Protestant values were challenged, and sometimes violently so. The Protestant domination of public education caused many Catholics to refuse to send their children to the public schools, which led to an alternative system of Catholic parochial schooling in the United States but also to a growing diminishment in the importance of the Protestant Bible in the school curriculum.[9]

Education for Capitalism. Beyond nationalism and Anglo-Protestantism, another major narrative proved to be powerful in the foundations and future of American schools. Capitalism, an economic system based in private investment and ownership of capital, heavily influenced early forms of schooling and decisions about who would be permitted schooling. The slave economies on which the early nation depended provided the justification for the laws in the early 1800s that forbade the education of enslaved people. The capitalist "free markets" of cotton production relied on the labor of enslaved people for maximum profit. Thus, in southern states, the economic welfare of the ruling class relied on enslaved people being kept submissive and ignorant. But capitalist values were infused in the schooling of free whites, since the newly developing capitalist economy required a population who believed in the value of hard work, thrift, savings, competition, individualism, and the sanctity of property

---

7. Quoted in Spring, *The American School*, 35.

8. This textbook first appeared in 1690 and was widely used throughout the 1700s. To see a sample of an 1805 version, go to www.gettysburg.edu/~tshannon/his341/nep1805contents.html.

9. For example, the Philadelphia Bible Riots in 1843—in which thirteen people died and a Catholic Church was burned to the ground—broke out in response to a school board's ruling that Catholic students could read their own version of the Bible in schools and be excused from other religious instruction. From Spring, *The American School*, 84.

ownership. Whereas the idea of the centrality of property was erased from Jefferson's writing of the Declaration of Independence seventy-five years before, by the mid-nineteenth century, the centrality of property found its way into this economic narrative. These values serve capitalism well, though their worth for democratic governance has long been debated, and so these values were built into early textbooks and teachings.

Contradictions: Freedom and Oppression

As historian James D. Anderson wrote, "Both schooling for democratic citizenship and schooling for second-class citizenship have been basic traditions in American education."[10] Historians point out that as Jefferson was attempting to make the connections between popular or common schooling and a free society in the state of Virginia, he was ignoring some 40 percent of the total number of Virginia's children, "who along with enslaved adults formed the basis of wealth for Jefferson, as well as for the state of Virginia."[11] The development of the common school ideal that began building in the 1800s took place alongside a successful campaign in the southern states to ban literacy for enslaved children and adults. Between 1800 and 1835, most southern states passed laws that made it a crime to teach enslaved people to read and write. Racism, therefore, was also an important factor in shaping the development of the educational system of the United States. As will be discussed in Chapter 15, *racism* refers to any act or program that results in the creation or maintenance of inequality or domination of a people based on race. Thus, the tensions of both democratic freedom and oppression were part of the development of common schools.

The victory of the Union Army in the Civil War freed those who had been legally enslaved, but free blacks believed that their true emancipation lay in developing systems of education for themselves and, most crucially, their children. In 1865, the federal government formed the Freedmen's Bureau to help set up school systems for free blacks, and many missionary societies from the northern states funded and sponsored teachers and schools throughout the South. But those who were formally enslaved were hungry for, and actively sought, universal, state-supported schools.

Those who had been enslaved emerged from their bondage with a deep respect for the powers of education and actively sought a literate culture for themselves. For the decade or so after emancipation, free blacks established a wide range of schools for themselves and with the assistance of entities like the Freedmen's Bureau. John W. Alvord, who was the national superintendent of schools for the Freedmen's Bureau, traveled across the South promoting educational systems for blacks. What he found in his travels, were practices of self-teaching and what he called "native schools" everywhere. He described one he found in Goldsboro, North Carolina: "Two colored young men, who but a little time before commenced to learn themselves, had gathered 150 pupils, all quite orderly and hard at study." All over the South, he found such native schools, initiated and maintained by people who had once been enslaved. Many of these schools were in places that had not been visited by the Freedmen's Bureau or any of the northern missionary societies. Educational historian

---

10. James D. Anderson, *The Education of Blacks in the South, 1860–1935* (Chapel Hill: University of North Carolina Press, 1988), 1.

11. Ibid.

James Anderson states, "Early black schools were established and supported largely through the Afro-Americans' own efforts."[12]

Common School Movement into the Progressive Era

Throughout the 1800s the nation grew in population and in diversity, and the arguments for common schools became more accepted. As the population and nation grew, more citizens began to accept the need for statewide systems of schooling. The era of the sometimes romanticized "little red schoolhouse,"[13] in which children from the same village or rural area would be all educated in the same room by one teacher, would be ending by the end of the nineteenth century.

In addition, the economy and rural-based lifestyle of the United States changed during the latter part of the nineteenth century. During the colonial era and through the early 1800s, America was still a largely rural and agrarian country. Family was the primary institution for education if it was available, desired, and affordable to them. But industrial capitalism gained more strength over the century and changed the nature of family life and the aims of education. Industrial and political leaders wanted children schooled for industrial and factory work.

The power of these industrial institutions and leaders shifted the educational focus of the society from families and villages to larger institutions, such as urban school systems. Families who worked in factories could not watch their children the way they could when they worked on farms. Workers in growing cities frequently left their homes in the dark and arrived home after dark; children were sometimes among those factory workers. As the economy moved toward industrialism, family life shifted, and the authority of the family decreased.[14] Moreover, the highly regimented nature of factory work required workers who could adapt and function within the new economy. The shifting economy of the nation pushed the agenda of the common school, a place where many industry leaders hoped that children would learn to be efficient, productive workers.

As populations and cities grew, the nation's landscape of schools fundamentally shifted from village schools to urban systems. The educational reformers of the late nineteenth century saw the division of labor in the factory, the coordination of modern businesses, the new technologies, and forms of organization as inspirational. They saw these new ideas as bringing control, order, rationality, and efficiency to the schools. These new ideas replaced the hard-to-control, parochial governance of the scattered array of village and rural schools

---

12. Ibid., 6–7.

13. Accounts of the physical state of many school buildings (falling apart, inadequately heated), the frequent corporal punishments administered, and the very parochial form of education provided in these village schools separate the myth from the reality of the "little red schoolhouse." For more information, see Richard J. Altenbaugh, *The American People and Their Education: A Social History* (Upper Saddle River, NJ: Merrill/Prentice Hall, 2003), 72–74.

14. "Industrial capitalism also wreaked havoc on the family. With the pre-industrial household gradually and grudgingly surrendering its manufacturing abilities, the family fragmented, and personal and work lives became bifurcated. Paternal, and often maternal, parents now trudged to and from the factories and home in the dark instead of casually entering the ten-footer. If the children did not work in the factory, they had to largely fend for themselves, and so the urban common schools began to adopt a custodial role, assuming some of the absent parents' responsibilities." Ibid., 71.

with the new, hierarchical systems of schooling. The reformers applied uniform standards across all schools and set standard ways of communicating, settling disputes, and running schools. As village and rural schools were consolidated into structured systems, patterns of both urbanization and industrialization greatly influenced the new school systems in that they shaped the thinking about what a "good school" was. As educational historian David Tyack notes, "efficiency, rationality, continuity, precision, impartiality became watchwords of the consolidators."[15]

One example of these new ideas was the introduction of the graded school, adapted from Prussian state school systems. Trying to teach many different ages of children in the same classroom was inefficient and, some thought, inhumane because lessons, desks, and activities could not be easily adjusted to fit the maturity of the pupils. It also didn't hurt that such graded schools allowed school systems to hire more female teachers, who were paid half the salary of their male counterparts, to teach the younger children. The Quincy School, opened in Boston in 1848, was dubbed an "egg-crate school" based on the new classification of pupils by grade, and by 1860, schools of most cities and town were graded.[16]

By the dawn of the twentieth century, school systems were in place around the new nation, and were free and open to many, though not all, children. African Americans, Asian Americans, Hispanic Americans, and Native Americans were still largely educated and socialized, when they were allowed to be educated at all, in segregated school systems, funded partially by the states or federal government. The kinds of learning provided in these segregated school systems were usually of a vocational nature and thus resembled socialization and training more than education, because it was widely believed that non-whites were not suited to intellectual kinds of learning and should instead be prepared for productive labor. Thus, while the "common schooling" era of the 1800s closed with a great deal of success in establishing wider access to equal opportunity to many of the nation's poor and immigrant citizens, it did not succeed in establishing fully universal and fully public schools. The twentieth and twenty-first centuries would see these battles continued.

The Legacy of the Common School Movement Today

We can see in the early history of American schooling a shifting but continuous struggle among at least three different narratives of public schooling: Education for Religious Morality, Education for Democracy, and Education for the Economy. Although these three narratives have altered to fit their specific moment in history, they have been prominent in the debates over public education in this country.

Those who attended public schools in the early 1960s were regularly read to from a Protestant Bible, recited the Christian Lord's Prayer (often in Protestant versions), sang Christian hymns (typically as sung in Protestant churches), and celebrated Christian holidays. One result of this emphasis on Protestant Christianity was the large and thriving Catholic Parochial School System. In the middle part of the 1960s, a series of court challenges brought by Catholics, Jews, and atheists brought to an end the use of public schools to promote

---

15.   David B. Tyack, *The One Best System: A History of American Urban Education* (Cambridge, MA: Harvard University Press, 1974), 28.

16.   Ibid., 44–45.

Protestantism and Christianity. The result of these court decisions, along with some other decisions such as racial desegregation, led to the burgeoning of a Protestant parochial school system (generally referred to as Christian schools) and a diminishing of size and importance (though not elimination) of the Catholic parochial school system. Another effect has been a political movement to allow public funds to support religious parochial education through public support of busing, textbooks, food, and other "noneducational" expenditures. It has also spurred the political effort to eliminate public schools as we know them and create a voucher system of funding where state funding follows the student wherever the student chooses to attend so that today we find public funding is being used for private education and public education is under enormous attack. So, while the narrative of religious morality has been greatly diminished inside public schools, the narrative is still quite alive in influencing education policy in America.

Though using public schools to advance religious ends was basically ended through court challenges, the silencing of the narrative of Education for Democracy to little more than a whisper has occurred during the relatively brief time span of the end of the twentieth century through to today. While we still find evidence of a narrative of democracy in the public schools, we find few policy-makers, parents, and students who connect public education as a necessary condition for a strong democracy. Americans seem to be more focused on Education for the Economy than on Education for Democracy. Still, the narrative of Education for Democracy is not dead. There are millions of Americans who still hold on to the idea that the American public school system must take its commitment to democracy seriously if we hope to maintain a free, vibrant, and just democracy into the future.

CHAPTER THIRTEEN

Narratives of Social Class and Education

Sociocultural Contexts for Interpreting Educational Texts

As explained in Chapter 3, to interpret a text requires the reader to read the text against other contexts. Chapters 5–12 developed three possible contexts for this task: philosophy and philosophy of education, socioeconomic ideology, and history. This chapter introduces a fourth possibility (sociocultural contexts including social class, race and racism, gender, and sexuality) and then zeroes in on social class as an example of one sociocultural context. The others will be treated in subsequent chapters.

Up to this point, I have kept the different contexts fairly separate from each other, treating each in isolation from the others. However, in practice none of these contexts exists separate from each other. In the last chapter, we see clearly the way in which both philosophical and ideological contexts arise in historical moments but continue to have their influence even in periods in which different narratives predominate. In this chapter, we shall see the way all three of the previous contexts become integral to the narrating of sociocultural contexts. Furthermore, even though different sociocultural contexts will be covered in different chapters, rarely do they arise in public discourse in isolation from each other. For example, social class and race are frequently narrated together and, particularly in the form of narratives of "single mothers" and "dead-beat dads," gender is narrated as integral to the stories of race and class. Narratives of gender and sexuality are often so intertwined that the stories often confuse one for the other. As with all of the previous topics, the separation of these different contexts serves a heuristic purpose designed to help students grasp the basics before reinscribing them into multivoiced narratives that draw from each other as well as from philosophy, ideology, and history.

An Introduction to Social Class

Whereas everyone has a general idea of what one means when speaking of social class, scholars are not in agreement as to the best way to explain the structural stratification of societies based on class. In educational scholarship, two predominant constructions of class vie for attention. One, socioeconomic status (SES), derives originally from the work of Max Weber, an early twentieth-century German sociologist. The second, Marxian theory of class, arises from the work of Karl Marx, the nineteenth-century German political, economic, and social theorist.

Marxian Theory of Class

Marxian theory defines class in terms of property, primarily ownership of or control over the means of production. In a capitalist society, capital controls production, so those with enough capital to own businesses and hire labor (the capitalists) share a class interest in opposition to the class interests of the laborers they hire (the working class). The working class does not control enough capital to own businesses and therefore workers must sell their labor to the capitalists. During Marx's time in the nineteenth century, a small middle class (or petite bourgeoisie), consisting primarily of small shopkeepers and professionals (i.e., teachers, doctors, lawyers, clergy, skilled artisans), existed but were so few in number as to have very little influence on the broader character of that historical moment. In the struggle between the capitalists and the workers, the middle class is relegated to choosing to work in the interest of one side or the other. In the capitalist societies, the middle class shares with the working class a dependency on those with sufficient capital to hire their services and so, to some extent, share some interests with the working class. On the other hand, because the middle class also provided services to others in the middle class and to the working class, those in that class also recognized some common interests with the capitalists.

During the twentieth century the middle class grew rapidly due to the bureaucratization of corporations so that by the 1950s, the middle class (small shopkeepers, professionals, and, now, a large and growing class of middle-level corporate bureaucrats) became an important player in the struggle between labor and owners. Being in the middle with a foot in both worlds, the middle class could swing their allegiance one way or another. Typically, Marxian theory argues that the middle class's dependence on stability in order to protect their small, but important, access to capital led them to side with the capitalists against the interests of the workers. However, given the explosion of corporate bureaucracies in the twentieth century, the growing middle class gained sufficient power to work in one of their unique class interests—a vibrant and well-funded system of high schools and higher education. But the significant downsizing of the American middle class and spectacular increase in the wealth of the capitalist class that began in the 1980s and continues to today has diminished further what little power the middle class had to influence education policy. Perhaps the defunding of public schools and universities that so marks the economic contexts of today's public institutions of education results from the decrease in the power of the middle class that stemmed from the rise of classical liberal/neoliberal policies in the 1980s and continues today under both Republican and Democratic congresses and administrations.

Socioeconomic Status (SES)

While a Marxian concept of class has an important place among educational scholars, educational policy-makers, media commentators, and school administrators and teachers overwhelmingly conceive of class as SES. Rather than defining class in terms of property, SES defines class as determined by two dimensions: the social and the economic.

The Social Dimension

According to SES, a continuum of power exists on a social scale marked by various resources of power that earn people different prestige or status. One can be seen as having much or little status depending on their unique combination of such resources of power as occupation; number of school degrees; prestige of the institution granting those degrees; one's ethnic or racial assignment; good looks; language, dialect, and accent spoken; religion; marital status; and many more factors. For simplicity's sake, most sociologists using an SES construct of class let occupation stand in for all of the others.[1]

The Economic Dimension

The economic dimension can be indicated by income or wealth (these are not the same things, which will be clarified below). The SES theory constructs class as the intersection of a people's placement on the social dimension with their placement on the economic dimension. Figure 13.1 visually represents an individual who possesses a middle social status and a middle economic position. We can see that the two lines intersect in the middle quintile. This is a typical location of the SES of teachers who tend to possess a middle social status and a middle economic position.

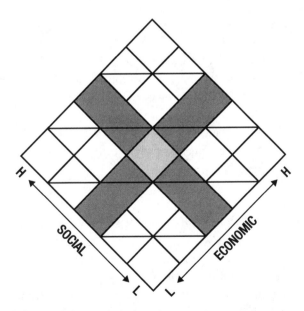

Figure 13.1 SES Determined by the Intersection of Social Status and Economic Position

---

1. For a sample ranking of occupation status, see James A. Davis et al., "Prestige Scores for All Detailed Categories in the 1980 Census Occupational Classification," National Opinion Research Center (NORC), http://ibgwww.colorado.edu/~agross/NNSD/prestige%20scores.html.

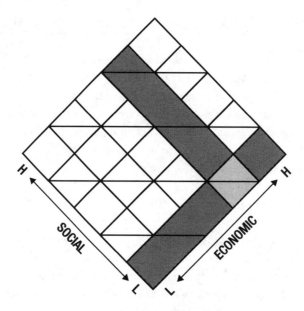

Figure 13.2 SES Determined by the Intersection of Social Status and Economic Position

Figure 13.2 represents an individual with a low social status and a relatively high income, perhaps a sex worker or a seller of illegal drugs.

Income. Sociologists tend to determine the economic dimension by measuring either income or wealth. Wealth will be defined below. *Income* refers to the money a person is paid for their work—their salary; wages; or, if running a small business, their profit. Typically sociologists and economists who use SES study income position by dividing the society into income quintiles where 20 percent of the population occupies one quintile. If we were to divide the 2007 American population into income quintiles, our table would look like Figure 13.3. According to the 2007 census, the bottom 20 percent of families of four had an income of less than $20,320 and the top 20 percent had an income of $97,030 or more.[2]

If we use income quintiles as a way to assign people's position on the economic dimension, a family of four with a 2007 income of more than $97,030 might be considered upper class. This would mean that approximately 20 percent of the population should be considered upper class. This has some obvious problems given that a family consisting of two married, experienced schoolteachers would be considered as having the same class position as the Bill Gates family. For many, it just does not seem to make sense to consider these two families as occupying the same class position. One solution to this problem is to simply choose a higher income dividing line. At this particular moment, many sociologists and politicians choose an income of $250,000 a year for a family of four to indicate the upper class. This figure suggests that approximately 3 percent of the American population in 2007 would be considered upper class.

---

2. Carmen DeNavas-Walt, Bernadette D. Proctor, and Jessica C. Smith, "Current Population Report: Income, Poverty, and Health Insurance Coverage in the United States: 2009," P60-238 (Washington, DC: US Census Bureau, 2010), www.census.gov/prod/2010pubs/p60-238.pdf.

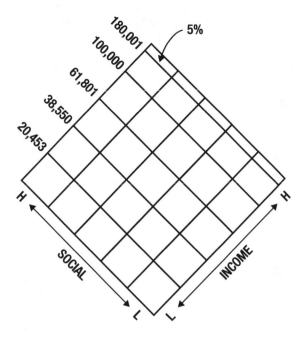

Figure 13.3 SES Determined by the Intersection of Social Status and Income Quintiles According to the 2007 Census

Furthermore, one's position in the middle three quintiles seems to have more to do with age than class. Most young families just entering the workforce will have incomes that place them in the second from the bottom quintile, but as their income rises with experience (especially those with salaried occupations), they also move up in quintiles.

On the other hand, one important factor made visible by the income quintile measure is the lack of mobility of those in the bottom and top quintiles. Those people born into a family in the bottom quintile are much less likely to move up even one quintile than members of the middle three quintiles. And those born into a family in the top quintile are much less likely to move down even one quintile than members of the middle three.[3]

Wealth. Many sociologists use income as a measure of economic position because it is easier to obtain or estimate than is wealth. *Wealth* refers to the differential between one's total assets and one's debts (i.e., wealth = total assets − total debts). Using wealth as a measure suggests a very different distribution of class positions for two important reasons. First, many families with relatively high income (for example, the family of two senior teachers mentioned above) also carry high debt due to the high cost of purchasing homes and paying for their children's college education. In fact, in 2012, 20 percent of the American people actually had negative wealth, meaning that their debts were larger than their assets.[4] Second, when using wealth as the economic measure of SES, the class divisions look quite different.

---

3. See *Pursuing the American Dream: Economic Mobility across Generations* (Washington, DC: Pew Charitable Trusts, 2012).

4. Diane Swanbrow, "Many U.S. Families Are Underwater with Debts: U-M Study" (Ann Arbor: University of Michigan, Institute for Social Research, 2012), http://home.isr.umich.edu/releases /many-us-families-are-underwater-with-debts-um-study/.

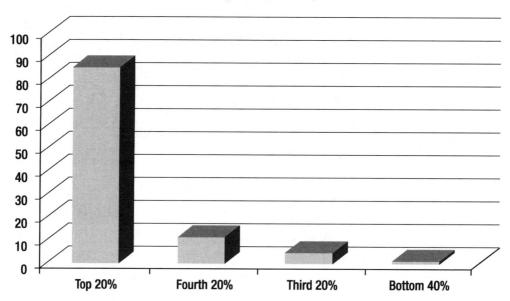

Figure 13.4 Percentage of Wealth by Quintiles Based on 2007 Census Data

Figure 13.4 presents a graph of the distribution of wealth by percentiles of the American population. Such a visual makes it easy to see that the bottom 80 percent of the American people have a small percent of the total wealth of the nation (only 15.1 percent).[5] As with income, the representation of wealth by dividing the population into equal quintiles may provide a misleading picture of the top 20 percent. Below is a graph that expands the top 20 percent in a manner that shows that the inequality at the top is also quite large.[6]

In fact, we are able to see that the top 1 percent of the population possesses more than one-third (34.6 percent) of all of the wealth in the nation, while the next lower 4 percent possesses more than one-quarter (27.3 percent). Together, the top 5 percent owns almost two-thirds of the wealth of the whole country. By breaking down the top quintile (see Figure 13.5), we may be able to develop a more useful understanding of the distribution of economic power in an SES construction of social class. Visually, we might consider the upper class to consist of the top 5 percent, the working class to consist of the bottom 40 percent, and the middle class to consist of the middle 55 percent. In this scenario, the combined economic power of the bottom 95 percent falls far short of the power of the top 5 percent.[7]

When reading education texts that address social class, we must try to determine what the authors mean by that. The first thing to determine is whether the author is using a Marxian or a Weberian (SES) concept of class or neither. If using SES, the next step is to determine whether the economic continuum is assumed to be based on income or wealth, and whether or

5. Edward N. Wolff, "Recent Trends in Household Wealth in the United States: Rising Debt and the Middle-Class Squeeze—An Update to 2007" (Annandale-on-Hudson, NY: Levy Economics Institute of Bard College, 2010).

6. Ibid.

7. Ibid.

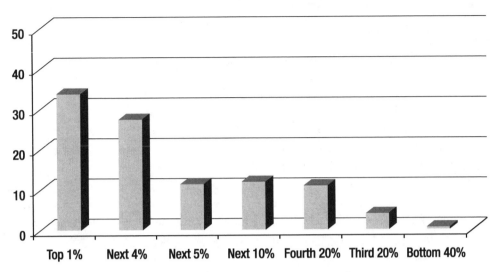

Figure 13.5 Percentage of Wealth with the Top Quintile Split Based on 2007 Census Data

not the author has complicated the social continuum or merely used occupation as the determinant factor. Once we have been able to develop a clearer understanding of which construct of social class is being used, we then need to draw on the various cultural narratives explicit or implicit in the text and, as a reader, your own assumed cultural narratives of social class. The next section explores some of the common narratives found in the education literature.

Narratives of Social Class and Education

There is certainly irony in the realization that of the many different cultural narratives about social class that permeate American society, the one that may be the best known and most frequently told denies the importance of class altogether. This cultural narrative is so associated with the United States that we might be tempted to call it "The Story That Is America." In fact, it is not just Americans who like to tell this story; people from all over the world sometimes use "America" or "the United States" as an ideograph to evoke this narrative—an ideograph that promotes the idea that anyone can make it in America. This idea, that the class position of one's parents is not what matters but rather one's individual ability and character determine a person's success, is so firmly etched in "The Story That Is America" that many of the poor from around the world dream of a ticket to the United States. In Chapter 4, I called this the Rags to Riches (RtR) narrative, a narrative often used as a way to suggest that social class in America is not very important. The narrative teaches that a person is more likely to climb out of poverty in America than in any other nation. It tells us that the United States is a middle-class society without the domination of the aristocracy that Europeans still must encounter and without the drag of poverty with which the story suggests South Americans and Africans must deal. In the United States, everybody seems to describe themselves as middle class. The rich dress down and the middle class copy the fashions of the inner-city poor. In America, social class just doesn't matter if you have talent and good character, or so the story goes. You often hear it in the phrase, "Only in America."

And certainly there is evidence that tellers of this narrative can use in support of their story. How about the one about the son of a single mom whose immigrant father left them to return to Africa and who grew up to be president of the United States? How about the teenager who had a great idea and a lot of determination and salesmanship who dropped out of college to start a computer software company and rose to become the richest man in the world? Surely, these specific narratives are but a couple of the hundreds we all know that appeal to this cultural narrative.

But while there are clearly specific anecdotes to support this cultural narrative, is there evidence of a broader sense to support it? What do the statistics tell us? Do they suggest that there is any truth to this narrative? If we look at world statistics, no other country can claim as many of the super-wealthy as does the United States. According to a research study from the United Nations University's World Institute for Economic Development Research, 25 percent of the world's top 10 percent and 37 percent of the world's top 1 percent wealthiest persons are Americans.[8] For many this shows that it is easier to become rich in the United States than in any other nation and confirms this cultural narrative.

But other people tell a different story supported by different data. They tell a story of a nation that fools itself and the world into thinking that class does not matter. This narrative, which I call the Transformation Not Reproduction (TNR) narrative, tells of a society in which social mobility is nowhere near as high as the RtR narrative would have us believe. In fact, the TNR narrative argues that the American class system permeates all American institutions from politics and the media to marriage and schools and that it results in the reproduction from generation to generation of a nation divided by class. This narrative promises that only a collective will of the people that challenges the RtR narrative can transform the nation to live up to its dream of equal opportunity for all regardless of class origin.

The TNR narrators have data on their side as well. They point out that having the greatest number of the super-wealthy is not a measure of opportunity but of inequality. They point to the Gini Coefficient, which is a measure of wealth inequality/equality, to show that the United States is far from having the most equality. According to the Central Intelligence Agency's *World Fact Book,* out of 136 nations, 40 have more inequality than the United States, but 95 have more equality than the United States, including such nations as Iran and Nigeria. No European nation is listed as having more inequality than the United States.[9]

The TNR narrators also point to intergenerational social mobility statistics, data that show the odds of moving up or down the income ladder, as evidence that class really does matter in the United States. According to Emily Beller and Michael Hout, the United States is actually below average in economic mobility and is significantly lower than nations such as "Canada, Finland, Sweden, Norway, and possibly Germany and the United States may be a less economically mobile

8. James B. Davies, Susanna Sandström, Anthony Shorrocks, and Edward N. Wolff, "The World Distribution of Household Wealth," Discussion Paper No. 2008/3, UNI-WIDER, February 2008, 15, at www.wider.unu.edu/publications/working-papers/discussion-papers/2008/en_GB/dp2008-03/_files/78918010772127840/default/dp2008-03.pdf.

9. "Distribution of Family Income—Gini Index," in *The World Fact Book 2013–2014* (Washington, DC: Central Intelligence Agency, 2013), www.cia.gov/library/publications/the-world-factbook/rankorder/2172rank.html.

society than Great Britain."[10] Beller also argues that the social mobility of American men born between 1965 and 1979 has actually declined from that of earlier generations in America.[11] These data, the tellers of the TNR narrative claim, show that the United States may have more inequality and less economic mobility than the RtR narrative would like us to believe.

The Great School Legend

So let us explore some of the common American cultural narratives that incorporate social class and focus especially on those that also include some aspect of education. The RtR narrative in the general population is often applied to our nation's creation of the first public mass education system. Earlier in the book I explored more fully the history of the creation of the American public schools; here I would like to address briefly one American cultural narrative. I call this the Great School Legend (GSL).[12] This narrative was perhaps the most prominent narrative about public schools during the twentieth century—at least up to the last couple of decades of that century. This cultural narrative tells of a young and unformed nation welcoming people from all over the world and from all walks of life and forging this diverse people into a great democratic nation with a common set of values, which included commitment to liberty, equality, and industry. Through a public investment in the education of all children regardless of their parents' background, we, as a nation, signaled our belief that the future of our nation lay in the hands of our children and also showed our clear belief that a "meritocracy" was superior to an "aristocracy."

This last point is sometimes misunderstood. All Americans are raised to understand that the founders of the nation were committed to liberty and to equality. However, they don't always realize that these terms did *not* mean that there was to be no social hierarchy but rather that the social hierarchy would be earned rather than inherited. In other words, the American experiment wished to build a society in which any child could rise to the top of the hierarchy based on her or his individual merit (hence meritocracy) rather than parents' social position (i.e., aristocracy). GSL tells us that the United States responded to this commitment of creating a social hierarchy based on individual merit by creating a public education system that would permit individuals to succeed based only on their abilities and character. Do well in school, and reap the nation's rewards. Do poorly in school, and find yourself, deservedly, on the bottom of the social and economic hierarchy.

Furthermore, one's social class was earned rather than inherited. In this way, the nation created a system to cultivate the best and the brightest to become its social, cultural, political, and economic leaders, which in turn led us to become the greatest nation on Earth. In this way, the GSL might be seen as a variation on the American Essentialism narrative presented in Chapter 4. Notice that the GSL also appeals to the Melting Pot narrative in that it suggests that another major purpose of public schooling is to forge a common American culture out of a disparate population both in terms of ethnicity and social class. And finally, notice that

10. Emily Beller and Michael Hout, "Intergenerational Social Mobility: The United States in Comparative Perspective," *Future of Children* 16, no. 2 (Fall 2006): 30.

11. Emily Beller, "Bringing Intergenerational Social Mobility Research into the Twenty-First Century: Why Mothers Matter," *American Sociological Review* 74, no. 4 (August 2009).

12. Colin Greer, *The Great School Legend: A Revisionist Interpretation of American Public Education* (New York: Basic Books, 1972).

it also appeals to the Stand on Your Own Two Feet narrative by assigning individual merit to those who succeed in the system and individual failure to those who do not. In other words, in the GSL, we see elements of at least three other cultural narratives, which helps reinforce the idea of the legitimacy of this story. If the GSL is a similar story to American Essentialism, the Melting Pot, and the Stand on Your Own Two Feet narratives, then it becomes easier to believe.

Also, notice that in the GSL, education is considered a *public* good. According to the GSL, it is in the interest of the nation to have a well-educated people, for it builds a common culture as well as provides the values necessary for a thriving democracy and provides the proper selection process for developing its most promising leaders. While individuals do receive their just desserts (i.e., they get what they deserve), the purpose of the public schools is a public one in the GSL cultural narrative. Its value accrues primarily to the public, not the private individual; hence they are called "public schools."

The Culture of Poverty Narratives

With the success of the civil rights movement, explaining school failure through genetics became an unfavored narrative in American society. In its place arose a Culture of Poverty narrative or, perhaps it is better to place it in the plural and say that there arose two Culture of Poverty narratives.

Culture of Poverty₁: The Cultural Deficiency Narrative

In his 1964 State of the Union address, President Lyndon Baines Johnson unveiled his War on Poverty, a collection of policies designed to reduce the nearly 20 percent poverty rate—a rate that was seen then as unacceptable by a large number of Americans.[13] Seen as an extension of Franklin Delano Roosevelt's New Deal, LBJ's Great Society expanded Keynesian economics to include the reduction of poverty as a public good that would result, it was claimed, in not only a more equitable society but an economically successful one as well. Johnson's (and President Richard Nixon's) policies, combined with the progressive tax structure of the middle twentieth century, helped to create a period of the greatest economic equality in the history of the United States.[14] Part of Johnson's War on Poverty included increased federal government support for education and youth support services. Educational agendas such

---

13. In contrast, in 2009, 21 percent of children lived in poverty, that is, more than 15 million children—an increase of 33 percent between 2000 and 2009. Rather than develop policies to reduce this poverty, today's policy-makers continue to adopt policies that increase the number of children in poverty. See Vanessa R. Wight et al., "Who Are America's Poor Children? The Official Story," National Center for Children in Poverty, 2011, www.nccp.org/publications/pub_1001.html.

14. Carol Higgs produced a graph that visually reveals the close relationship between the marginal tax rate of the top 1 percent and inequality in the United States during the twentieth century. The graph shows that the greatest period of equality occurred between World War II and the Reagan tax cuts. This period of high tax rates also produced the greatest growth in public infrastructure, including roads, bridges, and public schools as well as a period when almost anyone could afford college. See Carol Higgs, "Plutocracy Reborn: Re-Creating the Gap That Gave Us the Great Depression" (Washington, DC: Institute for Policy Studies and the Public Good. Reprinted in *The Nation,* June 30, 2008).

as Head Start and television programs such as *Sesame Street* were designed to "compensate" for an assumed deficiency among children of poverty. The idea that the culture of people living in poverty is deficient is an important element of the Culture of Poverty$_1$: Cultural Deficiency narrative.

In some ways the Cultural Deficiency narrative is itself a variation of the GSL, for it assumes that America's public schools provide an equal opportunity for all students regardless of family background. Given this assumption, if students fail, it could *not* be because the schools are failing the students but because there must be something deficient in the students themselves. If a category of students does not succeed in school (for example, children in poverty), there must be something about the students rather than the schools that causes their inability to succeed in an otherwise fair and equal system of schooling.

Of course, one could assume that what makes poor students deficient is genetics: that their parents are poor because they are not very smart, or they have bad character, and that both of these are traits inherited by their children. But the assumption that poor children, black children, Latino/a children, Irish children, Italian children, for example, failed at school because they were naturally intellectually and morally inferior is a race-based explanation that was in favor prior to World War II but that by the 1960s was no longer in fashion.

So, given that a race-based narrative was not an acceptable storyline to explain school failure of children in poverty, many people turned to a culture-based narrative of inferiority in its stead. Rather than suggesting that poor children were genetically inferior, the new story was that their culture was deficient. There were plenty of anecdotes published and circulated to support this narrative. Stories about the failure of parents to read to children or to even have books in the home, stories about parental disdain for education, stories about child neglect and even abuse, stories about poor nutrition based on poor buying choices rather than lack of money, and stories of poor parenting skills were all told and retold as ways to reinforce the basic cultural narrative that there exists a culture of poverty that is deficient in the qualities desired for success in school and in life in general. According to this narrative, it was no wonder these children failed and no wonder they ended up in lives of crime. Their home values are just inferior. It is certainly not the children's fault but rather the parents'. This story suggests that the good guys are the middle-class educated people who have good family values and who respect hard work and a good education. Teach these middle-class values and skills to the children of the poor (through programs such as Head Start and *Sesame Street,* for example) and you will make the goal of equal opportunity a reality.

We still find this narrative prominently told by many public figures. It is found in popular media as well. For example, *Lean on Me,* the 1989 movie based on the life of Joe Louis Clark and starring Morgan Freeman, retells this narrative through the story of a principal of a chaotic inner-city school who arrives with a big stick to bring order. Or consider *Stand and Deliver,* the 1988 movie starring Edward James Olmos that is based on the career of the late Jaime Escalante, the Los Angeles mathematics teacher of Bolivian descent who, through "tough love," brought the desire to achieve and the belief in self necessary for Latinos/as from the barrio to succeed and attend college. The Culture of Poverty$_1$: Cultural Deficiency narrative is found in teachers' lounges in such ideographs as "they come from families that don't value education," or "they don't believe in education because they think that they will just follow in their parents' footsteps." The narrative is even found on a bumper sticker that I happened to see: "Give them my work ethic; not my tax dollars."

The Culture of Poverty₂: Cultural Difference Narrative

Even though many Americans seem comfortable with calling the culture of people living in poverty deficient, others are made almost as uncomfortable with the idea of cultural deficiency as genetic deficiency. Some of these people have developed a different Culture of Poverty narrative: one that does not suggest that the culture of poor people is deficient, but only that it is different. And because it is different from the culture that is valued in schools, there is a mismatch between the culture of poor children and the culture of schools. Therefore, this mismatch of cultures results in poor children's lack of success. This story suggests that for poor children to succeed in school, they require educators to stop assuming the poor parents are deficient in child-rearing and that they have poor values and to recognize that they are raising their children to succeed in a world of poverty. Poor children require a different skill set and value orientation than children who expect to take their position in the middle class. Of course, according to this Cultural Difference narrative, while this culture of poverty helps kids survive poverty, it prevents social mobility into the middle class. Educators must be sympathetic to the children's and their parents' situation.

According to this narrative, educators should respect the cultural knowledge of surviving poverty that poor children bring to the school, but educators must also help these students understand the desirability of learning a new culture that will help them succeed in school, move out of poverty, and climb the ladder into the middle class. This narrative stops blaming the parents or the children and blames poor schools and poorly prepared teachers. According to the Culture of Poverty₂: The Cultural Difference narrative, if teachers could just understand the culture of poverty, they could intervene in poor children's education and lead them to master the values of the middle class, which would lead to success in school and life.

We find the Culture of Poverty₂: Cultural Difference narrative quite prominent in today's popular culture and in the politics of education. Popular movies such as *Dangerous Minds* (1995), starring Michelle Pfeiffer, and *Freedom Writers* (2007), starring Hilary Swank, seem to provide more sympathy for the cultures of the inner-city poor than did the earlier movies *Stand and Deliver* and *Lean on Me*. While still requiring the poor to give up their own culture and adopt that of the dominant middle class, these movies seem to suggest that there are rhyme and reason to the culture of these inner-city kids. Since the passage of No Child Left Behind and in its new guise as Race to the Top, the Cultural Difference narrative is central to Washington politics. Today's politicians refuse to permit educators to claim a Cultural Deficiency narrative to defend poor children's low school success; however, they do expect educators to replace the students' Culture of Poverty with a middle-class culture that is promoted through a common curriculum and measured through standardized tests. And these requirements are all elements of a Cultural Difference narrative.

Today, the most prominent promoter of this Cultural Difference narrative is Ruby Payne, who has developed a high-powered consulting business working with school districts all around the country to teach educators what she considers to be The Culture of Poverty in the hope that by understanding it, educators will be better able to appreciate and then to replace it with the middle-class culture that leads to success. Although Payne is often criticized for promoting a deficiency narrative, it is, I believe, really better understood as a difference narrative. Yet for many it does not really matter whether it is a deficiency or difference narrative because Payne is clearly advocating a Culture of Poverty narrative and that in itself is rejected in alternative narratives.[15] Also, notice that both versions of the Culture of Poverty narratives assume class as SES and place the important emphasis on the social continuum. In other words, the problem with poor children in schools is not their economic position but rather their social positioning. The problem with poverty is in its culture, not the reality of having little income and no wealth.

Reproduction Narratives

Economists Samuel Bowles and Herb Gintis provide an analysis of education and class that suggests that public schools serve the interests of the capitalist class by reproducing the class system from generation to generation by providing fundamentally different kinds of education for children of the different classes. The kind of education in working-class schools produces working-class labor. The kind of education in middle-class schools produces bureaucrats and professionals. The kind of education in schools for the children of the capitalists produces society's future leaders in business and civic affairs.

Resistance to Reproduction Narrative

Many scholars reject the existence of a culture of poverty. People living in poverty have different problems from those living in affluence, but they do not develop a different culture, they merely adopt different strategies for getting through the day. The most prominent critic of the culture of poverty explanation is William Julius Wilson, who has spent nearly thirty-five years documenting the lives of the poor of Chicago. His empirical research shows clearly that there is a distinct difference between poor people who live in economically devastated neighborhoods with a high percentage of people in poverty compared with poor people who live in economically viable neighborhoods with a low percentage of people in poverty.[16] In other words, it is not the individual family's poverty that predicts success in things like school and work as much as it is the neighborhood in which they live. This provides empirical evidence that there is no "culture of poverty" and argues instead that it is the geographic situation that provides some poor people opportunities and other poor people few opportunities. According to Wilson, it is not their culture but the class-segregated system within which they live that is the most important contributor to their success or failure.

So, if the failure of children living in poverty cannot be attributed to genetics or to a culture of poverty, how can we explain the statistical fact that children living in poverty continue to fail in schools? One possible way to explain this reality comes from a version of

15. For a presentation of Payne's ideas, see Ruby K. Payne, *A Framework for Understanding Poverty*, 4th ed. (Highlands, TX: Aha! Process, 2005). For a critique of Payne's "Culture of Poverty" as an inappropriate cultural deficiency narrative, see Paul Gorski, "The Classist Underpinnings of Ruby Payne's Framework," *Teachers College Record*, February 9, 2006; for Payne's response to Gorski's critique, see Ruby K. Payne, "Blog Entry: A Response to 'The Classist Underpinnings of Ruby Payne's Framework,'" *Teachers College Record*, July 14, 2006.

16. For example, see Loïc J. D. Waquant and William Julius Wilson, "The Cost of Racial and Class Exclusion in the Inner City," *The Annals of the American Academy of Political and Social Sciences* 501, no.1 (January 1989): 8–25.

the TNR cultural narrative discussed at the beginning of this chapter. This narrative tells a story of how there are mechanisms built into all social institutions that work to reproduce the status quo, including the social class system (and also the race, gender, and sexuality systems). In other words, built right into schools is a system that works to justify the present situation. In Chapter 8, I introduced the concept of hegemony, which suggests that the present inequitable status quo is maintained through a process in which the nation's institutions are harnessed in the interests of the dominant elites. The TNR narrative tells a story in which public schools work to reproduce the class system by convincing people that everyone has a fair chance for success, but, in fact, the system is fixed.

According to the TNR narrative, only a very few members of lower-status groups are provided a route to economic success. How else to explain, as an example that TNR narrators might point out, how the Ohio State Supreme Court has declared the funding of the state's public schools to be unconstitutional four times? Rather than address the concerns of the court, powerful Ohioans decided to replace the justices on the Supreme Court so that the state legislature can now safely ignore the court's directive. The result, according to the TNR narrative, is a system of education that is drastically unequal. For example, during the 2009–2010 school year, the Chagrin Falls, Ohio, public schools had a per-pupil expenditure of $11,912, whereas about thirty miles away, the Highland Local Schools had a per-pupil expenditure of $8,681.[17] Given that education is a state responsibility, not a local responsibility, the TNR narrative asks, how can we justify such unequal spending?

Some answer that question by suggesting that money is not what matters. We might call this the Money Doesn't Matter (MDM) narrative. This narrative points to a few schools in districts with low per-pupil expenditure that seem to get good results. But it is interesting that those who most fervently tell the MDM story choose to send their own children to schools in districts with a high per-pupil expenditure. If money doesn't matter, why not reduce the spending in their own schools so they can pay less in taxes?

The Resistance to Reproduction narrative is a version of the TNR narrative. The former tells of young people who intuitively understand that the schools are not designed for them. They grasp that even if they succeed in school, the best that could happen is for them "to escape" the poor neighborhoods. Success in today's schools is unlikely to lead to success for their community; it only leads to personal success. According to this narrative, these students sense in their gut that to succeed in school requires them to turn their backs on their family, friends, neighborhood, and people. It means they must give up their culture, their identity, and join the dominant group to maintain the suppression of otherwise deserving people. The result of the intuitive understanding that schools really are not working in the interest of students living in poverty is that many of them resist what the school teaches. They reject the celebration of middle-class and elite culture, language, and values because that culture, language, and values are really little more than self-serving justification for continuing the present inequitable and unfair class system. As Paul Willis pointed out, unfortunately, often it is their very resistance that leads to the reproduction of the status quo.[18] But not always.

---

17. "School Funding by District," Ohio General Assembly, 2013, http://ode.legislature.state.oh.us/index.php.

18. Paul E. Willis, *Learning to Labour: How Working Class Kids Get Working Class Jobs* (Farnborough, UK: Saxon House, 1977).

There are examples of students who resist the school's attempt to disempower the poor and other marginalized groups, resulting in their success rather than failure. For example, Mary Fuller presented the specific story of three Afro-Caribbean girls in a London high school who resisted the school's attempt to convince them that they could not succeed in school. They resisted by working together and supporting each other, which led to their academic success.[19] Dorinda Carter told of black students in an "upper-class, predominantly white, [American] suburban public high school," who resisted the school's conception of race and its assumption that the students could not succeed, and ended with the students achieving success in an otherwise hostile environment.[20] Na'ilah Suad Nasir provided an interesting tale of an American school that actually joined with a Muslim boy and his family to nurture the boy's resistance against a larger society that failed to show his family or him the respect that we would expect. By working with him, rather than trying to suppress his resistance, the school was able to provide him an education that did not force him to choose between success in school and his own identity.[21]

All three of these studies provide specific narratives of the cultural narrative that I am calling Resistance to Reproduction (a version of the TNR narrative). This cultural narrative typically is set in a hostile school environment for poor children and other members of disempowered groups. Its heroes are students and teachers who work with students to resist the dominant, hegemonic ideology that works to reproduce the status quo. Instead of resisting the hegemony in a negative way that leads to the kind of reproduction that Willis identifies, these heroes resist in a manner that rejects the dominant construction of education as solely the acquisition of technical skills (i.e., training for jobs) and the confirmation of middle-class values, and replaces it with an education of pride in self, people, and culture that leads to community and to solidarity with their class. It is this education for class identity, community, and solidarity that is necessary for the educational success of working-class students. Henry Giroux, one of the most important scholars advancing this narrative, emphasizes that not all oppositional behavior should be considered resistance. Some oppositional behavior actually works against the rebelling students' own interests. To avoid the kind of problem that Willis pointed to where students' oppositional behavior actually promoted their own class reproduction, Giroux argued that real resistance is politically aware and strategic. He wrote that

> the ultimate value of the notion of resistance has to be measured against the degree to which it not only prompts critical thinking and reflective action, but, more importantly, against the degree to which it contains the possibility of galvanizing collective political struggle around the issue of power and social determination.[22]

19. Mary Fuller, "Black Girls in a London Comprehensive School," in *Schooling for Women's Work*, ed. Rosemary Deem (London: Routledge & Kegan Paul, 1980), 52–65.

20. Dorinda J. Carter, "Achievement as Resistance: The Development of a Critical Race Achievement Ideology among Black Achievers," *Harvard Educational Review* 78, no. 3 (Fall 2008): 466–497.

21. Na'ilah Suad Nasir, "'Halal-ing' the Child: Reframing Identities of Resistance in an Urban Muslim School," *Harvard Educational Review* 74, no. 2 (Summer 2004).

22. Henry A. Giroux, *Theory and Resistance in Education: A Pedagogy for the Opposition* (South Hadley, MA: Bergin & Garvey, 1983), 111.

It is this resistance to class reproduction, one that teaches students to understand their political context and to develop the hope and strategies necessary to transform the nation and achieve its ideals of liberty and justice for all, that forms this narrative and should form the center of our educational work.

While this narrative is prominent in educational scholarship, it is more difficult to find examples of this narrative in movies popular today. However, in the 1960s, there were several movies where this narrative can be found, such as Tony Richardson's *The Loneliness of the Long Distance Runner* (1962), starring Michael Redgrave, which tells the story of a boy sent to a reform school who purposively rejects the favor of the establishment in order to remain in solidarity with his working-class inmates. Another example is Lindsay Anderson's *This Sporting Life* (1963), starring Richard Harris, which tells the story of a successful rugby player who becomes disillusioned when his success on the rugby pitch does not translate into a corresponding rise in social status. While we may have trouble finding contemporary dramatic films using this narrative, we can find it in documentaries, including *Precious Knowledge,* which recounts the resistance of faculty and students found in a Mexican-American Studies program in Tucson High School as they struggle against the Arizona state superintendent, who works to shut down their program.

Conclusion

This chapter has presented several competing cultural narratives that address social class and how they get retold as education narratives. One prominent cultural narrative is the Rags to Riches narrative (RtR), which celebrates the United States as a nation where social class does not really matter very much. In education, the RtR narrative gets retold in several different ways. We particularly find it in the Great School Legend, which attributes the public schools with creating the mechanism necessary to achieve a system based on merit rather than social class. We also see variations of the RtR narrative found in the two Culture of Poverty narratives, which account for the failure of the poor to take advantage of the schools for mobility as their own cultural deficiency or their cultural difference.

We also showed that the Transformation Not Reproduction narrative is often invoked as a counternarrative to the RtR narrative. In education, the TNR narrative often takes the form of the Resistance to Reproduction narrative, where students, teachers, and parents can help children in poverty to achieve success by helping them resist the reproductive teachings of schools and to help them develop class identity and solidarity as a way to stand together and succeed together.

If we are to understand the debates around social class in America, we must grasp the cultural narratives that underpin much of the discussion. This chapter has presented educational versions of cultural narratives that are frequently used by parents, teachers, policy-makers, and the media to couch their arguments. All too frequently the actual evidence necessary to develop a strong argument is missing in these discussions; therefore, the use of tropes and ideographs that call forth these cultural narratives often substitutes for real substantive engagement. The well-educated citizen, parent, and educator will recognize these cultural narratives right away and decide whether or not to require the presentation of premises necessary for a strong argument or to settle for the mere persuasiveness of the rhetoric that these cultural narratives can provide.

CHAPTER FOURTEEN

Narratives of Race

$\mathbf{M}$ost American college students studying race for the first time are astounded to find that race is not a category of the biological world but rather of the social world. For most Americans, regardless of the race they have been assigned, the biological basis of race is commonsense. In fact, to state otherwise seems to belie a natural fact that anyone can see just by opening their eyes and looking. For most Americans, it is obvious that nature divides humans into subcategories based on our inherited physiology. But in this case, "commonsense" is wrong, and "nature" turns out to be no more than a construction of society.

To state that human races are not determined by biology does not mean that what we call *race* has nothing at all to do with the physiology of human beings, but only that the schema that governs where the boundaries between racial categories are located and with which any particular human gets assigned to a particular category has no scientific basis. Rather than being located in nature, race is located in our socially constructed understanding of human groupings. This idea not only surprises most Americans, it also seems to contradict most people's own experience with the world, and so it is often quickly dismissed as wrongheaded and not to be taken seriously. For that reason, this chapter will start by trying to clarify the relationship between race and physiology and explain why contemporary scholars almost universally reject the idea that human race exists in the natural world.

The Nonscience of Race

Many people simply refuse to accept the idea that human races are not biological categories, but part of that refusal comes from not understanding the alternatives. To claim that race is not a *biological* category is not to suggest that people do not inherit their physiology from their parents. Of course they do. The claim that race is not a biological category is only a claim that the specific categories that we call "races" are *socially and culturally* constructed rather than *biologically* determined. For example, people inherit the color of their hair and eyes and their relative height and weight from their parents, but we do not categorize the human species into subspecies based on hair and eye color or height and body weight. There is no subspecies we call "giants" or "fairhairs." We just see these as characteristics of different groups of people distributed through physiological inheritance, not a basis upon which to divide the human species into a set of subspecies. There would be just as much legitimacy to treat blue-eyed blonds and brown-eyed brunettes as racial divisions as there is to divide the world into the categories that we now recognize as *race*.

Through the years, there have been many classifications of race. I remember my 1955 fourth-grade geography textbook specifically teaching that there were three human races: "Caucasian," "Mongoloid," and "Negroid"—a common understanding of race when I was a kid. Today, however, scientists overwhelmingly agree that these categories do not exist in the natural world. Again let me try to be clear: scientists are not suggesting that people do not differ physiologically, only that the ways in which we differ physiologically do not equate to what we call race.

There is no physiological indicator that occurs in everyone of one race that also fails to occur in people of a different race. Consider skin color, for example. Just by looking at people, we can see that some people have darker skin than other people. Isn't it obvious, some might ask, that there are some people who are "black" and some people "brown" and some people "white"? But the problem is where to draw the line between these races? When is a person's skin color so dark as to place them in one category or so light as to place them in the other? There are millions of people who are now classified as so-called Caucasians whose skin is darker than people who are classified as so-called Black. We do inherit our skin color from our parents, but that skin color has more to do with where our recent evolutionary ancestors clustered along the world's latitude rather than the result of belonging to a particular human subspecies. People who lived near the equator—regardless of where on the equator they may have lived—maintained the melanin in the surface of the skin. As the location of inhabitance moves away from the equator, the color of the skin gets lighter. At the present time, it is theorized that in northern climates, evolutionary processes selected those with lighter skin because of the human need for Vitamin D, which is produced by the body when sunlight strikes our skin. Those in latitudes far from the equator had less direct sunlight and, therefore, those with lighter skin produced more Vitamin D, resulting in a greater likelihood of reaching maturity and of reproducing. But this evolutionary change is one of the last to occur in the human species. Nearly all genetic variation had already occurred before humans migrated from the equatorial latitudes to the temperate ones. In other words, those whose skin was selected for its lightness in the northern latitudes already had all of the genetic variation of those from the equatorial latitudes. Or to reverse the sentence: nearly all of the genetic variation found in those from the northern latitudes also exists in those from the equatorial latitudes. The change in skin color is recent and lies, literally, on the surface of the body. It indicates nothing about the genetic makeup of a person below the skin.

"Well, what about diseases?" skeptics often ask. It is certainly true that the medical literature is beginning to recognize that different medical conditions and diseases are distributed differently across different so-called racial groups. Skeptics often raise questions about sickle cell anemia because many have believed that it is a medical condition of people of African descent. But that belief is inaccurate. Sickle cell is not distributed along lines that we now call race but along the lines of our recent evolutionary ancestors who lived in places with high incidence of malaria. That means not only Africa, but around Mediterranean Europe and the Middle East, South Asia, and Central and Northern-South America. Today we find sickle cell anemia in people whose ancestors came from regions including not only Africa but Sicily and other Southern Italian areas, Greece, Arabic countries, India, Malaysia, and Latin America. As with other alleged "indicators of race," sickle cell does not trace the so-called racial lines. Furthermore, those of African descent whose ancestors did not live in regions with high malarial incidence did not develop the sickling condition.

To reiterate, the point here is not that there is no physiological basis for the appearance of our human bodies. We do inherit them from our parents. It is to claim that the categories that we call "race" do not line up with any biological indicator or combination of indicators. Race, as we know, recognize, and claim it, just does not exist in the world of nature.

Race as Social Construction

If race is not a category of biology, what is it? Simply put, it is a category of our cultures. It is socially constructed within cultures and as cultures change across time and across geography so does race. If race were a category of biology, it would not change. It would remain stable. If a race existed in the natural world, then the categories would cross geographic boundaries. Puerto Ricans may assign a different word to the dog than Anglo Americans do, but to the Puerto Ricans, *el perro* is *el perro* and never *el gato,* just as to the Anglo American a dog is a dog and never a cat.

On the other hand, Puerto Ricans use a different racial classification than that traditionally used in the mainland United States. As stated above, according to the science of my youth, there were only three races. This three-part racial division has a legacy in the way in which the US federal government counts race. According to most government forms, "Hispanic" is an ethnic category and not a racial one. So, people are asked their race and then they are asked whether they are "Hispanic" or not. But on the streets of Puerto Rico, the category "Puerto Rican" is considered a racial category and not an ethnic one. For many in Puerto Rico, to be "Puerto Rican" is not just making a claim to ethnicity or nationality, but to race. Likewise, many who are natural-born citizens of Puerto Rico but clearly of European descent are reluctant to refer to themselves as "Puerto Rican" because it indicates a racial categorization to which they have not been assigned. Today, many young Americans use a racial categorization that is a lot closer to that of Puerto Ricans than the United States government because, in the last decade or so, the category "Latino/a" (or "Hispanic") has taken on a racial, and not just an ethnic, meaning. But it would be a mistake to treat the "Puerto Rican" category used by Puerto Ricans as the same as the "Latino/a" or "Hispanic" category used in the mainland United States because in Puerto Rico to be "Puerto Rican" is not to be Colombian or Mexican or Cuban. In other words, the racial divisions in Puerto Rico are distinct from the racial divisions in the mainland United States, which, in turn, are different from the racial divisions as constructed in Brazil or Argentina or South Africa.

In the United States today, white and black Americans have no trouble identifying "Asians" as a racial category, but these so-called Asians sometimes have trouble recognizing themselves as a racial category. Just as the idea of treating Americans of Mexican descent and those of Venezuelan descent and those of Panamanian descent as a single racial group called "Latino/a" (or "Hispanic") requires one to ignore not only cultural differences but physiological ones as well, so too Americans of Chinese, Japanese, Filipino, Indonesian, Hmong, Vietnamese, Cambodian, Sri Lankan, Indian, Bangladeshi, and Pakistani descent often have difficulty understanding themselves as members of one racial group. In their home countries, there are often racial distinctions made among these categories, but suddenly in the United States they learn that they are considered of one racial group. It can often be quite disturbing to a first-generation Chinese immigrant to find her daughter dating a Filipino, and vice versa.[1]

If race were a category of nature, rather than one of culture, we would find much more agreement across time and across geography about what constitutes racial categories. Even though there are surely physiological differences among people, these differences simply do not line up with the categories that different cultures assign to categories of race. For that reason, we must accept the realization that race is a category of culture and not biology.

Contemporary Racialization

One of the clearest pieces of evidence that race is a category constructed by sociocultural mechanisms rather than a category of biological necessity can be found in the present construction of new racial categories and the reconstruction of old ones. The process of the sociocultural construction of races is referred to as racialization. The term *racialization* has two different, but related, usages: In one meaning, racialization refers to the sociocultural processes that create races. This is the meaning that will be used in this section. (A second meaning refers to the recognition that race is a relevant category in understanding a particular social event or condition. This second meaning will be developed in the next chapter.) If we pay close attention, we can see racialization (of the first definition) at work in contemporary America as new races are constructed and old ones gain new boundaries and meanings.

The Racialization of Latinos/as

During the 1960s and 1970s, civil rights leaders representing the interests of the diverse populations descended from Latin American countries began to advocate for a single umbrella term to represent these different national identities. The term that became most accepted was *Hispanic.* Though the term itself refers to the culture of the Iberian peninsula (Spain, Portugal, Andorra, and Gibraltar), it began to be used to represent the peoples and cultures of Latin America as well. By having a single term to represent their overlapping common interests, people from nations as diverse as Cuba, Mexico, Puerto Rico, and Brazil could develop a political solidarity and assert more political leverage.

In 1980, the US Census added a question that asked people to identify themselves as Hispanic or Non-Hispanic. This question was followed by another question that asked the respondent to identify their race. In other words, one could identify as Hispanic and white, as Hispanic and black, as Hispanic and mixed-race, or as Hispanic and any other racial category available. In this way, the Hispanic category was separated from race. The census made clear that according to the US government, *Hispanic* was an indicator of national heritage or ethnicity, not of race.

---

1. See Nazli Kibria, "The Construction of 'Asian American': Reflections on Intermarriage and Ethnic Identity among Second-Generation Chinese and Korean Americans," *Ethnic and Racial Studies* 20, no. 3 (July 1997): 523–544.

The 2000 US Census found nearly 48 percent of Hispanics identified themselves as "white" while about 42 percent identified themselves as racially "other."[2] The 2010 US Census found an increase to 53 percent of Hispanics who identified themselves as white.[3] Reanne Frank, Ilana Redstone Akresh, and Bo Lu found that the high percentage of Latinos/as identifying as white on the 2003 New Immigrant Survey is closely connected to how light their skin is. Frank, Akresh, and Lu suggest that the increase in the percentage of Latinos/as identifying as white combined with the refusal of a large minority to choose one of the standard US racial categories suggests a new racial category is being constructed around darker-skinned Latinos/as who experience racial discrimination due to their skin color.[4]

Whether or not Frank, Akresh, and Lu are correct in their prediction of the Latino/a communities dividing along a "color line," it is clear that today many Latinos/as claim their own racial identity and reject being classified as white or black or Asian. As of yet, neither the US government, state governments, nor public schools recognize Latino/a as a racial category, but that doesn't stop the average American, whether Latino/a or not, from doing so. Being caught right in the middle of such a sociocultural change as the creation of a new race is often not easy to see, specifically because we are caught in the middle of it. But, if we step back and look at identities across time, we can draw no other conclusion than that the racialization of Latinos/as is occurring in the United States today.

The Re-Racialization of Asian Americans

Above I referred to the fact that American race scientists in the 1950s declared that humans were divided into three races. One of those races was called "Mongoloid." The so-called Mongoloid race purportedly consisted of people of Asian descent, including American indigenous peoples who, it was believed, had migrated from Asia during the last ice age. Today, this racial category no longer exists. It has been replaced with "Asian," "Asian and Pacific Islander," or "Asian American." But when shifting from "Mongoloid" to "Asian," not just the name was changed; so too were the boundaries that decided who is and is not to be considered "Asian." The process of racialization can group quite distinct nationalities, ethnicities, and cultures into a single category. As with the desire of Latino/a civil rights leaders working to construct the single category of Hispanic in order to gain more political leverage, today we find Asian American activists attempting to forge a common Asian identity in order to gain more political clout for those of Asian descent.[5]

---

2. See Elizabeth M. Grieco and Rachel C. Cassidy, "Table 10: Hispanic and Not Hispanic Population by Race for the United States: 2000," *Overview of Race and Hispanic Origin: 2000,* Census Brief (Washington, DC: US Census Bureau, 2001), www.census.gov/prod/2001pubs/c2kbr01-1.pdf.

3. See Karen R. Humes, Nicholas A. Jones, and Roberto R. Ramirez, "Table 2: Population by Hispanic or Latino Origin and Race for the United States: 2010," *Overview of Race and Hispanic Origin: 2010,* Census Brief (Washington, DC: US Census Bureau, 2011).

4. Reanne Frank, Ilana Redstone Akresh, and Bo Lu, "Latino Immigrants and the U.S. Racial Order: How and Where Do They Fit In?" *American Sociological Review* 75, no. 3 (June 2010): 378–401.

5. For an example of such an organized group of activists working to create this identity as a political pressure group, see "The 80-20 Initiative," www.80-20initiative.net/index.asp.

But think for a moment about the difficulty of this project. Consider the way in which in Asia (as in Europe and Africa), a long history of war and exploitation has created distrust, suspicion, and dislike of other Asian nations and their people. For example, the past militaristic aggression of the Japanese left a legacy of distrust among the Chinese, Koreans, and Filipinos. On the other hand, the Chinese have used their historical success at trade and market initiative to dominate economies in such nations as Indonesia and Malaysia, creating a legacy of dislike among the Indonesians and Malaysians for ethnic Chinese living in their countries. Much as European nations, many Asian nations carry old historic grudges.

Or consider that those from South Asia have little in common with those from Southeast and East Asia. The Indians, Bangladeshis, Pakistanis, and Sri Lankans have neither language nor physical similarity to other Asians and only a little overlap in religion. And what about the Pacific Islanders, who are traditionally located in this category? In what ways do the native Hawaiians or the Samoans or the Fijians share a culture or an identity with East, Southeast, or Southern Asians? And yet, in the United States, people from these otherwise distinct cultures and nations are often treated as if they were a single racial category. Often to their dismay, people of Asian descent in America find that they are treated alike by those who are not of Asian descent. In order to fight against the discrimination, many have found it desirable to overlook their cultural, ethnic, religious, and historical differences and forge a new racial identity. But this new "Asian" or "Asian American" racial category differs from the old "Mongoloid" category in that it no longer includes Indigenous Americans in the same category. American Indians seem to be becoming their own racial category—neither African American nor Latino/a nor Asian American, but something in itself. We are witnessing the racialization of the indigenous tribes of the Americas.

There also seems to be a beginning movement to racialize Muslims or Middle Easterners as evidenced in calls for profiling at airport security and suspicions of Arabic-language charter schools.[6] Even though "Muslim" is an indicator of one's religion, and like any religion it has nothing to do with one's biological heritage, since September 11, 2001, some Americans have begun to treat Muslims as if they were a racial group even though, as a religion, Islam is found around the world, and its adherents can look like they come from anyplace (and do). Some people use the term "Arab" to represent a racialized Muslim identity. But since Arabs make up a very specific ethnic community among dozens of others in the Middle East, using "Arab" as a general term to represent all people from the Middle East or all Muslims reveals a profound ignorance of Americans about other parts of the world. Whether or not "Muslim" or "Arab" does evolve into a racial category through the next decades, it should be clear that race is an ever-changing and -evolving set of culturally constructed categories, and that the processes of racialization are occurring as I write this chapter. Such social processes of racialization should be sufficient to convince even the most skeptical that race is not a category of the natural world.

Race as Narrative

As with other topics in this book, if race is a category of culture, then perhaps cultural narratives can better explain our understanding of race than do scientific findings. The following

6. See Devin Fehely, "Arabic Language Charter School Suffers Setback," Atlanta, GA, WXIA TV, 2011, www.11alive.com/news/article/200484/40/ALPHARETTA-Arabic-language-charter-school-suffers-setback.

section presents four unique cultural narratives that different people assume when they appeal to race in American society. I will not argue that any particular one of these is the correct narrative, only that these cultural narratives are quite prevalent in American culture and influence the way in which different Americans make sense out of this category we call race. Also, I do not claim that these four are the only narratives of race (they are not), but only that they are quite prominent narratives found in public discourse in the United States and provide another context with which to interpret texts about education.

The Race as Biology Narrative

I've just finished writing a long section clarifying how race is not a biological category, but just because nearly all scientists are agreed on this point does not mean that people do not appeal to a Race as Biology narrative whenever they talk about race. One way to understand this would be to point out that the use of the term *race* as a biological category depends on a weak scientific argument, since science makes an empirical claim and the empirical evidence in this case does not support the claim. On the other hand, rhetoric does not require evidence but commonsense for many people to accept it. Given that a high percentage of Americans still assume that race is a biological category then we must assume that when they use it, they assume the Race as Biology narrative. What could look more like commonsense than that? In other words, like other rhetorical devices, the appeal to biology when using the term "race" depends on a basic cultural narrative more than a reasoned scientific argument. As has already been pointed out in this book, rhetoric often trumps argument in the minds of readers.

According to the Race as Biology cultural narrative, there are three races located in the biological evolution of the human species. This story tells us that pre-human hominids migrated out of Africa and dispersed around the globe. At approximately the same time, but in three different locations on earth, *Homo sapiens* evolved from these pre-human hominids. According to this cultural narrative, one branch of the tree evolved in Africa and became the race we used to call "Negroid" but which today we more typically call "black." A second branch of the human tree evolved in Central Asia and became the race we used to call "Mongoloid," but today call "Asian." The third branch of the human tree evolved in the Caucasus Mountain region between the Black Sea and the Caspian Sea that, according to this narrative, became the race many still call "Caucasian."

According to this story, these three different evolutions created three different subspecies of *Homo sapiens*. The so-called Negroids settled Africa. The so-called Mongoloids settled Asia and migrated to the Americas, and the so-called Caucasians settled Europe. The result of this separate evolution resulted in three different kinds of humans with different strengths and weaknesses. During the height of popularity of this cultural narrative, believers argued that the three distinct evolutions resulted in not only different categories of humans but in a hierarchy of categories where Caucasians were considered the superior race and the so-called Negroids the most inferior race. This supposed hierarchy of races was used to justify everything from slavery to miscegenation laws to the eugenics movement to the Nazi Holocaust.

Today scientists have much evidence to suggest that this story just does not match the facts. While it is true that pre-human hominids did migrate around the world, contemporary evidence suggests that the evolution from pre-human to *Homo sapiens* occurred in one place—Africa. The migration of humans around the world occurred after this evolution making all human beings descended from the same people. Go back far enough, and we are all of African descent. So, while the Race as Biology cultural narrative is not supported by strong scientific argument, for some people, its commonsense narrative still makes a persuasive rhetorical device.

The Race as Ethnicity Narrative

In the early part of the twentieth century, Franz Boas, the leading American anthropologist of his time, began to publicly argue that there was no scientific evidence to support the idea that any human race was superior or inferior to any other due to nature. Instead, Boas argued that the appearance of inferiority and superiority was merely the result of social conditions backed by the power of the victor.[7] By the end of World War II, with the realization of the horror of the Holocaust, few scholars were ready to defend the scientific basis of race, and yet the textbooks used in America's elementary and secondary schools were apparently unwilling to acknowledge this growing consensus among natural and social scientists. Even today we find reluctance to assert strongly any counternarrative to the Race as Biology narrative in American science textbooks.[8] And yet, while many people may have been looking the other way, an alternative narrative has inserted itself squarely in the middle of the national conversation. I call this the Race as Ethnicity narrative.

The idea of ethnic groups is as old as the idea of races. *Ethnicity* means little more than a shared sense of peoplehood but the Race as Ethnicity narrative locates the human categories we call race in culture rather than in biology. In the Race as Ethnicity narrative, race either is recognized as one characteristic of a particular ethnic group, such as those who identify as Chinese culturally, or as the primary feature that identifies the shared sense of peoplehood, such as Asian American. The narrative of Race as Ethnicity can be told with many exemplar stories.

Consider the Irish in America. In the early part of the twentieth century, many considered the Irish to be a different racial category. The Irish were not considered "White." Nor were the Polish, the Slavs, or a whole host of people from Catholic countries in Southern and especially Eastern Europe. Nor were the Jews considered "White." World War II helped "whiten" these Americans. In many ways, this series of events seems to match The Melting Pot narrative described in Chapter 4.

When we no longer consider race to be biologically immutable, it reminds many people that at one time, so-called white ethnics were not considered really white. Yet, given time, hard work, and the G.I. Bill that helped pay for a generation of this group to go to college following WWII, by the 1970s nearly everyone recognized the Irish, Poles, Slavs, and others of this group to be white. And if the melting away of racial differences could occur then, then, at least according to the Melting Pot and Race as Ethnicity narratives, there is no reason not to think that it is continuing to happen with people who are considered racially different today.

7. Franz Boas, "The Real Race Problem from the Point of View of Anthropology," *The Crisis* 7 (December 1910).

8. Ann Morning, "Reconstructing Race in Science and Society: Biology Textbooks, 1952–2002," *American Journal of Sociology* 114, Supplement (2008): S106-S37.

In the late 1960s and early 1970s, civil rights activists worked to reconstruct the racial narrative used in this country. While just a few years earlier, young *Negroes* rejected that term and embraced the term *black* to represent themselves, some civil rights activists promoted the use of the obviously ethnic-sounding *Afro-American* term instead. Within a few years, *Afro-American* became *African American* and even more clearly appealed to a narrative of Race as Ethnicity. Today, it seems, the most accepted term in print to represent this group is *African American*. Gone is the referent to skin color and biology, and in its place a referent to geography has been inserted. In this way, African Americans are rhetorically just like Irish Americans, Italian Americans, and Polish Americans. According to this narrative, it is just a matter of time before this formerly racial category is seen as little more than an ethnic identity—something to put on and take off as the individual desires, just as some Irish Americans like to wear green every March 17th and make sure, every now and then, to drink a Guinness or bake a soda bread. They are Irish when they want to be and not when they prefer not to be. This is the promise of the Race as Ethnicity narrative.

And for some, the election of Barack Obama as president of the United States proved the truth of this narrative. Having an African American elected president seems to many to suggest that race has melted away; that we live in a "postracial" society in which race is something that people can put on and take off as they desire. To many, race does not really mean anything anymore. It seems to suggest that Dr. Martin Luther King Jr.'s dream has come true already: that his "four little children will one day live in a nation where they will not be judged by the color of their skin but by the content of their character."[9]

The Race as Caste Narrative

For many, the election of Obama and other evidence of success of African Americans and other people of color in the twenty-first century confirm the Race as Ethnicity narrative, but for many others, the apparent unique treatment of President Obama as not being American (i.e., the so-called birther movement), of being Muslim, of being a terrorist, and other code-worded comments, even from government officials elected to high national offices, proves the opposite to be true. It seems to many Americans that even a black elected to the highest office of the land is still considered by too many of their fellow citizens to be "a dangerous black man."

And while it is certainly true that for some blacks, life in America is better than it could ever have been for their parents, there is evidence to suggest that for many other black Americans, life is actually worse. According to the Census Bureau, the income of black Americans continues to decline. From 2008 to 2009, the average annual income of black Americans dropped 4 percent. During that same time, the percentage of black Americans living in poverty rose by 1 percent. The number of black Americans without health care rose by 2 percent to 21 percent.[10] Other statistics around test scores, high school dropouts, unequal punishment in schools, and college attendance suggest that things are not improving for black Americans in schooling either. And while the United States incarcerates a higher

---

9. Martin Luther King Jr., "I Have a Dream" (1963), accessed on May 30, 2013, at www.usconstitution .net/dream.html.

10. "Income, Poverty and Health Insurance Coverage in the United States: 2009," US Census Bureau, 2010, www.census.gov/newsroom/releases/archives/income_wealth/cb10-144.html.

percent of its population than any other nation (about 1 percent of the population), more than 2.5 percent of Hispanics and more than 6.5 percent of black Americans are in prison.[11] Statistics such as these leave many to question the narrative that race is just another indicator of ethnicity. Instead, it seems to them that race in America mirrors somewhat the caste system of ancient India.

In a caste system, a child is born into a caste and dies in the same caste. Although one can be more or less successful within a caste, one can never change castes. The caste a child is born into limits or promotes the possible occupations available to her or him. It helps determine a family's income, potential educational attainment, future occupation, and future lifetime partner. According to the Race as Caste narrative, race in the United States is much like this caste system: one is born into a race, and if one's parents happen to be of two different races, the race of less status is the one typically assigned to the child. So, for example, Obama, despite having a white mother; being raised in a white family; and attending elite, private, and almost completely white schools is considered a black man. So too is Colin Powell, former chair of the Joint Chiefs of Staff and the former secretary of state, whose mother of African descent and father of Irish descent immigrated to the United States from Jamaica.

In the United States, to be born black or Latino/a makes your chances of success in school, in income, and in health far less than to be born white. And while some categories of Asians in America seem to equal white Americans in some areas, some groups are more equivalent to blacks and Latinos/as than to whites; only Filipino Americans and Japanese Americans actually equal the average white American in personal income.[12]

Those who use the term *race* assume the narrative Race as Caste but do *not* desire that race be caste-like. They do *not* argue that race should be treated as caste. In fact, they argue that it should not be, but, they add, right now, in the United States, like it or not, race is a kind of caste system and until we acknowledge this fact, we will never be able to change that fact. They argue that before we can abandon the reality of race as caste, we must begin to acknowledge that the Race as Caste narrative most closely resembles the experience of race in America. Recognizing this reality, they hope, will lead people to seriously attempt to change the way race is built right into our institutions, into our system that creates the effect of caste even when people wish it to be otherwise. Pretending that race is mere ethnicity and that some future utopic postracial society is just around the corner, if not already here, can never come about, they argue, unless we first admit that right now, in the America of today, regardless of our hopes and dreams, race is just America's caste system.

The Race as Nation Narrative

For most people today, the term *nation* is just a synonym for the word *country* and indicates a political entity such as France or Germany or Italy. But these political entities are more properly called *nation-states*. Nation-states are decidedly a modern form of state. Prior to nation-states, there existed a wider range of states, such as kingdoms, principalities, and

---

11. Jenifer Warren, "One in 100: Behind Bars in America 2008," Pew Center on the States, February 2008, www.pewstates.org/uploadedFiles/PCS_Assets/2008/one%20in%20100.pdf.

12. C. N. Le, "Socioeconomic Statistics & Demographics," Asian-Nation: The Landscape of Asian America, www.asian-nation.org/demographics.shtml.

city-states. France is the name of the nation-state associated with the nation of the Franks. The unification of the German states did not occur until the latter half of the nineteenth century and, in fact, one reason Nazi Germany gave for its "legal" annexation of Czechoslovakia in 1938 was the "rightful" incorporation of the Germanic Sudetenland into the Germanic nation-state of Germany. In a similar way, the nation-state we now call Italy is the result of the unification of principalities in the Italian peninsula during the nineteenth century based on the claim that the Italian nation deserved its own unified state.

A "nation" is similar to an "ethnic group" in that both refer to a group of people who have a sense of peoplehood, a sense of common identity built upon a common culture and language. Unlike an ethnic group, however, a *nation* implies not just a sense of peoplehood but also a right to self-rule and often a right to a geographic locality. The idea that a nation deserves its own geographic state was one of the justifications for the creation of Israel and is now being used by Palestinians as a justification for a Palestinian state, and the desire for many Kurds for a Kurdistan to be made up of Kurdish territory in what is now Turkey, Iraq, and Iran. In the United States the right of nations to self-rule in a geographic location is found in the legal recognition of many of the indigenous people of America who have legal status and self-rule on the reservations that resulted from the treaties they were forced to sign with the government of the United States. The Navajo Nation, for example, has its own governing body, its own elections, its own police, its own courts, and its own schools. It is this right to self-rule that has permitted reservation tribes to start and run gambling casinos even in states where gambling is not legal.

Many American minority groups besides the native indigenous tribes claim nation status. For example, many Mexican Americans claim the right to nationhood since the territory we now call Texas, New Mexico, Arizona, and California were all part of the country of Mexico before the United States and its proxies forcibly annexed the land. Today, some in the Chicano movement claim the land as properly belonging to a nation of Mexican Americans, which they call "Aztlán" (the ancestral home of the Aztecs), and believe it is their ancestral right to the land and to self-rule.

But the idea of right to self-rule does not always demand control over a geographic location. The Miami Nation, for example, is a nonreservation tribe that, therefore, has no legal right to a geographic location, but it still maintains a legal tribal system of governance that provides some rights and responsibilities to its tribal members.[13] African Americans have had many "nationalist" movements through our history, from the Pan-African movement throughout the twentieth century to Marcus Garvey's Universal Negro Improvement Association and African Communities League in the 1920s, to the present-day Nation of Islam, to more culturally oriented movements such as the Harlem Renaissance of the 1920s and 1930s and the Afrocentrism advocated by many educators today.[14]

Afrocentricity makes a claim for the right of people of African descent to control their own culture, which includes the education of their children. According to the Afrocentric version of the Race as Nation narrative, the people of Africa have been dispersed throughout the world through an involuntary diaspora. In order for people of African descent to reclaim

13. See *kiiloona myaamiaki*, the webpage of the Sovereign Miami Tribe of Oklahoma, www.miamination .com/.

14. Make sure to check out this clip of Malcolm X explaining black nationalism, "Malcolm X Explains Black Nationalism," YouTube video, March 29, 1964, www.youtube.com/watch?v=TO6Co8v2XjY.

their legitimate place in the world, they must educate themselves and their children in the proud heritage that is the African people. As long as those of the African diaspora only know history through the eyes of their European and American conquerors, they will never understand the true value of their history and their culture because any history written by the victors necessarily distorts and omits the view of the vanquished. Or, as the Igbo proverb states it, "Until lions have their historians, tales of the hunt shall always glorify the hunter." According to the Afrocentric version of the Race as Nation narrative, only through viewing the world through the eyes of Africans and their descendants throughout the world can people of African descent develop the sense of pride in their own nation of people and take control of their own destiny. According to Afrocentricity, by understanding their own history and culture, those of African descent will be able to once again be responsible for their own lives and no longer be crippled by a forced reliance on the goodness of others. This Race as Nation narrative can be found in Afrocentric schools such as the Paul Robeson–Malcolm X Academy and the Marcus Garvey Academy in Detroit, the Betty Shabazz Charter School in Chicago, and the Columbus Afrocentric School in Columbus, Ohio.[15]

Conclusion

There are other narratives told that assume some different aspects of race. There are some that associate race with social class and others that see race as merely an ideograph used to justify the unequal distribution of power and wealth, but the four presented here are prominent in the educational literature. Hopefully, this brief discussion of four different ways in which race is narrated can help clarify some of the problems Americans have as they discuss the often intractable problem that is race in this country. Often we have people using a narrative based on the assumption of empirical validity that has, in fact, no scientific justification. Others prefer to use a narrative that equates race with the history of European immigrants, proffering an optimistic hope but, perhaps, ignoring a whole host of evidence to contradict the analogy. Others prefer what they consider to be an honest representation of the historical and the present reality of race in America, but in doing so, can appear to some to be pessimistic rather than realistic. Still others present a narrative that, though providing the hope of solidarity to members of racial minority groups, is sometimes interpreted as overly "militant" to members of the dominant groups.

My argument in this chapter is that before we are able to even address something as difficult as racism, we must first clear the brush around the idea of race itself. Only when we begin to communicate with each other with a clearer understanding that our use of the term *race* has built into it different narratives and, therefore, different histories and different entities, will we be able to understand the confusion that typically inhabits any texts about race. Whether it is written, videoed, or performed, people read race differently. They think they may be communicating one thing when they are communicating something else. They think they may believe one thing, but the cultural narrative upon which their text depends says another. Only when we begin to interrogate, unpack, and clarify the narratives that

---

15. See a trailer for a documentary on the Paul Robeson–Malcolm X Academy by Tiffany L. Williams at http://vimeo.com/21507211.

pass for commonsense in this nation may we begin to have a meaningful conversation to begin to remedy the legacy of our unique racial history.

As this chapter shows, race is not as obvious a category as most people assume. In this book, I will stipulate *race* to be a term used to refer to a category of our language and our social institutions that purports to classify people based on physiological groupings.

CHAPTER FIFTEEN

Narratives of Racism and Education

On May 1, 1992, Rodney King, a man whose beating by police after a routine traffic stop was captured on video and whose attackers were exonerated by a jury, sparking several nights of violence in the streets of Los Angeles, pleaded with the American people at a press conference, "I just want to say, you know, can we, can we all get along, can we, can we get along?"[1] King's plea tapped a desire that nearly all Americans have, and yet experience shows us that, as a nation and as a people, we have still not yet figured out how to "get along." There are an unlimited number of experts who are willing to tell us why we fail in this, but, in truth, there are a limited number of cultural narratives that these experts tap and formulate into their unique specific narrative. This chapter will begin by clarifying some language about racism and then will explore a few of the cultural narratives that Americans often draw upon when discussing educational issues. In this chapter, I focus on the issue of affirmative action in college admissions to provide a concrete example.

Exploring Some Terms

As defined in the last chapter, *race* is a term used to refer to a category of our language and our social institutions that purports to classify people based on physiological groupings. Hopefully this definition makes clear that when I talk about race, I am talking about something that exists in our language and in our society and culture, *not* in our biological constructions. In other words, as I use the term, race does not exist in biology. It is not a category of nature. However, race does exist; it exists in society.

Racism, Not Prejudice

I also wish to make a distinction between the terms *prejudice* and *racism*. These terms do not refer to the same thing. *Prejudice* refers to a belief or an attitude about a group of people based on an insufficient knowledge of the group. While we usually use the term as a negative attitude, people can also be prejudiced about a group of people in a positive way. Notice that,

---

1. Rodney King, "Can We All Just Get Along?" YouTube video, May 1, 1992, at www.youtube.com /watch?v=1sONfxPCTU0.

as an attitude or belief, prejudice exists *in the minds* of people. Prejudice is, then, a category of our minds, a psychological construct of individuals.

I will use the term *racism* to refer to any act or program that results in the creation or maintenance of inequality or domination of a people based on race. Notice that racism exists *in the world*; it does not exist in people's minds. It is an act that occurs in the social world, or it is a set of rules or codes that governs the way people act (i.e., a program). Racism is a sociological construct, located in the sociocultural aspects of societies.

This book addresses the sociocultural parts of our society. It is not a book in psychology. For that reason, in this book, I am interested in racism, not prejudice. It is not that I do not think prejudice is important. Rather, I think the way in which racism is realized in our sociocultural world is also important and is something that needs to be studied directly, not through the lens of a psychological construct such as prejudice. In other words, I will be discussing racism. Hopefully you will have the opportunity to consider prejudice from other texts.

Let me try to clarify this. If prejudice exists in individual minds and racism exists in actions and codes that govern actions, then we can create four theoretically possible categories of interaction between prejudice and racism (see Table 15.1) as outlined in four types: *W* can be prejudiced and engage in racist acts, *X* can be prejudiced and not engage in racist acts, *Y* can be unprejudiced and engage in racist acts, or *Z* can be unprejudiced and not engage in racist acts.

Most Americans equate prejudice with racism. The assumption is that if a person is prejudiced, then that person is racist and if a person is racist, then that person must be prejudiced. In this way, the discussion of racism is typically limited to Type W in the grid below. In this book, however, I am interested in both Type W and Type Y.

Type W: Prejudicial Racism

Prejudicial racism occurs when a person commits a racist act because of their prejudiced attitudes or beliefs. Just because a person is prejudiced does not mean that s/he has to act on those prejudices. In fact, it is nearly impossible for anyone to grow up in America without some prejudices. Consider again how we define prejudice as a belief or an attitude about a group of people based on an insufficient knowledge of the group. Do you have a belief or attitude of a group of people that you will acknowledge results from an insufficient knowledge of that group? How could you not? I certainly do. Don't we all? The problem for us here is not which one of us is prejudiced, but what the nature of those prejudices might be and, more importantly, do we act on our prejudices? Or, perhaps it is better to ask, *when* do we act on our prejudices? Because all of us have them and undoubtedly, at one time or another, act on our prejudices, what we really want to know is does that act caused by prejudice result in the creation or maintenance of inequality or domination of a people based on race and, if so, how pernicious is the racist act that results from that prejudice?

Given that racism requires action that creates or maintains inequality or domination, we need to know whether or not the action that we take because of our prejudice results in the

Table 15.1 Four Theoretically Possible Categories of Interaction between Prejudice and Race

	Racist	Not Racist
Prejudiced	W	X
Unprejudiced	Y	Z

creation or maintenance of inequality or domination based on race. If it does, then it moves beyond the psychological category of attitude and into the social world of action, and it is Type W racism. Prejudicial racism is pernicious. In its worst forms, it is more than ugly; it is destructive; it is murderous.

For example, on June 7, 1998, Lawrence Russell Brewer and two of his friends brutally beat James Byrd Jr., then chained his ankles and attached the chain to the back of their pickup truck and dragged him for three miles along a country road in East Texas. Byrd's crime? He was black, and the three white men took offense. Prejudicial racism must be addressed and stopped long before it gets to the point that resulted in James Byrd's death. Schools cannot tolerate such racism. But for all the damage done by prejudicial racism, I am more concerned about institutional racism because the incidents of prejudicial racism, even if frequent, are always located in the acts of individuals, whereas the effects of institutional racism are pervasive, continuous, and ultimately more damaging.

Type Y: Institutional Racism

Institutional racism occurs when a person acts in a manner that follows the rules or codes, either explicit or covert, that are institutionalized within the organizations and the structures of society when those codes lead to the creation or maintenance of inequality or domination of a people based on race. Because most Americans reduce racism to prejudice, they presume that if we could just get rid of prejudice, we would get rid of racism. But when racism refers to any act or program that results in the creation or maintenance of inequality or domination of a people based on race, then it should become clear that racism is being conducted on a daily basis by people who do not even realize they are engaged in racist acts. Racist acts are carried out by people who may not be acting on their prejudices at all, but may just be following the rules of their job. They may even be antiracists. They may even be members of the group that is the target of the racism.

For example, any teacher who taught American history in an American high school in 1993 and used any of the five best-selling textbooks would have taught that the history of America is the history of people of European descent in the Americas. At least one of those texts did have an introductory chapter on the pre-Columbian Americas. And one of the texts inserted alternative voices from different class and ethnic perspectives around several topics. But, overwhelmingly, the books explored not only the history of Americans of European descent as if their history is the history of the nation, but also told that history from the point of view of European-Americans. People of African, Asian, and Latin American descent and those descended from the First People of the Americas were not seen as integral to our history.[2] The effect of teaching a history that equates the history of the nation with the history of people descended from Europeans is necessarily to construct an inequality between Americans based on race. It is, therefore, by definition, a racist curriculum. Simply doing one's job as defined, simply following the textbook, simply teaching the curriculum, simply teaching to the AP test necessarily required the 1993 American history teacher to engage in racist action, to act as a racist. It makes no difference if the teacher had not been prejudiced against African Americans,

---

2. Michael Romanowski, "The Ethical Treatment of Japanese American Internment Camps: A Content Analysis of Secondary American History Textbooks," PhD diss., Miami University, Oxford, OH, 1993.

Asian Americans, Latinos/as, and Indigenous Americans; in fact, it didn't even make a difference if the teacher had been an African American, an Asian American, a Latino/a, or a Native American, they were engaging in racist acts simply by teaching the curriculum.

The same is true of the teaching of language, literature, science, and even math. Just by doing their job, most teachers are required to engage in racist acts. That does not mean that they are prejudiced. That does not mean that they are bad people or immoral people. It means that they live in a nation whose institutions were constructed at a time in which the country was overtly racist. Is there anyone who would deny that in the middle of the nineteenth century when the American public school system began, and at the beginning of the twentieth century when it became bureaucratized and institutionalized, that this nation was overtly a racist nation? Of course we were. So why are we surprised to learn that the structures upon which these institutions were built were riddled with racist codes? Given that today's institutions carry forth those same basic structures, why are we surprised that racism has been institutionalized into the very practices of our organizational life? Why are we surprised to find that our schools have built right into them codes that create or maintain inequality or domination based on race?

When we emphasize prejudicial racism and minimize institutional racism, we may begin to mistakenly think that if we could only get people to stop being prejudiced, we would end racism. But when we realize that once racism is built into the rules and codes of our institutions, one need not be prejudiced to produce racism, then we realize the necessity for examining and uncovering those racist codes. To do so, of course, requires us to look at race in a conscious way. To figure out what it is and where it does and does not influence practices, results in the creation or maintenance of inequality or domination of a people based on race. In order to successfully focus on race, we must engage in racialization.

Racialization

Chapter 14 presented the concept of racialization as having two different, but related, usages. The last chapter focused on *racialization*, defined as the sociocultural processes that create races. This chapter will focus on the other *racialization*: the recognition that race is a relevant category in understanding a particular social event or condition. Many people equate this kind of racialization with racism, but if we think carefully about it, we will realize that the act of racialization (recognizing that race is relevant) can be racist, but the failure to racialize can also be racist. This kind of racialization is racist whenever the racialization results in the creation or maintenance of inequality or domination of a people based on race. And the failure to racialize is racist whenever the refusal to recognize race as a relevant category results in the creation or maintenance of inequality or domination of a people based on race. In other words, in order to understand whether the act of racialization is or is not racist, we must decide whether or not the recognition of race as a relevant category maintains the inequalities of our legacy as a racist society or whether it works to transform that legacy. This idea will be developed further in a discussion of the narratives of racism that follows.

Privilege

Privilege is a term that we hear about more and more whenever someone addresses any of our social inequalities, such as race, gender, social class, sexuality, or ability. But the idea of privilege is often misunderstood both by those who wield the term as a sledgehammer against others as well as by those who deny its attribution to themselves.

For most people, privilege could be summed up by this quip from the commentator and columnist and then Texas commissioner of agriculture, Jim Hightower, who at the 1988 Democratic Convention said that the presumed Republican nominee for president, George H. W. Bush, had been "born on third base and thinks he hit a triple." To many Democrats, the line seemed to apply even more appropriately to his son, George W. Bush, and has become a common dismissal of those born of privilege. But while the quip might be good for a laugh, does it really help us understand privilege?

We all know that a large number of college students are privileged. For example, Su Jin Jez shows that in the United States, students from the top 10 percent income group are more than four times more likely to attend a four-year college than students from the bottom 10 percent. And I know that male students have heard that they benefit from gender privilege and that white students have heard that they benefit from white privilege. In fact, my experience is that most white students and male students have heard it so many times that they are tired of hearing about it—particularly when most of them do not feel that they enjoy any privilege whatsoever.

On the other hand, students from low-income groups and from racial and ethnic minority groups are likely to agree that a large number of their classmates are privileged. Many of them may think we have not talked about it enough. And finally, what of the realization that regardless of the class status of their family or their own race or gender or sexuality, any graduate of an American university possesses a kind of privilege when compared to the nearly 72 percent of Americans older than twenty-five without a college diploma?[3]

Let's get one thing straight from the start: to be privileged does *not* mean a person does not deserve their achievements. It does *not* mean that a person has not worked hard to accomplish what they have achieved. It does *not* mean that he is a bad, immoral, undeserving person. Take me as an example. I am a white, straight male from an upper-middle-class Protestant family who attended nothing but highly rated schools (private school through eighth grade, one of the "Top 10" public high schools in the country, and the University of Virginia). I have enjoyed enormous privilege throughout my life. Does that mean that I have not had to work to get where I am? Does it mean I can stop working now? Does it mean everything has been handed to me? Absolutely not. But what it does mean is that my whole life I have been able to believe that *if* I were to work hard that the system would pay off for me and, therefore, I had a lot of incentive to work hard. Furthermore, it has given me extra chances (retakes, if you will—yes, believe it or not, I have had to take advantage of several "retakes" in my life). It means that I "know people." Or if I don't, my father did or my mother or my uncles or my friends' parents or my headmaster. And we all know how much it is "who you know, not what you know" that greases the chain of success.

People who live without the kind of privileges that I have had have often had to act on faith, on the hope that if they work hard enough the system will pay off for them. They also have to walk a straight and narrow path. Mistakes are not permitted—party too much one semester, get pregnant, get caught smoking weed one time, get sick and get behind in your

---

3. "Bachelor's Degree or Higher, Percent of Persons Age 25+, 2008–2012," in *State and County Quick Facts* (Washington, DC: US Census Bureau, 2013), http://quickfacts.census.gov/qfd/states/00000.html.

coursework, and suddenly you find yourself in a ditch. Those without privilege may not be permitted back onto the path. Who do they know? Who is going to be able to work the school system to put the pressure on to get them into that honors class or to find the lawyer who can actually get their potential felony dropped to a misdemeanor? And even if they do everything right, who do they know who is going to find them that summer internship that will lead to the career that they are hoping for or get them that initial interview with that television station or bank or nonprofit that they hope to land?

Too many people (both those without much privilege as they lay that label on others as well as those who refuse to believe that the label is a legitimate description of their lives) think that privilege is like being born on third base and thinking you hit a triple. If I were to think that my privilege denigrated my own achievements, made me less moral, uncaring, or undeserving, well, I'd reject that label as well. But that is not what privilege gives most of us. Perhaps for some it does, but for most of us, privilege just opens doors; it doesn't wheel us across the threshold. It only throws the mattress under us when we fall; it doesn't keep us from falling. It only provides us a ladder to get back up; it doesn't climb it for us. No, those of us with class, race, gender, sexuality, able-bodied privileges still have to earn our own way. But, we have to admit, our path may not be quite the same path as those born without our privileges.

Another mistaken idea about privilege is that it is something we created for ourselves. This, of course, is the problem that Hightower's quip is zeroing in on. Too many of us with privilege actually do believe we did it all on our own, and anyone could do what we have done if they only had our talents and worked as hard as we did. But that misunderstands how privilege works. Here is the thing about privilege: those with privilege did not create their own privilege, nor can they give it away. I was born white in a nation that privileges whiteness. I was born in a nation that privileges males. I was born in a nation that privileges heterosexuality and middle-class values and Protestantism. I did not ask to be born into those categories. My privileges have been thrust upon me. They were given to me without my asking for them. And there is little I can do to give them away because they are not mine to give but belong to the others who place them upon me. I can pretend that I do not have those privileges, but at any time I can reclaim them and so, acting as if I am not privileged fools only me.

For those of us who have been anointed with these privileges, we are not to be blamed, nor are we to blame ourselves or feel guilty for what others have laid upon us. We are not to be held accountable for the fact that we have privileges. But, we can be held accountable, and we should be held accountable, for how we use the privileges that we have been granted. In whose interests do we use our privilege? Do we use these privileges to gain more privilege for ourselves and for those who already have plenty of privilege and the rewards of privilege, or do we use the privileges given to us to work with and for those with less privilege than we have? For those of us with race privilege, do we use our privilege to create or maintain inequality or domination of a people based on race? Or do we use our privilege to seek out, illuminate, and eradicate inequality or domination of a people based on race?

The truth is that every student at an American university has some privileges. Some have more than others, but every student has them. The students' task is to decide whether to deny their privilege, or whether to acknowledge it. And then, the students' task is to decide in whose interest they are going to use these privileges. Will they use their privilege to leverage more resources for themselves exclusively, or will they use it to work on behalf of the interests of other people? Luckily, for those who are in teacher education, speech and hearing, or social services, they have chosen a profession that will make it easy for them to use their privilege for others' benefits. But, they still must choose to do so. They still must decide to acknowledge their own privilege and to use it in others' interests. And if after coming to recognize their own privilege, they continue to deny it or continue to use their privilege for their own benefit alone, then others have a right to point out that they may not be living up to the moral obligations that come along with such social privileges.

Two Narratives about Affirmative Action

On March 6, 1961, when President John F. Kennedy issued Executive Order 10925 ordering all federal contractors to "not discriminate against any employee or applicant for employment because of race, creed, color, or national origin" and ordering contractors "to take *affirmative action* to ensure that applicants are employed, and that employees are treated during employment, without regard to their race, creed, color, or national origin," affirmative action was seen as an important mechanism for fighting racism.[4] But in 1996, when the voters of the state of California passed the California Civil Rights Initiative, known as Proposition 209, essentially ending affirmative action in the state of California; and in 1998, when the voters of the state of Washington passed the Washington State Initiative, known as Initiative 200, accomplishing much the same thing in Washington; and again in 2006, when the voters of Michigan passed the Michigan Civil Rights Initiative, known as Proposition 2, all but eliminating affirmative action in Michigan, affirmative action had come to be understood by many as a mechanism that did not fight racism but one that advanced a form of racism referred to as "reverse racism"—that is, racism against whites. How could this be? What changed between Kennedy's Executive Order and Proposition 2 in Michigan? And just as important, which is it? Is affirmative action racist or antiracist? Or is it both? Or, perhaps, neither? An examination of the cultural narratives that underpin this debate might help us answer those questions and bring clarity to an important educational issue that is typically blanketed in fog.

The Affirmative Action as Antiracism Narrative

The cultural narrative that is Affirmative Action as Antiracism includes many different themes, ideas, heroes, tropes, and ideographs. Any one person's use of it in the telling of a specific narrative will almost certainly not include everything that I am going to lay out in this section, but they will draw on some of it, and they would probably find themselves in agreement with much of it. The basic plot of the cultural narrative Affirmative Action as Antiracism might be stated this way: In our nation's past, we practiced and enforced explicit

---

4. "Executive Order 10925: Establishing the President's Committee on Equal Employment Opportunity" (Washington, DC: US Equal Employment Opportunity Commission, March 6, 1961), www.eeoc.gov/eeoc /history/35th/thelaw/eo-10925.html (emphasis added).

racism, but following World War II, a movement began demanding the civil rights of all regardless of race, which required not only that everyone begin to be treated equally, but that positive steps be taken to overcome the legacy that our earlier history of racism had created. Although it is understood to be a temporary transitional practice, until our racist legacy has been countered and dissipated, affirmative action must be continued.

Let us admit it plainly and openly and without rancor or guilt: the United States of America was, at least partly, founded on racism, and that unfortunate legacy still affects our lives today. Think about it. Following the invasion of the Americas by the Europeans, the indigenous people were nearly eradicated. Some have estimated that the population was reduced by as much as 95 percent as a result of disease, war, and enslavement. We might argue about the percentage of decline, about the cause of the decline, about whether it is evidence of genocide or not, but we cannot deny that following the arrival on the American continents by the Europeans, the indigenous people were nearly eradicated.

As the Affirmative Action as Antiracism narrative describes it, the interactions between the Europeans and the native population quickly became hostile with war and mutually murderous attacks—each side against the other. But it is a mistake to see these mutual acts of war as "both sides were to blame" because one side was a group of invaders attempting to steal others' land, and the others were trying to protect themselves and their land from these thieves. And also, from the beginning, the native people were treated as racially inferior, which the Europeans used to justify their thievery of the land and their slaughter of women and children. It was used to justify the trading of blankets treated with small pox in order to kill a whole tribe through disease.[5] (Might this be seen as an early case of a weapon of mass destruction?) Such racism was used to justify the practice of signing a treaty and then breaking it when the European population grew large enough to want to expand. This practice of the use of violence to steal people's land, to massacre villages, to enslave, and to force the survivors onto reservations in the most hostile and unproductive land on the continent can only be explained by the belief that the indigenous people were somehow racially inferior to the Europeans and their descendants and, therefore, not deserving of the normal protections of a "white people."

Furthermore, according to the Affirmative Action as Antiracism narrative, after the practice of enslavement of indigenous people proved to be difficult because too many of them died or escaped, the new Europeans in America turned to enslaved people who had been kidnapped from Africa and shipped across the ocean to work for them without pay and without the right to quit or, in fact, any rights at all. While Europeans and North African people around the Mediterranean and along the Atlantic coast had a long history of kidnapping and enslaving captives after raiding villages, the slave trade to the Americas took a much more violent and pernicious form than the traditional form of slavery—if for no other reason than in the early forms of European and Middle Eastern and North African slavery, enslaved people had some rights and they were still considered human beings and not mere chattel. But once slavery became justified by race, rather than the spoils of war, it ended any thought that slaves were fully human with the claim to any rights at all.

---

5. Peter d'Errico, "Jeffrey Amherst and Smallpox Blankets," Peter d'Errico's Law Page, http://people .umass.edu/derrico/amherst/lord_jeff.html.

In fact, while the so-called Indian problem died out by the end of the nineteenth century (due to the near extinction of the people) and the Civil War had put an end to overt slavery, American racism did not come to an end. The latter part of the nineteenth century and the first half of the twentieth century witnessed a combination of covert and overt forms of racism that today we often refer to under the umbrella Jim Crow. Legal segregation; legal discrimination in schooling and employment; law enforcement that protected the white while attacking the black, the indigenous, the Latino/a, and the Asian created a de facto inequality where some gained and others lost based on their so-called race.

According to the Affirmative Action as Antiracism narrative, it was only after World War II that the dominant European-descended people began to question the validity of such practices. Perhaps the change in mind of the American people of European descent was largely influenced by the horror of the Jewish Holocaust (especially when it became clear that the Germans' attempt to exterminate the Jews was justified by the American experience and practices of racism), or perhaps it was connected to the need of the United States to woo the people of Africa in the struggle against the Soviet Union in the Cold War.[6] Whatever the cause, the 1950s are often seen as the beginning of the American rejection of racism as a legitimate practice. By the 1960s, this movement had grown significantly strong to write into law that racism would no longer be tolerated and to demand the enforcement of those laws.

Most Americans, whichever narrative they use to describe affirmative action, will accept much of the narrative that was just told about America's racist history. They might argue about specifics, but the general story is agreed upon; the key differences come next. According to the Affirmative Action as Antiracism narrative, nearly 500 years of racism has left a legacy that cannot be undone by merely pretending everyone is white—which is what being "color blind" actually does. The racism has been built into our society and into our culture, where it languishes still, creating a very different life experience for people defined as white and everybody else. This racist legacy is built into what passes for our history and our language and our laws and our education. Its effects have created an unequal distribution of wealth and of rights that continues to affect everyone's lives. One does not have to go back to slavery to see evidence of this institutional racism.

For example, the Affirmative Action as Antiracism narrative reminds us that one of the important interventions of the federal government during the Great Depression of the 1930s was the creation of the Home Owners Loan Corporation (HOLC) to help financially stressed homeowners to refinance mortgages to escape foreclosure. In order to protect their own investment, the HOLC developed a formula for determining the "mortgage risk," which in turn was used by the banks to determine the requirements of the refinancing. An important part of determining the risk was whether or not the home was located in a segregated neighborhood or not. A completely segregated "native white" neighborhood (meaning no recent European immigrants such as Italians or Irish or Jews) received higher support than any mixed neighborhood, and a completely segregated black neighborhood was rated as too risky for any refinancing. This practice, called *redlining* for the maps that were created to show the various risk of neighborhoods, which used red for the "too risky for investment"

---

6. Derrik Bell, "*Brown v. Board of Education* and the Interest-Convergence Dilemma," *Harvard Law Review* 93 (1980): 518–533.

category, favored investment in the suburbs and helped create the segregation between the white suburb and black city.[7]

Following World War II, the federal government created the Servicemen's Readjustment Act, better known as the G. I. Bill, which attempted to help our nation adjust to a peacetime economy and to reward our soldiers by creating new opportunities for them. Everyone knows that the G. I. Bill made it possible for hundreds of thousands of soldiers, children of Southern and Eastern European immigrants and their Irish brethren, to attend college—something that had been nearly impossible for the largely working-class so-called ethnic whites to accomplish in large numbers before the war. Fewer, however, are aware that it also created a system that made it possible for these same people to purchase homes. One section of the G. I. Bill created a system whereby the federal government would guarantee loans from private banks to American veterans to purchase a home as long as the buyer and the home met certain criteria. Before this law, a prospective homebuyer had to put down as much as 60 percent of the cost of a home before a bank would loan them money for the purchase. Following the passage, banks could offer much better deals with lower down payments and lower interest rates. Using the new technology developed during the war for the civil engineering of barracks, roads, bridges, airbases, and other mass construction projects, the suburbs exploded. However, the regulations that made all of this possible did not treat all property the same. Using the same "risk assessment" practices as the HOLC maps of the 1930s, the federally guaranteed loans for veterans favored white neighborhoods, but by now children of European descent had been born in America and were, therefore, "native-born." They were now considered white enough to take advantage of the federally guaranteed mortgages and buy into the all-white suburban neighborhoods. On the other hand, the returning black servicemen and -women were restricted to buying in heavily black neighborhoods, which drove up the conditions and interest of their loans.

Understand that the practice of redlining made it all but impossible for blacks to even buy into an all-white neighborhood because even one black owner increased the so-called risk factor, reducing the worth of everyone's property in the neighborhood. Realtors refused to show such property to blacks since if it were sold, the reduction in worth of the other properties in the neighborhood would reduce their future commissions and even if they did show the property, the owners would not sell to a black family, since they did not want to hurt their friends and former neighbors financially. The practice of redlining combined with the G. I. Bill moved even more white families (now that the Irish and Southern and Eastern Europeans were considered white) out of the cities, and created even more segregation between the suburbs and the cities.

The practice of redlining was finally outlawed in the late 1960s, and by the middle 1970s the more blatant continuation of these practices was minimized. Today, informal and illegal redlining still occurs, and when caught, violators are punished, but (and this is key for understanding today's situation) the legacy of the practice of redlining still lives with us, not only in the segregation between heavily black inner-city neighborhoods, but with the discrepancy of family wealth based on race. Some scholars suggest that today's discrepancy

---

7. For a short explanation of redlining and the HOLC, see Lloyd Wynn, "The Birth of Redlining: The Real History of the Homeowners Loan Corporation," *The Black Commentator* 273, April 17, 2008, www .blackcommentator.com/273/273_sm_birth_of_redlining.html.

in wealth between white and black America (the median wealth of white Americans may be as much as twenty times greater than black Americans) results from the snowball effect that accrued to whites through their ability to acquire homes in the suburbs during this period while relegating blacks to being renters living in the inner city.[8] This, of course, continues to affect us as a result not only of the discrepancy of wealth, but of the quality of the schools that children living in the suburbs have when compared to the average student living in the inner city.

Those who tell the Affirmative Action as Antiracism narrative might point out that this reflects the present-day situation, in which many students of color find themselves living in pockets of high poverty and unemployment and low levels of nutrition and health care, which are the direct result of our nation's history of racism. Notice that no one today need be prejudiced. In fact, most of the players in the above narrative did not need to be prejudiced either. Once the HOLC created the racist maps[9] based on a "risk assessment," which racialized risk by assuming that risk was related to race, and once the G. I. Bill based their mortgage policies on these same maps, the actors did not themselves need to hold any racial prejudices at all. We can probably assume that many, perhaps even most, maybe even overwhelmingly most, were racially prejudiced, but *they did not need to be* in order to engage in racist acts. All they needed to do is to act to protect their own and their neighbors' economic well-being based on the rules built into the system. This is classic institutional racism.

And the racism that created the segregation between urban and suburban districts also created the favored suburbs with their higher real estate worth, which in turn resulted in white and wealthy schools educating mostly children who live in economic privilege. And it also created the non-white and less wealthy school districts that must struggle to educate a high number of children who live in poverty. Our nation's racist legacy has been built right into our present educational system. It does not require parents or legislatures to be prejudiced to maintain this racism. It only requires that they now ignore race, that they act "color-blind," and continue to work to make sure their own and their neighbors' and their constituents' children get the best education possible and let the parents and legislators in the neighboring districts do the same. The result is the maintenance of inequality based on race, creating white privilege for whites in the suburbs and victimization from racism for those students of color who live in the poorer urban districts with inadequate schools. Given the inequality that continues to appear in wealth, in influence, in status, and in the quality of schools, racism is institutionalized in the system as it is. According to those who tell it, the Affirmative Action as Antiracism narrative racializes the situation—that is, it recognizes that race still plays a role in the inequality of our housing and educational systems. The only way to overcome this heritage of racism is to take positive steps to counter racism's continued legacy and to continue, again in the words of President Kennedy, "to take *affirmative action*"

---

8. For a brief and clear explanation of the snowball effect in wealth accumulation, see "Interview with Dalton Conley, Background Readings for *Race: The Power of an Illusion*," PBS, www.pbs.org/race/000 _About/002_04-background-03-03.htm. For a discussion of the wealth gap between whites, blacks, and Hispanics, see Rakesh Kochhar, Richard Fry, and Paul Taylor, "Wealth Gaps Rise to Record Highs between Whites, Blacks, Hispanics," *Pew Research: Social and Demographic Trends* (Washington, DC: Pew Research Center, 2011), www.pewsocialtrends.org/2011/07/26/wealth-gaps-rise-to-record-highs-between-whites-blacks-hispanics/.

9. Remember that "racism" only requires the creation or maintenance of inequality or domination of a people based on race.

to ensure that all children regardless of their race have the opportunity to take advantage of our public education system in order to achieve all they are capable of despite that legacy.

And this legacy, the Affirmative Action as Antiracism narrative tells us, is found in admissions policies at universities when those admissions policies forbid the consideration of factors of race. So-called objective measures, such as standardized test scores, have this racist legacy built right into them, not because the tests ask bad questions, but because the tests measure only a limited aspect of what it takes to succeed in the university. The SAT tests can only explain about 20–30 percent of success in the first, second, third, or fourth year of college.[10] Furthermore, these tests appear to overestimate the success of some groups (primarily white males and Asian Americans) and underestimate the success of other groups (such as women, non-whites, and non-Asians).[11] A 2011 report based on results in Ohio claims that two of the four subsections of the ACT exam have no predictive value at all, though the other two do show some ability to predict students' college success.[12] Given the latent institutionalized racism in the education and economic situation of students of color, there continues to be the necessity for some kind of consideration to be given to attract and retain students who themselves still suffer from the racism institutionalized into our system. Once again, those who tell this particular narrative want to make sure that we understand that it does not require any present-day descendant of Europeans to be racially prejudiced. It does not suggest that children of the white middle class are racists themselves, but it does suppose that privilege bestowed upon them due to their race and class position and the privilege resulting from the high quality of their schools has influenced their high test scores.

If, as a nation, we wish to correct the half a millennium of racism upon which the present society still rests, we who may not have done the wrong, but who have certainly benefited from privileges without any fault of our own nor any merit either, will have to take positive measures, affirmative action, to right a wrong we did not create but from which today we still benefit.

The Affirmative Action as Racism Narrative

The Affirmative Action as Racism narrative does not have much disagreement with the first part of the story just told. Perhaps it would tell our early history with less stress on the racist part, but it certainly acknowledges that the early history of the United States was racist. It also acknowledges that while the Civil War ended slavery, Jim Crow laws and other such practices continued an overt and immoral racism for decades afterwards. Where the tellers

---

10. Jennifer L. Kobrin et al., "Validity of the SAT for Predicting First-Year College Grade Point Average," Research Report No. 2008-5 (New York: College Board, 2008); Krista D. Mattern and Brian F. Patterson, "Validity of the SAT for Predicting Second-Year Grades: 2006 SAT Validity Sample," Statistical Report No. 2011-1 (New York: College Board, 2011); Krista D. Mattern and Brian F. Patterson, "Validity of the SAT for Predicting Third-Year Grades: 2006 SAT Validity Sample," Statistical Report No. 2011-3 (New York: College Board, 2011); Krista D. Mattern and Brian F. Patterson, "Validity of the SAT for Predicting Fourth-Year Grades: 2006 SAT Validity Sample," Statistical Report No. 2011-7 (New York: College Board, 2011).

11. Leonard Ramist, Charles Lewis, and Laura McCamley-Jenkins, "Student Group Differences in Predicting College Grades: Sex, Language, and Ethnic Groups," Report No. 93-1 (New York: College Board, 1994).

12. Eric P. Bettinger, Brent J. Evans, and Devin G. Pope, *Improving College Performance and Retention the Easy Way: Unpacking the ACT Exam* (Washington, DC: National Bureau of Economic Research, 2011), http://faculty.chicagobooth.edu/devin/pope/research/pdf/Final%20AEJ%20Paper.pdf.

of this narrative veer off is in the aftermath of the civil rights movement of the 1950s and 1960s. According to this cultural narrative, the civil rights movement rightfully argued that a person's race should have no place in their treatment. It should not matter if a person is white, black, Asian, Latino/a, or a member of an Indigenous Nation, only her/his abilities and accomplishments as an individual should be taken into account.

Those who ascribe to this narrative argue that the problem with the Affirmative Action as Antiracist narrative is that in America, a person should be treated as an individual and not as a member of a group. A person should not benefit from who their father might be, but neither should he or she be punished for what their grandfather or great-grandfather might have done. He or she should be treated only on their own individual merit. It is true, they suggest, that in the past America was racist, but following a series of court cases and legislative actions in the 1950s and 1960s, those practices, thankfully, they might add, are in our past.

And they should stay in our past. What was wrong with the past practice was that an African American or a Mexican American or a Chinese American was denied entry to the nation's best colleges and universities due to their race. But, they ask, isn't taking into consideration an individual's race in affirmative action doing exactly the same thing? Isn't one person's being favored and another's being disfavored because of their race wrong, whether it is to advantage the advantaged or to advantage the disadvantaged? Let a person stand before the admissions committee as an individual with his or her own record, and not have to carry the burden of their ancestors' deeds as well.

But what about the point made in the Affirmative Action as Antiracist narrative that without affirmative action, the present-day African American and Latino/a and Native American is burdened by the very same legacy of racism that the European American now benefits from? Isn't the rejection of affirmative action merely institutionalizing the racist past in the present inequalities? Isn't it kind of like a relay race where one team is required to carry a weight of a hundred pounds on each leg and then, on the last lap, this admittedly unfair practice is removed, so that for the rest of the race no one is required to carry any extra weight? True, the last leg may be equal, but by then the team whose early legs carried the extra weight are far behind. How could we ever expect them to catch up to make the race fair unless we act in some way to overcome the past wrong?

The Affirmative Action as Racism narrative counters by suggesting that the moment we begin to take into consideration factors that are beyond the control of the individual, it is wrong. True, in the relay-race metaphor, the advantaged team may be far ahead at the time the weight is removed, but there is no last lap in the relay of life. Given enough time, those whose early runners were disadvantaged will catch up if they are worthy. They may have to make up ground a little at a time, but now they have an incentive to do so. Simply bringing them up to the front or adding hundred-pound weights to the legs of those in the lead removes such incentives. Besides, this isn't a relay race. Every race is a race among individuals. No, they counter, the best remedy to past wrongs is simply to stop the wrong practice.

Besides, they add, whenever you substitute the thinking of government bureaucrats for that of ordinary people, you get wrong thinking. The best adjudicator of quality is the marketplace. Let competition and the market determine who gets admitted to colleges and universities. "Playing the race card," many add, is not the solution. The only way to overcome racism is to stop racializing. Anytime you racialize, you introduce racism, they argue. So, take race out of it. Remember, race does not exist. It is not real, so why keep practices such as affirmative action to maintain the illusion that it is real? We need a color-blind policy in which everyone is treated as raceless.

The Model Minority Narrative

In 1960, Asian and Pacific Islanders constituted only one-half percent of the American population.[13] Since the 1920s, immigration laws made it very difficult for Asians to immigrate to the United States. This was not by accident but by design. In the 1920s, racial prejudice against Asians created an immigration policy calculated to keep Asians out. By 1965, however, the United States was deeply involved in a war in Southeast Asia, and combined with the successful domestic civil rights movements, and perhaps attempting to overcome the shameful internment of Japanese Americans during World War II, a new law opened up immigration to Asians. The result is that in the years since, Asian Americans have become the fastest-growing minority group by percentage, having a rate of growth of between 43 percent (people who identify as only of Asian descent) and 60 percent (people who identify as of mixed descent, including some Asian) from 2000 to 2010.[14] But whereas the overall growth rate may be quite high, Asian Americans still constitute a small percentage of the overall American population. The 2010 US Census data for Asian Americans and Pacific Islanders show 5 percent.[15] During this time, "Asian" as a racial category has been renarrated from the pre-WWII myth of Asians as the "Yellow Peril" (a story that told of Asians flooding the Americas, stealing their jobs, and taking over America with an incomprehensible culture) to the "Model Minority," which has come to be as much a burden for many Asian Americans as a boon.

The Model Minority narrative suggests that Asian Americans have succeeded in America as a result of a strong work ethic and a commitment to education. It points to statistics of high test scores and high rates of college and graduate school enrollment. For example, nationally, close to 43 percent of Asian Americans graduate from college compared with 25 percent of white Americans. Such statistics are often used to support the idea that other minority groups need to do only as the Asians have done and develop good morals and a strong work ethic; then they too can succeed as the Asian Americans have done.

One of the primary problems with this narrative is that it essentializes the category of Asian American, erasing distinctions among the subpopulations as well as ignoring their history. As mentioned in the last chapter, the category "Asian American" includes a wide range of people who often do not see much in common with each other until they find themselves in the racialized American society. Consider that this category, according to the US Census,

---

13. "Table 1: United States—Race and Hispanic Origin—1790 to 1990," *People and Households* (Washington, DC: US Census Bureau, 2002), www.census.gov/population/www/documentation/twps0056/tab01.pdf.

14. Padmananda Rama, "U.S. Census Show Asians Are Fastest Growing Racial Group," The Two-Way: Breaking News from NPR (Washington, DC: National Public Radio, 2012), www.npr.org/blogs/thetwo-way/2012/03/23/149244806/u-s-census-show-asians-are-fastest-growing-racial-group.

15. Karen R. Humes, Nicholas A. Jones, and Roberto R. Ramirez, "Table 2: Population by Hispanic or Latino Origin and Race for the United States: 2010" (Washington, DC: US Census Bureau, 2011), www.census.gov/prod/cen2010/briefs/c2010br-02.pdf.

includes the following different ethnic and national identities: Asian Indian, Bangladeshi, Bhutanese, Burmese, Cambodian, Chinese, Filipino, Hmong, Indo-Chinese, Indonesian, Iwo Jiman, Japanese, Korean, Laotian, Malaysian, Maldivian, Nepalese, Okinawan, Pakistani, Singaporean, Sri Lankan, Taiwanese, Thai, and Vietnamese.[16] Do we really expect all of these communities to experience the world in the same way?

In fact, the high success rates in education are not uniformly spread throughout these populations. Though a high percentage of Asian Indians, Chinese, Japanese, Koreans, and Pakistanis have high test scores and educational attainment, other Asians do not perform as well. For example, Vietnamese have a graduation rate closer to white Americans (about 20 percent), while Laotians, Cambodians, and Hmong have a graduation rate closer to Latinos/as, of 10 percent.[17]

Besides the difference in ethnic/national identity, the Model Minority narrative ignores the history of immigration and the structures that the 1965 immigration law created. For example, the 1965 law favors immigrants from the Eastern Hemisphere, including Asia, who already have high educational attainment, while there is no such bias for immigrants from the Western hemisphere. This means that the overwhelming percentage of Asian immigrants come to this country having already attained a high education in their home country. As we all know, because the best predictor of success in school is the social class of the parents, and that is, in turn, partly determined by parent educational attainment, we should not be surprised that the children of these highly educated Asians themselves succeed in school. What distinguishes the Vietnamese, Laotians, and Hmong from other Asians who immigrated to this country is that as a group, they have a much higher percentage of immigrants with low education attainment in their home country before immigration because of the large number who immigrated during the Vietnam War as refugees.

But even within those groups that have a high success rate, such as the Chinese, individual success is largely determined by social class and educational attainment of the student's parents. For example, those Chinese who immigrate to the United States largely to work in restaurants are not highly educated and their children do not, as a group, succeed particularly well in American schools. Effects of social class also can be seen in Korean Americans, where those of lower income do not perform well in school either.[18] In other words, the Model Minority narrative is only supported when we use selective data that erase national and ethnic identities and ignore social class.

Finally, the myth of the model minority places a burden on many Asian American youth who do not identify with this narrative. They find themselves trying to live up to a narrative that is unrealistic; the narrative is, in fact, a lie. For too many Asian American youth, this discrepancy between their own sense of self and educational success leads to a high degree of stress and depression, which in turn leads to high suicide rates.[19] While some Asian

---

16. Jessica S. Barnes and Claudette E. Bennett, "The Asian Population: 2000," Census Brief (Washington, DC: US Census Bureau, 2002), www.census.gov/prod/2002pubs/c2kbr01-16.pdf.

17. C. N. Le, "Socioeconomic Statistics & Demographics," *Asian-Nation: The Landscape of Asian America*, 2011, www.asian-nation.org/model-minority.shtml.

18. Jamie Lew, "Burden of Acting Neither White nor Black: Asian American Identities and Achievement in Urban Schools," *The Urban Review* 38, no. 5 (2006): 335–352.

19. Elizabeth Cohen, "Push to Achieve Tied to Suicide in Asian-American Women," CNN.com, 2007, www.cnn.com/2007/HEALTH/05/16/asian.suicides/.

Americans benefit from this myth, others are punished by it, and other minority groups such as Latinos/as and African Americans are stigmatized by it. If the Model Minority narrative is a myth even for Asian Americans, then how can it serve as a beacon of hope for Latinos/as and African Americans? It is a false story, one that provides false evidence for the Rags to Riches and the Individualism (Stand on Your Own Two Feet) narratives. As a result, the Model Minority narrative can be considered an example of institutional racism. An individual need not be prejudiced against Asians to believe in the narrative. Simply by the use of selective data that seem to support a widely held, but false, narrative, people may act in ways that work to maintain the racial oppression that many members of minority racial groups experience.

Conclusion

In the above telling of the two narratives of affirmative action, we see the rhetorical strategies of two sides as they tell their stories. We see tropes and ideographs called upon in order to make their narrative more persuasive. Hopefully, as we listen to these two narratives, we are able to see other commonly accepted narratives embedded in them. This is especially true of the latter narrative (Affirmative Action as Racist), which is why it requires so much less explanation or evidence for so many people to accept it. Because it uses many other narratives that people already accept, there is little need to make the argument. Notice, for example, how the Affirmative Action as Racist narrative takes up versions of the cultural narratives that I present in Chapter 4. We see elements of the narratives we called Stand on Your Own Two Feet and Market Fundamentalism. We also see oblique appeals through ideographs and tropes to the Melting Pot, the Balkanization, and the Minority as Problem narratives. On the other hand, we also find, at least some easily recognized cultural narratives in the Affirmative Action as Antiracist narrative. For example, we find this narrative to be fully compatible with, perhaps even a variation of, the narrative we called Cultural Pluralism. But it also obliquely suggests the Minority as Victim and the Radical Promise of Democracy narratives, and perhaps even a kind of variation on the American Jeremiad narrative (although in this case our origins were not completely pure—along with much good, we embedded wrong, and now it is necessary for us to get back onto the track of pursuing good).

The Model Minority narrative also depends heavily on widely accepted cultural narratives, including Rags to Riches and Individualism. Though analysis of the full set of facts refutes the implicit argument of the Model Minority narrative, it is rhetorically supported by cultural narratives, which lead people to assume its truth. When a specific narrative is supported rhetorically by widely accepted cultural narratives, it is easier to convince people to accept it. How many of you reading this chapter right now are still convinced the Model Minority narrative is essentially true? To refute myths based on widely accepted cultural narratives requires much more work than to advance them, making it much more difficult for opponents of institutional racism to convince people of its reality.

Of course, the use of rhetoric to make your argument more persuasive does not mean that the argument is not a strong one. Good rhetoric is a wise strategy for strong or weak arguments. I am not suggesting that we should eliminate rhetorical strategies from our public discussions. Rather, we relate these narratives because they are frequently called upon by our policy-makers, our politicians, and our news commentators to try to persuade Americans toward certain interests, and when we can spot them and separate them out from the basic arguments, we are in a better position to understand the fundamental issues and more wisely support one or the other side. Our task as readers of their texts is to be able to see what they are doing so that we can make our decisions based on the strength of their argument, rather than merely the persuasiveness of their rhetoric.

We also present these narratives so that we can come to recognize our own biases built into the narrative that we accept as "commonsense." If you accept one of these narratives as the obvious truth, then you will be more easily persuaded by a text that appeals to that narrative, even if the text's argument is weak. When a text's creator throws a narrative that we already accept into our face, we may often be blind to the text's argument. We may find ourselves accepting and agreeing with a text that, in reality, works against our beliefs and against our commitments simply because we did not unpack the text's rhetoric to examine its argument. Of course, the opposite is true as well. When we listen to an argument that seems to challenge cultural narratives that we hold to be true, we demand more evidence from the speaker than we do from those who support our narratives. Knowing this, we should learn to be more reflective of our own positions and demand just as much evidence from those who support our narratives as we do from those who challenge them.

When it comes to racism in this country, no one should be surprised that the rules and codes of our institutions are embedded with racism, nor should he or she be surprised that many of our narratives are equally infused with racism. How could it be otherwise? How could many of our cultural narratives with their origins in the nineteenth and early twentieth centuries not have hidden within them racist elements? Even if we ourselves are not racist, even if we are antiracist, even if we identify as members of a minority race, just by accepting and using these narratives without having carefully examined them, we can act in the interest of racism and continue to act in ways that result in the creation or maintenance of inequality or domination of a people based on race.

This chapter has examined at length a few cultural narratives, but there are plenty of other topics in education in which race and racism play parts. Consider the arguments around testing and the accountability system, around a common curriculum, around charter schools, around language instruction, around discipline, and around school funding, to name just a few. Each of these issues has proponents of one position or another whose texts appeal to cultural narratives with embedded racial narratives—some of these cultural narratives racialize in a way that works to maintain inequality or domination of racial minorities, while others racialize in a way to work against such domination and to transform our system of inequality. A smart, educated, and wise person will be able to recognize many of them. Pull the texts out and reconsider the value of the argument put forth in them. Hopefully, this section of the book will serve as a start in figuring out how to do this, but I acknowledge that it can only be a start. It requires all of us to reconsider our own beliefs to decide to what extent our beliefs have any real truth to them or are merely versions of a cultural narrative that we learned when we were young and now accept as true, as commonsense.

CHAPTER SIXTEEN

Narratives of Gender and Education

In the American colonial era, the education of girls and boys often occurred together. The Massachusetts School Law of 1647, frequently considered the world's first public school law, required education to be provided to *all children* in any Massachusetts Bay community of fifty or more households.[1] Of course, the purpose of "The Old Deluder Act" was to teach Protestant children to read the Protestant Bible and, therefore, by reading directly God's own words, arm them against the deceptions of Satan (who was presumed to take the form of the Pope) and his minions (i.e., Roman Catholic priests and nuns). All children, including girls, needed protection against Satan, and so girls and boys learned to read together.

But New England Puritans were not the only colonial Americans who advocated for the education of girls. For example, in Thomas Jefferson's "Bill for the More General Diffusion of Knowledge," written for the consideration of the Virginia state legislature in 1779, Jefferson included a provision for girls to be educated by the state alongside boys—but only for three years.[2] Jefferson wanted to ensure basic reading and writing for girls (which was the only goal of the Massachusetts Law of 1647 for all children), because girls would grow up to be mothers of sons and being literate would put mothers in a good position to teach their sons the most basic requirements of citizenship (which, of course, was not needed for daughters who had no legal right to practice citizenship).

According to historian John Rury,

> The years immediately following the American Revolution witnessed a surge of interest in female education and a growing perception that women had a critical role to play in the socialization of children of the new republic. This view—combined with a widely dispersed, largely agrarian population—helped to make coeducation a highly popular practice by the early nineteenth century, at least in the northern and western regions.[3]

---

1. "The Old Deluder Act (1647)," *Records of the Governor and Company of the Massachusetts Bay in New England* (1853), II: 203 (Austin, TX: Constitution Society), www.constitution.org/primarysources/deluder.html.

2. Thomas Jefferson, "A Bill for the More General Diffusion of Knowledge," in *The Works of Thomas Jefferson 1771–1779,* federal edition, Vol. 2, ed. Paul Leicester Ford (New York: G. P. Putnam's Sons, 1905), http://oll.libertyfund.org/title/755/86186.

3. John L. Rury, "Coeducation and Same-Sex Schooling," in *Encyclopedia of Children and Childhood in History and Society,* Faqs.org, 2008, www.faqs.org/childhood/Ch-Co/Coeducation-and-Same-Sex-Schooling .html.

In Ohio, for example, Oberlin College (1837) and Antioch College (1850s) became the first colleges to admit women. According to Rory, "By the 1890s, the vast majority of American school children enrolled in coeducational schools, a far higher percentage than in any other nation."[4] David Tyack and Elizabeth Hansot assert that

> The mixing of the sexes or "coeducation" (coined as an Americanism in the 1850s), for example, became the standard practice in American elementary schools during the first half of the 19th century, but it did not arouse much comment at the time. People did not debate it much until it had already become customary in the schools.[5]

But just because coeducation had become the rule in America does not mean that the practice was universally accepted. In the late nineteenth century, for example, a cultural narrative arose stating that "girls' reproductive organs" could be injured by attending school with boys and that their "delicate nerves" could become frayed when they had to attend school with boys. And in the early twentieth century, a cultural narrative began to circulate that female teachers emasculated, or weakened, their male students by feminizing the classroom.[6]

Even in the past, the majority of Americans have assumed that coeducation was good for girls and that higher education was safe for women, but narratives suggesting otherwise were prominent among a large minority. In fact, in revised form, these "unsafe" narratives still circulate today. Perhaps we have come to accept the idea that education and sports are not *medically* dangerous for girls, but if we pay careful attention, we do hear revised versions of this myth. For example, some narratives portray smart girls as unsexy. Other narratives tell us that athleticism is not feminine, or, at least, not unless the girl is a gymnast or swimmer. While not damaging girls physiologically, these contemporary narratives suggest that education may damage girls socially by making them too smart or too athletic.[7]

Luckily, we also see contemporary narratives that challenge these more traditional narratives so that many girls and their guy friends have no conflict between being smart and being sexy or between being an athlete and being feminine. But just because many college students may not accept the older, traditional narratives that make schooling socially "dangerous" for girls, many others do still accept them to be true. So, just as in the early twentieth century when the majority of Americans did not consider coeducation or higher education dangerous to girls, today a majority of Americans may not think being smart or an athlete reduces a girl's qualities; however, large minorities in both historical eras keep these minority narratives alive and influential.

Although there has been an important demise of the narrative that education is damaging to female physiology, the narrative that schools have become too feminized and unfriendly to boys is one cultural narrative that just won't go away. It is a very prominent cultural

---

4. Ibid.

5. David B. Tyack and Elizabeth Hansot, "Silence and Policy Talk: Historical Puzzles about Gender and Education," *Educational Researcher* 17, no. 3 (April 1988): 33.

6. Ibid.

7. Jarrah Hodge, "Smart Girls: For Girls Who Wear Glasses," *Gender Focus,* 2009, www.gender-focus .com/tag/smart-girls/; Ben Rubenstein et al., "How to Be Sexy While Playing Sports (Girls)," www.wikihow .com/Be-Sexy-While-Playing-Sports-(Girls).

narrative circulating today.[8] These narratives point to statistics of boys' problems in school, such as higher dropout rates, lower GPAs, and higher suspensions, and argue that schools are not "boy friendly." In fact, it is often argued that today's schools are anti-male. So, we can see that according to long-told cultural narratives, schools defeminize girls and emasculate boys—at the same time. It appears that, according to some of our prominent cultural narratives, schools are dangerous places for the development of our gender identity whether we are girls or boys. That not everyone accepts or retells these "dangerous narratives" does not reduce our need to recognize that they do still circulate in our culture and that millions of young girls and boys still pay the price.

Like any other topic, today's debates over gender and education tend to reflect differences in philosophies and economic-political ideologies. But before I explore the range of narratives about gender found in today's conversations about schools, I'd like to first present some basic information.

Boys, Girls, and Schools

Before going any further I would like to clarify some language that frequently gets confused in ordinary conversation, the popular media, and in fact even among scholars. I'm talking about the terms *sex* and *gender*. When I first started teaching college students, most people used the word *sex* when they probably should have used the term *gender*. Today, we find the opposite problem: many people use the term *gender* when they probably should use the term *sex*.

In the most common usage of these terms today, *sex* refers to the claimed biological categories of male, female, or intersex.[9] In other words, the term *sex* makes a claim about a person's biological classification.[10]

On the other hand, the term *gender* refers to socioculturally constructed expectations associated with a particular sex. Some performances we read as "feminine," others as "masculine," and still others as "androgynous."[11] In the recent past, a large number of people assumed that one's gender was determined by one's sex. They expected girls to be feminine and boys to be masculine. In fact, there are still a large number of people who make these same assumptions. But there is no particular reason why gender should be determined by sex because gender is a sociocultural construction and is, therefore, not biologically determined.

For example, I have listened to many discussions in which a female student will say that when she was young she was a "girly girl" or another who says that she was a "tomboy."

---

8. Gerry Garibaldi, "How the Schools Shortchange Boys," *City Journal,* Summer 2006, www.city-journal.org/html/issue_16_3.html.

9. "Intersex" refers to someone whose sex a doctor has a difficult time categorizing as either male or female. It refers to a person whose combination of chromosomes, gonads, hormones, internal sex organs, and/or genitals differs from one of the two expected patterns.

10. Of course, our understanding of biological categories itself might be understood to be located in culture more than in physiology. For example, see Judith Butler, *Gender Trouble: Feminism and the Subversion of Identity* (New York: Routledge, 1990).

11. Here the term "androgynous" refers to performances that reflect both feminine and masculine characteristics.

Saying that she was a girly girl is just another way to say that she performed as her culture stereotypically expects of girls and so was read as a feminine girl. Or to say that she was a tomboy is to say that she performed as her culture expects of boys and so was a masculine girl. Interestingly, these same student discussions usually find both the girly girl and the tomboy backing away from these identities in their present young adult performances. That is to say, they no longer think of themselves as acting as a stereotypically feminine girl or as a masculine girl but as something less stereotypical and more nuanced—perhaps we could call it a little more androgynous.

Many of today's college students (though clearly not all of them) intuitively accept that girls might benefit if they develop their "masculine side" and guys might benefit if they develop their "feminine side," or at the least, expand the performance a little bit. My point here is not to suggest that androgyny is more desirable than stereotypical feminine or masculine performances, but to encourage us to keep in mind that *gender* typically refers to a claim about a person's sociocultural performance, whereas *sex* typically refers to a claim about a person's biological classification. We should also keep in mind that these typical usages are challenged by both those who wish to hold on to the traditional usage in which one's gender is tied to one's biology as well as by those who wish to collapse the distinctions altogether and suggest that there are no biological categories outside of their sociocultural constructions.[12]

According to the US Census Bureau, in 2011, male and female educational attainment was quite similar: about 30 percent of men and women older than twenty-five have either a high school diploma or a GED (but no college) and about 14 percent of each have a bachelor's degree (but no graduate school). High school dropout rates are also about equal: about 1 percent more males (13.1 percent) drop out of high school than females (12.1 percent). The only meaningful differences are found on the high extreme where males are nearly twice as likely to have an advanced professional degree (such as law or medicine) or a doctorate: 3.9 percent male versus 2.2 percent female.[13]

The National Assessment of Educational Progress (NAEP), generally considered the only reliable measure of student achievement trends due to its consistent methods and measures, shows what most would consider a relatively small difference between boys and girls across the years.[14]

According to Lawrence C. Stedman,

> The gender gap in reading was the narrowest during the Reagan years and then nearly doubled, mostly due to slippage in boys' scores. Still, the gap remains small and, in 2004, both genders scored about where they had in the early 1970s. Contrary to stereotypes, the gender gaps in math have been tiny and the smallest of the four areas. The gender gap was largest in writing, with a female advantage that changed little in the 1980s and 1990s.[15]

---

12. For the most influential challenge to the idea of sex as a biological category, see Butler, *Gender Trouble*.

13. "Educational Attainment in the United States: 2011," in *People and Households* (Washington, DC: US Census Bureau, 2011), www.census.gov/hhes/socdemo/education/data/cps/2011/tables.html.

14. Lawrence C. Stedman, *The NAEP Long-Term Trend Assessment: A Review of Its Transformation, Use, and Findings* (Washington, DC: National Assessment Governing Board, March 2009), 12, www.nagb.org/content/nagb/assets/documents/who-we-are/20-anniversary/stedman-long-term-formatted.pdf: 22.

15. Ibid., 22.

While we can and should examine the persistent gaps in the performance of male students in reading and writing and the recent closing of gaps by female students in math and science, the small real differences by sex suggest to some that there are more important gaps, such as those experienced by different social classes, that we need to focus our attention on.[16]

Of course, there is more to education than achievement test scores, and even though these scores may not suggest much difference between male and female school achievement, that does not mean that men and women might not experience schools quite differently, leading to differences not easily measured in achievement tests. Some of these differences show up in the narratives used to describe girls and boys in schools and might help explain why so many Americans seem to accept that schools favor either one sex or the other. Or put a different way, the different experience of boys and girls in school may not be found in their achievement, but in all of the important aspects of being human not measured on an achievement test, such as character, self-confidence, and desire to participate in public life.

To Be a Girl: Narratives on Girlhood and Schooling

The Sugar and Spice and Good Girl/Bad Girl Narrative

Sugar and Spice
and everything nice,
That's what little girls are made of.

What American has not heard these lines from the nineteenth-century English poet Robert Southey's nursery rhyme?[17] Today's world of the WNBA, women astronauts, *Mean Girls,* Katniss Everdeen, and real-life tough women politicians such as Nancy Pelosi and Hillary Clinton lead many of us to find the idea that girls are all sugar and spice little more than amusing and old fashioned. But while it may be true that we have plenty of counterexamples in our contemporary life, the narrative that characterizes girls as the "gentle sex" who are "nurturing" and "caring" and love to dance, wear frilly things, cuddle stuffed poodles and live kittens, and are not supposed to create trouble has certainly not disappeared in the American culture.

One thing that we need to realize is that such gendered rhymes and other specific narratives are not just claims about what girls are, but they are narratives about how girls *should act.* One familiar American cultural narrative constructs a dichotomy between the "good girl" and the "bad girl." The sugar-and-spice girl captures the Good Girl part of this narrative. We also know the Bad Girl part of this narrative. We know that "bad girls" ruin their lives. Take a look at the 1903 print, "The Two Paths: What Will the Girl Become?" (Figure 16.1). A more stark and scary narrative could not be told. Take the sugar-and-spice route,

---

16. For example, Stedman wrote, "A focus on trends has obscured the persistent problem of low achievement. Our concern should not only be whether students are doing better than before but whether they are doing well enough to participate in the democracy, meet the demands of today's society, and fulfill their potential. NAEP's findings are telling.... On average, less than half of our 17-year-olds reach the 300 level and very few (2 to 10 percent) reach the 350 level ... ; yet, these are the levels purportedly needed for work, higher education, business, and government" (ibid., 22).

17. See The Mother Goose Society, www.delamar.org/mgs-long_folksmadeof.html.

THE TWO PATHS

WHAT WILL THE GIRL BECOME?

BAD LITERATURE AT 13

FLIRTING AND COQUETTERY AT 20

FAST LIFE-DISSIPATION AT 26

AN OUTCAST AT 40

Copyright, 1903, by J. A. Hertel.

STUDY AND OBEDIENCE AT 13

VIRTUE AND DEVOTION AT 20

A LOVING MOTHER AT 26

AN HONORED GRANDMOTHER AT 60

THE above cut represents a beautiful little girl at seven—as pure as a sunbeam—she comes from a fine Christian family. Going to the left you see her at thirteen reading "Sapho," a vile novel that was suppressed several years ago in New York—it had a bad effect on our model little girl; at nineteen *Flirting and Coquetry*; third stage, a step lower; at twenty-six, *Fast Life and Dissipation*—this tells the sad story; at forty she is *an outcast*—the miserable result of *Social Impurity*.

To the right we have a brighter picture—at thirteen, *Study and Obedience*; next a young lady in church—*Virtue and Devotion*; at twenty-six—*A Loving Mother*—a most inspiring and lovely scene; at sixty—*An Honored Grandmother*.

Figure 16.1 The Two Paths: What Will the Girl Become?

and become a respected and happy grandmother in your old age. Take the bad girl route, which starts by reading things like *Sapho*, and end up alone and a lonely outcast by the age of forty. But surely, many an early twentieth-century American girl read *Sapho* without ending up in the gutters of the Bowery; yet just as surely, due to such bad girl stories as depicted in this print, many an early twentieth-century American girl was frightened from even trying to read about, let alone perform as, anything other than a sugar-and-spice girl.[18]

18. Presumably, the reference in the print is to the infamous play *Sapho* by Clyde Fitch, produced by and starring Olga Nethersole, who became the iconic bad girl when she was put on trial as "a public nuisance that offended public decency." Fitch's play was, in fact, based on a French novel by Alphonse Daudet. You can read about the scandal in Ann Everal Callis, "Olga Nethersole and the *Sapho* Scandal" (master's thesis, Ohio State University, 1974), https://etd.ohiolink.edu/.

It may be that the narratives available today are more diverse, complex, and numerous than in the early twentieth century when this print was published, and yet the Good Girl/Bad Girl narrative still survives in some form in today's world and still has its impact.[19] If nothing else, we can see the Good Girl/Bad Girl narrative appealed to with the easy and frequent "slut" slur thrown at young women by men and women young and old. Such a slur invokes the Bad Girl narrative and is used to discipline bad girls and good girls alike.

Narratives of Girlhood and the Media

What are the narratives about girlhood that circulate in today's world? And where do we hear them? Certainly we hear many of these narratives from our parents, teachers, and friends, but just as surely we hear many of these narratives in the media. When we see the characterization of a girl in the media, how do we know that she is a girl? What do the producers, directors, actors, and artists use to let us know that the character is a girl and, therefore, what counts as appropriate for a girl?

How about Angelina Ballerina, the fictional mouse based on the 1980s English book series written by Katharine Holabird, illustrated by Helen Craig, and computer animated in its present form for broadcast on PBS stations across America? What narratives does this animated television series provide for young girls who are watching at precisely the age when they are becoming aware of gender performance? On AngelinaBallerina.com, Angelina Jeannette Mouseling is described as "an 8-year-old mouseling who is passionate about dancing and life. She is imaginative, clever, determined and is a feisty spirit bursting with energy." Is Angelina a sugar-and-spice girl, a bad girl, or something else? Explore the AngelinaBallerina.com website and identify the important elements of girlhood as presented in the videos and other representations at the website. What is your little sister, niece, or daughter learning about how to perform "girl" when she watches Angelina?

Then visit Dora the Explorer's video showcase on Nick Jr.'s website.[20] Besides the obvious early childhood gloss on vocabulary building and other educational benefits (including the teaching of Spanish), what does "tomboy" Dora teach kids about how to perform "girl"? In what ways does Dora's narrative overlap with Angelina's narrative, and in what ways do they differ?

Of the many things that could be identified in Dora's videos, I find it quite interesting that the Dora aesthetic is copied from computer games. Dora and her monkey friend are generally depicted walking down a path from left to right where she runs into problems to solve. It's not much different from *Mario* or 500 other video games. Do you think that the fact that the computer game industry has found it more difficult to attract girls than boys to the gaming world might have anything to do with its design? Does Dora's aesthetic set the stage to open up the performance of girl to include "gamer"? Is that a good thing?

In 2009, Mattel and Nickelodeon produced a new "Tween Dora" in hopes of holding on to their "aging" audience of young girls. Visit Dora's Explorer Girls website,[21] and consider how

---

19. "The Two Paths: What Will the Girl Become?" in *Social Purity,* ed. John W. Gibson (New York: J. L. Nichols, 1903), 58, www.loc.gov/pictures/item/2002716768/.

20. www.nickjr.com/kids-videos/kids-dora-the-explorer-videos.html.

21. www.nickjr.com/doragirls/home.jhtml.

Tween Dora expands the narrative of what it means to be a girl. According to the narratives found in Little Dora and Tween Dora, in what ways do girls change as they enter puberty? What is the difference between a girl-child and a girl-tween? Look at the appearance of the two Doras and what they actually do. What part of Dora's little girl character remains in her tween character, and what changes? What narrative do you think was read into the Tween Dora text by the parents who complained that the Tween Dora sexualized Little Dora and moved her away from a "tomboy" storyline? If they are right, does it tell little girls that it's okay to be a tomboy when a little girl but not when they become ten years old?[22]

Whether you agree or disagree with the parents' complaints about the new Dora, does the narrative underlying this controversy sound familiar? Is this a new version of the Good Girl/Bad Girl narrative? Are those who are complaining about the sexualization of Little Dora as she becomes Tween Dora reading too much into the change? Are they making the same old-fashioned mistake as the "Two Paths" print from 1903? How about those who complained about the Bratz dolls as presenting unacceptable sexualization? Are they making the same mistake of reading too much into it? Is the task force of the American Psychological Association making too big a deal when it states,

> One series of dolls popular with girls as young as age 4 are the Bratz dolls, a multi-ethnic crew of teenagers who are interested in fashion, music, boys, and image (see www.bratz.com). Bratz girls are marketed in bikinis, sitting in a hot tub, mixing drinks, and standing around, while the "Boyz" play guitar and stand with their surf boards, poised for action.... Moreover, Bratz dolls come dressed in sexualized clothing such as miniskirts, fishnet stockings, and feather boas. Although these dolls may present no more sexualization of girls or women than is seen in MTV videos, it is worrisome when dolls designed specifically for 4- to 8-year-olds are associated with an objectified adult sexuality. The objectified sexuality presented by these dolls, as opposed to the healthy sexuality that develops as a normal part of adolescence, is limiting for adolescent girls, and even more so for the very young girls who represent the market for these dolls.[23]

And if you think Tween Dora and Bratz are not an appeal to the Bad Girl narrative, how about the advertising campaign for the French lingerie company Fashionista's 2011 line of lingerie called *Jours Après Lunes* designed for girls four to twelve years of age or the French *Vogue* fashion shoot of ten-year-old Thylane Loubry Blondeau.[24] Watch the video on Blondeau and notice the multiple and contradictory narratives that this ad campaign seems to have evoked. For some, the Blondeau performance is little more than a disturbing celebration of the Bad Girl narrative, but for others, it is just an example of cultural difference. Is this progression from Little Dora to Tween Dora to Bratz to *Jours Après Lunes* and

---

22. For a discussion of the controversy surrounding the introduction of Tween Dora, see Associated Press, "Tween Dora Not a Tramp: Nick and Mattel Soothe Moms after Uproar," NYDailyNews.com, March 16, 2009, www.nydailynews.com/latino/tween-dora-a-tramp-nick-mattel-soothe-moms-uproar-article-1.372211.

23. "Report of the APA Task Force on the Sexualization of Girls," 2010, www.apa.org/pi/women/programs/girls/report-full.pdf.

24. www.huffingtonpost.com/2011/08/16/little-girls-lingerie_n_928219.html; video on Blondeau available at http://embed.5min.com/517138771/'/.

Thylane Loubry Blondeau an updated version of the "Two Paths" narrative of the print shown earlier, or is it something else altogether?

One of the positives of the Internet era is the possibility that ordinary people can get together and begin to challenge the dominance of corporate media, allowing for a wider diversity of narratives to circulate in our culture. Take a look at the SPARK website (www .sparksummit.com/). Here is how the website describes SPARK:

> SPARK is a girl-fueled activist movement to demand an end to the sexualization of women and girls in media. We're collaborating with hundreds of girls 13–22 and more than 60 national organizations to reject the commodified, sexualized images of girls in media and support the development of girls' healthy sexuality and self-esteem.[25]

What is the counternarrative that these girls and young women are trying to tell? How might a SPARK-influenced TV show for tweens permit a wider range of stories than even the supposedly tomboy Dora's Explorer Girls provide? Another very interesting site that presents counternarratives was created by and is designed for teenage girls. *Rookie Magazine*[26] explores contemporary life, including the news and culture, with articles and artwork by teens. It has been getting great reviews not only from teens but from adults as well.

Girlhood as Innocent

One does not have to accept the Sugar and Spice narrative or the Two Paths narrative to want to hold onto the narrative that tells us that childhood is innocent. The Innocence of Childhood narrative suggests that there is something that happens when we shift from child to teen that leads us out of innocence into culpability. Surely the Innocence of Childhood narrative can be seen in the controversy described above. Some people get quite upset when girlhood is not presented as "innocent." One interesting question is why it might be that so many of us are attracted to the story of childhood innocence despite all the evidence that children hardly live innocent lives. In the past several years, we have seen stories in which children have deliberately murdered people,[27] children as young as six have been convicted of sex crimes against other juveniles,[28] and all around the world we have seen an increase in the number of child soldiers[29] (though it is also important to realize that children have been soldiers for centuries, including in the American Revolutionary War).[30] For millions of boys and girls, childhood has no innocence whatsoever.

---

25. "Spark Change. Join the Movement," www.sparksummit.com/.

26. www.rookiemag.com.

27. John Dougherty and Anahad O'Connor, "Prosecutors Say Boy Methodically Shot His Father," *New York Times,* November 10, 2008, www.nytimes.com/2008/11/11/us/11child.html.

28. For example, see Wendy Koch, "Study: Many Sex Offenders Are Kids Themselves," *USA Today,* January 5, 2010, www.usatoday.com/news/nation/2010-01-03-kid-sex-offenders_N.htm.

29. "Child Soldiers: Global Report 2008," Coalition to Stop the Use of Child Soldiers, 2008, www.child -soldiers.org/global_report_reader.php?id=97.

30. David Rosen, "Child Soldiers: Victims or Heroes?" *FDU Magazine Online,* Summer/Fall 2005, www .fdu.edu/newspubs/magazine/05sf/childsoldiers.html.

The world's desperate desire to hold on to the narrative of the innocence of childhood despite the reality of children's lives has helped the Walt Disney Company grow to be the world's largest media conglomerate and, according to *Fortune Magazine,* the sixty-sixth largest corporation in America with revenues of more than 40 billion dollars in 2011.[31] Disney relentlessly pushes the Innocence of Childhood narrative, filling our screens with stories of princesses and their princes and their animal friends. Apparently we are desperate to have the innocent girlhood story told again and again, given that Disney comes out with another princess animated movie every few years—*Tangled* released in 2010 being the most recent. (While in fall 2010, Disney announced that it was ending production of all future princess movies, in winter 2011 it announced a new Disney princess for television, *Sofia the First,* which began broadcasting on the Disney Channel on January 11, 2013.[32])

But for all the apparent desire to narrate the world of childhood as innocent, that innocence is apparently not sufficient for the American people to believe that children's innocence relieves them of any culpability in their own sickness since, despite this love of the Innocence of Childhood narrative, between 1988 and 2005 approximately 17,000 American children likely died as the result of not having health insurance.[33] Far from being innocent, these children suffered the guilt of their parents for being poor. One must wonder how much their siblings and friends think of childhood as innocent when they watched their sibling or friend die for want of health insurance.

Scholar Henry Giroux[34] challenges the wisdom of such an essentialized and uncomplicated view of childhood. Giroux suggests that narratives of innocence often blind us to the real political interests at play. These interests promote the narrative of innocent childhood in order to distract us from the reality of the lives of children in contemporary American society. Giroux also suggests that a continued re-narrating of childhood as innocent leads us to fail to recognize the racism and sexism that are structured into these narratives helping to reproduce a racist and sexist society. Giroux forces us to reflect on the Disney narrative of girlhood. According to the Disney narrative, what does it mean to be a girl? Even the strong Mulan, who almost single-handedly saves a nation through her courage and physical power, returns home where she is finally "completed" by the attentions of a man. Is the Disney narrative as innocent as Disney and its fans proclaim?

31. "Fortune 500," *Fortune Magazine,* 2013, http://money.cnn.com/magazines/fortune/fortune500/2013/snapshots/2190.html?iid=F500_fl_list.

32. Dawn C. Chmielewski and Claudia Eller, "Disney Animation Is Closing the Book on Fairy Tales," *Los Angeles Times,* November 21, 2010, http://articles.latimes.com/2010/nov/21/entertainment/la-et-1121-tangled-20101121; Deadline Team, "Disney Unveils New Princess with 'Sofia the First,'" *Deadline Hollywood,* www.deadline.com/2011/12/disney-unveils-new-princess-with-sofia-the-first-tv-movie-series/.

33. Ekaterina Pesheva, "Lack of Insurance May Have Figured in Nearly 17,000 Childhood Deaths, Study Shows," Johns Hopkins Children's Center, www.hopkinschildrens.org/lack-of-insurance-may-have-figured-in-nearly-17000-childhood-deaths.aspx.

34. Henry A. Giroux, "Are Disney Movies Good for Your Kids?" in *Kinderculture: The Corporate Construction of Childhood,* ed. Shirley Steinberg and Joe Kincheloe (Boulder: Westview Press, 1997); see also Henry A. Giroux, *The Mouse That Roared: Disney and the End of Innocence,* Culture and Education Series (Lanham, MD: Rowman & Littlefield, 1999).

Narratives of Girl and of Scientist

Have you ever taken the Draw a Scientist Test (DAST)? If not, why not try it right now? It's easy. Get a piece of paper and draw a scientist. Don't worry about how good an artist you are, just draw it as best you can in just a few minutes. The DAST has been used since the 1980s to examine how people construct the image of "scientist" and has found remarkably similar results across ages, nations, and time. Most drawings show a man wearing a white lab coat, working alone with some kind of lab equipment, sporting glasses and crazy hair. Did your picture look anything like that? Interestingly, even studies as recent as 2006 suggest that college students are nearly as likely as elementary school students to draw such a representation of "scientist."

There is some controversy in the literature as to what these drawings actually mean. Some psychologists claim that they are windows into the minds of the test takers and reveal how these people actually imagine scientists. Others suggest that they have more to do with drawing the stereotyped vision represented in a culture's texts and may have little to do with how the person him- or herself actually imagines what a scientist looks like. But I am not particularly interested in what people actually think as much as I'm interested in the cultural narratives that circulate in our society that make possible the various specific narratives that people use when trying to make meaning of the world. Because this is my interest, it doesn't really matter whether the test takers actually believe the image represents real scientists or not, for they provide us a clue as to what they think the dominant cultural narrative might be.

If most people seem to draw a picture of a lone male in a white lab coat with crazy hair and glasses when asked to draw a scientist, then we might understand how it could be that so many teenage girls have a hard time imagining themselves as a scientist or, even worse, wanting to imagine themselves as a scientist. How many teenage girls want to become the female equivalent of that image, going through life in lab coat with crazy hair and glasses? Clearly, the cultural narrative of scientist depicted in most drawings created in the DAST seems to preclude or, at least, discourage girls from going into science.

Fermilab, a company in Batavia, Illinois, invited a seventh-grade teacher and her class to visit their labs. Before the field trip, the students were asked to draw a picture of a scientist and unsurprisingly produced picture after picture of men in white lab coats with crazy hair and glasses. But when the students visited the labs and met the scientists, including several women, the students were able to create a different shared narrative and, when asked to draw a scientist following the field trip, they produced a wide range of pictures of ordinary people—many of which depicted images that any teen girl could identify with and could aspire to become. Just as interesting as the pictures were the students' comments written to accompany their pictures. For example, one student, Amy, for her before picture describes a scientist as a hardworking, crazy-minded, and irritating male, but for her after picture she describes her scientist as a normal person outside of work doing a not-so-normal job (see Table 16.1). This serves as evidence, perhaps, that cultural narratives can be challenged by relevant personal experiences.[35]

---

35. See Amy's drawings at Marge Bardeen, "Who's the Scientist? Seventh Graders Describe Scientists Before and After a Visit to Fermilab," Fermilab, http://ed.fnal.gov/projects/scientists/amy.html.

Table 16.1 Amy's Comments Accompanying Her Pictures in the Draw a Scientist Test Before and After Her Class Visit to Fermilab

Before comment	After comment
I think of a scientist as very dedicated to his work. He is kind of crazy, talking always quickly. He constantly is getting new ideas. He is always asking questions and can be annoying. He listens to others' ideas and questions them.	I know scientists are just normal people with a not so normal job.... Scientists lead a normal life outside of being a scientist. They are interested in dancing, pottery, jogging and even racquetball. Being a scientist is just another job which can be much more exciting.

One issue plaguing science education is the disproportionate number of men in STEM (science, technology, engineering, and math) fields. According to a recent US Department of Commerce report, in 2009, only 24 percent of those working in STEM fields were women.[36] While there are multiple causes for the low representation of women in STEM fields, one cause is that the cultural narratives that construct what it means to be a "girl" and a "woman" do not overlap very much with the cultural narrative of what it means to be a "scientist." Because these narratives overlap so little, many a high school girl and college woman finds herself having to choose between the two as a basis for her own gender performance. We shouldn't wonder that many of them choose to perform "girl" or "woman" rather than to perform "scientist." Perhaps the class field trip to the commercial laboratory helped Amy and her female classmates develop a good counternarrative to the stereotyped scientist, and perhaps, this counternarrative will open up the possibility that one or more of them might think one does not have to choose between performing woman or performing scientist, but that there is actually a way to perform both. And that might lead one or two of them to enter a major in college that could lead to their becoming a scientist.

To Be a Boy

In January 2006, the narrative of the Boy Crisis in education reached a crescendo with story after story of the dismal state of American boyhood. These included a PBS documentary based on a best-selling book by Michael Thompson,[37] a cover story in *Newsweek*,[38] and major stories in *The New Republic*[39] and *Esquire*.[40] The Boy Crisis became a running narrative throughout 2006, showing up in numerous editorials, commentaries, magazine articles, and TV news segments. By December of 2006 the Boy Crisis narrative had entered commonsense. That

---

36. David Beede, Tiffany Julian, and David Langdon, "Women in STEM: A Gender Gap to Innovation" (Washington, DC: Economics and Statistics Administration, US Department of Commerce, 2011), www.esa.doc.gov/sites/default/files/reports/documents/womeninstemagaptoinnovation8311.pdf.

37. Michael Thompson, *Raising Cain: Boys in Focus,* Powderhouse and Oregon Public Broadcasting, 2006, videorecording.

38. Peg Tyre, "The Trouble with Boys," *Newsweek,* January 29, 2006, www.thedailybeast.com/newsweek/2006/01/29/the-trouble-with-boys.html.

39. Richard Whitmire, "Boy Trouble," *New Republic* 234, no. 2 (January 23, 2006): 15–18, www.newrepublic.com/article/boys-and-books.

40. Tom Chiarella, "The Problem with Boys ... Is Actually a Problem with Men," *Esquire,* July 1, 2006, www.esquire.com/features/ESQ0706SOTAMBOYS_94.

is to say, the narrative had been told so many times that many Americans now accepted that boys were in crisis in schools and no longer needed evidence to support the assertion. Not until 2008 did we see a major pushback against the Boy Crisis narrative. In May of that year, the American Association of University Women released "Where the Girls Are: The Facts about Gender Equity in Education." The AAUW report argued three major claims: that girls' educational success does not come at the expense of boys' educational success; that on average, both boys' and girls' achievement has increased; and that the real gap is an income gap, not a gender gap.[41] While recent reports continue to support the AAUW's three major claims, some of the subpoints used as premises to argue for the three major claims may be less accurate today. For example, while the AAUW's claim that the achievement in basic education continues to improve for both boys and girls, as of 2011, girls had reached parity with boys in mathematics in both the fourth and eighth grades.[42] On the other hand, in reading, the scores have not changed much in recent years, and the gap between boys and girls has stubbornly remained the same with the boys continuing to lag behind girls in both fourth and eighth grades.[43] In other words, the gender gap in mathematics has been closed while the gender gap in reading remains the same, suggesting that there really may be some kind of an achievement problem that needs to be addressed. But, while there may be a problem in a continued gap in math achievement, the data hardly suggest that there is a "crisis," at least when considering reading and mathematics achievement.

What are the elements of the Boy Crisis narrative? Interestingly, we need to ask which boy crisis we are talking about, because there is more than one.

Feminization of the Classroom Narrative #1: Blame the Feminists

One Boy Crisis narrative develops the theme that schools are too feminine as a result of the recent feminist movement. The feminization of the classroom narrative has been with us a long, long time. As mentioned earlier in this chapter, the feminization of the classroom narrative has been with us at least since the early twentieth century.[44] Interestingly, for those who tell versions of this narrative today, the feminization of the classroom is something that has happened in recent years. Of course, that the feminization is of recent occurrence is part of the narrative itself so that those who told versions of that narrative in the 1920s argued that the feminization resulted from the (then) new progressive education movement. Today the culprit for the apparent recent feminization of the classroom is the feminist movement, which, the narrative tells us, has caused a war to be waged against boys.

Philosopher Christina Hoff Sommers's turn-of-the-twenty-first-century best-selling book, *The War against Boys,* provides a version of the old feminization of the classroom narrative

---

41. Christianne Corbett, Catherine Hill, and Andresse St. Rose, "Where the Girls Are: The Facts about Gender Equity in Education" (Washington, DC: American Association of University Women, 2008), www .aauw.org/research/where-the-girls-are/.

42. "The Nation's Report Card: Mathematics 2011" (Washington, DC: National Center for Education Statistics, US Department of Education, 2011), http://nces.ed.gov/nationsreportcard/pdf/main2011/2012458 .pdf.

43. "The Nation's Report Card: Reading 2011" (Washington, DC: National Center for Education Statistics, US Department of Education, 2011), http://nces.ed.gov/nationsreportcard/pdf/main2011/2012457.pdf.

44. Tyack and Hansot, "Silence and Policy Talk."

updated for contemporary ideological politics. Sommers is well known for the development of a conservative feminist philosophy (which she calls "equity feminism") that positions itself against a cultural or radical feminist philosophy (which she calls "gender feminism"). By tying the old narrative of the feminization of the classroom to the new antifeminism narrative, Sommers was able to provide a clear and compelling narrative that served the interest of social conservatism and, therefore, found a ready-made audience and public relations apparatus en garde to advance her narrative.[45]

In order to show that there is a boy crisis, besides the achievement score gap discussed above, Sommers and others point to lower GPAs, higher dropout rates, more detentions and suspensions, higher numbers identified as learning disabled, and greater perpetrators of and victims of violence. All of these boy problems, according to Sommers and her allies, occur because cultural feminists have convinced schools to focus on the needs of girls and not boys. According to this narrative, the only time they do focus on boys is to berate them for being boys and try to get them to "get in touch with their feminine side." While these new narratives do lay out some evidence of areas where boys may be having trouble, they provide little to no evidence that these problems have anything at all to do with feminism. But lack of evidence has never stopped a cultural narrative from circulating and being used to justify people's ideologies.

Feminization of the Classroom Narrative #2: Boys Don't Want to Be Treated Like Girls

While Sommers's narrative argues that the "war against boys" results from the mistaken cultural feminist argument that feminine characteristics are superior to masculine characteristics, leading to the neglect and denigration of masculine boys, a second version of the Feminization of the Classroom narrative argues that the problem has little to do with feminism and more to do with the fact that women increasingly run the schools. Typically, according to this narrative, women just don't understand boys, thus the increased numbers of women in schools leads to the inevitable misunderstanding of boys. In other words, while the feminization #1 narrative argues that the problem lies with feminists, the feminization #2 narrative argues that the problem lies with women.

The failure of female teachers to understand boys leads them to treat boys like girls and, as a result, boys resist this attempt to emasculate them. According to this feminization of the classroom narrative, boys don't want to be treated like girls. This narrative suggests that boys act out more, talk frankly, have less intrinsic interest in school performance, and don't find much self-worth in pleasing the teacher.[46] These narrators sometimes draw on brain-imaging research to claim a biological difference between boys and girls that requires different classroom methods.[47] According to the Boys Don't Want to be Treated Like Girls narrative, we need more men teaching, and we need all-boy schools and classes. Schools need to be more "boy-friendly" by doing things such as having more frequent breaks, more active learning,

---

45. Christina Hoff Sommers, "The War against Boys," *The Atlantic,* May 1, 2000; Christina Hoff Sommers, *The War against Boys: How Misguided Feminism Is Harming Our Young Men* (New York: Simon & Schuster, 2000).

46. For a well-known example, see Gerry Garibaldi, "How the Schools Shortchange Boys."

47. For example, see the works of Michael Gurian, www.michaelgurian.com/.

and room for rough play. Actually, the Feminization of the Classroom narrative #2 sounds identical to the narrative found at the beginning of the twentieth century. Apparently when it comes to the feminization of the classroom and the unfriendly environment for boys, not much has changed in the century in between then and now.

The Tough Guise Narrative

You don't have to blame either feminists or all women to suggest that there is some kind of new problem facing boys. One contemporary narrative that does not blame either could be called the Tough Guise narrative.[48] Promoted by Jackson Katz, the Tough Guise narrative suggests that there has been a change in the culture that requires boys and men to perform in such a way as to display physical power and no weakness.[49] The Tough Guise narrative recognizes that males have a long history in many societies of having to perform as if they are strong, rational, calculating, invulnerable, macho, and heterosexual, but the Tough Guise narrative insists that what counts as being masculine today has become more extreme and more central to boys' and men's identity performances. This new culture has required boys and men to become hyper-masculine. The need for pumped-up bodies, unemotional and "cool poses,"[50] and a top-dog, cock-of-the-block attitude has created the idea that doing well in school is for sissies or nerds. Furthermore, the Tough Guise narrative suggests that this new hyper-masculinity has confused gender and sexuality, so that those boys who fail to perform a hyper-masculinity are not just failing to perform appropriate masculinity, but are, in fact, also failing to perform appropriate heterosexuality. This tying of gender performance with sexuality complicates an already difficult situation for adolescent males.

Above I described the difficulty many teen girls might have imagining themselves as scientists when the cultural narratives associated with scientists depict crazy-minded, bizarre-haired men with glasses. When you compare the typical desired image of an adult woman found in our media, the scientist comes off second-best to many teen girls. But much the same can be said for teen boys. While the boys can at least identify with the sex of the scientist, the cultural narratives that depict scientists in our society do not present a stereotypically masculine male for the boys to aspire to become. When given the choice between imagining themselves as a weird scientist versus a virile superhero, superstar, or star athlete, we can understand why many boys might be reluctant to embrace a future goal that will lead to their ostracism as a masculine male.

And this is part of the problem the Tough Guise narrative identifies for boys and most men. In the ever-increasing standard of what it takes to be considered a "real man," boys more than ever must up their performance of masculinity or find themselves victimized by their male peers and humiliated by their female peers. Unfortunately, this hyper-masculine performance is unobtainable to most boys and men and, according to the Tough Guise narrative, it also has little place for academic success in its characterization. In fact, just as many a seventh-grade girl feels that she has to choose between being a scientist or being a

48. Jackson Katz, *The Macho Paradox: Why Some Men Hurt Women and How All Men Can Help* (Naperville, IL: Sourcebooks, 2006).

49. Sut Jhally, *Tough Guise*, Media Education Foundation, 1999, videorecording.

50. Richard Majors and Janet Mancini Billson, *Cool Pose: The Dilemmas of Black Manhood in America* (New York: Simon & Schuster, 1993).

girl, many a seventh-grade boy feels that he has to choose between being a good student and being a boy. And, just as we shouldn't be surprised when a girl chooses to reject science and embrace girl, neither should we be surprised when a boy chooses to reject school and embrace boy.

Conclusion

This chapter has only addressed a few of the many narratives that circulate that help explain our experiences with gender and education. Some of these narratives have existed for over a century but are told today as if they are brand new. Some of these narratives are brand new and are providing counternarratives for young girls and boys to draw from as they attempt to learn how to perform their gendered identity. But while there does seem to be a wider range of narratives circulating today than in the early part of the twentieth century, thus providing more options, the dominant gender narratives are still very powerful for many girls and boys. These narratives can persuade many of them to harass and bully others who fail to conform and may induce many others to give in to this harassment and bullying and conform to the demands of the expectations of what it means to be a girl or to be a boy.

Who bullies and who conforms can be complicated by other identities and positionalities, such as social class, race, ethnicity, and sexuality. Some of these narratives are more likely to be found among rural, white, working-class schools, whereas others may be more likely to be found among suburban, Asian, middle-class schools, whereas others may be more likely found in other combinations of ethnicity, race, and social class. Hopefully, understanding that many of the narratives that circulate have little to do with evidence and everything to do with political ideologies can help us decide how schools ought to be responding. As a member of the public or as an educator or as a parent, how should we navigate through these conflicting narratives to advocate for educational policies and practices for girls and for boys?

CHAPTER SEVENTEEN

Narratives of Sexuality, Adolescence, and Education

From the point of view of adults, adolescence is understood as a problem to be managed, and the center of that problem is the adolescent body with its awakening desires and lack of discipline. Of course, that awkward age of early puberty in which the body begins to develop sexual desire and the brain moves toward abstract thinking has existed throughout human history, but not until the twentieth century did this period become identified as a unique stage in human development. Before then, puberty was indicative of change in status between childhood and adulthood. Romeo and Juliet may have been young lovers, but by the standards of the seventeenth century, they were also adult lovers.

The recognition of adolescence as a unique and individual stage in human growth and development accompanied the broad progressive ideas of the early twentieth century, but it was Sigmund Freud who did the most to turn the sexuality of this stage into a problem. Freud's theories are often misrepresented in contemporary popular culture, but one thing it gets right is Freud's belief that psychologically healthy adults maintained a careful balance between suppression and expression of their sexuality. Suddenly, following Freud, getting that balance right in adolescence became one central and essential key to developing into happy, mature adults.

This felt need to help adolescents find the right balance became a central theme of education in the 1950s. Perhaps it was the increased freedom made possible by the automobile or the independence made possible by the prosperous postwar American economy that led American adults to call on schools to help. Or, perhaps it was the fear promoted by the popular characterization of youth found in pop culture. Consider the 1955 movie *Blackboard Jungle,* where the Vic Morrow and Sidney Poitier characters promote the idea of youth out of control. Or consider the media promotion of James Dean as a visual ideograph of the brooding and dangerous adolescent male, and all of this topped off with Elvis Presley's "blatant sexuality" found in his swinging hips (which was reinforced when television banned showing Elvis from the waist down[1]). Whatever the cause, the 1950s saw an increased focus on addressing the "problems of adolescence" in schools.

In *The Education of Eros: A History of Education and the Problem of Adolescent Sexuality,* Dennis Carlson argues that four major "problems" became central concerns of American

---

1. See Alan Hanson, "As Seen on TV in the Fifties ... Elvis on the Living Room Screen," Elvis History Blog, September 2011, www.elvis-history-blog.com/karal-ann-marling.html.

high schools: the problem of becoming adjusted to normal family life and gender roles, the problem of the unwed teen mother, the problem of sexually transmitted diseases, and the problem of homosexuality.[2] Each of these "problems" generated its own narratives that worked to organize and pattern the conversation around sexuality and education during the 1950s and, in fact, every decade since. Later in this chapter, I will explore these narratives as they are told and retold in today's world, but before moving to these narratives, I would like to present some basic understandings assumed in this chapter.

Terminology and Sexuality

As in all topics of social identity and cultural politics, the representation of sexuality in our language has become an important site for care and reflection. In recent years, there has been a dramatic increase in the insertion of sexuality into public conversation. Once a topic relegated only to backrooms and psychologists' offices, sexuality is now openly discussed on television and in the newspapers. As a sign of the growing acceptability of public discussions of sexuality, on January 21st of 2012, President Obama used the word *gay* in his inaugural address, becoming the first president to do so. In this section, I am going to clarify some of the terms that we find in these conversations, but keep in mind that the use of these terms is rapidly evolving, and I make no claim that the usage presented in this chapter is the correct or final word on terminology.

LGBTQ is a collective acronym referring to those who identify as lesbian, gay, bisexual, transgender (or transsexual), or queer (or questioning). Sometimes the letter "I" is included to refer to those who identify as intersexed. According to Eli R. Green, Eric N. Peterson, and Josh Fletcher, these terms can be defined as follows:[3]

Lesbian: Term used to describe female-identified people attracted romantically, erotically, and/or emotionally to other female-identified people. (Many lesbians, though not all, object to being called "gay.")

Gay: 1. Term used in some cultural settings to represent males who are attracted to males in a romantic, erotic, and/or emotional sense. Not all men who engage in "homosexual behavior" identify as gay, and as such, this label should be used with caution. **2.** Term used to refer to the LGBTQI community as a whole, or as an individual identity label for anyone who does not identify as heterosexual.

Bisexual: A person emotionally, physically, and/or sexually attracted to both males/men and females/women. This attraction does not have to be equally split between genders, and there may be a preference for one gender over others.

Transgender: A person who lives as a member of a gender other than that expected based on anatomical sex. Sexual orientation varies and is not dependent on gender identity.

2. Dennis Carlson, *The Education of Eros: A History of Education and the Problem of Adolescent Sexuality*, Studies in Curriculum Theory (New York: Routledge, 2012).

3. This list was constructed by Josh Fletcher (Miami University, 2011–2012) and Richard Quantz (2013) from the following: Eli Green and Eric N. Peterson, "LGBTTSQI Terminology," LGBT Resource Center at UC Riverside, 2006, www.trans-academics.org/lgbttsqiterminology.pdf.

Transsexual: A person who identifies psychologically as a gender/sex other than the one to which he or she was assigned at birth. Transsexuals often wish to transform their bodies hormonally and surgically to match their inner sense of gender/sex.

Queer: 1. An umbrella term that embraces a matrix of sexual preferences, orientations, and habits of the not-exclusively-heterosexual-and-monogamous majority. *Queer* includes lesbians, gay men, bisexuals, transpeople, and intersex persons. **2.** This term is sometimes used as a sexual orientation label instead of *bisexual* as a way of acknowledging that there are more than two genders to be attracted to, or as a way of stating a non-heterosexual orientation without having to state whom they are attracted to.

Intersexed: Someone whose sex a doctor has a difficult time categorizing as either male or female. A person whose combination of chromosomes, gonads, hormones, internal sex organs, and/or genitals differs from one of the two expected patterns.

Sam Killerman[4] defines *questioning* as the process of exploring one's own sexual orientation, investigating influences that may come from their family, religious upbringing, and internal motivations.

Rethinking Gender

While it used to be thought that one's gendered performances "naturally" matched one's assignment to a sex, by now, most Americans have come to understand that a person's assignment to a biological category of sex and one's gendered identity are two different things. One can be assigned the category "male," for example, but perform in ways that a culture thinks are "feminine." In recent years, many people have tried to break down these things we call "sex" and "gender" in order to develop a way to think about them that more closely matches human experience. One of the more recent approaches suggests that our sex/gender identity can best be described as some combination of four different dimensions: gender identity, gender expression, biological sex, and sexual orientation (or to whom you are attracted). One particular version of the four dimensions approach suggests that each dimension is itself made up of two subdimensions, which themselves can be recognized as strong or weak influences, creating an enormous variety of ways in which individuals can construct their gender. So, for example, under the dimension gender identity, any individual might score high or low or in between on either or both of the "Woman-ness" and "Man-ness" scales. Or under the dimension of gender expression, any person might score high or low or in between on either or both of the "masculine" or "feminine" scales. Whether we use the four dimension approach or a two dimension approach or some other number of dimensions, most people today do seem to agree that gender, sex, and sexuality are somehow entwined in our socially constructed sense of self and others. Gone are the days when we think we can know a person by merely looking at them. Unfortunately, most schools have not yet begun to catch on to this complexity and continue to assume that all students are *cisgendered*—that is, the individual students all feel a clear alignment among gender identity, gender expression, biological sex, and sexual attraction.

---

4. Sam Killerman, "Comprehensive List of LGBTQ+ Term Definitions," It's Pronounced Metrosexual, 2011–2013, http://itspronouncedmetrosexual.com/2013/01/a-comprehensive-list-of-lgbtq-term-definitions/. This list also includes many of the terms on the Green and Peterson list with some different wording.

Some universities have begun to recognize that sex and gender are no longer to be considered straightforward and have adopted policies such as the availability of gender-neutral bathrooms and asking students to identify whether they wish to be addressed with gendered or gender-neutral pronouns such as ze or hir. Ze and hir are "alternate pronouns that are gender neutral and preferred by some gender diverse persons. Pronounced /zee/ and /here/, they replace 'he'/'she' and 'his'/'hers.'"[5] But while a few universities have responded to the recognized complexity of gender and sexuality, the number of high schools that do are few and far between.

Some junior high and high schools have been specifically created as a safe haven to gender diverse students. Careful to clarify that these schools are open to and enroll straight/cisgendered students, they nonetheless have a very high percentage of LGBTQ students. Perhaps the best known of these alternative high schools is the Harvey Milk High School, a New York City public high school located in the East Village that enrolls about 100 LGBTQ and straight/cisgendered students. The Alliance Charter School in Milwaukee, funded by the state of Wisconsin and designed to be LGBTQ friendly and that enrolls a little more than 150 students—about half of which identify as LGBTQ—gained much attention following a 2011 *Time* magazine article.[6] The Alliance School is one of the few gender diverse–friendly schools that enrolls students starting in the sixth grade. Some attempts to create such schools have not been able to survive the opposition from social conservatives who complain that public money should not be spent on protecting children just because of their sexuality when many other children are also bullied and harassed, as well as opposition from gay rights groups who argue that children should not have to be segregated to be safe and instead advocate for the creation of safe environments for LGBTQ children wherever they attend school.[7]

Some districts have encouraged the development of student support groups, such as Gay, Lesbian, and Straight Education Network (GLSEN) and such formal programs as SafeZone, to attempt to create a safer and more equitable environment for LGBTQ students. GLSEN was founded in 1990 to create a national alliance, as its name suggests, of LGBTQ and straight/cisgendered students, parents, and teachers interested in promoting safe environments for every member of a school community "regardless of sexual orientation or gender/identity expression."[8] GLSEN sponsors several well-known programs and projects, such as ThinkB4YouSpeak.com (a website designed to fight anti-LGBT language through advertising); gay-straight alliances (GSAs are student clubs located in schools); Ally Week ("a week for students to identify, support and celebrate Allies against anti-LGBT language, bullying, and harassment in America's schools"[9]); Day of Silence (a day in April in which students around the world take a vow of silence to ritually show the silencing of LGBT students); Changing the Game: The GLSEN Sports Project (which focuses specifically on elementary and secondary sports programs to promote respect for all athletes regardless of sexual

5. Green and Peterson, "LGBTTSQI Terminology."

6. Kayla Webley, "A Separate Peace?" *Time,* October 13, 2011, www.time.com/time/specials/packages/article/0,28804,2095385_2096859_2096805-1,00.html.

7. Karen Hawkins, "Plans for Gay-Friendly Chicago High School Nixed," *USA Today,* November 20, 2008, http://usatoday30.usatoday.com/news/education/2008-11-20-gay-high-school_N.htm.

8. "Our Mission," Gay, Lesbian, & Straight Education Network, www.glsen.org/values.

9. "Ally Week," Gay, Lesbian, & Straight Education Network, www.allyweek.org/about/.

orientation or gender identity/expression[10]); and Safe Space (a diversity training program to help educators develop a place where anti-LGBT language and action are not tolerated). All of these projects are designed to create a safe and respectful environment for all members of a school community.

Homophobia, Heterosexism, and Heteronormativity

Chapter 15 made a clear distinction between prejudice, prejudicial racism, and institutional racism. The terms homophobia, heterosexism, and heteronormativity are parallel terms applied to gender.

Homophobia refers to the fear or the hatred of homosexuals and homosexual behavior or of any gender-diverse identity or expression. Typically, the concept of homophobia implies that the hatred derives from an irrational fear. As such, homophobia, like racial prejudice, is a psychological concept and is often mistakenly used as a concept to explain social events. While there is little question that much too much anti-gay bullying and violence derive from individuals who suffer from an irrational fear of homosexuality, this book is more concerned with sociocultural causes for anti-gender-diverse behavior.

Heterosexism is a term that is used by some as another parallel term to racial prejudice, which, therefore, focuses on individuals' attitudes to gender-diverse people and action. This book, however, will use heterosexism as a parallel term for prejudicial racism. In this book, *heterosexism* refers to any act based on prejudice that results in the creation or maintenance of inequality or dominance of a people based on sexual orientation or gender identity/expression. In other words, in this book, I will reserve the term heterosexism for actions or programs based on homophobia, but not as a synonym for homophobia itself. As such, heterosexism is located in the sociocultural and not the psychological realm.

Heteronormativity refers to actions or programs that follow the rules or codes, either explicit or covert, that are institutionalized within the organizations and the structures of society when those codes lead to the creation or maintenance of inequality or domination of people based on sexual orientation or gender identity/expression. Heteronormativity assumes that heterosexuality is "normal," and all other forms of sexual orientation or gender identity/expression are not. Heteronormativity is built right into the institutions of our society so that one need not be homophobic to engage in practices that lead to the domination of gender-diverse people.

Obvious examples of heteronormativity can be found in the still-common practice of forbidding same-sex couples at proms, enforcing gender-aligned dress codes that deny transgendered individuals the right to self-expression, and the requirement of each student to identify him- or herself as a "him" or "her." But heteronormativity enters into schools in more formal ways, as when sex education teaches about "normal" sexual activity as located only between males and females. As is true with race—when we try to be race-blind, we actually end up treating everyone as if she or he were white—ignoring gender diversity results in treating all people as if they were straight or cisgendered. The fear that arises over

---

10. See "Changing the Game," Gay, Lesbian, & Straight Education Network, 2010–2013, http://sports.glsen.org/.

sexuality of any kind in schools, whether heterosexual or homosexual or other, leads most school people to try to eradicate references to sexuality from their classrooms. The attempt to do so, however, is of course futile because the refusal to recognize sexuality in the classroom merely imposes heteronormativity, which is clearly the recognition and privileging of one sexuality over all others.

Narratives of Sexuality

As with all of the other sociocultural positions addressed in this book, sexuality is appealed to through well-known cultural narratives. It is much easier for popular commentators, ideologues, and even well-meaning educators to try to convince students of one view or another by using these cultural narratives to persuade rather than actually developing well-reasoned, well-supported arguments. And it is certainly to the advantage of the entertainment industry to uncritically play up these cultural narratives in order to help pluck those ever-desirable dollars from the American family wallet.

The rest of this chapter presents just a few of the important cultural narratives found in our society that influence the conversation about sexuality in education. Perhaps it is important to reiterate that pointing out widely told cultural narratives is not to suggest that all of the narratives are "merely stories" that have no support in reality. Nor is it to suggest that all cultural narratives are equally mythologizing. Some cultural narratives are supported by scientists and scholars who study sexuality. Some cultural narratives make assertions unsupported by scientifically measured facts. Some cultural narratives are defensible through our experience; others are not. Like all of our discussions of cultural narratives, our purpose for focusing on the *narration* of sexuality, youth, and education, rather than empirical studies, lies in our recognition that facts and data have no meaning in and of themselves. We often become persuaded by texts less by their stated arguments and more by their appeal to cultural narratives that we already accept as true, but fail to recognize as influencing our commonsense understanding of the world.

The Narrative of Normal Family Life

As mentioned earlier in this chapter, in *The Education of Eros,* Carlson argues that sex education in the 1950s was designed primarily to address the problem of becoming adjusted to normal family life and gender roles. In order to recognize the potentiality of nonnormal family life, American culture obviously had to have some ideal family life to call "normal." While such ideas circulate in culture in many ways, one of the very influential mechanisms in the 1950s was the new mass medium of television, and TV's number-one family was almost certainly that of Ozzie and Harriet Nelson.

The Adventures of Ozzie and Harriet ran on television from 1952 to 1966 and starred the former big band leader, Ozzie Nelson; his band's lead female vocalist and real-life wife, Harriet; and their two real-life sons, David and Ricky. The sitcom centered around the stereotypical American ideal family consisting of a white man and white woman and their two white sons living in a quite nice, but relatively modest, suburban home. To create the illusion of realism, the show used outside shots of the family's real Hollywood Hills house with the interior of the house, where most of the action took place, replicated on the film studio lot. The plots of the shows also came out of the family's experiences, providing fodder for the comedy writers to poke fun at the loving, but mostly clueless, father as the couple raised their two very handsome, talented, and straight/cisgendered boys. The boys were often getting into cute jams leading to lessons of life for all involved. The father never seemed to work, or even leave the house. He was a well-mannered, gentle man with a soft voice. Harriet was a slim, well-groomed, and nicely dressed wise wife and mother who knew how to take the antics of her family with grace and charm. This was a very likeable nuclear family. It, of course, served as the basis for many other family sitcoms, including *Leave It to Beaver* and *Father Knows Best*.

Despite the fact that in the decades since the 1950s, Hollywood has attempted to "modernize" these family sitcoms by introducing elements of a changing family (think *Modern Family,* for example), the traditional values of the original 1950s programs were still visible through shows such as *My 3 Sons, The Brady Bunch,* and *The Cosby Show. While My 3 Sons* centered on a widower, *The Brady Bunch* focused on a blended family, and *The Cosby Show* starred an African American family, they were all built around domestic problems caused by the silly antics of children who need the guidance of a sometimes flawed, but always ultimately correct, middle-class parent.

The plotlines of this Normal Family narrative suggest that families might argue, but they ultimately love each other and come together to protect each other; that when we speak of family, we primarily mean a nuclear family with a husband and wife raising children; that they live in middle-class environments with middle-class homes; that they ignore politics; that they are not too intellectual but do want their children to do well in school; and for the purposes of this chapter, perhaps most importantly they represent untroubled gender identity/expression. In this narrative, all the characters are cisgendered.

The villains found in this narrative include all of those who would in some way or another threaten this ideal image of the nuclear family by introducing "dangerous" alternative lifestyles such as gay marriage, transgendered children, philandering husbands and their cheating wives, pregnant daughters, and economic vulnerability.

The Problems of the Unwed Teen Mother, STDs, and the Narrative of Teen Ignorance

In *The Education of Eros,* Carlson argues that the 1960s brought a change in the identification of the fundamental problem of sex education. Rather than the need to promote adjustment to normal family life, the 1960s began to define the problem as a lack of accurate information. Without accurate information, adolescents were vulnerable to things such as teen pregnancy and sexually transmitted diseases (or, in the language of the 1960s, VD—for venereal disease). As a result, sex education began to focus on delivering the information that was assumed young people did not always get at home. The teaching of facts and knowledge about sex did, as you might imagine, create quite a bit of controversy.

Those most objecting to the teaching of knowledge of sex in schools often identified themselves as social conservatives. Their narration of the unwed teen mother problem located its cause in the "dysfunctional family." Obviously, what makes the pregnant teen a problem is her unwed status. Nobody suggests that married teen mothers constitute a social problem. It is only the unmarried ones that carry the status of "problems." So one of the narrative solutions to the problem of the unwed teen mother lies in the Normal Family narrative. After all, if these adolescents could develop values consistent with the Normal Family narrative, they would understand that the purpose of sex is primarily procreation and that the primary purpose of the family as a social institution is to produce and raise children. Then the problem of unwed teen moms would be eliminated.

The same is certainly true of sexually transmitted diseases. As long as teens accept that sex out of wedlock is morally wrong, then presumably STDs would be stopped in their tracks. No sex until marriage and no sex out of marriage lead to only one partner each and, therefore, the very low percentage of risk of transmitting or receiving an STD.

This Normal Family narrative lost influence in education circles during the 1960s and 1970s but gained resurgence in the 1980s in the cultural narrative that underlies the Just Say No campaign of first lady Nancy Reagan[11] and exists to this day in the "abstinence only" curriculum that now dominates America's high schools. But, according to Carlson, in between those decades, during the 1960s and 1970s, sex educators zeroed in on lack of information as the source of the problems of unwed teen mothers and STDs, not inappropriate values or lack of role models (as implied in the Normal Family narrative).

In the 1960s, the problem of the unwed teen mother was addressed by a narrative with a plotline that tells us that teenage girls get pregnant because they and their boyfriends don't understand sufficiently the difficulties of being an unwed teen mother or the steps necessary to avoid pregnancy. While the Adolescent Ignorance narrative certainly recognizes that abstinence would solve this problem, it also suggests that abstinence is not the only way to address the problem of teen pregnancy. Knowledge about pregnancy and child rearing and access to birth control are also important elements in the battle against unwed teen pregnancy. It was during this time that we see fifth and sixth graders given a sack of flour to care for as their baby for a week. The youngsters gave their flour babies names and were required to carry them, change them, and feed them for a week in a simulation of baby care. It meant having to stay home Friday and Saturday night to care for their baby. I even know of teachers who would call their students at home in the middle of the night and tell them their baby was crying and they needed to feed her or change him or rock her back to sleep. Underneath this curriculum is the unmistakable narrative of adolescent ignorance. The exercise is designed to provide the experiential knowledge necessary to help adolescents realize that taking care of a baby is hard and exhausting work and help convince them that having a baby is something to be avoided at all costs. Because it dealt only with the results of unprotected sex and not at all with the facts of sex, this curriculum was deemed appropriate for children just entering puberty. Armed with the existential facts of caring for a baby, the hope was that these adolescents would make wiser choices when they were older.

---

11. While Mrs. Reagan's campaign started as an anti-drug advertising promotion, it was expanded to include premarital sex.

While the flour sack baby exercise was also seen in high schools, the older adolescents were primarily barraged with the dangers of sex and the need to take precautions. Birth control and condoms became a central aspect of the sex education curriculum. Movies about the ravages of syphilis, gonorrhea, and later HIV tried to scare adolescents with the facts. Of course, these movies and tales were supported by persuasive tropes and ideographs. Some high school health clinics began to offer free condoms and provide information on birth control. As can be seen, the narrative of teen ignorance promotes a theme that the problems of adolescent sexuality are technical ones rather than moral ones, and that require technical solutions rather than changes in moral values.

We can see then that the problems of the unwed teen mother and STDs can be addressed using two quite different cultural narratives. One of those cultural narratives is recognized as socially conservative and is integrally tied to the Normal Family narrative. The second narrative, often presented as a liberal solution, develops a narrative that avoids discussion of moral causes and instead presents storylines of teen ignorance. But the apparent ideological opposition between these so-called conservative and liberal narratives hides some other assumptions that point to deeper cultural narratives shared by both the Normal Family and Adolescent Ignorance narratives.

Notice that whether or not the solution is normal family values or factual information, the problem is assumed to lie in the adolescents' bodies. The Normal Family narrative assumes that the adolescents are morally corrupt and, as a result, lack the discipline to control their growing bodily desires. The Adolescent Ignorance narrative assumes that adolescents don't have the knowledge necessary to make wise choices as they give in to their growing bodily desires. In both cases, the "problem" is lack of restraint of sexual desire or lack of control of the adolescent body.

Another shared element in these cultural narratives is that they both insert problems of sexuality into racial and class-based contexts. Perhaps we could say that they urbanize dangerous sexuality. Whether the problems of teen pregnancy and STDs are narrated as dysfunctional families or adolescent ignorance, both narratives draw either directly or indirectly on language and images of the urban, black poor as the quintessential location of the problems. During the 1980s, this image was actively promoted by politicians through the trope of "welfare queen" and stories of mothers whose children each had a different father. Certainly, the stories and images of unwed teen moms seldom represented the suburbs or the white middle class. This narrative that urbanizes teen pregnancy is prevalent even though the few studies that compare the prevalence of teen pregnancy in urban and rural areas find the rates quite similar (however, at least one study did find that urban counties had slightly higher birth rates for teens[12]).

Narratives That Address Homosexuality and Gender Diversity

In *The Education of Eros,* Carlson argues that the "problem" of homosexuality has, for the most part, been peripheral to sex education curricula, primarily because prevention of

---

12. Carla Shoff, "Teenage Fertility: Does Place, Race, or Poverty Matter?" master's thesis, The Pennsylvania State University, 2009.

pregnancy had been the primary impetus for sex education, and homosexual activity does not cause pregnancy. But that does not mean that it was completely ignored. Certainly both the Normal Family narrative and the Adolescent Ignorance narrative speak to homosexuality.

The Gender Diversity Is Normal Narrative

Gay characters have existed in movies from the beginning of film, but nearly all gay characters were either in the closet, figures of ridicule, or both. For a good example of the last, check out 1912's *Algie the Miner,* a short ten-minute comedy with three credited directors including Alice Guy-Blaché, who is often credited as the first female director. *Algie the Miner* tells the story of a young straight man stereotyped as a gay man who is the object of ridicule, and who, in order to be permitted to marry the daughter of a tycoon, must "prove he is a man," so he travels to the West, becomes a cowboy, and returns to claim his bride. (You can stream or download it for free at http://archive.org/details/AlgieTheMiner.) Hollywood films are filled with such characters—some flamboyant, some subtle—providing a wink and a nod to the knowing audience. Though there is some disagreement, *The Boys in the Band* (1970) is often credited with being the first English-language movie with openly gay characters. While out of the closet and treated seriously, *The Boys in the Band* presented homosexuals without much diversity or complexity and as forced to live pretty miserable lives. An excellent history of gay characters in movie history is found in Vito Russo's *The Celluloid Closet: Homosexuality in the Movies* and the documentary film based on the book.[13]

Things were not any different in television. Though gay characters began to be seen in sitcoms in the 1970s and increasingly in the 1990s, it has only been recently that LGBT characters appear as regular characters on scripted television programs. Especially notable was the 1997 coming out of Ellen DeGeneres's character on *Ellen* so that DeGeneres's TV character and her real-life self came out at the same time. If we think about the popular television shows that helped construct the concept of the "normal family," we find no gays or lesbians in the family until the present *Modern Family* (1972's *The Corner Bar,* a workplace sitcom as opposed to a family sitcom, is frequently pointed to as having the first recurring gay character in prime time[14]). The Gay and Lesbian Alliance Against Defamation (GLAAD) estimates that during the 2012–2013 television season, "lesbian, gay, bisexual and transgender (LGBT) scripted characters represent 4.4% of all scripted series regular characters on the five broadcast networks: ABC, CBS, The CW, Fox, and NBC," which they state as a new high.[15] The increased presence of LGBTQ characters on television has helped promote a narrative in which gender diversity is characterized as merely one part of a person's normal self and part of a desired diversity for a society's normal community. This narrative often presents a trope that likens gender diversity with racial and ethnic diversity both in kind and in moral justification. The heroes in these

---

13. Vito Russo and Gene Woodling, *The Celluloid Closet: Homosexuality in the Movies,* Triangle Classics, rev. ed. (New York: Quality Paperback Book Club, 1995); Vito Russo, *The Celluloid Closet,* Sony Pictures Classics, Culver City, CA: Columbia TriStar Home Video, 2001.

14. Christine Sparta, "Emergence from the Closet," *USA Today,* March 11, 2002, http://usatoday30 .usatoday.com/life/television/2002/2002-03-11-coming-out-timeline.htm.

15. "Where We Are on TV Report: 2012–2013 Season," GLAAD, 2012, www.glaad.org/publications /whereweareontv12.

narratives are the out LGBTQ character and their straight and cisgendered allies and family. The villains are any who suggest that sexual orientation is a life choice or that queer identities are immoral. Particularly vilified are religious conservatives who justify their anti-LGBTQ positions as directed by God through sacred writings or church doctrine.

Modern Family can be seen as an example of the Gender Diversity Is Normal narrative. Its characters are consciously constructed to present *as normal* a family that *violates* many of the conventions of the Normal Family narrative. Even its name refers us back to the Normal Family narrative and suggests that it is presenting a new "Modern Family" narrative. The conventions of the family sitcom still exist in *Modern Family*: conventions such as continuous conflict among the characters; the silly antics of the kids; the doofiness of the parents, who despite their cluelessness eventually are shown to be right; and the endings that, despite all the conflict, show the characters all in solidarity with each other *as a family*. Many suggest that the increased circulation of the Gender Diversity Is Normal narrative that occurs through television and other entertainment media may be an important influence in the changing American attitude toward gay marriage. For example, a 2012 survey found that "In the past 10 years, the THR [*The Hollywood Review*] poll of likely voters across the nation found, about three times as many voters have become more pro-gay marriage as have become more anti-gay marriage—31 percent pro, 10 percent anti." Furthermore, the THR survey found that 27 percent of the respondents stated that gays on TV made them favor gay marriage, whereas only 6 percent stated it made them less favorable toward gay marriage.[16]

The Gay Agenda Narrative

But while we find a growing presence of a Gender Diversity Is Normal narrative in some media, there has been a counterforce that renews and retells the Normal Family narrative in other media and social institutions, such as the church and politics, and it is this narrative that still holds sway in public schools. One of the most active and influential countervoices to the Gender Diversity Is Normal narrative is found in the many activities of James Dobson's Focus on the Family.[17] Because the "normal family" is "normal," Focus on the Family has to create a narrative to explain the clearly visible existence of what it considers to be nonnormal sexual activity and gender identity. It does so by creating a narrative in which the "normal confusion" of adolescence is used by unscrupulous "recruiters" for "the gay lifestyle."

Focus on the Family promotes this intentionally political narrative as the Gay Agenda, which tells a tale of the infiltration of schools by these gay activists to recruit young people. Through its website, radio shows, and other communication networks, Focus on the Family has created a multipronged political agenda of its own to counter what it sees as the Gay Agenda. Among other things, Focus on the Family provides what it considers indicators of this agenda for parents to watch out for in their children's curriculum, textbooks, and school programs. It also provides support for parents willing to challenge schools when such indicators are found. Focus on the Family promotes campaigns to have books that are

16. Tim Appelo, "THR Poll: 'Glee' and 'Modern Family' Drive Voters to Favor Gay Marriage—Even Many Romney Voters," *The Hollywood Reporter*, November 3, 2012, www.hollywoodreporter.com/news /thr-poll-glee-modern-family-386225.

17. For a full list of Focus on the Family's activities see www.focusonthefamily.com/.

seen to normalize gender diversity (such as *And Tango Makes Three*[18]) removed from school libraries and to fight the adoption of sex education programs that are seen as promoting the gay agenda. Partly because of the cultural activism of Focus on the Family and other social conservative organizations, many public schools are hesitant to adopt any sex education other than abstinence only programs, feeling that anything else may just cause too much disruption.

Organizations such as Exodus Global Alliance[19] and Jews Offering New Alternatives for Healing[20] (JONAH) offer an alternative to the Gender Diversity Is Normal narrative by providing a variety of activities for those who consider their own or a family member's same sex attraction (SSA) as not normal. These groups also accept the Gay Agenda narrative to explain the discomfort of some people to their own same sex attraction. Some groups reject the normality of gender diversity to such an extent that they promote what they call "interventions" conducted by "therapists" and family and community members when an adolescent shows persistent indicators of gender-diverse activity. These interventions build around what is called "conversion therapy," "reparative therapy," or "sexual orientation therapy" and often involve parents' sending their adolescent to a camp designed to bring them back to "normal" identity and behavior. While the state of California has attempted to outlaw such conversion therapy, as of the writing of this chapter, the courts have not agreed on whether such bans are legal or not. The Southern Poverty Law Center states that there are nearly seventy conversion therapists operating in twenty states. It also claims that such attempts at "conversion" result in "increased anxiety, depression, and in some cases, suicidal ideation."[21]

Conclusion

The narratives discussed in this chapter are hardly the only cultural narratives that work to form our understanding of sexuality (consider, for example, the recent prominence of the Gays Are Victims of Bullying narrative), but the ones discussed here are prominent narratives found in the media consumed by youth and influential in the way in which schools address sexuality. At the present time, American public schools have chosen to implement sex education based primarily around basic reproductive facts and abstinence only programs. One primary reason for this choice is that the approach rarely brings out irate parents and citizens to the school board meetings, whereas the introduction of other curricula typically does. Perhaps when those growing numbers of people who fail to define adolescent sexuality as a "problem" start to show up to school board meetings to raise a ruckus when their school's sexuality education curriculum continues to promote the Normal Family narrative, school administrators will be forced to choose a curriculum that they think is more justified through scientific research and ethical reasoning rather than picking the least controversial approach as sufficient. Until that time, American public school students are likely to have to rely on gaining their knowledge and understanding of sexuality from their families, friends, and the popular entertainment media.

---

18. Justin Richardson, Peter Parnell, and Henry Cole, *And Tango Makes Three* (New York: Simon & Schuster Books for Young Readers, 2005).

19. See Exodus Global Alliance at www.exodusglobalalliance.org/.

20. See JONAH International: Institute for Gender Affirmation at http://jonahweb.org/index.php.

21. Southern Poverty Law Center, "Conversion Therapy," www.splcenter.org/conversion-therapy.

CHAPTER EIGHTEEN

Conclusion

Education and Democracy

According to the present American commonsense, the purpose of public schooling is to train workers to get jobs and create a strong economy. Ask most high school students why they should complete high school, and they will tell you that they need a high school diploma to get a good job or to get into a university so they can get a better job. Ask most students at a public university why they are in college, and they will tell you that it is to get a good job. Ask most Americans why we need to have a strong system of public education, and they will tell you so that America can compete in the world marketplace. Whether we are talking about the Reagan administration's Nation at Risk, the George W. Bush administration's No Child Left Behind, or the Obama administration's Race to the Top, the overwhelming understood purpose of public schools is to provide the engine for the capitalist economy.[1] The present-day, billionaire-funded educational reforms—such as those advocated by Microsoft's Bill Gates; the oil refinery Koch Brothers; the financial, communication, and media mogul Michael Bloomberg; the Walmart Walton family; and Amway's Richard DeVos—have clearly assumed that the primary, if not only, purpose of schooling is to train workers for a competitive market.[2] In this commonsense, *public* schools are understood to be institutions harnessed for *private* purpose, assuming that a democratic public space can take care of itself.

But even though today's American commonsense all but excludes schools from contributing to a well-functioning democracy, it has not always been so. As discussed in Chapter 12, throughout most of our history since becoming a democratic nation, public schools were

---

1. *A Nation at Risk: The Imperative for Educational Reform: A Report to the Nation and the Secretary of Education, United States Department of Education* (Washington, DC: National Commission on Excellence in Education, 1983), http://datacenter.spps.org/uploads/sotw_a_nation_at_risk_1983.pdf; George W. Bush, *No Child Left Behind: Communication from the President of the United States Transmitting a Report for Nationwide Education Reform Entitled "No Child Left Behind"* (Washington, DC: US G.P.O., 2001), http://hdl.handle.net/2027/umn.31951d019720020; "Race to the Top Program Executive Summary" (Washington, DC: US Department of Education, 2009), www2.ed.gov/programs/racetothetop/executive-summary.pdf.

2. Kevin K. Kumashiro, "When Billionaires Become Educational Experts: 'Venture Philanthropists' Push for the Privatization of Public Education," *Academe* 98, no. 3 (May–June 2012), www.aaup.org/article/when-billionaires-become-educational-experts#.UdlpqT6gnSw; Peter Dreir, "Why Are Walmart Billionaires Bankrolling Phony School 'Reform' in LA?" in *Moyers & Company*, New York: WNET, March 2, 2013, http://billmoyers.com/2013/03/02/why-are-walmart-billionaires-bankrolling-phony-school-reform-in-la/.

seen, in one way or another, as serving its democratic interests. Thomas Jefferson's sentiment, "If a nation expects to be ignorant and free, it expects what has never been and will
never be," captures much of the earlier American commonsense that existed up until the
second half of the twentieth century.[3] In this previous commonsense, *public* schools primarily served *public* purposes. At the very least, prominent policy-makers understood that the
educational needs of democracy were equal to the training needs of capitalism. Certainly
there was recognition that one purpose of our public schools might be to serve the private
interests of individuals and of corporations, but there was a clear understanding that the
public interests of our democracy also needed nurturing.

In the first chapter of this book, I discussed John Dewey's distinctions between the public
and the private and between the idea of democracy and the mechanisms of democracy. As
a reminder, Dewey wrote, "The public consists of all those who are affected by the indirect
consequences of transactions to such an extent that it is deemed necessary to have those
consequences systematically cared for."[4] Acts remain private when they affect only those who
have a direct role in the actions. When consequences of actions begin to affect people who
do not participate directly in those actions, they become public, and when these public acts
reach sufficient impact on the nonparticipating members, they must be regulated by some
mechanism designed to represent the interests of the nonparticipants.

In a liberal democracy such as the United States, public acts are understood to require
democratic means. In other words, when private spaces such as families, churches, and
corporations act in ways that only impact members of their own group, they are free to act
democratically or not. For example, most American families operate with a kind of benevolent
dictatorship of one or two parents, although surely there are some that operate in the spirit of
democracy.[5] Some churches in the United States operate democratically while others do not.
Few corporations operate in a manner normally considered democratic, but the possibility
for such corporations to do so is available.[6] In other words, private space may be organized
democratically or not, as the participants determine. But in public space where people may
be significantly affected by decisions made by others, no such option exists: public spaces
must always be democratic spaces, or we abandon democracy.

Dewey suggested that many people confuse the mechanisms that we create to implement democracy with the idea of democracy itself. Too many people think that democracy
is equated with elections, representative legislatures, supreme courts, and constitutions,
whereas Dewey points out that those are just mechanisms that we have opted for as a way
to implement the idea of democracy itself. Dewey's concept of democracy is often referred
to as *deliberative democracy* in that he argued democracy requires those who are affected by
public actions to have a voice in the decisions that affect them. They should have a chance to

----

3. Quoted in a letter from Thomas Jefferson "To Colonel Charles Yancey, January 6, 1816," in *The Works
of Thomas Jefferson,* Federal Edition, Vol. 11 (New York: G. P. Putnam's Sons, 1904–1905), 497.

4. John Dewey, *The Public and Its Problems: An Essay in Political Inquiry* (Chicago: Gateway Books, 1946),
15–16.

5. For example, see Blaise T. Ryan, *Democratic Parenting for Kids Aged 1–12: Evolving beyond Authoritarian
and Permissive Parenting,* ed. Bruce Spurr (ParentLearningClub.com, 2011).

6. For example, see Russell Lincoln Ackoff, *The Democratic Corporation: A Radical Prescription for Re-
creating Corporate America and Rediscovering Success* (New York: Oxford University Press, 1994).

participate in the deliberations that affect their lives. If we live in a situation in which some people make decisions that affect other people without their having a part in the deliberations, then we are violating the idea of democracy. The solution is not to reject democracy itself, such as turning public functions over to private enterprises, but to replace the mechanisms being used with ones that are better able to nurture democracy.

But Dewey's delineation of public space does not address where the limits of such spaces might exist. When things become public, who must deliberate? Everyone? Or just those potentially affected by the decision? Is there one gigantic "public" made up of everyone? Or might we consider the idea that there are many different "publics," and only the publics relevant to the decisions being made need to be consulted? For example, who should participate in the decisions regarding American Electric Power's Cardinal Power Plant near Brilliant, Ohio, whose coal-fueled power plant is responsible for releasing hundreds of pounds of mercury into the air, helping to contribute to the poisoning of the Great Lakes?[7] Is this simply a private matter for the corporation to decide for itself? Or do the people who live around the Great Lakes have a say in its policies? How about the people hundreds of miles away on the East Coast and in New England where the pollution from the plant creates acid rain that is destroying their forests and lakes? Or is this a matter that everyone in the nation should participate in, even those out West who are not directly affected by the coal burning?

How about public schools? Who is the "public" for the schools of Topeka, Kansas? Certainly the students in the Topeka schools are affected and, therefore, the students' parents and guardians, but who else? The teachers and staff? How about the citizens of the local school district? How about the citizens of the state of Kansas? How about those of the nation? Of course, the US Supreme Court decided that the protection of racial minority groups was a national public interest when it ruled in *Brown v. Topeka Board of Education* that the Topeka schools must desegregate their schools. But what about, for example, a common core curriculum for every public school in the United States? How about equal funding?

Philosopher of education Kathleen Knight Abowitz argues that public schools need to nurture and develop their publics. Following Dewey, Abowitz argues that a public arises whenever an issue affects multiple interest groups to the extent that the people affected feel the need to try to influence the situation. But the initial, nascent public that arises in moments of controversy does not develop into a fully functioning public unless people actually speak and listen to each other so that all participants grow and learn about the effects of the decision on all interests. It is the joint consideration and collaborative solutions that lead to a fully functioning democratic public. Unfortunately, too often, public debate in public school districts is reduced to each side speaking and neither side listening. If we keep in mind Dewey's distinction between the idea of democracy and the mechanisms of democracy, Abowitz suggests that the failure of a school district to find fair and ethical practices that incorporate all interests, including those of minority groups, might require new mechanisms for the implementation of democracy rather than the abandonment of democracy by replacing public space with private enterprise. Instead of turning to profit-seeking corporations and private markets, Abowitz suggests that we adopt procedures that develop and maintain

---

7. Vicki Stamper, Cindy Copeland, and Megan Williams, *Poisoning the Great Lakes: Mercury Emissions from Coal-Fired Power Plants in the Great Lakes Region*, ed. Theo Spencer (Natural Resources Defense Council, 2012).

the idea of democracy where people come together in an honest attempt to figure out how to live and work together in public space.

But for such truly democratic public spaces to develop, Abowitz argues, we must nurture particular habits that are central to the development and maintenance of deliberative publics. For her, "habits are developed dispositions for established forms of action and thought."[8] In the Deweyan sense, *habits* are learned and developed in and through experience and lead people to think and to act in particular ways. She identifies four habits crucial to deliberative democracy: communication, leadership development, power building, and collaborative creation. Democratic communication requires that participants not only speak with clarity, reason, and purpose, but that they grow and learn by listening to others. Abowitz argues that for too long, educational leaders have been equated with individuals who hold formal positions in schools (such as principals and superintendents) and who tell others what to do. Instead, she argues, democratic leadership should be considered a kind of activity rather than a position that includes actions such as organizing people to fight for recognition that their interests are legitimate, supporting others when the going gets difficult, or persevering as required to follow an issue through to a satisfactory conclusion. In this sense, anyone can be an educational leader, whether a school administrator, teacher, staff person, student, parent, or interested community member. Abowitz defines power "as the ability to authentically participate and exercise influence in decision-making processes."[9] Without the knowledge, skills, and dispositions necessary to understand issues and to represent their interests, people are locked out of deliberations, and truly democratic publics cannot be formed. Collaborative creation exemplifies the tendency to work with others to bring to life the idea of democracy in specific contexts. It requires citizens who are inclined to work with others, both those who share their interests as well as those who represent different interests, to bring democracy to life. For Abowitz, democratic spheres require people who are inclined to genuine communication, to the development of leaders, to the building of legitimate power, and to the creation of genuine collaboration. These necessary habits of democracy are not inherent but acquired through educational experience.

Lonnie Sherrod argues that an activist orientation is another of the dispositions necessary for democracy to thrive. His research has found that urban youth, regardless of race, ethnicity, and social class, tend to identify two basic rights and responsibilities as important qualities of citizenship. His research found that urban youth tend to expect certain entitlements (such as education and health care) as one kind of right and certain freedoms (such as freedom of speech and of religion) as another. Furthermore, urban youth tend to identify citizenship as requiring the giving back to the community (or helping other people) as one responsibility and political participation and patriotism as another. Different categories of youth may emphasize one of these more than others (for example, according to Sherrod, girls tend to emphasize prosocial qualities more than boys), but in large, there is wide agreement about the range of expectations associated with good citizenship.

But, Sherrod argues, an important aspect of citizenship is not fully acknowledged by youth: the requirement to act for social justice. Good citizens do not permit civic institutions

---

8. Kathleen Knight Abowitz, *Publics for Public School: Legitimacy, Democracy, and Leadership* (Boulder: Paradigm Publishers, 2013), 93.

9. Ibid., 105.

to act unjustly without feeling the responsibility to change those practices. Sherrod calls this *activism* and argues that democracy "depends on citizens who make informed judgments about the fairness of existing laws and who at times object to policies and even (as in many movements for social justice) disobey unjust laws."[10] Aaron Schutz agrees that activism is a central element to good democratic behavior and argues that organized protests are necessary to advance the interests of those groups, such as the working class, who have less formal power in society. Action, according to Schutz, is just as important in democratic space as voice.[11]

What Abowitz, Sherrod, and Schutz agree on is the necessity for public education to develop the knowledge, skills, and dispositions required of citizens in a democracy. We might suggest that these qualities must be central to the goals of public schools if they are to serve the public interest. One cannot help but wonder where these knowledge, skills, and dispositions are going to come from if the public school curricula have abandoned such controversial topics as sustainability, social class, race, ethnicity, and sexuality for the safety of that which can be tested on multiple choice tests. When the only legitimate school knowledge is assumed to be that with which everyone agrees or, at least, that with which the experts all agree, then how are our citizens to develop the habits necessary to achieve the kind of well-developed publics that Abowitz argues are necessary for public schools themselves? How are they to develop the disposition to activism that Sherrod and Schutz argue is central to democracy itself?

Failure to place as much importance on the qualities necessary for democratic community engagement as we do on the qualities necessary for economic gain invites the dismantling of the American experiment in democracy. This book has explored many of the issues that arise in contemporary public education in a manner that reveals the multiple positions often advanced by different interest groups when school decisions and practices become sites of community engagement. All members of our communities, but especially educators, parents, and community leaders, must have the knowledge, ability, and willingness to participate in the kinds of deliberations that are the heart of democratic societies. Demystifying the rhetoric, identifying the narratives, and reasoning our way through the difficult issues become essential qualities to be developed in our public schools. Being able to study the issues and make reasoned and ethical commitments to positions on these concerns must become major goals of our public education. Speaking and listening carefully, intelligently, fairly, and critically to those who share our public space in order to find ways for us to live and work together in these public spaces become the single most important responsibility of public education to its students and its publics. All public educators must place a full and complete commitment to democracy at the center of their professional conscience and at the top of their professional practice.

10. Lonnie R. Sherrod, "Promoting Citizenship and Activism in Today's Youth," in *Beyond Resistance! Youth Activism and Community Change: New Democratic Possibilities for Practice and Policy for America's Youth*, ed. Shawn Ginwright, Pedro Noguera, and Julio Cammarota (New York: Routledge, 2006), 291.

11. Aaron Schutz, *Social Class, Social Action, and Education: The Failure of Progressive Democracy* (New York: Palgrave Macmillan, 2010).

Bibliography

Abdullah, Fizan, Yiyi Zhang, Thomas Lardaro, Marissa Black, Paul M. Colombani, Kristin Chrouser, Peter J. Pronovost, and David C. Chang. "Analysis of 23 Million US Hospitalizations: Uninsured Children Have Higher All-Cause in-Hospital Mortality." *Journal of Public Health, Advance Access Publication* 32, no. 2 (October 2009): 236–244.

Abowitz, Kathleen Knight. *Publics for Public School: Legitimacy, Democracy, and Leadership.* Boulder: Paradigm Publishers, 2013.

Ackoff, Russell Lincoln. *The Democratic Corporation: A Radical Prescription for Recreating Corporate America and Rediscovering Success.* New York: Oxford University Press, 1994.

"Active Living Research: Using Evidence to Prevent Childhood Obesity and Create Active Communities." www.activelivingresearch.org/files/Active_Ed.pdf.

Adler, Mortimer. "Labor, Leisure, & Liberal Education." *Journal of General Education* 6 (1951): 35–45.
———. *The Paideia Proposal: An Educational Manifesto.* New York: Macmillan, 1982.

Agee, Mark. "Texas Teens Most Likely to Learn Abstinence in Schools, Become Young Mothers." *Star-Telegram,* September 22, 2008.

"Ally Week." Gay, Lesbian, & Straight Education Network. www.allyweek.org/about/.

Alperovitz, Gar. "The Question of Socialism (and beyond!) Is about to Open Up in These United States." Truthout, April 12, 2013. www.truth-out.org/news/item/15680-the-question -of-socialism-and-beyond-is-about-to-open-up-in-these-united-states.

Altenbaugh, Richard J. *The American People and Their Education: A Social History.* Upper Saddle River, NJ: Merrill/Prentice Hall, 2003.

Anderson, James D. *The Education of Blacks in the South, 1860–1935.* Chapel Hill: University of North Carolina Press, 1988.

Appelo, Tim. "THR Poll: 'Glee' and 'Modern Family' Drive Voters to Favor Gay Marriage—Even Many Romney Voters." *The Hollywood Reporter,* November 3, 2012.

Arendt, Hannah. *The Origins of Totalitarianism.* New York: Harcourt, 1966.

Associated Press. "Tween Dora Not a Tramp: Nick and Mattel Soothe Moms after Uproar." NYDailyNews.com, March 16, 2009, www.nydailynews.com/latino/tween-dora-a-tramp-nick-mattel -soothe-moms-uproar-article-1.372211.

"Bachelor's Degree or Higher, Percent of Persons Age 25+, 2008–2012." In *State and County Quick Facts.* Washington, DC: US Census Bureau.

Bagley, William C. "An Essentialist's Platform for the Advancement of American Education." *Educational Administration and Supervision* 24 (1938): 241–252.

Bardeen, Marge. "Who's the Scientist? Seventh Graders Describe Scientists Before and After a Visit to Fermilab." Fermilab. http://ed.fnal.gov/projects/scientists/index.html.

Barnes, Jessica S., and Claudette E. Bennett. "The Asian Population: 2000." *Census Brief.* Washington, DC: US Census Bureau, 2002. www.census.gov/prod/2002pubs/c2kbr01-16.pdf.

Barr, Andy. "Oklahoma Bans Sharia Law." Politico, November 3, 2010. www.politico.com/news /stories/1110/44630.html.

Bealer, Hannah C. "Bill Would Allow Guns on Campus, in Church." *Springfield News-Sun,* June 22, 2011.

Becker, Marc. *Indians and Leftists in the Making of Ecuador's Modern Indigenous Movements.* Latin American Otherwise. Durham: Duke University Press, 2008.

Beede, David, Tiffany Julian, and David Langdon. "Women in STEM: A Gender Gap to Innovation." Washington, DC: Economics and Statistics Administration, US Department of Commerce, 2011.

Bell, Derrik. "*Brown v. Board of Education* and the Interest-Convergence Dilemma." *Harvard Law Review* 93 (1980): 518–533.

Beller, Emily. "Bringing Intergenerational Social Mobility Research into the Twenty-First Century: Why Mothers Matter." *American Sociological Review* 74, no. 4 (2009): 507–528.

Beller, Emily, and Michael Hout. "Intergenerational Social Mobility: The United States in Comparative Perspective." *The Future of Children* 16, no. 2 (Fall 2006): 19–36.

Bennett, William J. "The Book of Virtues." *Booknotes.* C-SPAN, 1994. Video Interview.

Berman, Ari. "Mitt Romney's Neocon War Cabinet." *The Nation,* May 21, 2012. www.thenation.com /article/167683/mitt-romneys-neocon-war-cabinet#axzz2dYnzIDvs.

Bernstein, Basil. *Class, Codes and Control.* 2nd ed. Volume 3: *Towards a Theory of Educational Trans-missions.* Primary Socialization, Language and Education series. London: Routledge & Kegan Paul, 1977.

Bettinger, Eric P., Brent J. Evans, and Devin G. Pope. *Improving College Performance and Retention the Easy Way: Unpacking the ACT Exam.* Washington, DC: National Bureau of Economic Research, 2011. http://faculty.chicagobooth.edu/devin.pope/research/pdf/Final%20AEJ%20Paper.pdf.

Bialik, Carl. "Ill-Conceived Ranking Makes for Unhealthy Debate." *Wall Street Journal,* October 21, 2009.

Biesta, Gert. "'Mind the Gap!' Communication and the Educational Relation." In *No Education without Relation,* ed. Charles Bingham and Alexander Sidorkin, 11–22. New York: Peter Lang, 2004.

Biesta, Gert, Charles Bingham, Frank Margonis, Alexander Sidorkin, Jaylynne Hutchinson, Bonnie Lyon McDaniel, Cherlyn M. Pijanowski, et al. "Manifesto of Relational Pedagogy: Meeting to Learn, Learning to Meet." In *No Education without Relation,* ed. Charles Bingham and Alexander Sidorkin, 5–7. New York: Peter Lang, 2004.

Bingham, Charles, and Alexander M. Sidorkin, eds. *No Education without Relation.* New York: Peter Lang, 2004.

———. "The Pedagogy of Relation: An Introduction." In *No Education without Relation,* ed. Charles Bingham and Alexander Sidorkin, 1–4. New York: Peter Lang, 2004.

Boas, Franz. "The Real Race Problem from the Point of View of Anthropology." *The Crisis* 7 (December 1910): 22–25.

Boehner, John. "Boehner on MSNBC: The American People Want No Part of Dems Govt Takeover of Health Care." YouTube video. 2010. www.youtube.com/watch?v=aYs3YRpspFY.

Borg, Linda. "Student 'Zombies' March on R.I. Department of Education in Protest." *Providence Journal,* February 13, 2013.

Bound, John, Michael F. Lovenheim, and Sarah Turner. "Increasing Time to Baccalaureate Degree in the United States." In *Education Finance and Policy,* 375–424, Cambridge, MA: MIT Press, 2012.

Boyles, Deron. *American Education and Corporations: The Free Market Goes to School.* Garland Reference Library of Social Science. New York: Garland, 1998.

Buber, Martin. *I and Thou.* Translated by Walter Arnold Kaufmann. The Scribner Library Philosophy/Religion. New York: Scribner, 1970.

Bush, George W. *No Child Left Behind: Communication from the President of the United States Transmit-ting a Report for Nationwide Education Reform Entitled "No Child Left Behind."* Washington, DC: US G.P.O., 2001. http://hdl.handle.net/2027/umn.31951d019720020.

Bushaw, William J., and Shane J. Lopez. "A Time for Change: The 42nd Annual Phi Delta Kappa/ Gallup Poll of the Public's Attitudes toward the Public Schools." *Kappan* 92, no. 1 (2010): 9–26.

Butler, Judith. *Gender Trouble: Feminism and the Subversion of Identity.* New York: Routledge, 1999.

Cabrera, Nolan L., Jeffrey F. Milem, and Ronald W. Marx. "An Empirical Analysis of the Effects of Mexican American Studies Participation on Student Achievement within Tucson Unified School District." Tucson: University of Arizona, 2012.

California Postsecondary Education Commission. "Changes in Student Fee Levels in California's Public Postsecondary Education Systems." *Commission Fact Sheet 04-02,* 2004. www.cpec.ca.gov /FactSheets/FactSheet2004/fs04-02.pdf.

Callis, Ann Everal. "Olga Nethersole and the *Sapho* Scandal." Master's thesis, Ohio State University, 1974.

Carlson, Dennis. *The Education of Eros: A History of Education and the Problem of Adolescent Sexuality.* Studies in Curriculum Theory. New York: Routledge, 2012.

Carlyle, Thomas. *Sartor Resartus: The Life and Opinions of Herr Teufelsdrockh* (Project Gutenberg, 1890). www.gutenberg.org/files/1051/1051-h/1051-h.htm.

Carter, Dorinda J. "Achievement as Resistance: The Development of a Critical Race Achievement Ideology among Black Achievers." *Harvard Educational Review* 78, no. 3 (Fall 2008): 466–497.

"Changing the Game." Gay, Lesbian, & Straight Education Network. http://sports.glsen.org/.

Chiarella, Tom. "The Problem with Boys … Is Actually a Problem with Men." *Esquire,* July 1, 2006.

"Child Soldiers: Global Report 2008." Coalition to Stop the Use of Child Soldiers, 2008.

Chmielewski, Dawn C., and Claudia Eller. "Disney Animation Is Closing the Book on Fairy Tales." *Los Angeles Times,* November 21, 2010.

Clinton, Bill. "Transcript: Bill Clinton's Democratic Convention Speech." *ABC News.* http://abcnews .go.com/Politics/OTUS/transcript-bill-clintons-democratic-convention-speech/story?id=17164662.

Clinton, Hillary Rodham. *It Takes a Village: And Other Lessons Children Teach Us.* New York: Simon & Schuster, 1996.

Cohen, Elizabeth. "Push to Achieve Tied to Suicide in Asian-American Women." CNN.com. 2007. www .cnn.com/2007/HEALTH/05/16/asian.suicides/.

Cohn, Jonathan. "The Bailout That Worked." Newrepublic.com. 2010. www.newrepublic.com/blog /jonathan-cohn/78781/obama-gm-detroit-auto-bailout-worked.

Collins, Marva. "Marva Collins Seminars, Inc." www.marvacollins.com/comments.html.

"Conversion Therapy." Southern Poverty Law Center. www.splcenter.org/conversion-therapy.

Corbett, Christianne, Catherine Hill, and Andresse St. Rose. "Where the Girls Are: The Facts about Gender Equity in Education." Washington, DC: American Association of University Women, 2008.

Council of Learned Societies in Education. "Standards for Academic and Professional Instruction in Foundations of Education, Educational Studies, and Educational Policy Studies." 1996. www.unm .edu/~jka/csfe/standards96.pdf.

Counts, George S. *Dare the School Build a New Social Order?* The John Day Pamphlets, No 11. New York: Day, 1932.

Cuban, Larry. *How Teachers Taught: Constancy and Change in American Classrooms, 1890–1990.* 2nd ed. Research on Teaching Series. New York: Teachers College Press, 1993.

Dantley, Michael E. "Successful Leadership in Urban Schools: Principals and Critical Spirituality, a New Approach to Reform." *Journal of Negro Education* 79, no. 3 (2010): 214–219.

Darder, Antonia. *A Dissident Voice: Essays on Culture, Pedagogy, and Power.* Counterpoints: Studies in the Postmodern Theory of Education. New York: Peter Lang, 2011.

Davidson, Adam. "Vote Obamney!" *New York Times Magazine,* October 9, 2012.

Davis, James A., Tom W. Smith, Robert W. Hodge, Keiko Nakao, and Judith Treas. "Prestige Scores for All Detailed Categories in the 1980 Census Occupational Classification." National Opinion Research Center (NORC). http://ibgwww.colorado.edu/~agross/NNSD/prestige%20scores.html.

Deadline Team. "Disney Unveils New Princess with 'Sofia the First.'" Deadline Hollywood, www.deadline .com/2011/12/disney-unveils-new-princess-with-sofia-the-first-tv-movie-series/.

DeNavas-Walt, Carmen, Bernadette D. Proctor, and Jessica C. Smith. "Current Population Report: Income, Poverty, and Health Insurance Coverage in the United States: 2009." P60-238. Washington, DC: US Census Bureau, 2010. www.census.gov/prod/2010pubs/p60-238.pdf.

DeParle, Jason. "Harder for Americans to Rise from Lower Rungs." *New York Times,* January 4, 2012.

d'Errico, Peter. "Jeffrey Amherst and Smallpox Blankets." Peter d'Errico's Law Page, 2010. http://people.umass.edu/derrico/amherst/lord_jeff.html

Dewey, John. *The Child and the Curriculum.* Chicago: University of Chicago Press, 1902. www.gutenberg.org/files/29259/29259-h/29259-h.htm.

———. *Democracy and Education.* New York: Macmillan, 1916.

———. "My Pedagogic Creed." *School Journal* 54 (1897): 77–80.

———. *The Public and Its Problems: An Essay in Political Inquiry.* Chicago: Gateway Books, 1946 [1927].

Dickens, William T., and James R. Flynn. "Black Americans Reduce the Racial IQ Gap: Evidence from Standardization Samples." *Psychological Science* 17, no. 10 (2006): 913–920.

DiPrete, Thomas A. "Is This a Great Country? Upward Mobility and the Chance for Riches in Contemporary America." *Research in Social Stratification and Mobility* 25 (2007): 89–95.

"Distribution of Family Income—Gini Index." In *The World Fact Book 2013–2014.* Washington, DC: Central Intelligence Agency, 2013. www.cia.gov/library/publications/the-world-factbook/rankorder/2172rank.html.

Dougherty, John, and Anahad O'Connor. "Prosecutors Say Boy Methodically Shot His Father." *New York Times,* November 10, 2008.

"Dream Act: Summary." National Immigration Law Center. http://nilc.org/dreamsummary.html.

Dreir, Peter. "Why Are Walmart Billionaires Bankrolling Phony School 'Reform' in LA?" Moyers and Company, March 2, 2013. http://billmoyers.com/2013/03/02/why-are-walmart-billionaires-bankrolling-phony-school-reform-in-la/.

Du Gay, Paul. *Doing Cultural Studies: The Story of the Sony Walkman.* Culture, Media and Identities. Thousand Oaks, CA, and London: Sage, in association with the Open University, 1997.

Eligon, John. "A State Backs Guns in Class for Teachers." *New York Times,* March 8, 2013.

Elwell, Frank. "Verstehen: The Sociology of Max Weber." www.faculty.rsu.edu/~felwell/Theorists/Weber/Whome.htm.

Engel, Angela. "Exposing the Myths of High Stakes Testing." In *FairTest: The National Center for Fair and Open Testing.* 2007. www.fairtest.org/exposing-myths-high-stakes-testing.

Farkas, George. "How Educational Inequality Develops." National Poverty Center Working Paper Series, #0609. Ann Arbor, MI: National Poverty Center, 2006. www.npc.umich.edu/publications/working_papers/.

Fehely, Devin. "Arabic Language Charter School Suffers Setback." Atlanta, GA: WXIA TV, 2011.

Felty, Don. "The Bully Pulpit: Presidential Rhetoric and National Education Agenda in the Reagan Administration, 1981–1984." PhD diss., Miami University, Oxford, OH, 1992.

Ferguson, Ronald F., Jens Ludwig, and Wilbur Rich. "A Diagnostic Analysis of Black-White GPA Disparities in Shaker Heights, Ohio." Brookings Papers on Education Policy. Washington, DC: Brookings Institution, 2001.

Fortino, Ellen. "Lane Tech Students Hold Morning Sit-in to Protest *Persepolis* Book Ban." *Progress Illinois,* March 18, 2013. www.progressillinois.com/quick-hits/content/2013/03/18/lane-tech-students-hold-morning-sit-protest-persepolis-book-ban.

"Fortune 500." *Fortune Magazine,* 2013. http://money.cnn.com/magazines/fortune/fortune500/2013/snapshots/2190.html?iid=F500_fl_list.

Frank, Reanne, Ilana Redstone Akresh, and Bo Lu. "Latino Immigrants and the U.S. Racial Order: How and Where Do They Fit In?" *American Sociological Review* 75, no. 3 (June 2010): 378–401.

Freire, Paulo. *Pedagogy of the Oppressed.* New York: Seabury Press, 1970.

Freire, Paulo, and Donaldo P. Macedo. *Literacy: Reading the Word & the World.* Critical Studies in Education Series. South Hadley, MA: Bergin & Garvey Publishers, 1987.

Fuller, Mary. "Black Girls in a London Comprehensive School." In *Schooling for Women's Work,* edited by Rosemary Deem, 52–65. London: Routledge & Kegan Paul, 1980.

Garibaldi, Gerry. "How the Schools Shortchange Boys." *City Journal,* Summer 2006. www.city-journal .org/html/issue_16_3.html.

Giroux, Henry A. *Theory and Resistance in Education: A Pedagogy for the Opposition.* South Hadley, MA: Bergin & Garvey, 1983.

———. "Are Disney Movies Good for Your Kids?" In *Kinderculture: The Corporate Construction of Childhood,* edited by Shirley Steinberg and Joe Kincheloe, 53–69. Boulder: Westview Press, 1997.

———. *The Mouse That Roared: Disney and the End of Innocence.* Culture and Education Series. Lanham, MD: Rowman and Littlefield, 1999.

Goldberg, Jonah. "Do Away with Public Schools." *Los Angeles Times,* June 12, 2007. www.latimes.com /news/opinion/commentary/la-oe-goldberg12jun12,0,6103226.column.

Goldenberg, Suzanne. "US Supreme Court Rules for Monsanto in Indiana Farmer's GM Seeds Case." *The Guardian,* May 13, 2013.

Gorski, Paul. "The Classist Underpinnings of Ruby Payne's Framework." *Teachers College Record,* February 9, 2006.

Green, Eli, and Eric N. Peterson. "LGBTTSQI Terminology." LGBT Resource Center at UC Riverside, 2006. www.trans-academics.org/lgbttsqiterminology.pdf.

Greer, Colin. *The Great School Legend: A Revisionist Interpretation of American Public Education.* New York: Basic Books, 1972.

Grieco, Elizabeth M., and Rachel C. Cassidy. "Table 10: Hispanic and Not Hispanic Population by Race for the United States: 2000." In *Overview of Race and Hispanic Origin: 2000.* Census Brief. Washington, DC: US Census Bureau, 2001. www.census.gov/prod/2001pubs/c2kbr01-1.pdf.

Grossman, Zoltan. "From Wounded Knee to Libya: A Century of U.S. Military Interventions." http:// academic.evergreen.edu/g/grossmaz/interventions.html.

Gudrais, Elizabeth. "Unequal America: Causes and Consequences of the Wide—and Growing—Gap between Rich and Poor." *Harvard Magazine,* July–August 2008.

Hanson, Alan. "As Seen on TV in the Fifties ... Elvis on the Living Room Screen." Elvis History Blog, September 2011. www.elvis-history-blog.com/karal-ann-marling.html.

Harrison, David. "Are 'Charter Universities' the Future of State-Funded Higher Ed?" *Stateline.* Washington, DC: Pew Charitable Trusts, 2011. www.pewstates.org/projects/stateline/headlines/are-charter -universities-the-future-of-state-funded-higher-ed-85899376842.

Hawkins, Karen. "Plans for Gay-Friendly Chicago High School Nixed." *USA Today,* November 20, 2008.

"Health Expenditure, Total (% of GDP)." The World Bank Group, 2014. http://data.worldbank.org /indicator/SH.XPD.TOTL.ZS.

Heath, Shirley Brice. *Ways with Words: Language, Life, and Work in Communities and Classrooms.* New York: Cambridge University Press, 1996.

Higgs, Carol. "Plutocracy Reborn: Re-Creating the Gap That Gave Us the Great Depression." Institute for Policy Studies and the Public Good, Washington, DC, reprinted in *The Nation,* June 30, 2008.

Hirst, Paul Heywood, and R. S. Peters. *The Logic of Education.* The Students Library of Education. New York: Humanities Press, 1970.

Hochschild, Jennifer L. "Social Class in Public Schools." *Journal of Social Issues* 59, no. 4 (2003): 821–840.

Hodge, Jarrah. "Smart Girls: For Girls Who Wear Glasses." Gender Focus, 2009. www.gender-focus .com/tag/smart-girls/.

Hofstadter, Richard. *Anti-Intellectualism in American Life.* New York: Knopf, 1964.

Holliday, Darryl. "Students Stage 'Die-in' at School-Closing Protest." *DNAinfo Chicago,* May 15, 2013. www.dnainfo.com/chicago/20130515/woodlawn/students-stage-die-at-school-closing-protest.

Hopkin, William R., Jr. "*Roe v. Wade* and the Traditional Legal Standards Concerning Pregnancy." *Temple Law Review* 47 (1974): 715–738.

Humes, Karen R., Nicholas A. Jones, and Roberto R. Ramirez. "Table 2: Population by Hispanic or Latino Origin and Race for the United States: 2010." In *Overview of Race and Hispanic Origin: 2010*. Census Brief. Washington, DC: US Census Bureau, 2011.

Hundley, Kris. "Billionaire's Role in Hiring Decisions at Florida State University Raises Questions." *Tampa Bay Times,* May 9, 2011.

Hutchins, Robert M. *The Conflict in Education in a Democratic Society.* New York: Harper & Row, 1953.

"Income, Poverty and Health Insurance Coverage in the United States: 2009." US Census Bureau, 2010. www.census.gov/prod/cen2010/briefs/c2010br-02.pdf.

"Infant Mortality Rate." In *The World Fact Book 2013–2014*. Washington, DC: Central Intelligence Agency, 2013. www.cia.gov/library/publications/the-world-factbook/rankorder/2091rank.html.

"Interview with Dalton Conley, Background Readings for *Race: The Power of an Illusion*." PBS, www.pbs.org/race/000_About/002_04-background-03-03.htm.

Jefferson, Thomas. "A Bill for the More General Diffusion of Knowledge." In *The Works of Thomas Jefferson 1771–1779*, edited by Paul Leicester Ford. New York: G. P. Putnam's Sons, 1905.

———. "To Colonel Charles Yancy." In *The Works of Thomas Jefferson,* Federal Edition, Vol. 11. New York: G. P. Putnam's Sons, 1904–1905, 493–497.

Jhally, Sut. *Tough Guise.* Media Education Foundation, 1999. Videorecording.

Johnson, Carole E. *Introduction to Auditory Rehabilitation: A Contemporary Issues Approach.* The Allyn & Bacon Communication Sciences and Disorders Series. Boston: Pearson, 2012.

Johnson, Richard. "What Is Cultural Studies Anyway?" *Social Text* 16 (1986/87): 38–80.

Katz, Jackson. *The Macho Paradox: Why Some Men Hurt Women and How All Men Can Help.* Naperville, IL: Sourcebooks, 2006.

Kennerly, Maxwell S. "*Ebay v. Newmark*: Al Franken Was Right, Corporations Are Legally Required to Maximize Profits." *Litigation & Trial,* September 13, 2010. www.litigationand trial.com/2010/09/articles/series/special-comment/ebay-v-newmark-al-franken-was-right-corporations-are-legally-required-to-maximize-profits/.

Kibria, Nazli. "The Construction of 'Asian American': Reflections on Intermarriage and Ethnic Identity among Second-Generation Chinese and Korean Americans." *Ethnic and Racial Studies* 20, no. 3 (July 1997): 523–544.

Killerman, Sam. "Comprehensive List of LGBTQ+ Term Definitions." It's Pronounced Metrosexual, 2011–2013. http://itspronouncedmetrosexual.com/2013/01/a-comprehensive-list-of-lgbtq-term-definitions/.

———. "The Genderbread Person V2.0." It's Pronounced Metrosexual, 2012. http://itspronounced metrosexual.com/2012/03/the-genderbread-person-v2-0/.

King, Martin Luther, Jr. "I Have a Dream." 1963. www.usconstitution.net/dream.html.

King, Rodney. "Can We All Just Get Along?" YouTube video, 1992. www.youtube.com/watch?v=1sONfxPCTU0.

Kinnickell, Arthur B. "Ponds and Streams: Wealth and Income in the U.S., 1989 to 2007." In *Finance and Economics Discussion Series*. Washington, DC: Federal Reserve Board, 2009–2013. www.federalreserve.gov/pubs/feds/2009/200913/200913abs.html.

Kinzer, Stephen. *Overthrow: America's Century of Regime Change from Hawaii to Iraq.* New York: Times Books, 2006.

Kobrin, Jennifer L., Brian F. Patterson, Emily J. Shaw, Krista D. Mattern, and Sandra M. Barbuti. "Validity of the SAT for Predicting First-Year College Grade Point Average." Research Report No. 2008-5. New York: College Board, 2008.

Koch, Wendy. "Study: Many Sex Offenders Are Kids Themselves." *USA Today,* January 5, 2010.

Kochhar, Rakesh, Richard Fry, and Paul Taylor. "Wealth Gaps Rise to Record Highs between Whites, Blacks, Hispanics." In *Pew Research: Social & Demographic Trends*. Washington, DC: Pew Research Center, July 26, 2011.

Kristol, Irving. "The Neoconservative Persuasion." *The Weekly Standard* 8, no. 47 (August 25, 2003).

Kumashiro, Kevin K. "When Billionaires Become Educational Experts: 'Venture Philanthropists' Push for the Privatization of Public Education." *Academe* 98, no. 3 (May–June 2012).

Le, C. N. "Socioeconomic Statistics & Demographics." Asian-Nation: The Landscape of Asian America, 2011. www.asian-nation.org/demographics.shtml.

Lew, Jamie. "Burden of Acting Neither White nor Black: Asian American Identities and Achievement in Urban Schools." *The Urban Review* 38, no. 5 (2006): 335–352.

Lincoln, Abraham. "A House Divided against Itself Cannot Stand." The National Center for Public Policy Research. www.nationalcenter.org/HouseDivided.html.

Liptak, Adam. "U.S. Prison Population Dwarfs That of Other Nations." *New York Times,* April 23, 2008.

Liston, Barbara. "Florida Lawmaker Hands out Belts under Saggy Pants Ban." Reuters, August 30, 2011.

"Little Change in Public's Response to 'Capitalism,' 'Socialism': A Political Rhetoric Test." Washington, DC: Pew Research Center, 2011.

Lleras, Christy, and Claudia Rangel. "Ability Grouping Practices in Elementary School and African American/Hispanic Achievement." *American Journal of Education* 115, no. 2 (2009): 279–305.

Lubin, Gus. "The Five States Where Teachers Unions Are Illegal Have the Lowest Test Scores in America." *Business Insider,* February 23, 2011.

Majors, Richard, and Janet Mancini Billson. *Cool Pose: The Dilemmas of Black Manhood in America.* New York: Simon & Schuster, 1993.

Makwana, Rajesh. "Neoliberalism and Economic Globalization." In *Share the World's Resources: Sustainable Economics to End Global Poverty.* London: Share the World's Resources, 2006.

"Malcolm X Explains Black Nationalism." March 29, 1964. YouTube video. www.youtube.com /watch?v=TO6Co8v2XjY.

Marx, Karl, and Friedrich Engels. *The German Ideology.* New York: International Publishers, 1970.

Mattern, Krista D., and Brian F. Patterson. "Validity of the SAT for Predicting Fourth-Year Grades: 2006 SAT Validity Sample." Statistical Report No. 2011-7. New York: College Board, 2011.

———. "Validity of the SAT for Predicting Second-Year Grades: 2006 SAT Validity Sample." Statistical Report No. 2011-1. New York: College Board, 2011.

———. "Validity of the SAT for Predicting Third-Year Grades: 2006 SAT Validity Sample." Statistical Report 2011-3. New York: College Board, 2011.

"*McCleary v. State of Washington.*" Hot Topics: Current Education Issues in Plain Language, April 2013. www.k12.wa.us/Communications/HotTopics/HotTopic-McCleary.pdf.

McLaren, Peter, and Ramin Farahmandpur. *Teaching against Global Capitalism and the New Imperialism: A Critical Pedagogy.* Lanham, MD: Rowman & Littlefield, 2005.

Meier, Deborah. *The Power of Their Ideas: Lessons for America from a Small School in Harlem.* Boston: Beacon Press, 2002.

Miller, T. Christian. "Contractors Outnumber Troops in Iraq." *Los Angeles Times,* July 4, 2007.

Moffatt, Mike. "Would 0% Unemployment Be a Good Thing?" About.com. http://economics.about .com/od/helpforeconomicsstudents/f/unemployment.htm.

Molnar, Alex. *Giving Kids the Business: The Commercialization of America's Schools.* Boulder: Westview Press, 1996.

Moore, David W. "Half of Young People Expect to Strike It Rich, but Expectations Fall Rapidly with Age." Gallup Poll News Service, 2003. www.gallup.com/poll/7981/Half-Young-People-Expect -Strike-Rich.aspx.

Morning, Ann. "Reconstructing Race in Science and Society: Biology Textbooks, 1952–2002." *American Journal of Sociology* 114, suppl. (2008): S106–S137.

Moustafa, Margaret. "Foundations of Universal Literacy." In *Reading Process and Practice,* edited by Constance Weaver, 365–377. Portsmouth, NH: Heinemann, 2002.

Nasir, Na'ilah Suad. "'Halal-ing' the Child: Reframing Identities of Resistance in an Urban Muslim School." *Harvard Educational Review* 74, no. 2 (Summer 2004).

A Nation at Risk: The Imperative for Educational Reform: A Report to the Nation and the Secretary of Education, United States Department of Education. Washington, DC: National Commission on Excellence in Education, 1983. http://datacenter.spps.org/uploads/sotw_a_nation_at_risk_1983.pdf.

"The Nation's Report Card: Mathematics 2011." Washington, DC: National Center for Education Statistics, US Department of Education, 2011.

"The Nation's Report Card: Reading 2011." Washington, DC: National Center for Education Statistics, US Department of Education, 2011.

"NEA Code of Ethics." National Education Association, 1975. www.nea.org/home/30442.htm.

Newby, Joe. "La Raza Student Mob Storms Tucson School Board, Shuts Down Meeting." Examiner.com, April 11, 2011. www.examiner.com/article/la-raza-student-mob-storms-tucson -school-board-shuts-down-meeting.

Noddings, Nel. *Caring: A Feminine Approach to Ethics & Moral Education.* Berkeley: University of California Press, 1984.

———. *The Challenge to Care in Schools: An Alternative Approach to Education.* Advances in Contemporary Educational Thought Series. New York: Teachers College Press, 1992.

———. "An Ethic of Care and Its Implications for Instructional Arrangements." In *The Education Feminism Reader,* ed. Lynda Stone. New York: Routledge, 1994.

"North Dakota Lawmakers Approve Measure That Could Ban Abortion." Reuters, March 22, 2013. www.reuters.com/article/2013/03/22/us-usa-abortion-northdakota-idUSBRE92L19Z20130322.

Novak, Michael. "A Closet Capitalist Confesses." *The Washington Post,* March 14, 1976.

Obama, Barack. "Remarks at a Campaign Rally in Green Bay, Wisconsin." In John Woolley and Gerhard Peters, *The American Presidency Project,* 2012, transcript. www.presidency.ucsb.edu/ws/index .php?pid=102560.

O'Connor, Sandra Day, and Roy Romer. "Not by Math Alone." *Washington Post,* March 25, 2006.

"OECD Programme for International Student Assessment." PISA 2009 results, www.oecd.org/edu /pisa/2009.

"Ohio Governor Signs Law Allowing Guns in Bars." Reuters, June 30, 2011. www.reuters.com /article/2011/06/30/us-ohio-guns-idUSTRE75T7BX20110630.

"Old Deluder Act (1647)." From *Records of the Governor and Company of the Massachusetts Bay in New England* (1853), II: 203. Austin, TX: Constitution Society.

Orton, Beth. "Last Leaves of Autumn." On *Sugaring Season,* ANTI Records, 2012. Compact disc.

"Our Mission." Gay, Lesbian, & Straight Education Network. www.glsen.org/values.

Partanen, Anu. "What Americans Keep Ignoring about Finland's School Success." *The Atlantic,* December 29, 2011.

Payne, Ruby K. "Blog Entry: A Response to 'The Classist Underpinnings of Ruby Payne's Framework.'" *Teachers College Record,* July 14, 2006.

———. *A Framework for Understanding Poverty.* 4th ed. Highlands, TX: Aha! Process, 2005.

Pesheva, Ekaterina. "Lack of Insurance May Have Figured in Nearly 17,000 Childhood Deaths, Study Shows." Johns Hopkins Children's Center. www.hopkinschildrens.org/lack-of-insurance-may-have -figured-in-nearly-17000-childhood-deaths.aspx.

Plato. *Apology.* Translated by Benjamin Jowett. Auckland: The Floating Press, 2011.

———. *Plato's Meno.* Translated by Benjamin Jowett. Rockville, MD: Serenity, 2009. http://books.google .com/books?id=5VZYxRiErO0C&printsec=frontcover&dq=meno&hl=en&sa=X&ei=CJs_Udw KgdjSAbyQgcgE&ved=0CDMQuwUwAA.

Poplin, Mary, and Joseph Weeres. *Voices from the Inside: A Report on Schooling from Inside the Classroom.* Claremont, CA: The Institute for Education in Transformation at the Claremont Graduate School, 1992.

Pursuing the American Dream: Economic Mobility across Generations. Washington, DC: Pew Charitable Trusts, 2012. www.pewtrusts.org/uploadedFiles/wwwpewtrustsorg/Reports/Economic_Mobility /Pursuing_American_Dream.pdf.

Quantz, Richard A. *Rituals and Student Identity in Education: Ritual Critique for a New Pedagogy.* Education, Politics, and Public Life series, edited by Henry A. Giroux and Susan Searls Giroux. New York: Palgrave Macmillan, 2011.

"Race to the Top Program Executive Summary." Washington, DC: US Department of Education, 2009. www2.ed.gov/programs/racetothetop/executive-summary.pdf.

Rama, Padmananda. "U.S. Census Show Asians Are Fastest Growing Racial Group." The Two-Way: Breaking News from NPR. Washington, DC: NPR, 2012. www.npr.org/blogs/thetwo-way/2012/03/23/149244806/u-s-census-show-asians-are-fastest-growing-racial-group.

Ramist, Leonard, Charles Lewis, and Laura McCamley-Jenkins. "Student Group Differences in Predicting College Grades: Sex, Language, and Ethnic Groups." Report No. 93-1. New York: College Board, 1994.

Rand, Ayn. "The Meaning of Money." In *For the New Intellectual: The Philosophy of Ayn Rand,* vii. New York: Signet, 1963.

———. "What Is Capitalism?" In *Capitalism: The Unknown Ideal,* edited by Nathaniel Branden, Alan Greenspan, and Robert Hessen, 1–29. New York: Signet, 1967.

Ratcliffe, David T. *The Six Nations: Oldest Living Participatory Democracy on Earth.* Roslindale, MA: Rat Hous Reality Press, 1995–2013. www.ratical.org/many_worlds/6Nations/.

Reagan, Ronald. "Farewell Address to the Nation." The American Presidency Project. www.presidency.ucsb.edu/ws/?pid=29650.

"Report of the APA Task Force on the Sexualization of Girls." American Psychological Association, 2010. www.apa.org/pi/women/programs/girls/report-full.pdf.

Richardson, Justin, Peter Parnell, and Henry Cole. *And Tango Makes Three.* New York: Simon & Schuster Books for Young Readers, 2005.

Romanowski, Michael. "The Ethical Treatment of Japanese American Internment Camps: A Content Analysis of Secondary American History Textbooks." PhD diss., Miami University, Oxford, OH, 1993.

Rosen, David. "Child Soldiers: Victims or Heroes?" *FDU Magazine Online,* Summer/Fall 2005.

Rosenkrans, Nolan. "Kasich Funding Formula Favors Suburban Schools; TPS, Other Urban Districts, Mostly Flat under Governor's Plan." *The Blade,* February 8, 2013.

Rousmaniere, Kate. "The Forging of Common Public Schools." Lecture, Miami University, Oxford, OH, March 12, 2012.

———. "Questioning the Visual in the History of Education: Or, How to Think about Old Pictures of Schools." Miami University, 1998. www.units.muohio.edu/eduleadership/kate/kate1.html.

Rousseau, Jean-Jacques. "The Social Contract." In *Internet Modern History Sourcebook,* edited by Paul Halsall. www.fordham.edu/halsall/mod/rousseau-soccon.asp.

Rubenstein, Ben, Sondra C. Eshafer, Nicole Willson et al. "How to Be Sexy While Playing Sports (Girls)." www.wikihow.com/Be-Sexy-While-Playing-Sports-(Girls).

Rucker, Philip. "Romney Questions Obama Commitment to 'American Exceptionalism.'" *Washington Post,* March 31, 2012.

Rury, John L. "Coeducation and Same-Sex Schooling." *Encyclopedia of Children and Childhood in History and Society,* 2008. faqs.org.

Russo, Vito. *The Celluloid Closet, Sony Pictures Classics.* Culver City, CA: Columbia TriStar Home Video, 2001. DVD, 101 min.

Russo, Vito, and Gene Woodling. *The Celluloid Closet: Homosexuality in the Movies.* Rev. ed. New York: Quality Paperback Book Club, 1995.

Ryan, Blaise T. *Democratic Parenting for Kids Aged 1–12: Evolving beyond Authoritarian and Permissive Parenting,* edited by Bruce Spurr. ParentLearningClub.com, 2011.

Salazar, Karina. "Nogales Border Safe, Open for Business, Residents Say." *Arizona Daily Sun,* April 18, 2011.

Sands, David. "Detroit Walkout: High School Students Suspended for Leaving School Start Freedom School." *HuffPost Detroit,* April 27, 2012.

Santoni, Ronald E. *Bad Faith, Good Faith, and Authenticity in Sartre's Early Philosophy.* Philadelphia: Temple University Press, 1995.

Shah, Anup. "World Military Spending." July 7, 2010, www.globalissues.org/article/75/world-military-spending.

"School Funding by District." Ohio General Assembly, 2013. http://ode.legislature.state.oh.us/index.php.

Schutz, Aaron. *Social Class, Social Action, and Education: The Failure of Progressive Democracy.* New York: Palgrave Macmillan, 2010.

Shaw, Pete. "Local High School Students Stand against Standardized Testing." *Portland Occupier,* April 30, 2013. www.portlandoccupier.org/2013/04/30/local-high-school-students-stand-against-standardized-testing/.

Sherrod, Lonnie R. "Promoting Citizenship and Activism in Today's Youth." In *Beyond Resistance! Youth Activism and Community Change: New Democratic Possibilities for Practice and Policy for America's Youth,* edited by Shawn Ginwright, Pedro Noguera, and Julio Cammarota, 287–300. New York: Routledge, 2006.

Shoff, Carla. "Teenage Fertility: Does Place, Race, or Poverty Matter?" State College: Pennsylvania State University, 2009.

Siegel, Jim, and Joe Vardon. "15 Years—No School Funding Fix." *Columbus Dispatch,* March 25, 2012.

Smith, Beau. "Art Is Life." Ezine @rticles, February 28, 2008. http://ezinearticles.com/?Art-Is-Life&id=1013832.

Sommers, Christina Hoff. "The War against Boys." *The Atlantic,* May 1, 2000.

———. *The War against Boys: How Misguided Feminism Is Harming Our Young Men.* New York: Simon & Schuster, 2000.

"Spain." In *The World Fact Book 2013–2014.* Washington, DC: Central Intelligence Agency, 2013. www.cia.gov/library/publications/the-world-factbook/geos/sp.html.

Sparta, Christine. "Emergence from the Closet." *USA Today,* March 11, 2002.

Spring, Joel H. *The American School, 1642–1993.* 3rd ed. New York: McGraw-Hill, 1994.

Stamper, Vicki, Cindy Copeland, and Megan Williams. *Poisoning the Great Lakes: Mercury Emissions from Coal-Fired Power Plants in the Great Lakes Region,* edited by Theo Spencer. Natural Resources Defense Council, 2012.

Stedman, Lawrence C. *The NAEP Long-Term Trend Assessment: A Review of Its Transformation, Use, and Findings.* Washington, DC: National Assessment Governing Board, March 2009.

Steele, Claude. "Thin Ice: Stereotype Threat and Black College Students." *The Atlantic Magazine,* August 1999.

Swanbrow, Diane. "Many U.S. Families Are Underwater with Debts: U-M Study." Ann Arbor: University of Michigan, Institute for Social Research, 2012.

Taylor, Paul, and Rakesh Kochhar. "America's Changing Workforce: Recession Turns a Graying Office Grayer." In *Social and Demographic Trends Report,* edited by Rich Morin. Washington, DC: Pew Research Center, 2009.

Thayer-Bacon, Barbara J. "Personal and Social Relations in Education." In *No Education without Relation,* ed. Charles Bingham and Alexander Sidorkin, 165–179. New York: Peter Lang, 2004.

Thompson, Michael. *Raising Cain: Boys in Focus.* Oregon Public Broadcasting, 2006.

Toulmin, Steven, Richard D. Rieke, and Allan Janik. *An Introduction to Reasoning.* 2nd ed. New York: Macmillan, 1984.

Tritch, Teresa. "How the Deficit Got This Big." *New York Times Sunday Review,* July 23, 2011.

"Two Paths: What Will the Girl Become?" In *Social Purity,* edited by John W. Gibson. New York: J. L. Nichols, 1903.

Tyack, David B. *The One Best System: A History of American Urban Education.* Cambridge, MA: Harvard University Press, 1974.

Tyack, David B., and Elizabeth Hansot. "Silence and Policy Talk: Historical Puzzles about Gender and Education." *Educational Researcher* 17, no. 3 (April 1988): 33–41.

Tyre, Peg. "The Trouble with Boys." *Newsweek,* January 29, 2006.

von Hayek, Friedrich A. *The Constitution of Liberty.* Chicago: University of Chicago Press, 1960.

————. *The Road to Serfdom.* Chicago: University of Chicago Press, 1944.

Wade, Nicholas. "Chimps, Too, Wage War and Annex Rival Territory." *New York Times,* June 21, 2010.

Waquant, Loïc J. D., and William Julius Wilson. "The Cost of Racial and Class Exclusion in the Inner City." *The Annals of the American Academy of Political and Social Sciences* 501, no.1 (January 1989): 8–25.

Warren, Jenifer. "One in 100: Behind Bars in America 2008." Pew Center on the States, 2008.

Weaver, Constance. *Reconsidering a Balanced Approach to Reading.* Urbana, IL: National Council of Teachers of English, 1998.

Webley, Kayla. "A Separate Peace?" *Time,* October 13, 2011.

West, Cornel. *The Cornel West Reader.* New York: Basic Civitas Books, 1999.

————. *Race Matters.* 2nd ed. New York: Vintage Books, 2001.

"Where We Are on TV Report: 2012–2013 Season." *GLAAD,* 2012. www.glaad.org/publications /whereweareontv12.

"Where Your Income Tax Money Really Goes." War Resisters League. www.warresisters.org/pages /piechart.htm.

Whitmire, Richard. "Boy Trouble." *New Republic,* January 23, 2006, 15–18.

Wight, Vanessa R., Michelle Chau, and Yumiko Aratani. "Who Are America's Poor Children? The Official Story." New York: National Center for Children in Poverty, 2011.

Willis, Paul E. *Learning to Labour: How Working Class Kids Get Working Class Jobs.* Farnborough, UK: Saxon House, 1977.

Wolff, Edward N. "Recent Trends in Household Wealth in the United States: Rising Debt and the Middle-Class Squeeze—An Update to 2007." Annandale-on-Hudson, NY: Levy Economics Institute of Bard College, 2010.

Wood, George. "The Lessons of a Rural Principal." *Teaching Tolerance* 38 (Fall 2010): 25–27, www .tolerance.org/magazine/number-38-fall-2010/lessons-rural-principal.

Wynn, Lloyd. "The Birth of Redlining: The Real History of the Homeowners Loan Corporation." *The Black Commentator* 273 (2008). www.blackcommentator.com/273/273_sm_birth_of_redlining .html.

Index

About the Author

Richard A. Quantz is professor of social foundations of education in the Department of Educational Leadership at Miami University, Ohio. A former elementary school teacher, he has spent the last thirty-five years actively teaching undergraduates and teachers how to critically understand the classrooms and schools that they inhabit and work within. His scholarship focuses on the sociocultural aspects of education, with a particular interest in cultural studies. He is the author of *Rituals and Student Identity in Education: Ritual Critique for a New Pedagogy,* Education, Politics, and Public Life (New York: Palgrave Macmillan, 2011), winner of the 2011 AESA Critics' Choice Book Award.